Dilemmas of Scale in America's Federal Democracy

National and local traditions vie within the American federal system and the American experiment with self-government. Bringing together contributions from history, political science, and sociology, this book focuses primarily on the local tradition, seeking to recapture its origins, explain its current impact, and assess its worth.

Martha Derthick is Julia Allen Cooper Professor in the University of Virginia's Woodrow Wilson Department of Government and Foreign Affairs.

WOODROW WILSON CENTER SERIES

Continued on page following index

WOODROW WILSON INTERNATIONAL CENTER FOR SCHOLARS

WOODROW WILSON CENTER PRESS

The Woodrow Wilson Center Press publishes books written in substantial part at the Center or otherwise prepared under its sponsorship by fellows, guest scholars, staff members, and other program participants. Conclusions or opinions expressed in Center publications and programs are those of the authors and speakers and do not necessarily reflect the views of the Center staff, fellows, trustees, advisory groups, or any individuals or organizations that provide financial support to the Center.

Woodrow Wilson Center Press
Editorial Offices
One Woodrow Wilson Plaza
1300 Pennsylvania Avenue, N.W.
Washington, D.C. 20523
telephone: (202) 691-4010

Dilemmas of Scale in America's Federal Democracy

Edited by
MARTHA DERTHICK

WOODROW WILSON CENTER PRESS

AND

PUBLISHED BY THE PRESS SYNDICATE OF THE UNIVERSITY OF CAMBRIDGE
The Pitt Building, Trumpington Street, Cambridge, United Kingdom

CAMBRIDGE UNIVERSITY PRESS
The Edinburgh Building, Cambridge CB2 2RU, UK   http: //www.cup.cam.ac.uk
40 West 20th Street, New York, NY 10011-4211, USA   http: //www.cup.org
10 Stamford Road, Oakleigh, Melbourne 3166, Australia

First published 1999

Printed in the United States of America

Typeface Sabon 10/13 pt. *System* QuarkXPress [BB]

A catalog record for this book is available from the British Library.

Library of Congress Cataloging-in-Publication Data
Dilemmas of scale in America's federal democracy / edited by Martha
Derthick.
p.   cm. — (Woodrow Wilson Center series)
Includes index.
ISBN 0-521-64039-3 (hc.)
1. Federal government—United States.   2. Federal-city relations—
United States.   3. Democracy—United States.   I. Derthick, Martha.
II. Series.
JK325.D555   1999
324.6'3'0973—dc21   98-46762

ISBN 0-521-64039-3 hardback

Contents

Tables

Acknowledgments

The Project on Local Self-Government was sponsored by the Division of United States Studies of the Woodrow Wilson International Center for Scholars with financial assistance from the Smith Richardson Foundation. The participants are grateful to Michael J. Lacey, director of the division, and George Wagner, his assistant, for making the project possible, encouraging an interdisciplinary effort, and bringing us together in workshops that enabled us to reflect on what we were trying to do. This support was invaluable, as everyone who attended the workshops will attest. After Mr. Wagner's departure, Susan Nugent picked up the pieces and graciously helped us reach publication. In addition, as editor I thank the White Burkett Miller Center of the University of Virginia and its director, Kenneth W. Thompson, for supporting my participation in this project.

Martha Derthick

Foreword

MICHAEL J. LACEY

"The world of public affairs is so old," Woodrow Wilson once observed, that no person can know it "who knows only that little segment of it which we call the present." In keeping with this insight, the American program of the Woodrow Wilson International Center for Scholars, the nation's official memorial to Wilson as a scholar and statesman, is concerned mainly with research on the history of American society and politics. It is devoted to furthering critical reflection on the relations between ideas and institutions in modern America, particularly the institutions of government. It aims to provide a forum in Washington, D.C., for the presentation and assessment of new scholarly perspectives on the American experience, and to do what it can—through its fellowships, scholarly working groups, conferences, and publications—to develop our knowledge of those long-term, fundamental, underlying issues and problems that have shaped and continue to shape our understanding of the national community.

The progress of scholarship requires collaborative creativity. One of the duties of the American program is to facilitate collaborative creativity by providing the administrative leadership for large-scale, cooperative projects that arise from time to time out of the scholarly discussions that take place among the Center's staff, its fellows, and its advisers. This book is an example. Its editor, Martha Derthick, has been a long-term adviser to the program, and the plan for the volume arose out of discussions with her during a time when she was in residence as a guest scholar of the Center. The volume is the result of a working group that met on several

Michael J. Lacey is director, Division of United States Studies, Woodrow Wilson International Center for Scholars.

occasions under her direction. Participants wanted to exploit the possibilities of cooperation among scholars with different backgrounds and special competencies who shared an interest in the dynamics of American federalism and the problems presented by them to the stability, capacity, and social worth of local communities, the importance of which looms so large in the nation's social and political thought.

Special thanks are due to the authors and all who participated in critical discussion of the component essays as they emerged, but particularly to the editor, who conceived this project and brought it to fruition, for her patience and skill in determining the changing needs of the work as time went on. The Center is also pleased to acknowledge with gratitude the support of the Smith Richardson Foundation, whose generosity and confidence in the long-term importance of this kind of work is much appreciated.

Introduction

MARTHA DERTHICK

In the classical political thought of the West, it was supposed that democracies must be small and direct. Democracy was a form in which all citizens must participate, thus it could exist only on a very circumscribed scale—that of the Greek city-state, in which, ideally, an assembly was limited to the range of the human voice.

As modern nations arose, there arose as well the alternative conception that democracy could be *representative*. Democracies could be republics—things *of* the public but not identical with it. The populace could control officeholders through periodic elections. Democracies were governments in which officeholders had acquired their authority through a competitive struggle for the people's vote.[1] The people were assured of opportunities to render judgment on the officeholders' conduct of office.

Nonetheless, the idea survived that democracy was purer and more attainable on the small scale than on the large and that its survival on a small scale was indispensable to its attainment on a larger scale. The classic statements of this proposition are to be found in the work of Alexis de Tocqueville, who derived them from his observations of the United States, set forth in *Democracy in America,* and of the English liberal philosopher John Stuart Mill.[2]

---

[1] For a recent treatment of democracy—its evolution, practice, and prospects—see Robert A. Dahl, *Democracy and Its Critics* (New Haven: Yale University Press, 1989). For a more specific discussion of the scale of democracies, see Robert A. Dahl and Edward R. Tufte, *Size and Democracy* (Stanford: Stanford University Press, 1973).

[2] In Tocqueville, Chapter 5 is crucial, but the theme is stated throughout—as, for example, in Chapter 2: "In the laws of Connecticut, as well as in all those of New England, we find the germ and gradual development of that township independence which is the life and mainspring of American liberty at the present day." *Democracy in America* (New York: Vintage Books, 1956), vol. I, 42. Mill's statement is brief and incidental to his main theme, which is a defense of individual liberty. *On Liberty* (New York: Henry Holt, 1877), 194.

But there are native statements of the idea as well, for it has had particular power in the United States. The idea is conventionally associated with Thomas Jefferson, even though his exposition was fragmentary rather than extended.[3] Fuller expositions came in the work of Progressive social thinkers, notably John Dewey and Mary Parker Follett.[4]

It is no accident that Progressive thinkers contemplated "the dilemma of scale," as Samuel H. Beer has termed it[5]—that is, the question of whether democracy can be realized on a grand scale—for it was not until the Progressive Era that it was posed in the United States in a stark, inescapable form. The Framers had waged an intense theoretical debate over it, with the Anti-Federalists arguing the classical position that democracies had to be small (even if not necessarily as small as Athens) and the Federalists, in a bold stroke executed by James Madison, arguing just the reverse—that large scale was essential to realizing effective self-government because it alone could protect against the pathology of democracy, which was majority tyranny.[6]

Until after the Civil War, it was not certain that the United States would endure on a large scale. Before then, the Anti-Federalists' prediction that social heterogeneity would threaten the existence of the nation and make domestic government unstable had proved true. Also, before the Civil War domestic government in the United States had been extremely decentralized. It lay scattered in isolated hamlets—little rural republics, at least in New England and New England's offshoots in the Midwest. Southern places, which were oligarchical, were not in the same

[3] The principal statement is in a letter to Joseph C. Cabell, Feb. 2, 1816, in Adrienne Koch and William Peden, eds., *The Life and Selected Writings of Thomas Jefferson* (New York: Random House, 1944 and 1972), 660–62.

[4] John Dewey, *The Public and Its Problems* (Denver: Alan Swallow; copyright by Henry Holt, 1927, and Mrs. John Dewey, 1954), chap. V; Mary Parker Follett, *The New State* (New York: Longmans, Green, 1918).

[5] Drawing on Machiavelli, Beer states the dilemma as follows: "On the one hand, if a state—any state—is to avoid internal disruption, its governing body must be small. On the other hand, if it is to be strong enough to cope with external threats, it must be able to summon large numbers to its defense. For republics, which by definition are governed by the people, these imperatives of scale create an insuperable dilemma. If the republic is small enough to govern itself peaceably, it will be too weak to defend itself, while if its numbers are great enough for defense, they will be too many for self-government." *To Make a Nation: The Rediscovery of American Federalism* (Cambridge, Mass.: Harvard University Press, 1993), 86ff.

[6] The position of the Anti-Federalists on scale is conveniently summarized in Herbert J. Storing, *What the Anti-Federalists Were For* (Chicago: University of Chicago Press, 1981), chap. 3; Madison's classic statement in defense of the extended sphere is of course *The Federalist*, No. 10.

sense or to the same degree self-governing, but there too government was quite decentralized. It was concentrated at the level of the county. Everywhere, state legislatures set the framework for local government—their legal superiority was never in doubt—but state governments' capacity for supervision was minimal. Domestic government in nineteenth-century America was local government.

All of this changed dramatically in the several decades after the Civil War, as the population multiplied, large cities formed, the economy industrialized, transportation was revolutionized by the railroad and then the car, society grew more riven and stratified, and the nation, now confirmed in its nationhood, essayed imperial adventures.

Progressive political thinkers then confronted with passion, urgency, and the overbearing earnestness of well-meaning Protestants the question of whether democracy really existed in their country, with its ideal of popular sovereignty. They mounted ambitious projects of reform at every level of the federal system—local, state, and national—in an attempt to perfect it. Although today's scholarship typically understands them to have been nationalists primarily, even the most nationalistic among them, Herbert Croly, took the trouble not to attack the principle of federalism frontally.[7] Many of them honored the small-scale place, beginning with the neighborhood, and worried about how to maintain its vitality in the new urbanizing, more complex and impersonal society.[8] Moreover, as social and political activists, they practiced what they preached. They were active in settlement houses and municipal governments, as well as in the Progressive movement at the level of national party politics.

An example was Frances Perkins, who became secretary of labor in Franklin Roosevelt's administration after years of activism and officeholding at the municipal and state levels. In the 1940s, she remarked on the experience:

I only knew the state. I was much more aware of New York and of belonging to it than I was of belonging to the U.S.A., which perhaps is wrong and unpatriotic,

---

[7] For example, Eldon Eisenach, *The Lost Promise of Progressivism* (Lawrence: University of Kansas Press, 1994) and Michael S. Joyce and William A. Schambra, "A New Citizenship, a New Civic Life," in Lamar Alexander and Chester E. Finn, Jr., eds., *The New Promise of American Life* (Indianapolis: Hudson Institute, 1995). For Croly's denial that nationalization of society necessarily meant centralization of government, see *The Promise of American Life* (New York: E. P. Dutton, 1963; copyright by Macmillan, 1909), 273, 275, and *Progressive Democracy* (New York: Macmillan, 1914), 241–42.

[8] See especially Follett, *The New State*.

but I honestly believe that's how people develop. You become responsible for a small area you can see. You gradually know the rest.[9]

Tocqueville never put it more vividly, or convincingly.

The assumption on which this volume rests is that Tocqueville, Mill, Dewey, Follett, and Perkins were not wrong. Without vigorous local governments in which they learn the rudiments of democracy and become attached to the polity in a small area they can "see"—see in the sense that they experience it, not just watch events staged for their viewing on TV—citizens are unlikely to become reliably attached to the larger polity. They are likely to become distrustful, to think that they are being misled or ignored or, worse, taken advantage of by self-serving officials in a remote national capital. That describes the attitude of many Americans today, and although there are probably many causes for this deep and persistent disaffection, which polls and political scientists have been reporting for approximately thirty years,[10] I would guess that one contributing cause is the drastically diminished importance of local government in the modern American polity, compared with, say, the early twentieth century. That belief on my part, which rests on no concrete evidence, inspired the project that led to this volume. I do not know to what extent the contributors may share that belief, but all have brought to this work respect for the claim that the health of democracy on a small scale is important for the health of it on a large scale. That shared point of view gave coherence to the undertaking.

How one thinks about the place of local democracy in the larger American democracy depends crucially on how one thinks about the place of local governments in the federal system, within which they are embedded. The very existence of local governments is contingent: Constitutionally, they are creatures of state governments. On the other hand, state governments, their nominal creators, are not creatures of the national government, but have a constitutionally protected right to exist independently. At least vis-à-vis the national government, then, local governments share in this independent right to exist, insofar as state governments permit them to enjoy it.

One can view American federalism from two quite different theoretical

[9] George Martin, *Madam Secretary: Frances Perkins* (Boston: Houghton Mifflin, 1976), 164.
[10] For a leading report, see Seymour Martin Lipset and William Schneider, *The Confidence Gap* (New York: The Free Press, 1983). For a brief update, see Burns W. Roper, "Democracy in America: How Are We Doing? We're Doing Our Best to Make the Answer 'Badly,'" *The Public Perspective* 5, no. 3 (March/April 1994): 3–5.

perspectives, which have been explicated by Beer. One theory is that of contractual federalism; the other he calls "national federalism." Under contractual federalism, several sovereign and independent states enter into a contract or treaty under which they delegate specified and limited powers to a general government. They retain their sovereignty. Under national federalism, a federal system is not based on a contract among separate sovereigns, but derives from "an order by the single sovereign power, the people at large of the whole country, who create two levels of government, a general government and several state governments, delegating to each certain limited powers." According to Beer, both systems are federal in the sense that each "provides for a territorial division of authority between a general government and several state governments, protected by some sort of exceptional [presumably constitutional] legal provision."[11]

Beer argues that national federalism was the theory embraced by the American Framers, Madison principally, against a background of its development by the English political philosopher James Harrington. The warrant for this interpretation is found above all in a powerful passage with which Madison opened *Federalist* No. 46. He is addressing the question of whether the federal government or state governments will hold the advantage in the new union—and that, he says, will depend on the decision of the sovereign people, who are the common superior of all of them:

Notwithstanding the different modes in which they are appointed, we must consider both of them as substantially dependent on the great body of the citizens of the United States. . . . The federal and State governments are in fact but different agents and trustees of the people, constituted with different powers and designed for different purposes. The adversaries of the Constitution seem to have lost sight of the people altogether in their reasonings on this subject; and to have viewed these different establishments not only as mutual rivals and enemies, but as uncontrolled by any common superior in their efforts to usurp the authorities of each other. These gentlemen must be reminded of their error. . . . The ultimate authority . . . resides in the people alone.[12]

In Madison's theory, the federal principle becomes, along with separation of powers, an "auxiliary precaution" by which the people maintain control over the government.[13] In a representative government, the prin-

---

[11] The full argument appears in Beer, *To Make a Nation*. I have drawn here from a summary of it—a speech entitled "Federalism and the National Idea: The Uses of Diversity"—that was published in the *Harvard Graduate Society Newsletter* (Fall 1991): 8–9, 20–24.

[12] *The Federalist Papers* (New York: New American Library, 1961), 294.

[13] The phrase appears in *Federalist* 51, ibid., 322.

cipal means of control remains the government's direct dependence upon the people. As organs of government created by the people, state governments and their local subdivisions became a means by which the people could check and balance the power of the national government. But in Madison's view, which is also emphatically Beer's view, the smaller places are no more purely democratic by reason of being small. On the contrary, democracy would be perfected—and principles of justice and the general good would be arrived at—by rational debate and discussion on the large scale. In this view, diversity did not cripple democracy in a great nation. Rather, "diversity was welcomed as an indispensable condition for strengthening the foundations and widening the horizons of public opinion."[14]

Throughout American history, compact-based, essentially conflictual theories of federalism have competed with theories that emphasize the oneness of the nation and the need for cooperation among all of its legal and social parts. For a long time, the Supreme Court operated with the postulates that the two centers of government were "sovereign" and hence "equal," and that the relation of the two levels of government with each other was one of tension rather than collaboration. By 1950, these postulates of "dual federalism," as the late Edward S. Corwin called it, were dead.[15] States were no longer seen as sovereign or equal, and the normal relation between the different levels of government was now presumed to be cooperation. Intergovernmental cooperation, in the form specifically of grants-in-aid, had been practiced at least since 1862, when the Morrill Land-Grant College Act was passed to assist states in establishing colleges in the agricultural and mechanical arts. Cooperation was the prescription of Progressive political thinkers such as Croly and Follett. As constitutional practice, it received powerful confirmation with passage of the Federal Aid Highway Act in 1916 and then the Social Security Act of 1935, with which Congress and the New Deal administration of Franklin D. Roosevelt fashioned a public policy for poor relief. Although that act created for the benefit of retired workers the purely national program that we now know as Social Security, it also entrusted public support of the poor to federally aided but state-run programs for the aged and for dependent children. Intergovernmental coop-

[14] *Harvard Graduate Society Newsletter:* 22.
[15] "The Passing of Dual Federalism," in *American Constitutional History: Essays by Edward S. Corwin,* ed. Alpheus T. Mason and Gerald Garvey (New York: Harper Torchbooks, 1964), 145–64. The original article appeared in the *Virginia Law Review* (February 1950).

eration is deeply, irrevocably embedded in the practice of American government.

But even if collaboration has become the norm in governance, tensions between small-scale polities and the large-scale one persist. As constitutional scholar Herman Belz has suggested, these tensions are associated in American political thought with rival conceptions of freedom, which the Founding generation contested. There is the liberty of self-governing communities, which have an obligation to make citizens virtuous and on which they depend for happiness and well-being. Competing with it is a conception of liberty resting on natural rights, which asserts the primacy of individual liberty over community consensus.[16]

American practice initially favored the first of these conceptions. Historical accounts convincingly show that at the beginning of the experiment with self-government, at least in New England, individuals were tightly bound to, and observed the norms of, the small-scale societies to which they belonged. The medieval historian Peter Riesenberg, bringing a fresh eye to the American Founding, finds the explanation for Americans' embrace of republicanism partly in their practice of self-government on the small scale, which he compares with the practices of ancient Greece:

What predisposed so many colonists to choose some form of republicanism as the basis for their new country? Though surely not the whole answer, perhaps part of it lies in the fact that in 1776 the overwhelming majority of Americans still lived in the kind of small-scaled community whose life and values we have seen were essentially stable since the Greeks. In terms of law, social theory, and reality, and the relationship of secular and religious authority, Concord [Massachusetts], for example, resembled an English village of the late Middle Ages, or, indeed, ancient Sparta. In the size of its population, its acceptance of community values and the community's regulation of public, economic, and personal life, in its constant search for the basis of harmony in the making of corporate decisions, its need for unity and homogeneity in religious affairs, its dependence upon shame to assure conformity, its intolerance of novelty and idiosyncrasy, its dependence upon citizens for the temporary but recurrent exercise of public office—in all these critical ways and matters the similarity of the colonial town to the ancient polis is remarkable.[17]

However, such tightly bound communities were no sooner established in the New World than they began to come apart. A vividly detailed

---

[16] Herman Belz, "Constitutionalism and the American Founding," in *The Framing and Ratification of the Constitution,* ed. Leonard W. Levy and Dennis J. Mahoney (New York: Macmillan, 1987), 344.

[17] Peter Riesenberg, *Citizenship in the Western Tradition* (Chapel Hill: University of North Carolina Press, 1992), 269.

monograph by historian Helena M. Wall shows how powerfully constraining these early American communities were—and how stressful and
oppressive life in them was.[18] No wonder the frontier beckoned. No wonder the search for republican liberty soon took the form of separating the
public from the private, and eventually using public power radically to
protect the private. The second conception of freedom, which was very
much present at the framing, gained strength with time and today prevails, though not without challenge.[19]

As Americans broke out of the early communal mold, they held fast
nevertheless to the idea that they had a right to self-government on the
small scale. Communities on the frontiers of settlement defined themselves rather than being defined by central governments.[20] Woodrow Wilson, with customary rhetorical flourish, spoke of "self-originated, self-
constituted, self-confident, self-sustaining, veritable communities,"
which had "sprung up of themselves," rather than having been invited to
exist "like plants in a tended garden." The American garden of communities in Wilson's image was untended, spontaneous, a bit wild. This spon-
taneity and variety, he said, "this irrepressible life of its communities,"
had given the United States its extraordinary elasticity.[21]

Today, the United States still gropes to find an accommodation between
the great nation and parts of smaller scale that are defined in space and en-
dowed with their own institutions of government. This is an effort to realize equality and justice without sacrificing liberty and elasticity. Or, in
Belz's terms, harking back to the framing, it is an effort to reconcile two
competing conceptions of liberty. The search for accommodation, sometimes conflictual, sometimes cooperative, is the central subject of this volume. The nation makes more powerful claims on the attentiveness of citizens than it once did, and its government reaches far more deeply and
pervasively into their everyday lives. But the residue of the country's his-

---

[18] *Fierce Communion: Family and Community in Early America* (Cambridge, Mass.: Harvard University Press, 1990). An "afterword" on "transformations" (126–50) describes
the disintegration of that early community. The disintegration was itself very early.

[19] For recent challenges, see Michael J. Sandel, *Democracy's Discontent* (Cambridge, Mass.:
Harvard University Press, 1996) and Alan Ehrenhalt, *The Lost City: Discovering the Forgotten Virtues of Community in the Chicago of the 1950s* (New York: Basic Books, 1995).

[20] See the description of how "outlivers"—persons separated by distance, religion, resent-
ment of taxes, or whatever—seceded from New England towns and set up towns of their
own, with their own church and meeting, in Kenneth A. Lockridge, *Settlement and Unsettlement in Early America* (Cambridge: Cambridge University Press, 1981), 39–43.

[21] *Constitutional Government in the United States* (New York: Columbia University Press,
1908), 182–83. But Wilson appears to have been referring to states, not localities.

toric localism remains evident in many of its governmental structures and public attitudes. Many thousands of general-purpose local governments exist in this country, which—by comparison with other Western nations—has been unusually resistant to abolishing them.[22] As trust in the federal government to do a good job has plummeted since the late 1960s and early 1970s, trust in local governments has remained fairly stable; as of the early 1990s, it was well above the level for the federal government.[23]

Although the essays in this volume all rest on some measure of respect for the claims of locality in American public life, they focus variously on the several themes that I have identified: the contribution that small-scale democracy may make to the larger democracy; the nature of American federalism and intergovernmental relations; and the values of community as they come into conflict with claims of individual right and entitlement. Even if we hoped to produce essays that were theoretically informed and informative, this volume is not meant primarily as a contribution to the literature of political theory, one important body of which today pits "liberals" against "communitarians." Rather, for the most part we concentrated on the empirical task of showing how dilemmas of scale and the definition of political community have entered into politics and policy-making in the United States, both historically and presently, forming one dimension of the democratic dialogue by which governing takes place.

Today, unlike the Founding generation and those successors who fought a civil war, we take the existence of a powerful national government as a fact of political life. A strong national government developed for many compelling reasons: to promote and regulate commerce on a large scale; to respond to demands for economic stability and security; to combat discrimination with guarantees of fundamental rights; to protect against foreign enemies, which grew more menacing as physical isolation diminished. But this development also occurred because the "national idea"—the idea that the nation is the primary political community, superior morally as well as legally to the lesser ones—took hold.[24] Building on

---

[22] *Local Government Reform and Reorganization,* ed. Arthur B. Gunlicks (Port Washington, N.Y.: Kennikat Press, 1981).

[23] Everett Carll Ladd, ed., *America at the Polls, 1994* (Roper Center for Public Opinion Research, 1995), 34.

[24] Samuel H. Beer, "The National Idea in American Politics," lecture delivered to the faculty and officers of Boston College, Chestnut Hill, Mass., April 21, 1982. For a sharp critique of the national idea and its effects, see Michael S. Joyce and William A. Schambra, "A New Civic Life," in Michael Novak, ed., 20th anniversary edition of Peter L. Berger and Richard John Neuhaus, *To Empower People: From State to Civil Society* (Washington, D.C.: AEI Press, 1996), 11–29.

foundations laid primarily by Alexander Hamilton speaking for the Federalists and Daniel Webster speaking for the Whigs, the leaders of Progressivism early in the twentieth century argued the necessity of a national political community of shared social ideals. Thereafter successive liberal Democratic presidents advanced the cause of nationalism, and modern social science contributes to the devaluation of political community on the small scale by interpreting local government mainly as an instrument for realizing selfish economic advantage and racial exclusion.[25]

Our shared purpose in this volume is to show that self-government on a small scale is a legitimate, even indispensable, portion of the American political inheritance. As readers will see, this does not mean that contributors necessarily embrace the present arrangements of American local government. On the contrary, several are severely critical. Like any political institution, local governments in the American mold may be perverted and used for unworthy ends. We want to suggest nonetheless that there are still grounds for honoring this peculiarly American inheritance and attempting to perfect it. Although the growth of national government has been necessary and in many respects beneficial, few students of government would deny that centralization and the development of mass democracy have had costs. As Sidney Milkis argues, Americans have been left without adequate means of "common deliberation and public judgment." They are also alienated and distrustful. Though big government is more honest, professional, fair, and egalitarian than what it replaced, it is also more remote and impersonal. Once cared for by politicians in face-to-face relations, citizens are now manipulated by them through mass media—and they respond with boredom, cynicism, and distaste. Government has ceased to engage the citizenry as it once did.[26]

One place—we do not insist the only place—to seek repair may be in political institutions on a small scale; as Stephen Elkin argues, local government uniquely affords citizens the experience of "deliberating and struggling over the content of the public interest"—and thereby learning how to judge others (elected officials at all levels) who are supposed to do such deliberating on behalf of the rest of us. How best to improve local political institutions is open to debate. Contributors to this volume have varying views on that subject.

[25] See, for example, Nancy Burns, *The Formation of American Local Governments: Private Values in Public Institutions* (New York: Oxford University Press, 1994).

[26] For an extremely evocative account of this change in its Southern context, see Jimmy Carter, *Turning Point: A Candidate, a State, and a Nation Come of Age* (New York: Times Books, 1992).

We begin in Part I with two essays (Wilson, Elkin) that consider the benefits to be realized by nurturing citizenship in the local polity, the ways in which that might be done, and the need in the modern nation to find a way to reconcile the claims of the rights-defining and rights-enforcing national government (for so it appears in this volume, for good and ill) with the more pragmatic, concrete, and grounded politics and society of the smaller place. Wilson states the moral importance of local communities: "a set of shared expectations and living arrangements that exist to express and enhance the social nature of mankind." And he defends their differences: "People ought to be free to seek out and take pride in the differences that exist among communities." Elkin, on the other hand, while making a forceful argument for local politics as a school of citizenship, holds that the actual localities of the United States are poor schools because they are balkanized and sharply differentiated by their socioeconomic conditions. This eliminates the need for hard choices about the public interest in prosperous places and sharply narrows the opportunity for choice in very poor ones. If local governments are to be relied on for sustaining a republican regime, Elkin believes, they must be reformed.

Following this introduction, in Part II a group of historical essays analyzes the grounding of local self-government in early American experience (Maier); the attenuation of the localistic tradition over time as the nation developed, Progressivism fostered plebiscitary democracy, and the federal system became centralized (Milkis, Derthick); and the persistence of that tradition nonetheless in many thousands of institutions of local government (Doherty and Stone).

Maier's essay, though cast as a critique of Tocqueville, does not challenge his observation that local self-government was uniquely vital in British North America. She finds the explanation for that in the colonists' English heritage and in the exigencies of governing a very extended territory. Milkis argues the importance of political parties in sustaining local self-government, and traces the decline of parties to Progressive Era reform, with its commitment to pure democracy. In his view, Progressivism was critical in turning the United States from a decentralized republic into a mass democracy. My essay purports to show how important and persistent local government was in the United States. Well into the twentieth century, American domestic government was largely local, but this changed under the impact of Progressivism, the New Deal, and the modern rights revolution. Doherty and Stone, though sharing the view that local government is "heavily infused with private values and calculations about private advantage," hold that "because of their proximity to the everyday life of citizens, local governments hold the best hope for engaging citizens in self-governance; that local institutions have the *potential* for being places of reinvigorated participation, citizenship, and community; and that, in a country increasingly disillusioned and dissatisfied with politics, this potential needs to be explored." That is the task they undertake.

In Part III a series of papers examines the interplay of the national and the local in several currently contested policy arenas: land use (Altshuler); environmental protection (Landy); schools (Weiher and Cookson); voting rights (Valelly); and criminal justice (Hagedorn and DiIulio).

Altshuler's essay describes and explains the persistence of land-use regulation as a function of local government, and illuminates the dilemmas that this poses for a society whose public ideology, if not its private practices, rejects inequality and segregation. Landy seeks to discover what might constitute the appropriate limits of the strong national policy apparatus that has developed since the early 1970s in the field of environmental protection. He asks at what point the harms wrought by increased policy centralization exceed its benefits. Weiher and Cookson ask, apropos the schools, whether "some arrangement can be found that preserves the affective influence of local communities without sanctioning meanness toward those who, while being outsiders in the organic sense, are nonetheless fellow Americans"—and then wrestle with the dilemma both theoretically and by reference to experience. Valelly shows how national intervention via voting rights policy has produced gains in local self-government in the South. In the last chapter of this section, Hagedorn and DiIulio by contrast set forth a highly critical view of the federal government's role in administering criminal justice. They find that much federal judicial intervention in state and local government is unjustified and harmful. Each policy arena has its own set of dilemmas. All of these authors struggle with the pros and cons of centralization in a historically decentralized polity.

As the Center's Project on Local Self-Government proceeded, the workshop participants came to focus more intently on the need for a reconciliation between large-scale and small-scale polities, and for conceptions of community and federalism that would facilitate one. Society's everyday struggle became our intellectual struggle; we found ourselves groping for balance, a middle way. Hence we welcomed the afterword by Philip Selznick—a benign, helpful observer at the project's workshops—whose recent work had addressed, from the perspective of sociology and philosophy, questions that we were approaching as historically oriented political scientists—or, in the case of Maier, as a politically oriented historian.[27]

Selznick's afterword bespeaks the aspirations of the participants generally, even though it is an independent contribution, composed after listening sympathetically to the project members' struggle with the intellectual dilemmas of scale and the polarities of the particular and the universal. His brief essay, which emphasizes the value in any community of unity that preserves the integrity of the parts, at least conceptually points the way for a constructive resolution of long-standing dilemmas of American democracy.

[27] Philip Selznick, *The Moral Commonwealth: Social Theory and the Promise of Community* (Berkeley: University of California Press, 1992).

I

Citizenship and local self-government

1

City life and citizenship

JAMES Q. WILSON

Cities occupy an ambiguous place in American federalism. Constitutionally they do not exist; that document recognizes and protects the existence of states, their representation in the Senate, and their right to a "republican form of government." Nowhere are cities mentioned. They are the creatures of state law and, in theory, might be abolished or changed by state legislatures.

But people regard cities—or more accurately, communities—as the foundation of the political system. They view their members of the House chiefly as representatives of local areas with an obligation to serve local needs; they jealously assert the right of a community to exercise control over schools, police, and land-use policy; when asked which level of government gives them their money's worth, they put cities ahead of states and Washington;[1] when they engage in volunteer action, it is typically in communities, with community needs in mind.

This conflict between the legal and the affective status of communities suggests that federalism in the United States has two quite distinct and sometimes competing meanings. Federalism is about both levels of authority and realms of life. Cities, especially the small ones (or the communities that make up large ones), are scarcely visible as a level of legal authority, but they are all-important as a domain of human life. The conflict between these two meanings of "city" lies at the heart of many of our most passionate debates. Legally, a city is a concentration of people governed by a municipal corporation created to deliver services. Membership in such a state-chartered corporation has, in theory, no effect on citizenship, rights, or obligations; these matters are determined uniformly for a

---

[1] *Los Angeles Times* poll data as cited in *The Public Perspective*, April–May 1995: 28.

17

whole nation (or, in the view of a few writers, the entire world). Morally, a city is a set of shared expectations and living arrangements that exist to express and enhance the social nature of mankind. People like or dislike their cities precisely to the extent that they produce decent citizens, encourage desirable careers, and punish deviant behaviors; these matters are powerfully shaped by local circumstances, and people ought to be free to seek out and take pride in the differences that exist among communities. The great struggles over civil rights have been between these two meanings of community.

In the ancient view, the city—the polis—was necessary to the perfection of human nature. Man could not acquire virtue except as part of a community; his community ought to be judged good or bad to the extent that it produced virtue. Men had rights, but these rights did not exist in or derive from a prior state of nature; they derived from membership in a community and could not exist apart from it.[2]

This view was replaced in the West with the idea that human nature exists apart from the communities in which particular men live and that men have rights that derive from some pre-social status. This belief lies at the heart of the Enlightenment and of the political arrangements spawned by that movement. The Declaration of Independence gave memorable expression to the idea; the Constitution provided a mechanism by which it could be vindicated. But the theory that one could, in the abstract and without regard to membership in a community, be a citizen and have the rights of a citizen is still not a familiar one, I suspect, to the vast majority of people who now live or who ever lived.

Most Americans believe in the promise of the Declaration and endorse the arrangements of the Constitution, but they are ambivalent about the underlying principle. They agree that people are in a legal and moral sense created equal, but in every practical sense they are manifestly unequal—in talents, actions, beliefs, and aspirations. Those differences affect how people will live together in communities that are central to the happiness and well-being of most of their residents. The Declaration is a cosmopolitan proclamation, but people are by nature locals. An increasing fraction of them have become cosmopolitans—that is, persons whose lives are oriented toward the national or global world of ideas, occupations, and commerce—but they remain only a fraction, and even that fraction spends much time worrying about conditions in their neighborhoods.

It could scarcely be otherwise. For most of his time on earth, man has

---

[2] Fred D. Miller, Jr., *Nature, Justice, and Rights in Aristotle's Politics* (New York: Oxford University Press, 1995).

lived in communities that rarely exceeded a few dozen people. Evolution has made us neighbors (*neighbor:* literally, "the next farmer").[3] Our interest in local matters dominates our concern for national or international ones. The space given to local news is three times as great as that given to cosmopolitan news even in a cosmopolitan newspaper such as the *Los Angeles Times;* it is undoubtedly much greater in less ambitious journals. A typical 11 P.M. television newscast will contain four times as much local as national news; an all-news radio station will broadcast more local news than any other kind.[4]

It is sometimes said that voting turnout is higher in big cities than small ones. That finding, however, confounds individual and communal effects. Big cities have higher proportions of people with high incomes and much schooling—traits that are correlated with political participation. Controlling for these traits, Sidney Verba and Norman Nie found that residents of rural areas and isolated communities (that is, towns not part of a metropolitan area) vote in elections at a higher rate than do residents of big cities. When forms of participation other than voting—writing letters, going to meetings, calling officials—are included, small-town participation is even higher.[5]

People are right in assigning importance to communal affairs. They care about the demeanor of their neighbors because it affects them directly and, in the short run, more profoundly than almost any national or world event. Their safety and peace of mind are determined by how the boys down the block behave; the value of their property is affected by how neighbors maintain property nearby; the confidence they have in their own children's schooling is influenced by the conduct of other people's children in that school.

Americans tell pollsters that they think crime and disorder are desperately serious problems, but many of them also say that crime is not a great problem in their own neighborhood.[6] Critics seize on this discrepancy as

---

[3] Note that the Old English for a peasant, "boor," has now become the word for a clownish rustic. A contemporary cosmopolitan often thinks of his neighbors as tiresome boors.

[4] Estimates made by Heather Elms.

[5] Sidney Verba and Norman H. Nie, *Participation in America* (New York: Harper & Row, 1972), chap. 13. My attention was drawn to this finding by Richard Dagger, "Metropolis, Memory, and Citizenship," *American Journal of Political Science* 25 (November 1981): 724.

[6] In 1993, the Gallup Poll found that 86 percent of interviewees believed crime was an important issue, but only 5 percent thought their neighborhoods had more crime than the average amount of crime; 57 percent thought their areas had less than the average amount. *The Gallup Poll: Public Opinion, 1993* (Wilmington, Del.: Scholarly Resources, 1994), 177, 204.

evidence that the fear of crime reflects hysteria or media manipulation more than any daily reality. But that criticism misses the point. People take the crime rate seriously even though it may not touch them directly for the same reason they take the unemployment rate seriously even though they have a job: A high level of crime (or unemployment) suggests that the community (or the nation) is ill. Human satisfactions are to a significant degree interdependent; we cannot be entirely happy if people with whom our fate is intertwined are unhappy, and we cannot be confident about our future if the future of people like us is clouded.

THE RECIPROCAL CONSTRUCTION OF CITIZENSHIP

Crime and disorder are to neighborhoods what cancer and infection are to organisms. If the immune system of other communities is weak, we suspect that of our own community is also weak. As a result, we often evaluate neighbors by stricter standards than we evaluate acquaintances who do not live near us. The behavior of the former shapes our lives in ways the conduct of the latter cannot. An acquaintance living at a distance may have all manner of annoying eccentricities, but we are prepared to overlook or chuckle about many of them because they do not affect how we live, and are more than offset by traits that we find engaging or lovable. But similar oddities among neighbors affect our communal life, and we are less prepared to overlook them or offset them against more appealing qualities. We select our friends but not our neighbors, so the latter are to some degree strangers in our midst; we deal with them because of where, not who, they are.

We teach our neighbors and they teach us. Frequent face-to-face contact and the regular observation of one another's conduct shapes how we act toward them and they toward us. We hope that by things said and unsaid, by direct gaze or averted eyes, by reproach and suggestion we can increase the chances that they will live quietly, reciprocate favors, avoid excess, respect privacy, maintain property, and acknowledge rights. They have similar hopes for us, though their standards may differ from ours. A neighborhood is a school for civility, if not for citizenship. A good neighborhood—good, that is, because standards are widely shared, commonly enforced, and generally observed—is a public asset, one that induces pride and sustains loyalty. A bad neighborhood—bad because standards are in conflict or command no general support—is a curse.

This process of teaching civility is enhanced by the conditions of small-town life. Many years ago, Stanley Milgram found that city dwellers were, compared with people in small communities, less polite, more suspicious, and less helpful.[7] Since this finding accords with popular opinion and everyday experience, it is probably true. Small-town relationships are fostered—or, if you prefer, induced—by such simple things as eye contact. People in Parkesburg, Pennsylvania, a town of 2,700 residents, are much more likely to make eye contact with and speak to strangers than are people in Philadelphia or even Bryn Mawr. (Though small, Bryn Mawr is part of the Philadelphia metropolitan area, whereas Parkesburg is isolated.)[8]

Though civility may be the first virtue of a good neighborhood, civility can lead to citizenship. People with a shared sense of community will be more likely, I conjecture, to have a shared sense of efficacy. People who feel they can influence their neighbors will be more likely to feel they can influence distant officials, if for no other reason than their ability to mobilize neighbors to act upon officials. Small towns are more likely than big cities to produce the civilizing effects of neighborhood, and definable neighborhoods in big cities are more likely to do this than indistinct or contested neighborhoods in those cities.

The kinds of citizenship that results will depend on the size of the city in which it is produced. For example, conflicts among people in small communities or discrete neighborhoods in big cities will often be especially impassioned. Many neighbors fight more bitterly and bear grudges longer than urban activists. The former quarrel as individuals, the latter as representatives of groups; the former are weakly organized, the latter highly organized; the former commit their entire personality to the issue, the latter play specialized roles; the former are mobilized by issues that affect them personally, the latter by ones that involve them ideologically. Big-city politics is like national politics: Owing to the existence of cross-cutting cleavages and organizational roles, activists can fight without much rancor and change allies without any shame. In this respect large-scale politics may be more likely to teach moderation and prudence. But small-scale politics teaches something else—the importance of direct knowledge, firsthand experience, long-term commitments, and communal preservation. Localistic politics is rarely about abstractions, the knowledge that informs it is not controlled by the media, and the participants must live with the conse-

---

[7] Stanley Milgram, "The Experience of Living in Cities," *Science* 167 (1970): 1461–8.
[8] Joseph Newman and Clark McCauley, "Eye Contact with Strangers in City, Suburb, and Small Town," *Environment and Behavior* 9 (December 1977): 547–58.

quences. It is about the quality of local schools, the use of local land, and the protection of familial interests.

THE REVOLT AGAINST LOCALISM

Because localism produces bourgeois civility and parochial politics, we should not be surprised to discover that cosmopolitans, and especially intellectuals, would view it skeptically. And indeed they have. As others remark in this volume, the approval of small-town life found in Thornton Wilder's *Our Town* is nearly drowned out by the contempt for it expressed in Sinclair Lewis's *Main Street*, Sherwood Anderson's *Winesburg, Ohio*, and Grace Metalious's *Peyton Place*. What may be surprising is that intellectuals ever had much good to say about localism.[9] Yet some did.

At one time, scholars such as Ferdinand Toennies deplored the replacement of the idealized communal life of rural villages (gemeinschaft) with the anonymous, calculating life of big cities (gesellschaft), but they were soon replaced by writers such as Émile Durkheim, who applauded the opportunity created by the growth of cities.[10] To the latter, the individualistic cohesion of big-city life—"organic" solidarity—would replace the stultifying conformity of village life—"mechanical" solidarity.

In this century, the study of the city for a while seemed to be guided by a sense of the lost neighborhood. In 1938, Louis Wirth published his famous essay, "Urbanism As a Way of Life," in which he lamented the extent to which the size, density, and heterogeneity of big cities led to the depersonalization of human relations, the decay of mutual support, and the erosion of traditional values.[11]

The Durkheimian reaction was not long in coming. A new generation of scholars celebrated the very features that Wirth (and before him, Toennies) deplored. Cities, indeed, lead to an erosion of old values—and a good thing, too. Villagers are intolerant, urbanites tolerant; village life emphasizes conformity, city life opportunity; villages require interaction, cities

---

[9] Of course, some intellectuals have viewed localism abroad with a tolerance never displayed toward it at home. Village life in primitive cultures (or village life in a romanticized Western past) has often elicited praise from cosmopolitans who would never dream of living in such conditions in contemporary America or Europe.

[10] Ferdinand Toennies, *Community and Society* (New York: Harper & Row, 1963, first published in 1887); Émile Durkheim, *The Division of Labor in Society* (New York: Free Press, 1964, first published in 1893).

[11] Louis Wirth, "Urbanism As a Way of Life," *American Journal of Sociology* 44 (1938): 1–24.

permit privacy. And besides, big cities are collections of urban villages; community is alive and well in New York, but each community is one that its members have chosen, so each is an expression of a personal lifestyle.

There was much truth in all of these rejoinders. Indeed, their premise had been defended by none other than James Madison when he explained that liberty would be more secure in a large republic because oppressive majority factions would be harder to form in large as opposed to small polities.[12] But the average citizen need not read the *Federalist* papers to grasp the point; anyone with unusual opinions, an exotic lifestyle, or unconventional tastes will find more opportunities and less censure on Broadway than on Main Street, in Cleveland than in Winesburg. (This is not to deny the existence of small-town refuges for the offbeat; the hot tubs of Mill Valley have become a modern, albeit minor, legend.)

Madison's argument in favor of an extended republic and his involvement in writing an apparently mechanistic and libertarian Constitution have prompted a lasting and important debate over what role, if any, the Founders assigned to virtue and character formation. The most plausible answer, I think, is that they intended to create a national government of few and defined powers, leaving to other levels of government and to private arrangements—village and church life in particular—the task of helping shape a decent citizenry. But I confess that it is hard to find much in the writings of the most prominent Founders to indicate that they spent much time thinking about this question.[13] Conservatives often regret the Founders' inattention to virtue, liberals their neglect of community. I think these regrets overstate matters a bit. Before the Constitution was even written, the Northwest Ordinance had been passed by the Continental Congress (it was reaffirmed by the First Congress). That law asserts that "religion, morality, and knowledge being necessary to good government and the happiness of mankind, schools and the means of education shall forever be encouraged." As Charles Kesler notes, by the 1930s this commitment had led to setting aside more than 145 million acres of public land to endow public education.[14] Some states, such as Massachusetts, had anticipated the Ordinance; others were not long in following this

[12] *Federalist* No. 10.
[13] For a spirited argument that the Founders so neglected virtue as to create an "ill-founded" regime, see George F. Will, *Statecraft as Soulcraft* (New York: Simon & Schuster, 1983).
[14] Charles R. Kesler, "Education and Politics: Lessons from the American Founding," *University of Chicago Legal Forum* 1991: 101–22.

lead, in almost every case for purposes of moral improvement as well as technical training.

Nonetheless, the new regime undeniably created a regime based on rights, and big cities in time became the places in which those rights could be most vigorously asserted. Over the years, big and small cities alike had practiced segregation, rounded up vagrants, jailed drunks, and forcibly treated the mentally ill. But big cities contained organized groups that could contest issues that in small ones were left to informal understandings. When the courts set about ending segregation, striking down laws against vagrancy and public drunkenness, and deinstitutionalizing the mentally ill, they found allies in big cities but not small ones. When mayors began building high-rise public housing projects and mounting slum-clearance programs, there existed in big cities both supporters (people demanding new housing, business groups eager to revitalize central business districts) and opportunities (neighborhoods that lacked effective political-defense systems) to a greater degree than in small cities. The national government is sometimes characterized as acting on (and even against) big cities and big-city interests, but a closer inspection of the action usually reveals that Washington agencies are acting with certain factions within cities—housing or school officials, for example—and against other factions within those cities.

Modern life has become urban life. But even in the big city, the old distinction between locals and cosmopolitans remains important. Urban locals are those who came to the metropolis searching for work and opportunity but retain a localistic attitude toward neighborhood. They pay great attention to those who live around them, prefer areas with shared cultures to those with diverse ones, join block clubs and neighborhood groups, and worry about whether the neighbors worry enough about what others think of them. Cosmopolitans also come to the big city for opportunity, but they have little interest in their neighbors. As long as the neighborhood (which for them may mean the apartment building) is safe and attractive, what the neighbors do or think is of no importance. Cosmopolitans are oriented to the world of fashion, ideas, and career, and to friends who live in different neighborhoods or even distant cities. To them, the city is a refuge from the forced intimacy of the small town.

For locals, citizenship means voting, obeying the law, being a good neighbor, and (occasionally) joining neighborhood causes; to the cosmopolitan, it means voting, obeying the law, not bothering neighbors, and participating in causes and careers that, typically, have no territorial base. Sometimes it means even more. Alan Ehrenhalt's splendid account of small-community life in the 1950s within the Chicago area reveals how, even inside a huge metropolis, neighborhoods could combine small businesses, local churches, and particular schools into an intensely local lifestyle even though these homespun areas were within an easy drive of the cosmopolitan lures of The Big City.[15]

My conjecture that locals outnumber cosmopolitans even in big cities is consistent with the fact that most people, I think, prefer small-town and suburban life. But one need not rely on conjecture; far stronger evidence is available from the movement of the population. For decades, central cities have lost population while suburbs gained it. Between 1960 and 1990, the percentage of the population living in cities with 25,000 to 50,000 inhabitants grew by 18 percent; the percentage living in cities with 500,000 to 1,000,000 residents fell by 31 percent.[16] The ideal urban residence for many Americans is a city of single-family homes, little traffic, one high school, and a small, accessible city hall.

For a long time, federal policy has supported this preference by means of subsidized mortgages (FHA and GI home loans) and the interstate highway system. The middle class was encouraged to leave the city; the poor who remained behind were provided with public housing projects close to downtown. In the late 1950s, that policy began to change. The combined effect of middle-class flight to the suburbs and lower-class concentration in urban ghettos deprived the central business district of affluent customers and left city hall scrambling for tax revenues. Urban-renewal programs were created to keep (or lure back) the restless middle class, urban mass transit systems received federal subsidies once reserved almost entirely for the interstate highway system, and the ability of the suburbs to maintain a homogeneous population was challenged by legal and political attacks on "snob zoning" ordinances. In some states, people who worked downtown but lived in the suburbs were forced to help pay for services for big-city residents by means of a central-city tax on income earned in that city.

COMMUNITY, RIGHTS, AND RACE

The shift from a federal policy encouraging towns to one subsidizing cities was inconsistent in part because, like many national policies, the new was added to the old without abandoning the old: FHA mortgages

---

[15] Alan Ehrenhalt, *The Lost City: Discovering the Forgotten Virtues of Community in the Chicago of the 1950s* (New York: Basic Books, 1995).
[16] *Statistical Abstract of the United States, 1992*, 35.

and highway construction continued apace while a new policy was created to counter their effects. But it was also inconsistent in another sense.
Hard on the heels of the effort to save the central cities came the rights
revolution. Civil-rights laws were passed that forbade racial or ethnic discrimination in buying or selling housing and in school admissions. To the
extent that these laws were enforced (and the school-desegregation laws
certainly were), people began to worry that the social meaning of neighborhood was being jeopardized. Some of this concern was an expression
of overt racism and some an expression of symbolic racism (a name given
to the theory that opposition to school or neighborhood integration,
though justified by claims of individual merit or local autonomy, is in fact
a polite way of expressing, perhaps unconsciously, a deeply ingrained
racism).[17] But some of this concern may also have reflected a genuine belief that a neighborhood can exist only on the basis of a shared culture
and common experiences. Accompanying this belief was the empirical
generalization that racial or ethnic identity, though legally and morally
unimportant, may be correlated, imperfectly but significantly, with other
traits (social class, the probability of having a criminal record, the likelihood of valuing school achievement) that are important.

Whatever the underlying motive (and it probably involved some complex combination of all of the above), the resistance to some aspects of the
rights revolution was bound to be serious. Rights and community are, to
a degree, naturally at odds. Rights attach to individuals; they are prior to
and abstracted from communities; they entitle a person to defy both unjust laws and oppressive conventions; they protect, in the extreme case,
rebels and nonconformists. A community, on the other hand, is the property of a collectivity, not an individual; it requires some measure of conformity, whatever one's rights; it tolerates some level of deviance (but not
much), reacting to rebels much as the body's immune system reacts to in-
fections.

Locals are on the grinding edge of this conflict; cosmopolitans stand
above it and condemn many of those caught up in it. To a local, a community is territorial, valuable, and vulnerable; it requires defense. To a
cosmopolitan, a community is accidental, questionable, and replaceable;

---

17 The theory of symbolic racism has been developed by David Sears and his co-workers.
See, for example, David O. Sears, Carl P. Hensler, and Leslie K. Speer, "Whites' Opposition to 'Busing': Self-Interest or Symbolic Politics?" *American Political Science Review*
73 (1979): 369–84. For a criticism of this theory see Howard Schuman, Charlotte Steeh,
and Lawrence Bobo, *Racial Attitudes in America* (Cambridge, Mass.: Harvard University Press, 1985) and Paul M. Sniderman and Michael Gray Hagen, *Race and Inequality: A
Study in American Values* (Chatham, N.J.: Chatham House, 1985).

it deserves challenge. The former lives among neighbors, the latter chooses friends. Gerald Suttles described the struggle by white ethnics to defend
their neighborhoods against both urban redevelopers and racial integra-
tors as springing from the shared view that government had abandoned
their prized local community.[18] Jonathan Rieder quotes a white carpenter
in Brooklyn who complains about people (he described them as "rich liberals," but in fact he was referring to cosmopolitans of many different
ideologies) who "look down on my little piece of the American dream,
my little backyard with the barbecue," but "we've invested everything we
have in this house and neighborhood."[19]

To blacks and other minorities, of course, matters looked very different. They had their own stake in the American dream and saw banks, re-
altors, and neighborhood associations mobilized to deny it to them. Each
side in the battle over territory had legitimate claims, but the generals
who precipitated and to a degree directed that battle—judges, attorneys,
government officials, intellectuals—assigned very little value to territory
and a very high one to rights. As in many wars, the generals had the strategy but the foot soldiers felt the pain.

The rights revolution soon extended beyond the fight over schools,
busing, and neighborhood change in ways that began to affect the generals as well as the privates. Beginning in the mid-1960s, the mentally ill
were deinstitutionalized on the theory that they had a right to live in the
community and in the belief that they would find better treatment there
than in institutions. But not enough treatment centers were created to
provide adequate treatment, and the rights the ill now enjoyed made it
difficult to keep them in existing centers.[20]

At about the same time, the laws against vagrancy, loitering, and public
drunkenness were either repealed, narrowed, overturned, or left unen-
forced. In 1972, the Supreme Court held that a city ordinance making vagrancy illegal was unconstitutionally vague;[21] a decade later, it struck
down a California statute banning loitering.[22] Lower courts have held that
a law banning loitering for the purpose of begging is an unconstitutional

---

[18] Gerald D. Suttles, *The Social Construction of Communities* (Chicago: University of
Chicago Press, 1972).
[19] Jonathan Rieder, *Canarsie: The Jews and Italians of Brooklyn Against Liberalism* (Cambridge, Mass.: Harvard University Press, 1985), 200. See also E. J. Dionne, Jr., *Why
Americans Hate Politics* (New York: Simon & Schuster, 1991), 92–3.
[20] For a careful analysis of the impact of deinstitutionalization of mental patients on urban
street life, see Christopher Jencks, *The Homeless* (Cambridge, Mass.: Harvard University Press, 1994), chap. 3.
[21] *Papachristou v. City of Jacksonville*, 405 U.S. 156 (1972).
[22] *Kolender v. Lawson*, 461 U.S. 352 (1983).

infringement of free speech.[23] Laws banning public drunkenness have survived constitutional scrutiny,[24] but their enforcement remains controversial. In only a few courts have laws against sleeping on the streets been struck down[25] (but their use is heavily contested). Reviewing these and other cases, George L. Kelling and Catherine M. Coles have concluded that, though many legal issues remain to be decided, the consequence of the extension of constitutional protection to vagrants, loiterers, panhandlers, and (in a few cases) the homeless, coupled with organized efforts in some cities to protect street people from police control, has inhibited law-enforcement agencies from doing much to contain the problem.[26]

The result varies from place to place depending on local conditions and government energy, but in several big cities people in the most fashionable areas encounter the homeless asleep on the sidewalks and panhandlers begging aggressively. This aspect of the rights revolution struck at the cosmopolitans as well as the locals. Street people have brought home to cosmopolitans the costs of expanding rights in ways that school and neighborhood integration never did. Now they, like everyone else, must struggle to find ways of reconciling freedom and order in public places. But unlike the locals, the cosmopolitans are not attempting to defend threatened communities in which they participate in important social exchanges; they are simply trying to get to the subway, the theater, or the office without undue interference. Cosmopolitans bring greater political resources but lower stakes to the struggle to define the proper scope of rights.

The rights revolution also has placed under siege the ability of towns to control the class composition of their communities. As Martha Derthick notes in her chapter, this development has been the product of state rather than federal court decisions. The New Jersey Supreme Court has imposed "numerical fair shares on low-income housing on local places."[27]

---

[23] *Loper v. City of New York Police Department*, 802 F. Supp. 1029 (1992).
[24] See, for example, *Powell v. Texas*, 392 U.S. 514 (1968).
[25] *Tobe v. City of Santa Ana*, 27 Cal. Rptr. 2d 386 (1994) and *Pottinger v. Miami*, 810 F. Supp. 1151 (1992) found constitutional objections to ordinances restricting the activities of homeless persons; both have been appealed. The Santa Ana holding has been overturned by the federal Court of Appeals (892 P.2d 1145 [1995]) and the Pottinger case has been remanded (40 F.3d 1155 [1994]).
[26] George L. Kelling and Catherine M. Coles, *Fixing Broken Windows* (New York: Free Press, 1996).
[27] Derthick, "How Many Communities?" this volume. The case was *Southern Burlington County NAACP v. Township of Mount Laurel*, 67 N.J. 151 (1975) and 92 N.J. 158 (1983).

As proponents and critics of community autonomy press their cases, the sometimes unspoken subtext is race. Though many of the same issues would exist in American cities were there no African-Americans at all, the existence of a large black minority and the history of its painful struggle for equal opportunity have powerfully shaped the debate and constrained the range of available solutions.

Suppose that African-Americans were randomly distributed throughout the population such that about 12 percent of the inhabitants of every city and town were black. What we now think of as the urban problem (or the crime problem or the welfare problem) would look very different. There would be no predominately black central cities (such as Atlanta, Cleveland, Detroit, and Washington, D.C.) surrounded by predominately white suburbs. "Big city" would no longer mean "black city"; "small town" would no longer mean "lily-white suburb." There might still be a black underclass (though if the theory of William Julius Wilson is correct, it might be much smaller owing to the closer proximity between black settlements and attractive jobs), but that underclass would be much less threatening to those who live in it or near it.[28] Neighborhoods, black or white, with a few disorganized families are safer and more cohesive than ones with a high fraction of them.[29] Less dense areas have, other things being equal, less reliance on welfare: Rural welfare recipients, black or white, got off sooner than their big-city counterparts because they felt the stigma of welfare more keenly.[30] In a nation of random racial distribution, there would be fewer black elected officials (because there would be fewer majority-black districts), but all white elected officials would have to take into account black views (since all would have constituencies that were roughly one-eighth black).

Such a world would be very different from the one we have now, or are ever likely to have. There has been, from all accounts, a considerable in-

---

[28] William Julius Wilson, *The Truly Disadvantaged* (Chicago: University of Chicago Press, 1987).

[29] On the effect of the size of the poverty population in a neighborhood on the homicide rate, see Steven F. Messner and Kenneth Tardiff, "Economic Inequality and Levels of Homicide: An Analysis of Urban Neighborhoods," *Criminology* 24 (1986): 297–317. The density of poor people and the percentage of single-parent families were more powerfully associated with homicide than either race or income inequality. See also Ora Simcha-Fagan and Joseph E. Schwartz, "Neighborhood and Delinquency: An Assessment of Contextual Effects,"*Criminology* 24 (1986): 667–703, and Robert Sampson, "The Community," in *Crime,* ed. James Q. Wilson and Joan Petersilia (San Francisco: ICS Press, 1994), 193–216.

[30] Mark R. Rank and Thomas A. Hirschli, "A Rural-Urban Comparison of Welfare Exits: The Importance of Population Density," *Rural Sociology* 53 (1988): 190–206.

crease in the proportion of white Americans who are willing to accept some black neighbors, but there may not have been a large change in the preferences of black *or* white Americans about the kind of neighborhood in which they would prefer to live. William A. V. Clark has published the results of a survey of 2,644 Los Angeles households carried out in 1987. The households were asked "what mixture of people" they would prefer in a neighborhood in which they wished to live, assuming houses were affordable in that neighborhood. The results are not surprising: White Anglos prefer neighborhoods that are 70 percent or more white Anglo; blacks prefer neighborhoods that are roughly 50 percent black and 50 percent either white Anglo or white Hispanic. Hispanics prefer predominately Hispanic neighborhoods.[31]

Much the same results were obtained by David J. Armor, who, with his colleagues, surveyed the residents of at least eight large cities. Despite the range of places—Cincinnati, Hartford, Kansas City, Little Rock, Los Angeles, Milwaukee, a North Carolina county, and Omaha—the results were quite similar. The vast majority of whites prefer majority-white neighborhoods with a roughly 20 percent black membership, whereas the vast majority of blacks prefer neighborhoods that are half white and half black. Both racial groups prefer some racial mixing, but blacks prefer more of it.[32]

These preferences have changed and may change more in the future. White preferences for white neighborhoods may decline a bit as black or Hispanic crime rates decline, as white education levels improve, or as people come to believe that persons of roughly the same economic class will behave in similar ways. But as Thomas Schelling has shown, any feasible changes are unlikely to move our society very far in the direction of random ethnic distribution. So long as there are even very small preferences for certain kinds of neighborhoods, with normal relocation moves, neighborhoods will over time tend to become overwhelmingly of one ethnic group or another.[33] Even starting with a random distribution, slight preferences will in time exert a powerful effect. At first, this tiny prefer-

---

[31] William A. V. Clark, "Residential Preferences and Residential Choices in a Multiethnic Context," *Demography* 29 (1992): 451–65. See also Clark, "Residential Preferences and Neighborhood Racial Segregation: A Test of the Schelling Segregation Model," *Demography* 28 (1991): 1–19.

[32] David J. Armor, *Forced Justice: School Desegregation and the Law* (New York: Oxford University Press, 1995), 136–8.

[33] The classic demonstration is Thomas C. Schelling, "Dynamic Models of Segregation," *Journal of Mathematical Sociology* 1 (1971): 143–86. For a plain-language explication, see Schelling, "On the Ecology of Micromotives," *The Public Interest* 25 (1971): 59–98.

ence may cause just one person to move next door to a similar person. But that small change will make the neighborhood much more (or much less) attractive to the next person contemplating a move, who then moves accordingly. The effect of that move is to make neighborhood composition even less random; this affects the next mover, and so on. Soon neighborhoods will be overwhelmingly black or white or Hispanic, even though no individual mover intended that result.

The ineluctable logic of Schelling's analysis makes it clear why school- and neighborhood-integration efforts have not yielded better results; why, indeed, schools have become even more segregated in some places as a result of efforts to integrate them. Coercive measures can reduce the effect of individual preferences, but only very high levels of coercion can prevent them from operating altogether. As telecommuting and the like make it ever easier to live far from some jobs, this process of stratification will accelerate.

Federal policy is largely powerless to change this, however much federal officials may lament it. The result may be more and more big cities that resemble Atlanta or Detroit. To manage this disparity, there has emerged what Peter Salins has called a Faustian bargain: Big-city leaders manage big-city poorhouses in exchange for subsidies extracted by state and federal tax authorities from suburban residents.[34] To cope with this, Salins suggests nationalizing income-maintenance programs, equalizing city fiscal capacities, preventing the use of land-use controls for population screening, and decentralizing the management of urban services. He admits that all would meet with political resistance. On that he is surely correct, especially with respect to land-use controls.

There have been efforts to distribute public-housing residents, especially blacks, more evenly across the metropolis. The best-known of these is the so-called Gatreaux program. When a federal judge (and ultimately the Supreme Court) found the Chicago Housing Authority (CHA) to be unconstitutionally segregating its black tenants, the CHA began to issue housing vouchers to tenants (now numbering several thousand) for use anywhere in the Chicago metropolitan area. After a few years, researchers tracked down a sample of those who had moved—some to houses in Chicago, others to houses in the suburbs. The two groups seemed roughly similar in most observable traits—black females with (typically) two or three children, most long-term Aid to Families with De-

---

[34] Peter D. Salins, "Cities, Suburbs, and the Urban Crisis," *The Public Interest* 113 (1993): 91–104.

pendent Children (AFDC) recipients. Nonetheless, those who had moved to the suburbs were more likely to get a job—and their children were more likely to finish high school and attend college—than was true of those who had stayed in the city.[35] The difficulty with accepting this result, of course, is that the movement of the two groups of women—some within the city, some to the suburbs—was not randomly assigned, meaning these people may have differed importantly in ways that affected how their children later turned out.

The Department of Housing and Urban Development wishes to make greater use of housing vouchers to achieve Gatreaux-like results on a larger scale. But two problems stand in its way: uncertainty as to whether moving (as opposed to maternal attitudes and behavior) produced the Gatreaux changes, and the intense resistance found in many neighborhoods to any massive relocation program. In Baltimore, for example, whites in blue-collar suburbs opposed what they feared would be an invasion; in other cities, black politicians have opposed efforts to break up their constituencies.[36]

DIVERSITY AND TERRITORY

Cities, suburbs, and towns will inevitably differ in their social composition. Indeed, we already celebrate part of this diversity. Drive the freeways of Los Angeles and you will encounter signs, erected by the state, that direct motorists to neighborhoods labeled "Little Tokyo," "Little Korea," "Little Saigon," and "Chinatown." (There is no sign for "Little Mexico City" or "Blacktown.") What we celebrate, we ought to encourage. We are pleased to find strong neighborhoods with involved citizens regulating one another's behavior by social exchanges; we are frustrated by our inability to produce more of them.

The federal government has no almost no means at its disposal for producing what so many people want. The Constitution was written to create a limited government checked by rival ambitions and guaranteed rights. Liberty was our goal; its pursuit had to be moderated to preserve

[35] James E. Rosenbaum, "Black Pioneers: Do Their Moves to the Suburbs Increase Economic Opportunity for Mothers and Children?" *Housing Policy Debate* 2 (1991): 1179–213, and Rosenbaum and Susan J. Popkin, "Employment and Earnings of Low-Income Blacks Who Move to Middle-Class Suburbs," *The Urban Underclass*, ed. Christopher Jencks and Paul E. Peterson (Washington, D.C.: Brookings Institution, 1991), 342–56.

[36] See Karen De Witt, "Housing Voucher Test in Maryland Is Scuttled by a Political Firestorm," *New York Times*, March 28, 1995, A14.

order, but not to enhance virtue. A liberal democracy—and America was the first—leaves the cultivation of virtue to personal habits and private arrangements. Though Americans often have good things to say about how Singapore or Saudi Arabia enforce virtue, not many seem eager to live in those places—perhaps because they have noticed that there is not much political freedom in either place, and no liquor in the latter.

Even though our national government is not designed to cultivate virtue, it has the capacity to make it harder for other institutions to do that cultivating. Everybody in national office professes to love families and neighborhoods and to deplore crime and disorder, and no doubt they are sincere. But no national agency has it in its power to do much for families and neighborhoods or against crime and disorder, and I doubt we would want to create any agency that had the kind of power that achieving these goals would require. So when it comes to enhancing the communal context of character formation and citizenship development, the most we should expect is a good deal of hand-wringing.

But state and national agencies do have it in their power to create difficulties for institutions involved in (and essential to) the cultivation of character and citizenship. They can make certain that as little tax money as possible goes to churches or church-related organizations. They can actively oppose, or give aid and comfort to the enemies of, meaningful school-choice programs. They can equip individuals with rights not only against the national government, but against communal institutions—the disciplinary authorities in public schools and the order-maintenance functions of the police. They can encourage the deinstitutionalization of the mentally ill and discourage the local restraint of pornography. They can announce programs designed to support community-based policing, having first issued court orders that make one goal of such policing—the reduction in disorder occasioned by vagrancy and panhandling—difficult to achieve. They can deplore the spread of drug trafficking while excluding from the trial of arrested traffickers any evidence that was gathered in ways that did not conform to the most precise, detailed, and complex rules of search and seizure. They can make divorce and single-parenthood as easy as possible, and adoption as difficult as possible. State authorities can strip local school districts of much of their autonomy; state courts can insist that towns be economically integrated, no matter how great the correlation of behavioral dispositions with class differences.

There is little hypocrisy in any of this. There is, instead, a commitment to individual freedom that, however overextended, is at root commendable. The American version of rights is, however, more radically individualistic than that which is found in most other free societies.[37] To some commentators, the way to correct this excessively individualistic view is to equip communities or institutions with rights. A school should have the "right" to maintain an orderly classroom, a police officer the "right" to maintain order on his beat. This approach is, I think, mistaken. The problem is not to increase the number of entities claiming rights and thus enlarge the power of the institution, the judiciary, that umpires those claims, but to acknowledge and support local and especially nongovernmental entities that are engaged in building character.

That support might in part be financial, not by giving more federal grants to churches and voluntary associations, but by making it easier for people to give more. Suppose, for example, that the tuition to church-related schools were deductible on one's federal income tax (just as local property taxes are now), or that individuals could allocate, up to some limit, part of their federal tax liability to approved local, private, social-welfare associations. Suppose that state laws were drafted making it easier to compel drug abusers to enter treatment programs and to keep homeless mental patients in hospitals. Suppose that the receipt of AFDC (now renamed Temporary Assistance to Needy Families) by an unmarried teenage mother were made contingent on her living for the first few years of her child's life in a group home or family shelter under adult supervision. Suppose that local ordinances made it easier for neighborhoods to tax themselves for the purpose of hiring additional security guards (from either local police agencies or private firms), perhaps with tax subsidies for the poorest neighborhoods that chose this option.

The object would be to endow neighborhoods and neighborhood institutions with a greater share of the resources and roles now held by large government agencies—all subject, of course, to the restriction that these resources and this authority could not be used in ways that violated the fundamental rights of all citizens. To make that constraint something other than a license for endless judicial meddling, the federal courts would have to return to a distinction that has become blurred during the last several decades—the distinction between any right one might value and those rights so fundamental as to be "implicit in the concept of ordered

---

[37] On this, see Mary Ann Glendon, *Rights Talk* (New York: Free Press, 1991). Robert Bellah and his colleagues have suggested that our current rights talk is different from what it was in premodern America; see Bellah et al., *Habits of the Heart* (Berkeley: University of California Press, 1985), 20.

'liberty.'" [38] This issue lies at the heart of the question of incorporation: To what extent are the rights mentioned in the first ten amendments to the Constitution, together with their subsequent judicial expansion, fully incorporated in the due process clause of the Fourteenth Amendment and thus made applicable to the states? [39] Whatever the merits of any theoretical resolution of this issue, in fact the Supreme Court has steadily made almost every right against federal power a right against state power, and what federal courts have been reluctant to do some state courts have been eager to accomplish.

Given the courts' position on this matter, there is no way to correct it save by constitutional amendment (virtually impossible) or judicial restraint (unlikely but not impossible). Absent one or the other of these eventualities, it will remain the case that appointed judges will sustain a radically rights-based view of communal life at the very time when elected officials seem increasingly disposed to assert a different view.

Federalism was designed in part, I think, to insure local control over, and local diversity among, the processes of village life on which moral development depends. As long as that effort succeeded, the national government did not need to be overly intrusive; it could assume that "there is a portion of virtue and honor among mankind"; [40] indeed, republican government "presupposes the existence of these qualities in a higher degree than any other form." [41] In saying "presupposes," the Framers took for granted the existence of qualities they did not think the government could or should try to produce. What worried them was not whether men could be reasonably decent, but whether liberty could be adequately protected and prosperity generally achieved.

Today, the national government finds itself in exactly the opposite position from what the Framers intended. It has protected and extended liberty beyond anything that could be imagined in 1787 and has achieved a level of prosperity that is the envy of most of the world. But its citizens criticize it for having failed to protect and enhance virtue, and they hold it accountable for the increase in crime, drug abuse, out-of-wedlock births, and communal disorder. The government finds itself in a position that is politically untenable and constitutionally suspect.

---

[38] *Palko v. Connecticut*, 302 U.S. 325 (1937).
[39] For an analysis of what the authors of the Fourteenth Amendment intended in this regard, see Charles Fairman, "Does the Fourteenth Amendment Incorporate the Bill of Rights?" *Stanford Law Review* 2 (1949): 5.
[40] *Federalist*, No. 76.   [41] *Federalist*, No. 55.

It is in this position, I believe, because the culture of the West—and especially that of the United States—has moved dramatically over the last hundred years toward a more radically individualistic conception of liberty. From graffiti to crime, from illegitimacy to drug abuse, most of the problems that trouble us are not the result of governmental failures. We have these problems in common with most other industrialized nations in the world; the differences in policies among these regimes seem, at best, to produce only small differences in outcomes.

The government is now asked to overcome or compensate for a vast cultural change. It is as if we were to ask engineers to build retaining walls that could stem the seismic shocks of relentlessly shifting tectonic plates. Neither enterprise is likely to succeed. At best, the government can (1) moderate its decades-old drive to expand rights without regard to communal consequences; (2) temper the expansion of individual claims on fragile communal institutions; and (3) enhance the capacity of neighborhood institutions to perform their traditional functions. Seismic events can be neither prevented nor resisted, but people, like sticks, can be made safer if they are bound together in ways that enable them to bend without breaking.

2

Citizen and city

Locality, public-spiritedness, and the American regime

STEPHEN L. ELKIN

Why is local political life of great potential importance for the American regime? The broad answer has long been clear. John Stuart Mill said that "free and popular local and municipal institutions" are part of "the peculiar training of a citizen, the practical part of the political education of a free people."[1]

Mill's formulation suggests that local politics affords an opportunity for citizens to consider a wide range of public matters, and thus to develop the skills and outlook necessary to be effective participants in the larger political life of the regime. We may say that local political life can help to form the character of the citizenry.

What should the character of the American citizenry be? Assuming that we as Americans wish to become a more or less fully realized republican regime,[2] an answer must begin with a sketch of this regime's theory of political constitution. Such a theory sets out the major organizing institutions of the regime, the manner in which they need to work, and the forces that make it probable that they will work in the necessary ways. With these features of the regime in mind, we can discuss what is necessary to make the institutions work in the appropriate way. This, in turn, will lead us to consider the character the citizenry must have.

James Madison's theory of political constitution, as it appears in *The Federalist* and other writings, is the appropriate theory to guide us. Those who participate in the founding of some great undertaking are particularly valuable guides to its underlying theory because in trying to bring

---

[1] John Stuart Mill, *On Liberty* (New York: Penguin, 1981), 181.
[2] See Stephen L. Elkin, *City and Regime in the American Republic* (Chicago: University of Chicago Press, 1987), chap. 6, and Stephen L. Elkin, "The Constitution of a Good Society: The Case of the Commercial Republic," in *The Constitution of Good Societies,* ed. Karol E. Soltan and Stephen L. Elkin (State College, Pa.: Penn State Press, 1996).

about this new enterprise they are forced to think in depth about its foundations. What must be changed, they ask, if we are to proceed? Unlike those who come later, those present at beginnings have before them the old as a living presence—and the comparison with the new helps bring clarity to their thinking. For those of us who come after, such comparisons can be only imaginary.

In the case of Madison, there is a second compelling reason to start with his account of the theory of political constitution. It is simply the most comprehensive and compelling account we have[3]—as well as being the most authoritative in the sense of being the one most commonly consulted when we seek guidance about how the American regime is to work.[4]

There are six essential features of the Madisonian constitution:[5] 1) institutions that are designed to prevent faction, particularly majority faction, which Madison believed was the principal disease of popular government; 2) institutions that are designed to promote deliberative ways of lawmaking, which are necessary to "refine"[6] the people's voice; 3) more specifically, institutions that are designed to encourage lawmaking that gives concrete meaning to a substantive conception of the public interest; 4) a citizenry capable of choosing lawmakers who are disposed to deliberate on the concrete meaning of the public interest; 5) laws that bind not only the citizenry but those who make the laws; and 6) a social basis for the regime that would make all this possible—in particular, men of standing and property whose self-interest overlaps with the public interest, and who might be induced to take a large view of their interests, thus increasing the overlap.

It is elements 2 through 4—the institutions and the citizenry that make possible deliberative ways of lawmaking that give concrete meaning to the public interest—that are of particular importance for an analysis of citizenship and the city. Because one central task of a republican regime is to give concrete meaning to the public interest, it is appropriate to start with an account of its substantive elements.

Madison's discussion of the public interest is less than explicit. How-

[3] Cf. Edmund S. Morgan's comments that "Madison wrote not only the United States Constitution, or at least most of it, but also the most searching commentary on it that has ever appeared." "The Fixers," New York Review of Books, March 2, 1995: 25.
[4] This is not to say that Madison's theory of political constitution is not flawed. I believe that it does require reworking. See Elkin, "Madison and After: The American Model of Political Constitution," Political Studies 44 (1996): 592–604.
[5] For this discussion I draw freely on my paper "Madison and After."
[6] Alexander Hamilton, James Madison, and John Jay, The Federalist, ed. Jacob E. Cooke (Middletown, Conn.: Wesleyan University Press, 1961), No. 10.

ever, one element of the public interest for Madison was, almost certainly, that government should secure civil, political, and property rights.[7] To do so is not simply a matter of subjecting government to strict limits, as if government itself were the enemy of the liberty that these rights define. To the contrary, the enemy of liberty is not government per se but tyrannical (or weak) government. Moreover, it may take considerable exertions of governmental authority to secure rights.[8] Thus, the problem for the public interest is to define the kinds of actions government must take to make rights a concrete reality in the day-to-day life of the society.

In addition, given Madison's concern for the prevention of factional rule, it seems plausible that he would be concerned about the extent of private power. Popular government is just as much in danger from powerful private interests as it is from arbitrary actions by government officials. Once public authority becomes an extension of private interest, the rights of the citizenry are in danger—and any claim that lawmaking serves the larger good becomes implausible. Not only can the public subvert the private, but the private can corrupt the public.

Beyond these two aspects of the public interest, we may be reasonably certain that Madison at least acquiesced in Alexander Hamilton's judgment that lawmaking in the public interest must foster a commercial society. Commerce was to be the engine for the prosperity that Hamilton thought both valuable in itself and necessary for the stability of the republic.[9] At a minimum, this means that republican lawmaking should aim to promote material prosperity through an organization of wealth production that has a significant role for private ownership of productive assets and for markets.[10] On balance, lawmaking should support and encourage private ownership of these productive assets. Among other things, this means taking account of the fact that, if there is to be significant material prosperity, controllers of productive assets must have considerable discretion in how to deploy them. Without such discretion, they are unlikely to invest at a level that will promote significant and widespread material prosperity.[11]

---

[7] *Federalist* No. 10.
[8] *Federalist* No. 37. See also Herbert Storing, "The Constitution and the Bill of Rights," in *How Does the Constitution Secure Rights?* ed. Robert Goldwin and William Schambra (Washington, D.C.: American Enterprise Institute, 1985).
[9] *Federalist* Nos. 11, 12, and 30.
[10] I here draw freely on my "Constitution of a Good Society."
[11] See Charles E. Lindblom, *Politics and Markets: The World's Political Economic Systems* (New York: Basic Books, 1977), esp. chap. 13, and Adam Przeworski, *Capitalism and Social Democracy* (Cambridge: Cambridge University Press, 1985), chap. 4. Cf. also Elkin, *City and Regime in the American Republic*, chap. 7.

To summarize, we may say that, for Madison, the central feature of a republican regime is that it is a regime of limited powers, where the limitations are defined by the manner in which rights are to be secured, private power regulated, and a commercial society promoted. The purposes and the concomitant limitation on governmental power define the regime: If we wish for a republic, we must value these concerns, and it is in their constitutive nature that the warrant is found for treating them as part of the public interest. The public interest is a complex judgment about how and to what purposes political authority can be exercised to promote the good and the well-being of the public.

There will be other elements in a full account of the public interest of a commercial republic, but I have said enough for the discussion here of local political life to proceed.

Given the public interest as I have defined it, how should republican lawmaking be organized? Madison suggests that it must be deliberative in form. It is difficult to see how else a broadly defined public interest can be given meaningful expression. If lawmaking is anything other than deliberative—for example, if it is organized around bargaining—the public interest can be served only by chance, as an accidental by-product of the bargaining. Similarly, if the broad contours of the public interest are to be given concrete meaning, this can be accomplished only through the exercise of practical reason—in short, through deliberation.

Unless it is supposed that the only limits on public authority worth caring about are the ones that courts feel comfortable with, the legislature too must be capable of deliberative ways of lawmaking. A central problem, therefore, in the design of the American regime is how to ensure that the legislature engages in deliberative ways of lawmaking—not to the exclusion of other modes of lawmaking, but at least on those occasions when the public interest is at issue.[12] If the legislature is to do so, representatives must be capable of discussing how the dimensions of the public interest can be brought to bear in particular choices.

What will prompt lawmakers to engage in deliberative ways of law-

[12] It is not possible here to consider the content of such a distinction, but in a complex society—indeed, plausibly in any modern society—there will be many matters that, for one reason or another (including some quite bad ones), become subjects of lawmaking but have little bearing on the public interest of the regime. For such matters, it seems eminently reasonable to have them decided by various devices that simply aggregate whatever preferences lawmakers—and, by extension, citizens—happen to have, including ones that are narrowly self-interested. But a significant part of lawmaking will indeed consider matters in which the content of the public interest is at stake, and it is here that deliberative ways of lawmaking are needed.

making in the public interest? Any complete answer must be complex and beyond the scope of the discussion here. An important part of the answer, however, is that the legislature as an institution can teach; it can help to form the outlook of lawmakers and thus be a school for learning the arts of deliberative lawmaking. The legislature, however, cannot be the proper sort of school without the right pupils. Otherwise said, a legislature largely composed of abject self-interested mediocrities cannot by some hidden hand turn itself into a lawmaking body of great distinction. John Stuart Mill tartly said in this regard that

a school of legislative capacity is worthless, and a school for evil, instead of good, if through want . . . of the presence within itself of a higher order of character, the action of the body is allowed, as it so often is, to degenerate into an equally unscrupulous and stupid pursuit of self-interest of its members.[13]

However unsettling the thought, therefore, the citizens of a commercial republic must in their way be as capable as its lawmakers. They must have those qualities of judgment that allow them to say which prospective lawmakers understand lawmaking to be, in significant part, a deliberative process and which of them also have either the skills necessary to make it so work or the inclination to learn them.[14] In short, citizens must be public-spirited.

A PUBLIC-SPIRITED CITIZENRY

Public-spiritedness is a disposition to give significant weight to the public interest. It consists of the not-very-demanding belief that there is a public interest and that political life should devote significant effort to giving it concrete meaning.

For present purposes, a principal expression of public-spiritedness is the inclination to judge lawmakers by whether they show a concern for both the public interest and its necessary corollary deliberative ways of lawmaking. If they cannot make such judgments, lawmakers will easily work out that if they *say* they are concerned about the public interest and provide small displays of wanting to reason about its content, this will do the trick. Voters can't tell the huckster from the great lawmaker.

The problem for constitutional design, however, is not only to educate

---

[13] *On Liberty and Other Essays,* ed. John Gray (Oxford: Oxford University Press, 1991), 417.
[14] Elkin, "The Constitution of a Good Society."

citizens to the fact that there is a public interest and to foster the development of the skills necessary to judge whether lawmakers have a disposition to engage in deliberative lawmaking. Citizens must also have some
conception of the substantive elements of the public interest. Public-spirited citizens thus have two characteristics: They have some knowledge of
the broad elements of the public interest and a concern that lawmaking
gives it concrete meaning; and they believe that lawmaking must, therefore, be deliberative. Public-spirited citizens expect lawmakers to engage
in practical reasoning to give concrete meaning to the public interest, and
they have both the capacity and the inclination to judge whether prospective lawmakers are likely to do so.

If these are the qualities that republican citizens must have, a central
problem for a republican regime is how these qualities are to be fostered.
It cannot be assumed that, as a matter of course, we as a citizenry have the
ability to make the necessary judgments about our lawmakers.[15] If we are
to judge the qualities of our lawmakers, we must ourselves—in concert
with others—have some experience of attempting to give concrete meaning to the public interest. We must, in short, have some experience of deliberative ways of lawmaking in which the content of the public interest is
at issue.

The underlying proposition here is, as Madison pointed out, that we
cannot rely on our lawmakers' being statesmen. Republican lawmakers
will be more ordinary mortals; they will need to have incentives both to
deliberate and to deliberate about the right things, namely the concrete
meaning of the public interest. A crucial set of such incentives will need to
come from a citizenry able to reward by election those they believe have
the disposition to engage in deliberative lawmaking in the public interest.

Mill points to where we must look for the education of a republican
citizenry, particularly for fostering its public-spiritedness. It is only in the
context of local political life, he suggests, that any significant number of
citizens can gain the experience necessary to choose republican lawmakers.[16] A crucial component of the theory of the political constitution of
the commercial republic must then be its design for local government.

---

[15] It is not easy to come by evidence on the matter. For two discussions see Elkin, *City and Regime*, chaps. 7 and 8, and William Galston, *Liberal Purposes: Goods, Virtues, and Diversity in the Liberal State* (Cambridge: Cambridge University Press, 1991).
[16] Cf. Norton Long's characterization of the views of John Dewey that "only in the local community could the public discover itself and in doing so realize its shared common purposes that alone make possible real democracy." "Dewey's Conception of the Public Interest," paper delivered to the Midwest Political Science Association, April 1980.

LOCAL POLITICAL LIFE IN A REPUBLICAN REGIME

If citizens of a republican regime are to judge the inclinations and capacities of their lawmakers, an essential feature of local government is that it afford them the experience of deliberating and struggling over the content of the public interest. They must themselves, I have said, have some experience of trying to answer the question, "What is the public interest here in this case?" Because these are complicated matters to judge, and because the incentive on the part of present and aspiring lawmakers to sham will be great, a citizenry that lacks this experience will be easily misled. As V. S. Naipaul says, "When men cannot observe they don't have ideas: they have obsessions."[17] If we substitute "participate in deliberative processes" for "observe," the possibility for mischief and worse is apparent. Walter Lippmann simply said that "the kind of self-education which a self-governing people must obtain can only be had through its daily experience."[18]

There is nothing very difficult to understand in all of this. We enter the politics of a free government, and simply by having to answer questions that invite, indeed require, that we talk in terms of broader interests than our own, we end up thinking about what these interests might be. From perhaps knowing little and caring less about these public interests, we now find ourselves trying to find the words of the public interest to cloak our narrow interests. We now know more than we did—and, as in learning anything, we come imperceptibly to see the point of at least some of these public interests. We are on our way to becoming more fully public-spirited.[19]

In much the same way, and more mundanely, we become more adept at spotting bad arguments and learn something of how to craft good ones. That is, we come to understand that being effectively involved in the broad range of matters encompassed by the public interest requires us to

---

[17] Quoted in Roger Shattuck, "The Reddening of America," *New York Review of Books,* March 30, 1989: 5.

[18] "The Constitution of a Good Society," 263.

[19] Think of the small-town Rotarian who enters local political life in order to advance his business and soon finds himself worrying about the state of the schools and local health care, neither of which (the school being part of a regional system) has much effect on his local taxes. Cf. Jon Elster's comment that "over time one will become swayed by consideration of the common good. One cannot indefinitely praise the common good *du bout des lèvres,* for . . . one will end up having preferences which initially one was faking." *Sour Grapes: Stories in Subversion of Rationality* (Cambridge: Cambridge University Press, 1983), 36.

rely on the judgment of those who have thought long and hard about these matters. We thus learn to spot who is genuinely knowledgeable and has an eye open to larger, public interests; and we learn that open and vigorous debate soon exposes shoddy arguments based on rank prejudice. In short, we learn to be better deliberators ourselves—and, by extension, to identify those who show the requisite talent and inclination. The design of republican local government institutions must then provide the possibility for widespread participation in deliberation over public matters.

There is a good deal to be said about how the public interest manifests itself in local political life, what motives can be harnessed to draw citizens into a local politics that considers it and tries to give it concrete meaning, and what the structure of local political institutions must be. We already know some things of importance about these matters,[20] so I will turn to a question that has been given very little consideration: what citizens must bring to local political life if local politics is to work in the participatory, deliberative, and public-interested manner required to foster public-spiritedness.

THE QUALITIES CITIZENS MUST BRING
TO LOCAL POLITICAL LIFE

The formal structure of institutions does not ensure that they will work in the manner desired. To be sure, institutions help form the outlook and dispositions of those who work within them, but they cannot do so for just any sort of individuals. What is worse, institutions that are designed to be participative and deliberative—as I have said local governments must be in a republican regime—can easily turn into teachers of cynicism and frustration if those who operate them are ill-equipped and disinclined to make them work in the appropriate ways. Moreover, even if those who participate are receptive to what the institutions might teach through their operations, participants need other qualities if they are to act on these lessons in public-spiritedness.

What qualities must citizens bring to local political life if its institutions are to foster public-spiritedness? There are at least six:

1. Citizens must come to these institutions with the beginnings of the idea that there are public as well as private interests.
2. They must have a significant measure of prideful independence.

---

[20] For my own efforts in this regard, see Elkin, *City and Regime in the American Republic.*

3. They must come to political life with some degree of trust in other citizens.
4. They must have the capacity to make moderately complex judgments about public matters—that is, they need some measure of cognitive complexity.
5. They must have some degree of respect for other citizens, and thus there must be a substantial degree of mutual respect among the citizenry.
6. They must be concerned with the esteem in which others hold them—and central to the granting of such esteem must be a reputation for reasoned analysis of public matters.

The beginnings of public-spiritedness

To even get started on the project of fostering public-spiritedness, we must assume that a significant number of citizens have some inclination to judge political life in terms of larger concerns than their own and those of their immediate circle. They may be only weakly inclined, but this disposition cannot be absent. They may also have only the weakest idea of how to go about such judging and what its content should be, but there must be something to build on. Political life can only reinforce or diminish what is already present; it cannot create dispositions from scratch. People who cannot imagine why they shouldn't litter or why they ought to help frail people across a busy intersection are people for whom political life can do little—except, possibly, to secure their possessions and act as a source of largess that will make their lives and the lives of their intimate circle more comfortable.[21]

What will be the sources of even these minimal concerns for the good of something larger than oneself? Presumably from the usual places. Among the first lessons we learn if we are emotionally healthy is that there are other people in the world, and that the well-being of some of them is important to us. Call this a functioning family. Sometime later we learn that we are part of larger groups—of neighbors, of members of a religious congregation,[22] of families connected by a common workplace—

---

[21] For an object lesson in the form of a highly colored portrait of a group of people whose understanding of their obligations reaches little beyond their immediate circle, see Edward C. Banfield, *The Moral Basis of a Backward Society* (New York: Free Press, 1967). An overview of the whole question can be found in Robert D. Putnam, "Bowling Alone: America's Declining Social Capital," *Journal of Democracy* 6 (January 1995): 65–78.

[22] Cf. Tocqueville's comment that "religion, which never intervenes directly in the government of American society, should therefore be considered as the first of their political institutions. . . ." *Democracy in America*, vol. 2 (Garden City, N.Y.: Doubleday, 1969), chap. 9.

and we come to see that our well-being is tied to the fate of those others. Call this community.[23] Although not everyone will grow up this way, a great number must if there is to be a public-spirited citizenry.[24]

A concern for the public interest starts, then, with a basic connection being made in the outlook of the child between his or her own interests and those of others. Self-interest is stretched to include the well-being of others. On this foundation, an interest in civic life can grow: The child moves into adulthood and becomes a part of the various groups and organizations that compose civil society—those groupings that are not of the state but concerned with public matters. Such experience reinforces the idea that the interests and well-being of others deserve serious consideration—that my well-being requires attending to the well-being of others.

Concern for the well-being of others need not, of course, go any further than fostering a realization that I share my private interests with others, and that we can act together to serve them. But civic organizations can be more than interest groups, as they engage in informal social problem-solving and common work whose effects reach beyond those who are characterized by a specific set of interests. And on the basis of this initial stretching, a concern for the political good of the political community can be built: The fostering of such a concern reinforces and stretches further the connection between one's own good and the good of a larger whole.[25]

There is more. Since any conception of the public interest will be a partial one—no one person is capable of thinking through its complete concrete meaning—if we are to be public-spirited we must also have the self-confidence to face the fact that our view is only one among several. This may not be the only source of the tolerance necessary for living with conflict over how to interpret the public interest, but it is certainly an important one. And again, we must look to the family, neighborhood, and church—that is, to the contexts in which our identities are first formed. If we do not see ourselves as belonging to some grouping larger than our-

---

[23] It seems likely that religion plays a key role here. We learn to connect our own well-being to that of others not only by participating in a particular religious congregation but also through direct religious teaching.

[24] Cf. James Q. Wilson's remark that there are "understandings that arise spontaneously out of, and necessarily govern, human relationships: the need to show some concern for the well-being of others, treat others with minimal fairness, and honor obligations." "The Moral Sense," *American Political Science Review* 87 (March 1993): 8. Consider also Aristotle's comment that it is "in the household first [that] we have the sources and springs of friendship, of political organization, and of justice." *Eudemian Ethics* 1242 bl.

[25] For the classic discussion see Tocqueville, *Democracy in America* Vol. I, 63–70; 512–13; 525–30.

selves, we are unlikely to feel able to give meaning to and act upon a good as complex as the public interest. If our feet are not anchored somewhere, we cannot lift our eyes to the horizon.

Prideful independence

However public-spirited citizens may be, it will matter little to their behavior if they do not have confidence in their own opinions. They must think that these deserve to be heard, that their views ought to affect public action, and that their efforts will meet with some success.[26]

Only those who have faith in their own abilities—who are *proud* of their independent powers of judgment—can act in a public-spirited fashion.[27] They will think it their right to judge their lawmakers and not be overawed by them or by the size of the task. As men and women who respect their own abilities and accomplishments, however, they will also understand that being a lawmaker is a demanding job, difficult to do well, and that a cavalier dismissal of the job and those who do it is beneath them.

The roots of prideful independence are to be found, in part, in the world of work[28]—among other things, in the experience of non-routine, complex, loosely supervised work that, in allowing workers to exercise considerable discretion, fosters the self-respect and independence of judgment that are at the core of prideful independence. Because both of these traits are also necessary for mutual respect and the ability to make complex judgments—virtues I will consider below—the structuring of jobs and the broader world of work is of the greatest possible moment for the political life of republican government.[29]

Markets also engender some degree of prideful independence because they offer the regular possibility of exercising independent judgment.

[26] I am here concerned only with the manner in which prideful independence affects public-spiritedness in the context of local political life. Prideful independence has other, independent effects. For example, it is needed if citizens are to be careful guardians of their private interests.

[27] Cf. Thomas Pangle's comment that republican citizens need a "combination of pride and humility." Thomas Pangle, *Enobling of Democracy: The Challenge of the Post Modern Era*, (Baltimore: Johns Hopkins University Press, 1992), 177.

[28] The effects of the organization of work on character were well understood by Adam Smith, who, at the dawn of the industrial revolution, argued that dull, repetitive work can only undercut the self-respect that is at the core of the capacity for independent judgment. *The Wealth of Nations* (New York: Modern Library, 1937), 716–40.

[29] See Robert Lane, *The Market Experience* (Cambridge: Cambridge University Press, 1991), 198–9. See also Judith Shklar, *American Citizenship: Quest for Inclusion* (Cambridge, Mass.: Harvard University Press, 1991).

They also help to foster a sense that there is some connection between one's exertions and a desired result—what Robert Lane calls "self-attribution." One learns that one can affect one's environment; a sense of efficacy develops, and this is crucial to a sense of independence.[30]

It is much the same with the question of job security. The traditional argument was that independence came from owning property—that is, some portion of the productive assets of the community through which one could learn a living. This source of independence is now effectively gone: Few of us own productive property of the kind that we ourselves can deploy to make a living. For economic security, most of us must rely on wages and salaries. Thus many of us are prey to the economic insecurity that arises from a lack of steady, reasonably paying work with the consequence that a sense of pride and independence is undercut.[31]

It matters, therefore, for republican government how the distribution of wealth and income is generated. The same distribution—in one case characterized by gross economic insecurity among a substantial part of the citizenry, in another by relative economic security—produces quite different environments: The insecure environment is much less hospitable to republican government.

Additional sources of prideful independence are to be found in deliberative lawmaking itself. It bolsters a sense of prideful independence, because such lawmaking treats citizens as if they have the ability to understand and profit by the reasoning that goes into the making of law. Consider, by contrast, a politics that treats citizens as objects to be manipulated by spin doctors—that is, one which treats them as if they are too stupid to understand what is being done to them, and so lacking in self-respect as not to resent it.[32] If the only consistent message citizens get is that lawmakers think they are fools,[33] those citizens are unlikely to take seriously that there is a public interest. How citizens are addressed is especially crucial in a continent-sized republic like ours, where national political life is remote for most people and the rhetoric of public leaders is often the only message that reaches them.

---

[30] See Lane, *The Market Experience*, chaps. 9–10.

[31] See Donald Moon in *Democracy and the Welfare State*, ed. Amy Guttman (New York: Free Press, 1958); Shklar, *Citizenship;* and Michael Walzer, *Spheres of Justice* (Princeton, N.J.: Princeton University Press, 1988).

[32] Cf. Louis Brandeis's comment that "for good or for ill, [government] teaches the whole people by example." *Olmstead v. United States,* 277 U.S. 438 (1928), Brandeis dissenting.

[33] Cf. V. O. Key, Jr., *The Reasonable Electorate: Rationality in Presidential Voting* (Cambridge, Mass.: Harvard University Press, 1966), chap. 1.

Finally, participation in a vital civic life brings individuals into concrete, day-to-day contact with public matters, with questions that touch on more than their own private interests. If this experience *is* concrete and regular, it will plausibly promote a sense of confidence that one has something to say about public life.

Trust

Trust is one of our principal orientations to the social world. It concerns whether we believe, with due regard to circumstances, that we can expect others to act with some concern for our interests and not to take every opportunity to serve their own interests at the expense of ours. More generally, it concerns whether we suppose that those doing the work of the world can be relied upon to do something like their best most of the time and to attend to larger interests rather than their own and those of their immediate circle. The more trusting we are, the more we believe these things.

If citizens have little trust, it is doubtful they will feel inclined to join others in deliberating about public matters. Nor are they likely to trust remote national lawmakers about whom they have little detailed knowledge and with whom they have even less contact. Citizens without trust in their lawmakers may be humbled by the power these officials project through carefully managed mass media, and this may quiet distrust for the moment. However, as soon as things go a bit wrong, distrust quickly dissolves the trappings of office and turns them into the perquisites of unearned privilege—in the process engendering a kind of all-purpose cynicism that is infertile ground for a politics of the public interest.[34]

As with public-spiritedness, the deepest roots of trust are in family and neighborhood. It is difficult to imagine a child growing into a trusting adult who has learned early in life that one cannot trust even those to whom one looks for love and bodily comfort. In much the same way, a child growing up in a neighborhood filled with predatory inhabitants is unlikely to feel drawn into cooperative dealings later in life.

It would be surprising if popular culture and the mass media did not also have some effect on children's and adults' sense of trust. Thus, if the reporting of violent crime strongly implies that each of us is in imminent

[34] On trust see Edward C. Banfield, *The Moral Basis of a Backward Society* (New York: Free Press, 1967, 1958); and James Q. Wilson, *The Moral Sense* (New York: Free Press, 1993).

danger,[35] this can only reinforce feelings of mistrust of our fellow citizens. If the ordinary fare of television and the movies is that elected officials take bribes and cut deals to further the interests of wealthy constituents, and that businessmen regularly and illegally dump toxic waste at the first opportunity, many of us will suppose that, in fact, this is the way things are. After all, television and movies are vivid in the way that our timid little surmises about how the world really works can never be.

Those lucky enough to grow up in an environment where feelings of trust emerge as a matter of course are to some degree inoculated against the cynical maneuvering, naked displays of self-interest, and failures of policy that are the inevitable and frustrating features of even the best-designed political orders. They are less likely to take these parts for the whole, and more likely to believe that mendacity and foolishness will inevitably garner more public attention than the earnest, little-noticed, plodding competence that characterizes most of our work in the world.

Complex judgments

Without some measure of cognitive complexity,[36] it is unlikely that citizens can make the kind of judgments about lawmakers that I have said is necessary. They will not only be unable to judge what elements of the public interest are at stake in any particular effort at lawmaking, they will also find it difficult to judge whether lawmakers have any real concern with the public interest.

A principal source of the ability to make complex judgments—of cognitive complexity—is likely again to be in the world of work. Although it may be too much to claim that having complex, non-routine, loosely supervised work can promote such capacity, it is at least plausible that the lack of it dulls what powers people have. Because work consumes the largest portion of most adults' waking hours, if the experience there does not reinforce a capacity for cognitive complexity, most people are unlikely to develop it to any high level. Here again, Adam Smith is suggestive. He comments that the "understandings of the greater part of men are necessarily formed by their ordinary employments" and that the person engaged in repetitive industrial work "becomes as stupid and ignorant as it is possible for a human creature to be."[37]

---

[35] Which, even with higher crime rates, most of us are not.
[36] See Lane, *The Market Experience*, especially chap. 7.
[37] Smith, *The Wealth of Nations*, 734–5. Thus the poor are doubly handicapped. They do not have complex, demanding work (if they have any work at all), and their participation

Mutual respect

A deliberative mode of association must rest on a foundation of mutual respect among citizens. Unless citizens regard one another as equals, they are unlikely to deliberate, whatever the formal rules of the institutions require.[38] Mutual respect is the minimum form equality must take, and it can be roughly understood as respect for persons as opposed to their abilities or attainments. Mutual respect is especially important if the natural inequality of reasoning ability—and reasoning is the center of deliberation—is not to subvert the education of judgment that flows from participation.

The fundamental feeling at the heart of mutual respect is that I am as good as you—no better, perhaps, but certainly no worse. The enemy of mutual respect is a sense of power so great among some that they think they are in a position to inflict cruelties on others and a corresponding sense of servility and fear among the others.[39]

A measure of material equality is likely to be a minimum condition of mutual respect. How much material equality is necessary to sustain mutual respect? Perhaps a modest amount will suffice—more than characterizes the United States, say, but less than any strong egalitarian standard would call for.[40] The prospects for a deliberative local politics depend on how stringent a standard must be met, since any great degree of material equality will probably be difficult or even impossible to achieve within the minimum requirement of a commercial republic—that is, within some form of the private ownership of productive assets.

The dimensions of the problem that economic inequality poses for mutual respect are the following. It seems likely that persons in families with incomes around the current median household income of just under $37,000 are not likely to be overawed by someone who comes from a household with an income of $150,000. They inhabit something like the same world economically, and differential incomes can plausibly be at-

in the marketplace is limited in other respects as well; money is the passport to market participation, and this is, of course, what the poor lack.

[38] These matters are sometimes discussed under the heading of political equality, and my discussion should be read as assuming that all citizens have at least formal legal equality.

[39] See Judith Shklar's discussion of Rousseau in this respect. *Men and Citizens* (Cambridge: Cambridge University Press, 1969), 19.

[40] But see the Federalist (!) Noah Webster's comment that "an equality of property, with a necessity of alienation, constantly operating to destroy combinations of powerful families, is the very soul of a republic. . . . An equal distribution of property is the foundation of a republic. . . ." "Examination into the Leading Principles of the Federal Constitution," in *Pamphlets on the Constitution of the United States Published During Its Discussion by the People 1787–88*, ed. Paul Leicester Ford (Brooklyn, N.Y., 1888).

tributed to differences in talent and luck. The better-off person, in turn, is unlikely to think of the less-well-off person as someone who lacks character and talents worth respecting.

The problem for mutual respect is likely to lie with those at the top and bottom of the income distribution. At the moment in the United States, when those in the bottom two deciles, with a top income of $17,000, come in contact with those in the top 2 to 3 percent—and even with those in the top decile (the lower limit for the top 5 percent of families is well over $100,000)—they are meeting people who inhabit another world. They are all too likely to be deferential to those they think have won the economic race. As the political economy is now organized, moreover, the top 10 percent holds, and will continue to hold under virtually any set of reforms now possible, the major organizing positions in the society. Additionally, the top 10 percent are more or less completely insulated from contact with the poor and near-poor, and being so, some number of them will become fearful of the motives of those at the bottom. Mutual respect is unlikely to be a feature of relations between the two groups.

A real difficulty for republican government, therefore, is not so much the size of the top income strata (the 2 to 3 percent) but their fear of a bottom that is too large for comfort—and to whom they mostly respond without generosity. Their wealth is not the problem. Rather, it is their response to the bottom: The substantial political influence they wield is not often mobilized to bring the poor into the system of mutual respect. Even more problematical for republican government is simply the number of the poor and near-poor. Something like a quarter of the population—those living in households with yearly incomes under $15,000—is outside the system of mutual respect. In short, a political economy like that of the present United States—characterized by an income distribution in which a significant part (the lowest two deciles) lives in poverty and near poverty, whereas the top decile consists of people whose income is ten to several hundred times greater than that of those in the lowest deciles—is not likely to be a place in which mutual respect can flourish.

The difficulty of achieving some measure of material equality is eased by the reasonable assumption that the core of mutual respect is self-respect. Although material circumstances in a commercial society plainly have some bearing on self-respect, it is unlikely that they are determinative. Think of the effects that possessing a skill or a body of specialized knowledge has on a person. The relatively low-income specialist in ancient Greek philosophy is less likely to feel overawed by the rich merchant

banker than will the moderately well-paid middle manager of a corporation. Similarly, to take an extreme case, the violin-maker is unlikely to
think that he or she is a lesser person than the rich corporate raider.

To have a skill means to have the ability to create something—and,
where such a skill is of a complex sort, those who have it are given or naturally have a sense of their own worth and are likely to be accorded respect by others. We may suppose, therefore, that those of modest
means—they cannot have little or nothing by way of income—and secure
skills will have a good measure of self-respect; and this in turn will not
only be communicated to those of greater material means, but the latter
will probably to some degree share their evaluation of skills and knowledge. A basis for mutual respect is in place.[41]

Here, then, is one recipe for mutual respect: Each person is to have income sufficient for that measure of self-respect that will result in mutual
respect. This formulation does not point to anything like strong economic equality. But it does suggest that our present distribution of income and
wealth is too unequal, given that mutual respect is necessary for republican citizenship. Moreover, it is entirely possible that the measure of equality that *is* required is within our economic means.[42]

But two points must be emphasized. First, self-respect is unlikely to be
very strong among persons with little or no income, regardless of their
skills—at least not in a commercial society. In much the same way, their
self-respect is likely to be eroded if they have so low a level of economic
security that it will take little to tumble them into poverty.

Second, many—perhaps most—people in a commercial society will
not have a level of skill sufficient in itself to promote self-respect, nor will
they possess the kind of knowledge that is in short supply. The basis for
their self-respect is thus likely to be closely tied to their material circumstances, including income and the prestige of the job they do. There is still
some room here to get quit of the tyranny of money, since there is a good
deal of evidence[43] that once people rise above a certain modest level of income, the amount of discretion they have on the job becomes more im-

[41] Cf. Charles Anderson, *Pragmatic Liberalism* (Chicago: University of Chicago Press,
1990), chap. 7.
[42] "Too much" equality is no good either, since it will likely undercut prideful independence. Substantial equality can probably be achieved only by wholesale government
transfers, and that will almost certainly undercut the sense of pride in one's accomplishments if the principal way in which people earn their living is through paid work. Nor
will wholesale transfers do much for the prideful independence of those from whom the
transfers are taken.
[43] See Lane, *The Market Experience*.

54   STEPHEN L. ELKIN

portant in determining their sense of well-being. People who can exercise initiative, or are not treated as replaceable parts in a giant human-mechanical machine, are likely to feel more fully human and thus have a greater degree of self-respect. The potential here in the reorganization of work is obvious.

The central questions concerning mutual respect and self-respect are apparent in the remarks of Franklin Roosevelt:

> Our aim is to recognize what Lincoln pointed out: The fact that there are some respects in which men are clearly not equal; but also to insist that there should be an equality of self-respect and mutual respect—at least an approximate equality in the conditions under which each man obtains the chance to show the stuff that is in him compared to his fellows.[44]

If the relation between mutual respect and economic equality is likely to be modest, if real, that between the distribution of complex, demanding, and loosely supervised work and mutual respect is likely to be greater. Again, self-respect is the crucial link.

Consider remarks by the great economist Alfred Marshall: "The business by which a person earns his livelihood fills his thoughts during by far the greatest part of those hours in which his mind is at its best: during them his character is being formed by the ways in which he uses his faculties at work."[45]

Nonroutine, complex, loosely supervised work is important for self-respect. Those whose work is closely monitored, whose jobs are so routine as to require little of them, will need to look for self-respect elsewhere. They may indeed find it or simply carry it with them from childhood, but the burden on other domains grows as work is barren.

How much mutual respect is needed for the kind of local politics that will engender the capacity for judgment that republican citizens need? If a commercial republic needs very substantial displays of mutual respect, it probably cannot succeed. If, on the other hand, mutual respect can be of the kind found among decent people who are encouraged to act in mutually respectful ways—by, for example, a modest measure of material equality—then the prospects are brighter.

[44] From remarks delivered to the U.S. Congress in support of an inheritance tax, June 19, 1935. Quoted in Nelson Aldrich, Jr., *Old Money: The Myths of America's Upper Class* (New York: A. A. Knopf; Random House, 1988), 235.
[45] Alfred Marshall, *Principles of Economics,* 8th edition (New York: Macmillan for the Royal Economic Society), 1–2.

The esteem of others

Citizens can be drawn to reason-giving and deliberation out of concern for enjoying the esteem of others. Concern for the esteem of others, as Tocqueville pointed out, is a powerful motive in all popular regimes.[46] A significant number of citizens must come to local political life with the following view: that those among them who show an awareness of interests larger than their own, who try to give content to such interests, who attempt to demonstrate why such larger interests should be attended to, and who listen attentively to the views of others on these matters should be held in high esteem. Conversely, a significant number of citizens must also believe that those who never rise above their own interests, who unrelentingly pursue their own immediate and direct interests, are citizens from whom decency requires that one avert one's eyes.

Concern for the esteem of others is a motive that can be harnessed in the context of local political life. Indeed, this is probably the only context where such a private-regarding motive can be systematically employed in ways that will lead republican citizens to engage in a deliberative politics.[47]

Conclusion

Local political life—and political life generally—cannot perform miracles of transformation. Deeply self-interested, unreflective citizens unable to think very hard about political life will defeat virtually any effort to induce them through constitutional design to think more carefully about public matters. The world of family and work is where the foundations for a public-spirited citizenry are laid. It would be very odd indeed if it were otherwise. Political life is much like any other undertaking: What we learn as children has a powerful impact there. And work takes up much more of our time than politics and more powerfully affects our day-to-day lives. If it helps to form our character in ways that are deeply adverse to the requirements of republican citizenship, it is unlikely that very much can be done about it.[48]

---

[46] See the discussion in Elkin, *City and Regime.*
[47] See Elkin, *City and Regime,* chaps. 8 and 9.
[48] What about people who don't work? If they are retired, there is no problem; they will have worked. But what about the ill and infirm, the long-term unemployed, and those

LOCAL POLITICAL LIFE AND THE PROSPECTS FOR
A REPUBLICAN REGIME

It is entirely likely that even if citizens come to local political life with all of the qualities I have discussed, unless that politics is structured very differently than it presently is, little public-spiritedness will be fostered.

Briefly, the present character of local political life promotes a narrowness of concern on the part of citizens; concomitantly, it does little to stretch self-interest to a concern with broader, public interests.[49] Citizens quickly learn that local politics is about the advancement of private interests; naturally enough, they conclude that their interests, too, should be given serious attention. Although local inhabitants may sometimes be inclined to rise above the pursuit of their own, their neighborhood's, or their other group interests, they will typically find little encouragement in the decision-making that lies at the center of local political life.

The present pattern of politics, moreover, offers few opportunities for deliberation. What is more, it stands in the way of opening up more opportunities. Much of the workings of local politics takes place not in the public forum of the local legislature but in an executive-centered process that revolves around the mayor and his chief administrators. It is, in short, the antithesis of a deliberative politics.

Equally serious, in a significant number of localities it is currently unlikely that citizens can be drawn into a consideration of the concrete meaning of the public interest. This is particularly the case for homogeneous, well-to-do suburbs and towns. The residents of these municipalities are the beneficiaries of a political economy that insulates them from the need to face the question of how to deal with the interconnections among the elements of the public interest.

Although others must struggle with this question (and, struggling or not, they are strongly affected by the tensions among elements of the public interest),[50] for the citizens of more or less uniformly prosperous communities local political life is all of a piece: Those who run business corporations can have very wide discretion in how they employ their assets,

who never intend to enter the labor market? There is no easy way around the point that in a commercial republic, employment is crucial to republican citizenship—and not just for the reasons I have been considering here. See the very useful discussion by Shklar in *American Citizenship.*

[49] For some evidence and argument that supports the characterization of local political life in this and the next paragraph, see Elkin, *City and Regime,* chaps. 8 and 9.

[50] See the discussion above on the public interest as Madison likely understood it.

local prosperity can be high, and government can be limited. By contrast, those living in other kinds of communities will face questions such as these: If business corporations have wide discretion in how they employ their assets, they may decide to leave the locality, thus significantly reducing local prosperity; should then the powers of local government be used to reduce such discretion? And how will such an effort fit with a concern that government should be limited?

Rather than being drawn into a local politics that teaches the citizenry something of such tensions among elements of the public interest, those who live in homogeneous, prosperous communities can move happily through life, indifferent to these tensions. Indeed, they have the luxury of responding in a puzzled way when someone points out that serving the public interest is a difficult matter. After all, for them the pieces of the public interest fit together rather nicely.

Whereas citizens of prosperous localities need not face the question of how to understand the elements of the public interest, those in other communities cannot. Their socioeconomic condition allows them few if any choices. They too are homogeneous: A substantial majority of their citizens are poor or nearly poor.

Thus, at present, East St. Louis and East Cleveland operate in a different world from Bronxville, New York, and Winnetka, Illinois. East St. Louis and East Cleveland cannot pay their bills, much less devote resources to weighing how best to manage their local economies. Property values in East St. Louis have fallen to less than $50 million from $200 million since the mid-1960s. Its per capita income is now one-third that of the United States as a whole, and two-thirds of its residents receive some form of public assistance.[51]

East St. Louis may be the extreme, but other localities share many of the same problems. Such localities are, for all intents and purposes, economically and politically bankrupt. Their politics are much more likely to teach futility than what is at stake in giving concrete meaning to the public interest. Given this state of affairs, the citizens of such communities will simply be left out of local politics as a school of citizenship—or they will be assigned, as it were, to the wrong school. But a nontrivial number of citizens live in such localities, so the loss to a public-spirited citizenry is significant.

Finally, local political life is now balkanized by special districts and

---

[51] For these data, and for a general discussion, see *New York Times*, April 4, 1991 and October 30, 1994.

separate governing boards for a number of services. If local political life remains thus fragmented, it will be exceedingly difficult for citizens (and those who speak for them) to consider the full range of concrete matters relevant to the public interest.

If we desire a more fully realized republican regime, we must extensively reform local political life. This conclusion is likely to be resisted for all the usual reasons. Even more troubling, however, is that it is likely to be resisted by many who understand themselves to be friends of the American regime, devoted to a full realization of its republican character.

Such people may well accept the above characterization of local politics as more or less accurate, but still argue that we need not extensively reform local political life. Local politics, they will say, is simply not that important for fostering public-spiritedness—and thus for securing a flourishing republican regime. If the reforms called for are extensive, as they must be, then we should not undertake the task. The costs will be great and the gain little.[52]

The issue here is why local political life is fundamental for fostering public-spiritedness, and why nothing else can take its place. Again, Mill points the way. After saying that "free and popular local and municipal institutions" are part of "the peculiar training of a citizen," Mill adds that without the habits of mind learned through participation in local political life—specifically, the inclination to act from "public or semi-public motives"—"a free constitution can neither be worked or preserved."[53]

Mill's formulation suggests, first of all, that local politics is the only forum that affords an opportunity for citizens to consider a wide range of public matters, and thus to develop the skills and outlook necessary to be effective participants in the larger political life of the regime. Only local government offers an array of public decisions wide enough to draw citizens into the full range of matters encompassed by any plausible conception of the public interest. Local political institutions are the only context in which a significant number of citizens can put into practice their inclination to be public-spirited—and, in doing so, reinforce and refine it.

---

[52] They might argue as well that public-spiritedness itself is not as important as I have suggested for the realization of a republican regime. To deal with this response would require elaborating further the theory of political constitution that I have sketched above.

[53] Mill, *On Liberty,* 181. Tocqueville said that "municipal institutions constitute the strength of free nations. Town meetings are to liberty what primary schools are to science: they bring it within the people's reach, they teach men how to use and enjoy it. A nation may establish a free government, but without municipal institutions it cannot have the spirit of liberty." Tocqueville, *Democracy in America,* vol. 1, 62–63.

Local political life is also especially important in a regime like ours because fostering public-spiritedness must be done through indirect, "mild" means—that is, through experience rather than through tutelary or even harsher methods. To rely on such direct and even coercive means is to undercut one of the fundamental purposes of the regime, namely, securing the rights of its citizens.

Again, local government offers the only possibility for large numbers of citizens to become involved in exercising public authority—that is, to take responsibility for the use of powers that will affect others, many of whom will not share their views on matters of policy. Civic associations cannot do the job: The element of authority is missing. To be responsible in such a fashion is likely to prompt a healthy skepticism concerning whether one's own views are quite so obviously right as they seem. Such judiciousness is necessary if a politics of the public interest is not to degenerate into a deep conflict that will pull the regime apart.

Finally, if properly structured, local government makes plain that there is no easy escape from our fellow citizens. If the most powerful and wealthy among us are prevented from building legal walls around themselves, the message that we are all in this together—that there is something more than the interests of me and mine, that there is a common or public interest—becomes not an abstraction but a fact of everyday life. A nation—or even a state or region within it—is too big to make this point in any concrete, regular way. And if the point *is* made in these larger contexts, the sheer size and complexity of the larger political system impede the ability to respond to it.[54]

Tocqueville sums up the crucial point about the relation between local political life and republican government when he comments that "the most powerful way, and perhaps the only remaining way, in which to interest men in their country's fate is to make them take a share in its government."[55] We may extend the thought by saying that for citizens to have any concern for the public interest of the regime, they must have the experience of grappling with its elements. For any significant number of citizens this can happen only through local political life.

Those who profess their allegiance to the realization of an American

---

[54] Participating in the exercise of public authority also reinforces prideful independence. To feel a sense of responsibility—to learn to weigh interests and concerns that are not one's own—is humbling, but it provides a realistic foundation for self-respect: I can participate intelligently in so important a matter. Again, local government is the only place where large numbers of citizens can learn this lesson.

[55] Tocqueville, *Democracy in America,* 66.

republic need then to consider arguments of the kind I have just set out. Even more important, if they are to be convincing in their dismissal of the critical importance of local political life for a fully realized republican regime, they will need a theory of the political constitution of the American regime such as the one I sketched in the opening pages. If that theory is deeply flawed, they must supply a better one. Otherwise, those who profess to be friends of the regime can have no serious account of whether or not a reformed local political life is essential to make it flourish. Nor, in consequence, can they be good friends of the regime.

II

Local self-government in American political history

3

The origins and influence of early American local self-government

Democracy in America reconsidered

PAULINE MAIER

Studies of American local institutions are haunted by the spirit of Alexis de Tocqueville, and for good reason. In the famous fifth chapter of *Democracy in America,* Part I (1835), he presented a compelling argument that local self-government provided an essential foundation for America's democratic political culture. Tocqueville based his conclusion on two kinds of information: what came from his own observations during a tour of the United States he made with Gustave de Beaumont between May 1831 and February 1832 and what he received from others, either orally or on paper. Whenever he discussed American manners or habits, Tocqueville drew on his own observations. In describing American local government, however, he relied for the most part on secondary information. And there his sources were skewed; he depended primarily on a group of New England enthusiasts, among them historian and editor Jared Sparks, who firmly believed that New England, with its town-meeting form of local government, was the "cradle of American democracy."[1]

Because he came from a nation with a highly centralized administration, Tocqueville was struck by the vitality of New England's town government. Having encountered that unexpected phenomenon, however, he quickly became aware of how ignorant he was of the French system, whose workings he had more or less taken for granted, but which he needed to understand in order to make sense of American practices. "On a multitude of points," Tocqueville wrote a French friend, "we don't know what to ask, because we are ignorant of what exists in France and because, without comparisons to make, the mind doesn't know how to

[1] See particularly George Wilson Pierson, *Tocqueville and Beaumont in America* (New York: Oxford University Press, 1938), chap. 30, "Sparks—and Local Self-Government," 397–416.

proceed." He was fully aware, Tocqueville told his father, "that with us the government concerns itself with almost everything," but although "a hundred times the name *centralization* has been dinned into my ears," it had never been explained. He therefore implored correspondents to explain precisely how French government worked. What exactly did the 1,200 employees of the Ministry of the Interior do? How much independence remained to the commune? And what powers were exercised by the various departments and arrondissements?[2]

At about the same time—in September 1831—he plied Bostonians with similar questions and received in return not only spoken answers but written materials, among them a gift from Harvard President Josiah Quincy, a little book called *Town Officer* that explained local officials' duties. In his discussion of local government in *Democracy in America,* Tocqueville cited that book and also relevant provisions in state codes of law. But those sources were insufficient, it seems; from Cincinnati in December he wrote Sparks, who had first met Tocqueville during a visit to Paris in 1828, asking more detailed questions. Tocqueville wanted to know not just what the law said, but what was done in fact; he wisely observed, there is "a big difference between the letter of the law and its execution." The farther he traveled from Massachusetts, Tocqueville wrote Sparks, the more he regretted not having stayed there for a longer period, because nowhere had he found communal institutions approaching those of New England. In reply, Sparks composed a tract—"Observations on the Government of Towns in Massachusetts"—that described the evolution and workings of Massachusetts local government for an audience "but little informed on the subject."[3]

Tocqueville is innocent of the charge that he thought all of America was like New England. He not only explicitly denied that towns and counties were organized identically throughout America, but devoted a section of his fifth chapter to describing local systems of government elsewhere in the Union and how they differed from that of New England—or, more exactly, from that of Massachusetts, which he assumed was in all essential respects the same as local governments elsewhere in New England.

[2] Ibid., 403–5.
[3] Ibid., 402; Alexis de Tocqueville, *Journey to America,* ed. J. P. Mayer, trans. George Lawrence (Westport, Conn.: Greenwood Press, 1971 [reprinted 1981]), esp. 45–8; and Tocqueville to Sparks, December 2, 1831, Sparks's "Observations," and other related documents in *Jared Sparks and Alexis de Tocqueville,* ed. Herbert Baxter Adams, Johns Hopkins University Studies in Historical and Political Science, Series 16, No. 12 (Baltimore: Johns Hopkins University Press, 1898), 9–13 (quotation at 11), 17ff., and passim.

But he took only a "broad look at the rest of the country," and devoted the bulk of his discussion to "one of the states of New England," Massachusetts, where principles basic to the formation of local governments throughout the American nation were, he asserted, "carried further with more far-reaching results than elsewhere" and so "stand out there in higher relief and are easier for a foreigner to observe."[4] It seems likely, however, that Tocqueville chose to concentrate on Massachusetts less for the reason he stated than because he had in hand a mass of information on it that was presented in a form readily adaptable to his purposes—information that had been generously supplied by men whose conviction of the preeminent influence of New England on American politics and culture shaped not only Tocqueville's views but those of several generations of American historians.

Modern scholars have information at hand that is more comprehensive and more "objective" than what Tocqueville had at his disposal. Given the continuing influence, explicit and implicit, that *Democracy in America* has exerted on discussions of American government, it seems worthwhile to examine Tocqueville's position against modern knowledge, asking the same questions he asked: How, and why, did administrative responsibility come to rest at the local level in the United States? And what difference did that make? The underlying issue is whether, once one "corrects" Tocqueville's data, his conclusions still stand and, beyond that, what impact local self-government in fact had upon the character and functioning of American democracy.

For Tocqueville, the question of how and why localities came to govern themselves seemed hardly worth pursuing. He considered the township a basic human institution "so well rooted in nature that whenever men assemble it forms itself," as if by the hand of God. But once more complex political systems developed, such primitive forms of association were, he thought, almost impossible to sustain unless they had become deeply rooted in the customs and habits of a people. Nations attract the services of men whose talents fit them for the work of government, but localities remain in the hands of "coarser elements" whose "numerous blunders" cause disgust among "enlightened" people. As a result, townships almost inevitably lost their independence as societies became more "civilized." Municipal freedom was for Tocqueville essential to a free society: "Local

---

[4] Alexis de Tocqueville, *Democracy in America*, ed. J. P. Mayer (Garden City, N.Y.: Doubleday, 1969), 80–4 and 63.

institutions," he wrote, "are to liberty what primary schools are to science; they put it within the people's reach" and accustom them to use it and appreciate its benefits. Yet local governments were so vulnerable to encroachments from above, he asserted, that they had failed to retain their historic power and significance in any nation of contemporary Europe.[5]

Tocqueville's account of political evolution from a "semibarbarous" to "civilized" or "enlightened" society had a marked resemblance to early social scientific models of human social development. It also coincided nicely with Sparks's description of the emergence of town government in early New England. The first New England town, Sparks said, was established by the settlers of Plymouth when they were still "surrounded by a vast wilderness, uninhabited except by a few savages" and so, with regard to "the rights and forms of government," in a "state of nature." The system of regulation they set up "for mutual convenience and security" was "the simplest form of a republic," one in which each person had a voice and the majority ruled. Officials were given limited powers, and their duties "were prescribed by the people themselves." Subsequent groups of colonists, who took up lands distant from that original settlement, followed Plymouth's example in establishing local governments that were, in effect, "independent republics." They "soon acquired the knowledge and habits of local government," which became so deeply embedded in the region's customs that they were "never abandoned" and remained the foundation of New England's nineteenth-century municipal system. Provincial (or, later, "state") government emerged subsequently, Sparks explained, as the separate towns found it "convenient . . . to unite under some form of government . . . to protect themselves from the Indians, and for other advantages," but the towns remained unwilling to grant that "union" any more power than was "essential to the general interests." Central government was therefore a creation of the towns, who yielded power grudgingly, carefully reserving their "primitive rights" and preserving the "local forms of government already established." That process, Sparks said, illustrated a basic principle of American institutions—"that a superior government exercises such powers only as are delegated to it by an inferior, or, in other words, by the people."[6]

These remarks, which appeared at the start of Sparks's "Observations" on Massachusetts town government, restated a point he had made earlier in person to Tocqueville, who dutifully recorded Sparks's words in

[5] Ibid., 62–3.
[6] Sparks, "Observations," in *Jared Sparks and Alexis de Tocqueville,* 17–18.

his notebook: "Almost all societies, even in America, have begun with one place where the government was concentrated, and have then spread out around that central point. Our forefathers on the contrary founded *the locality before the State*. Plymouth, Salem, Charlestown existed before one could speak of a government of Massachusetts; they only became united later by an act of deliberate will." The "fact" that all superior authority was built upon delegations of power from towns explained for Sparks the powerful "spirit of locality" that he thought distinguished New Englanders as well as their "republican principles"—that is, their conviction that legitimate authority depended upon popular consent. Tocqueville echoed Sparks: New England's political life, he said, was "born in the very heart of the townships," each of which was at first "a little independent nation." The towns were not creatures of a central state, but "surrendered a portion of their powers for the benefit of the state," to which they eventually became subordinate. That central power emerged as a creation of the towns, rather than the reverse, was for Tocqueville an important fact that he cautioned readers always to bear in mind. It explained for him why the United States had managed to avoid the loss of communal freedom that Tocqueville considered characteristic of most civilized nations.[7]

Sparks's description of seventeenth-century political development was probably influenced overmuch by the revolutionary creation of a federal government with authority taken from what had been sovereign states (although the question of whether the states or the nation came first was disputed in his time, most notably in the Webster-Hayne Debates of 1830). More important, with regard to the creation of local governments and their relationship to central or provincial authority, modern scholarship tells the story of a more complex development than Sparks described, one in which *central authority came first,* even in those New England colonies that Sparks knew best.

Start, like Sparks, with Plymouth, an independent colony that was absorbed into Massachusetts in the late seventeenth century by act of the British Crown. The course of Plymouth's development was not as Sparks said; indeed, it conformed more closely to the model Sparks associated with societies *outside* New England. The original settlement at the town of Plymouth did become a center from which other settlements spread out, but as that happened Plymouth became the home of a central gov-

---

[7] Tocqueville, *Journey to America,* 47–8, and *Democracy in America,* 67.

ernment that conferred political authority on new towns and brought them together in a larger whole. By 1630, ten years after Plymouth's founding, people had begun moving onto lands to its north that would later be organized into towns by permission of the Plymouth General Court. In October 1636, that body voted that

the towne of Scituate be allowed (vizt, the purchasers & freemen) to dispose of the lands beyond the North River, except that wch was before disposed on to others. And also it be allowed them to make such orders in their towneship for their convenient & comfortable living as they shall finde necessary, provided they have, in case of justice, recourse unto Plymouth, as before.

By 1687, some twenty towns extending eastward across Cape Cod to the island of Nantucket and westward toward Narragansett Bay were similarly authorized and granted governmental power by the Plymouth General Court, which in 1638 became a representative body of delegates elected by householders in the various towns.[8]

The dispersion of population within Plymouth Colony did not, in truth, always occur within a process that was so carefully ordered, with Plymouth organizing and conferring powers on the colony's developing towns. Several small communities grew and prospered without official recognition, and the colony gradually came to consist of a somewhat miscellaneous set of towns, clusters of farms, and isolated homesteads spread over an extensive territory. But that development was not considered normal or commendable. The colony's historian and longtime governor, William Bradford, regarded the scattering of Plymouth's peoples "under one pretense or other" with deep regret—mainly, it seems, for religious reasons. "This I fear," he wrote, "will be the ruin of New England, at least

---

[8] John Demos, *A Little Commonwealth: Family Life in Plymouth Colony* (New York: Oxford University Press, 1970), 7, 9–11. See also note 13 on p. 11, which lists "the towns of Plymouth Colony, in the order of their incorporation: Plymouth, 1620; Scituate, 1636; Duxbury, 1637; Barnstable, 1639; Taunton, 1639; Sandwich, 1639; Yarmouth, 1639; Marshfield, 1641; Rehoboth, 1645; Eastham, 1646; Bridgewater, 1656; Dartmouth, 1664; Swansea, 1667; Middleborough, 1669; Edgartown, 1671; Tisbury, 1671; Little Compton, 1682; Freetown, 1683; Rochester, 1686; Falmouth, 1686; Nantucket, 1687." Demos's use of the word "incorporation" is not, I think, technically correct, since in British law incorporation was a prerogative of the Crown, which in the colonial period created only a handful of colonial corporations including, for example, those of New York and Philadelphia. The term is, however, at least metaphorically correct insofar as the towns were legally organized only with the permission of central authority and exercised certain powers of self-government similar to those of legally constituted corporations. The quotation in the text is from *Records of the Colony of New Plymouth in New England,* ed. Nathaniel B. Shurtleff, Court Orders: vol. 1, 1633–1640 (Boston: Press of W. White, 1855), 44.

of the churches of God there, and will provoke the Lord's displeasure against them."[9] For Puritans, whether in Plymouth or Massachusetts Bay, God's people were supposed to remain "knit together" in close communities where they could give each other guidance and support in living according to His edicts. Clearly, the creation of isolated "independent republics" was not an accepted norm. Bradford and the founders of Plymouth believed in tightly organized societies with central authority; for them, the governmental powers of the towns were not original but secondary, founded on grants from Plymouth's General Court.

The history of the Massachusetts Bay Colony is essentially the same, with a few idiosyncratic variations. Salem did exist prior to the establishment of a Massachusetts government, as Sparks said. Like Plymouth, it grew out of an earlier attempt at colonization. The first settlers of Massachusetts Bay landed there in June 1630, but Salem, wrote a member of that expedition, "pleased us not." And so, five days later, Massachusetts Governor John Winthrop and his assistants set out to find a new location for "Boston," the name already chosen for the centralized community they planned to found. Deciding where to "plant" the new colony proved difficult, and in July the settlers moved to a temporary location on a peninsula between the mouths of the Charles and Mystic Rivers, which would become Charlestown. Disease spread through the encampment; a rumor arrived that the French were about to attack. As a result, between late July and September 1630 groups of colonists dispersed into what would become seven towns in the vicinity of Massachusetts Bay: Watertown, Roxbury, Dorchester, Medford, Saugus, Charlestown, and, on the Shawmut Peninsula, Boston. The settlers worked desperately to provide shelter before the onset of winter. Then, having "built already," they were unable "to build again" at still another place, so the scattering of colonists became a settled fact of life.[10]

The process of town formation in the Massachusetts Bay Colony was therefore more rapid than at Plymouth, but central authority was never absent or insignificant to the process. The colony had a set of officers—a governor, a deputy governor, and a "Court of Assistants"—in place when the first settlers arrived at Salem. The assistants, all men of respectable rank, became leaders of the several Massachusetts towns, which meant

[9] Demos, *Little Commonwealth*, 10–11; William Bradford, *Of Plymouth Plantation, 1620–1647*, ed. S. E. Morison (New York: Knopf, 1952), 254, 333.
[10] Account and quotations from Darrett B. Rutman, *Winthrop's Boston: Portrait of a Puritan Town, 1630–1649* (Chapel Hill: University of North Carolina Press, 1965), 23–9.

that at first central and local authority rested in much the same hands. As justices of the peace (or, as they came to be known, "magistrates"), the assistants exercised various judicial and executive responsibilities within the towns; they also presided over the distribution of land. Acting as the colony's Court of Assistants with its governor and deputy governor, they appointed constables who worked with them in enforcing the law on the local level.

The Court of Assistants tried to contain population dispersal. On September 7, 1630, it called back settlers who had pushed north to Aggawam (later the town of Ipswich) and decreed that "noe person shall plant in any place within the lymitts of this Pattent, without leave from the Governor and Assistants, or the major parte of them." New towns within the patent were thereafter organized, as at Plymouth, with the permission of the colony's central government and exercised powers that it granted and defined.[11]

Central authority therefore came first, but as the towns grew in number and size, the townsmen themselves gradually assumed responsibility for their affairs. They did so, it seems, not over the opposition of the assistants but with their support (and perhaps even to their relief). In 1634 the "freemen of every plantation" were ordered "to chuse two or three of each towne" to meet with the assistants at the next General Court and speak for their constituents "in the publique affayres of the commonwealth," including the passing of laws, granting of lands, and election of provincial officials. The towns thereby became, as at Plymouth, a constituent part of the colony's central government, one which later took on independent power as town delegates began to sit apart from the assistants as a lower house of assembly.

On March 3, 1635/36, the General Court formally gave the towns power to regulate their own internal affairs—to dispose of their lands and woods, to make laws and ordinances compatible with those of the General Court, to exact penalties from lawbreakers (which could not, however, exceed 20 shillings), and to choose their own officers, including consta-

---

[11] Ibid., 41–4, and *Records of the Governor and Company of the Massachusetts Bay in New England*, ed. Nathaniel B. Shurtleff, vol. 1, 1628–1641 (Boston: W. White, Printer to the Commonwealth, 1853), 76. On the determination of the early governments of Massachusetts to retain supervisory power over the towns whose creation they authorized, see also David Thomas Konig, "English Legal Change and the Origins of Local Government in Northern Massachusetts," in *Town and County: Essays on the Structure of Local Government in the American Colonies*, ed. Bruce C. Daniels (Middletown, Conn.: Wesleyan University Press, 1978), 12–43.

bles, "surveyors for the high wayes, & the like." By then, the towns had already become the collectors of provincial taxes, which they had to do in ways specified by the General Court—for example, by assessing a man's share according to the size of his estate. They had also become an arm of the central government in providing for its defense. They were told, for example, to assure that local men had "good & sufficient armes" and to furnish such armaments at town expense if necessary (1630/31), to provide places to store ammunition (1634/35), and, sometimes, to supply men to work on colonial fortifications (1635/36). The General Court ordered the towns to appoint two night watchmen for at least a stated period of time (1634), to keep standard weights and measures (1635), to decide who could sell "wine & strong water" (1637/38); it charged them with keeping land transaction and other records. Thereafter the responsibilities entrusted to the towns continued to grow by the same process of delegation from the center.[12]

Again, the process of decentralization was not always so carefully ordered. The General Court seemed at times two steps behind its land-hungry people. Moreover, those religious refugees from Massachusetts orthodoxy who founded Rhode Island did settle in towns that remained so independent of one another that the modern historian G. B. Warden questions whether in the mid-seventeenth century a "Rhode Island" existed above and beyond the separate settlements it supposedly comprised. Several towns, including Providence and Portsmouth, were governed under civil covenants that reflected "a crazy quilt of . . . antithetical political and religious views" and so were "almost mutually exclusive."[13] Connecticut was also founded by people who left Massachusetts Bay, and, in

[12] Shurtleff, *Records of Massachusetts Bay*, vol. 1, 118–9, 172 (order on town powers of 1635/36). On assessments, see 77, 120; on arms, ammunition, and fortifications, 84, 138, 166; also 85 and 120 (the watch), 148 (weights and measures), 221 (liquor), and 116 and 176 (records). On the process by which towns came to exercise control over liquor licenses and, in general, on the expansion of town powers, see Rutman, *Winthrop's Boston*, 222–3 and 62–4. The order of 1635 giving towns power over their affairs is worth comparing to the Township Act of 1670 in *The Colonial Laws of Massachusetts* (Boston: Rockwell and Churchill, 1887), 147–8. The wordings are in many places the same or similar, but the 1670 act is more capacious, and provides more details on the selection and qualifications of local officers such as selectmen, jurors, and constables. See also *General Laws of Massachusetts, From the Adoption of the Constitution, to February, 1822* (Boston: Hillard, Gray, Little, and Wilkins, 1823), vol. 1, 250–5 for "An Act for regulating Towns, setting forth their Power, and for the choice of Town Officers," passed in 1785.
[13] G. B. Warden, "The Rhode Island Civil Code of 1747," in *Saints and Revolutionaries: Essays on Early American History*, ed. David Hall et al. (New York: Norton, 1984), esp. 139–42.

at least one notable example, without asking the General Court's permission—and even against its wishes. Later the settlers created a common, central government similar to that of Massachusetts by a process that seemed to follow the model Sparks and Tocqueville presented: The settlers first founded towns, which then confederated under the Fundamental Orders of Connecticut (1739). However, a historian of Connecticut, Bruce C. Daniels, says that in fact the towns "deliberately gave up their sovereignty to a General Court, and it was under this court's guidance that the towns were organized." Moreover, Connecticut towns exercised no power but those delegated to them by the colonial government at Hartford, which also created most town offices. As such, Daniels says, "the court formed those towns in substance and not vice versa." But over time, as the population grew, town government increased in size and power, and became increasingly independent of outside intervention until, by the time of the Revolution, Connecticut's towns had reached "a semi-autonomous stage of development."[14] To the extent that Connecticut towns were "independent republics" by the end of the colonial period, they had achieved that identity over time by receiving responsibility for one public function after another from the colony's General Court.

Despite Sparks's apparently authoritative assertions, then, local institutions were generally the creations, not the creators, of central government in New England. And that same pattern of development, with central governments predating and fueling the development of local government, seems to have prevailed elsewhere. Virginia first established a system of local government under county courts in 1634, more than a quarter century after the colony was originally settled in 1607. Thereafter the General Assembly proceeded to grant counties one responsibility after another, until the colony experienced "a fundamental decentralization and dispersal of power." County courts first received jurisdiction over minor civil and criminal cases, then became responsible for maintaining bridges and ferries (1642/43); before long they were empowered to probate wills, and their juridical authority was extended to all cases in common law and equity (1645). They were allowed to enact local bylaws (1661/62) and, in general, became responsible by the late seventeenth century for administration, the maintenance of order, and the keeping of records. County officials collected provincial as well as local taxes, and were charged with raising, training, and equipping the militia and so became the main agent of the colony's defense. The justices of the peace,

[14] Bruce C. Daniels, "The Political Structure of Local Government in Colonial Connecticut," in Daniels, *Town and County*, 44, 67–8.

sheriffs, and clerks who exercised these extensive powers were commissioned by the royal governor, whose appointments were, however, confined by custom and sometimes by statute to persons nominated by current justices and therefore drawn from members of ranking local families. For that reason, local officeholders both brought a "paternalistic flavor to county government" and kept it "responsive to community needs."[15]

In Maryland, too, local government was entrusted not to towns but to counties. As Tocqueville observed, "the farther one goes from New England," particularly in a southerly direction, "the more the county tends to take the place of the township in communal life." Counties in New England were late-developing units of government and remained relatively unimportant, but in Maryland they became primary centers of administration. There, acts of Assembly passed between 1654 and 1671—well after the 1630s, when Maryland was founded—granted county justices "most of the administrative responsibilities that made their courts into local governments." Again, once begun, that transformation occurred with striking rapidity. As Lois Green Carr notes, by 1689—when Maryland's proprietary government was overthrown—the counties were able to keep order and provide essential services alone, without a central government.[16]

The local institutions and development patterns of local governments did not everywhere conform to the Massachusetts and Virginia models. Rhode Island, as already noted, held true to its long-standing reputation as "the eccentric deviation from everything considered normal among its neighbors."[17] Moreover, the other colonies had a sufficient variety of local governments and institutional histories to make the pronouncement of any general rule a perilous enterprise. Note, for example, that colonial South Carolina invested limited powers of local self-government in parish vestries, churchwardens, and road commissions, not towns or counties; that local government included counties, townships, "boroughs," and a chartered city in colonial Pennsylvania, where "decentralization" in the eighteenth century took the form of an enhancement of borough responsibilities at the cost of counties; and that the evolution of strong local gov-

[15] See the excellent brief summary in Warren M. Billings, *The Old Dominion in the Seventeenth Century: A Documentary History of Virginia, 1606–1689* (Chapel Hill: University of North Carolina Press, 1975), 69–82, and also Robert Wheeler, "The County Court in Colonial Virginia," in Daniels, *Town and County,* 111–33, esp. 111.

[16] Tocqueville, *Democracy in America,* 81, and, on counties in New England, 70–1, 76–7; Lois Green Carr, "The Foundations of Social Order: Local Government in Colonial Maryland," in Daniels, *Town and County,* 72–110, esp. 84, 73.

[17] Warden, "Rhode Island Civil Code," 139.

ernment in New York was impeded by the fact that its Dutch and then its
original, seventeenth-century English rulers—particularly James, Duke of
York, who, after becoming King James II, was forced from the throne in
1688/89—objected strongly to sharing the powers of government with
localities.[18]

If, however, some underlying "principle" of organization wound
through this maze of institutions and formative experiences, it was surely
not the priority of local to central authority. The experiences of the flag-
ship colonies Massachusetts and Virginia, and of others as well, suggest
that the vitality of local government that Tocqueville observed in the
1830s had begun two centuries earlier, when provincial legislatures created local institutions and then, act by act, year by year, regularly enhanced
their responsibilities until what Tocqueville called administrative decentralization had become "the American way."

Why did provincial governments transfer power to towns and counties? Since colonial assemblies were composed of delegates elected by
towns or counties, that transformation might well be described as a
seizure of power rather than as a surprising gift of state prerogatives to
lower levels of government. In truth, however, neither of those alternative
conceptions contributes much toward understanding a process that was
in good part a logical response to growth and expansion.

As the colonies' population multiplied and spread out geographically,
many essential services could no longer be performed at the center with
any convenience or efficiency. And as settled areas extended ever farther
from the center of government, provincial officers became less familiar
with local men and situations, so the advice of local officials naturally
rose in influence. Delegating tasks to local governments also relieved
provincial officials of responsibilities that became increasingly burdensome as their colony grew. In Virginia, for example, the governor and
council exercised all the powers of government while settlers remained
near Jamestown. Before long, however, colonists took up lands along the
upper reaches of the James River; by the mid-1630s, they were moving
north beyond the York River. Eight counties seemed sufficient in 1634,
when the Virginia legislature first established county courts for the more
regular and consistent government of its people; but by 1668, when Vir-

---

[18] Richard Waterhouse, "The Responsible Gentry of Colonial South Carolina: A Study in
Local Government, 1670–1770"; Wayne L. Bockelman, "Local Government in Colonial
Pennsylvania"; and Nicholas Varga, "The Development and Structure of Local Government in Colonial New York," in Daniels, *Town and County,* 160–85, 216–37, and
186–215.

ginians had crossed not just the York but the Rappahannock River and founded plantations beside the Potomac, the colony had twenty counties. So extensive a territory could not be governed well from any one central place given the primitive state of communications and transportation. Moreover, many governmental tasks—registering deeds, for example, or probating wills—were essential but tedious to perform, and the burden multiplied with the population. The convenience of both provincial officials and private citizens was therefore served by having such tasks performed locally.[19]

The importance of expansion to the creation of strong local governments is confirmed by the case of colonial South Carolina, where government remained remarkably centralized. The reason, according to Richard Waterhouse, is that, "at least before 1760, the colony's population remained confined to the low country, and the relative closeness of most inhabitants to Charles Town made for ease of access to the Courts of Common Pleas and General Sessions which met there: the establishment of county courts with judicial powers comparable to those of Virginia was therefore unnecessary." And since there was no felt need for strong local judicial institutions until the very end of the colonial period, such courts could not take on administrative powers, as happened in the Chesapeake. Once population spread into the backcountry, however, South Carolina began to create local institutions like those of other British North American colonies.[20]

The process of decentralization was not, however, a phenomenon in all colonial empires. It failed to occur in New France, where the "habitants"—who remained far fewer in number than the English settlers to their south—"had a reputation for being as independent and impatient of outside authority as any British colonist, but administration remained

[19] Billings, *Old Dominion,* 69–70, 75.
[20] Waterhouse, "Responsible Gentry," 163–4, 161. See also 179–80: "The fact that such strong institutions of local government as existed in Virginia and Massachusetts failed to develop in South Carolina resulted neither from indifference on the part of merchant and planter elite nor from the phenomenon of a jealous Commons House of Assembly's declining to share its right and privileges with local institutions. Rather, this failure was the consequence of settlement patterns, which in turn resulted from geographic circumstances. Carolina society was much smaller and more compact than, for example, Virginia's, and as long as the population remained confined to the low country, the relative proximity of most colonists to Charles Town, combined with the excellent road and river system, made for ease of access to the legislative, administrative, and judicial institutions in Charles Town." Migration to the backcountry in the 1750s and 1760s altered the situation: Settlers stimulated by "the sheer distance of the new areas of settlement from Charles Town" demanded "strong institutions of local government," and in 1769 the assembly responded by creating four circuit courts "with highest jurisdiction in both criminal and civil matters" (180).

centralized in the French tradition." And in Spanish America, the Crown carefully repressed tendencies toward local independence and self-government such that local governments became weaker until by 1700, as Charles Gibson put it, "very little remained of the municipal autonomy that was traditional in the earlier Hispanic world."[21] Strong local self-government was a distinguishing characteristic of British North America and manifested the colonists' English heritage. Everywhere the colonists attempted to reconstruct the familiar institutions of English government; even the differences among their local institutions reflected in part variations in the English communities from which settlers came.

American colonists were, moreover, as dedicated to local prerogatives as their seventeenth-century English ancestors, who executed one king and replaced another to check intrusive monarchical central government and strengthen the House of Commons, which provided a platform for the defense of local or "country" rights. During the 1760s and 1770s, the Americans went one step further, opposing Parliament itself and fending off efforts to weaken the powers of their representative assemblies. The Massachusetts Government Act of 1774, which attempted not only to alter the structure of provincial government but to prevent the convening of town meetings, seemed to threaten local self-government throughout the thirteen colonies. "Why did you go to the Concord Fight, the 19th of April, 1775?," Mellen Chamberlain asked Capt. Levi Preston, a ninety-one-year-old veteran of the Revolutionary War from Danvers, Massachusetts, in 1827. "Young man," Preston replied, "what we meant in going for those red-coats was this: we always had governed ourselves, and we always meant to. They didn't mean we should."[22] The statement makes no sense except as a defense of local government. On the provincial level, the people of Massachusetts in 1775 shared governing power with a royal governor appointed by the King. Only within the towns could they be said to have governed themselves.

What difference did the tradition of strong local self-government make? It had, first of all, profound significance for the structure of American government, but in ways that defy simple explanations. Traditionally it has been assumed that central power atrophied as critical powers were delegated to subordinate authorities. The state, as Tocqueville put it,

[21] W. J. Eccles, *France in America* (New York: Harper and Row, 1972), 127–8; Gibson, *Spain in America* (New York: Harper and Row, 1966), 95–9.
[22] Mellen Chamberlain, *John Adams: The Statesman of the American Revolution: With other Essays and Addresses. Historical and Literary.* (Boston: Houghton Mifflin, 1899), 248–9.

became an "obscure and placid entity" of only "secondary importance," and national authority—once it was established—remained "an exception."[23] Local governments performed the functions that affected people's day-to-day lives: schooling, maintaining roads, keeping the peace, administering justice, keeping records of wills, indentures, and land titles—even collecting taxes and providing defense against outside enemies. But at the same time, we know, colonial legislatures, modeling themselves on the English House of Commons, grew in power,[24] which makes it unlikely that such ambitious institutions would strengthen localities in ways that weakened their authority. To posit a struggle for ascendancy between provincial legislatures and local governance also overlooks the fact that both were answerable to the same constituents—those people of the towns or counties who elected the members of provincial assemblies.

Tocqueville in fact understood the roles of state legislatures and towns as more complementary than conflictual. The General Court of Massachusetts exercised what he called the power of "government" in passing general laws ordering, for example, the collection of taxes or the establishment of schools. But the "administration" of those orders was entrusted to the towns, which retained the right to regulate matters of concern to them alone, and which were also left substantial flexibility in adapting state laws to local circumstances. "Administration" for Tocqueville therefore implied substantial independent power, far more surely than if the towns had been asked simply to execute laws in a mechanical or bureaucratic manner.[25] Towns might be "constrained to obedience" by state laws that sometimes defined their administrative responsibilities in detail. But the state imposed that obligation "in principle only," Tocqueville said, and "in its performance the township resumes all its independent rights. Thus taxes are . . . voted by the legislature, but they are assessed and collected by the township; the establishment of a school is obligatory, but the township builds it, pays for it, and controls it." The Massachusetts School Act of 1647, for example, ordered towns to establish basic schools to teach reading and writing when they had fifty house-

---

[23] Tocqueville, *Democracy in America*, 69, 61. Note, however, that on page 74 of the Lawrence translation Tocqueville refers to local officials as "secondary authorities" because they were often bound by "a multitude of detailed obligations strictly defined" by their state legislature.

[24] See, for example, Jack P. Greene, *The Quest for Power: The Lower Houses of Assembly in the Southern Royal Colonies, 1689–1776* (Chapel Hill: University of North Carolina Press, 1963).

[25] On this point, see Martin Diamond, "The Ends of Federalism," *Publius* 3 (1973): 129–52, esp. 138–42.

holders and "grammar schools" to prepare students for the university
when their populations increased to one hundred families or householders. However, the towns were left free to hire the teachers, decide whether
they would be paid by students' parents or by "the inhabitants in general," and determine the length of the period in which instruction was offered. Some towns seem to have gone a step further; they took it upon
themselves to decide whether or not they would comply with what the
law clearly demanded.[26]

Municipal freedom was further protected by the absence, which Tocqueville noted, of state agencies to monitor and enforce town or county
compliance with legislative mandates. Local officials who neglected to
perform their statutory obligations could, however, be called to account
and punished in either the ordinary courts or county courts of sessions.
That mechanism of enforcement was so inconspicuous that it sometimes
seemed nonexistent to foreign observers, but the apparent determination
of the states to keep their "governmental authority . . . out of sight" did
not detract significantly from their power; administrative orders, which
were "almost always concealed under a judicial mandate," took on, according to Tocqueville, "that almost irresistible force which men accord
to due process of law."[27]

The relationship of the states to local governments was therefore very
different from that of the states to the nation, at least after 1789 and ratification of the federal Constitution. Both the state and the federal governments received directly from the people the authority and power to execute carefully defined, distinct tasks; neither depended on the other for its
existence. Moreover, both could enforce their authority directly on individuals, without relying on the other for the "administration" of its laws.
But that "mature" form of American federalism emerged from an earlier
system in which the states' relationship to the nation was similar in many
ways to the states' power over localities. The first government of the United States, the Second Continental Congress, which assembled on May 10,

---

[26] Tocqueville, *Democracy in America,* 67–68, 74; on the subject of governmental versus
administrative centralization, see 87–92; on Massachusetts in particular, see 80: "Above
the level of the county officials there is really no administrative power, but only the power of the government." See also 83, where Tocqueville says it is possible to see the beginning of administrative centralization in some states, and cites as an example (note 40)
New York's creation of a board of regents to supervise its educational system. Massachusetts School Act of 1647 quoted in Lawrence A. Cremin, *American Education: The
Colonial Experience, 1607–1783* (New York: Harper & Row, 1970), 181–2. The law, it
seems, was widely copied elsewhere in New England, but honored within Massachusetts
in a somewhat haphazard manner; see p. 82.
[27] Tocqueville, *Democracy in America,* 74–80, 82.

1775, as the news of Lexington and Concord spread through the continent, depended on its member colonies to implement the measures it adopted. It asked provincial assemblies or extralegal conventions not only to supply soldiers and funds but to perform other tasks. On October 6, 1775, for example, it voted to recommend that the several provincial assemblies or conventions, acting with their councils or committees of safety, "arrest and secure every person in their respective colonies, whose going at large may, in their opinion, endanger the safety of the colony, or the liberties of America."[28]

Despite its dependency, Congress seems to have been not only respected but given substantial authority—far more, certainly, than the colonies were willing to grant Parliament. For example, in May 1775, when royal government had collapsed in Massachusetts, that colony's provincial convention asked Congress's "most explicit advice" on how it should proceed. Six months later, in November 1775, New Hampshire and South Carolina asked the same question, as did Virginia in December. Congress told each of those colonies how to establish temporary civil governments. Then, on May 10 and 15, 1775, when independence had become inevitable, Congress called on the colonies to suppress all exercises of authority under the British Crown and create new governments "under the authority of the people."[29]

On the basis of those resolutions, the American people founded new state governments under the world's first written constitutions. That process supports Daniel Webster's argument of 1830 that the nation came before the states, since the first state governments were founded under the direction of Congress (although the states were left to determine, as they insisted, the precise forms of their republican political institutions). Again, as with town governments in Massachusetts and Connecticut and county government in the Chesapeake, *central authority came first*—although it was exercised in ways that respected local prerogatives over local affairs.

The original relationship between states and nation nonetheless proved problematic from the first. During the revolutionary war, the states honored Congress's requests imperfectly at best, and their compliance became so unreliable thereafter that, in the spring of 1787, James Madison listed among the "Vices of the Political system of the U[nited] States" the "want of sanction" to its laws "and of coercion in the Gov-

---

[28] *Journals of the Continental Congress, 1774–1789*, ed. Worthington C. Ford (Washington D.C.: U.S. Government Printing Office, 1905), vol. 2, 280.
[29] Ibid., 79, 83–4; vol 3., 319, 326–7, 403–4; vol. 4, 342, 357–8.

ernment of the Confederacy." There was, he recognized, a certain similarity between the relationship of the Confederation Congress with the states and that of the state with local governments, but there was also a crucial difference. "If the laws of the States, were merely recommendatory to their citizens, or if they were to be rejudged by County authorities," he asked, "what security, what probability would exist, that they would be carried into execution?" Unlike state laws, acts of Congress, "tho' nominally authoritative," were "in fact recommendatory only."[30] The Constitution of 1787 solved that problem by granting federal authorities independent power received directly from the sovereign people in areas of policymaking that affected the people of the United States collectively, as well as independent power to enforce its laws on individuals through a federal judicial system independent of state courts with both primary and appellate jurisdiction. Those institutional innovations distinguished the United States of 1788, Tocqueville argued, from all previous confederacies, in which member states retained the right to "direct and supervise" the execution of union laws. When the government of the United States levies a tax, he noted, "it does not turn to the government of Massachusetts, but to each inhabitant of Massachusetts. . . . It has its own administrators, courts, officers of justice, and army," so the "federal government can do what it has been given the right to do." And in that way—essentially by centralizing federal administrative authority—the Americans, Tocqueville said, "amended their laws and saved their country."[31]

Henceforth administrative decentralization would apparently be confined within the states. But the relationship between states and localities was also redefined, or defined with greater precision, in the wake of independence, when state legislatures forcefully reasserted their power over lower units of government. That development was well known to Tocqueville, who recognized that the once "independent republics" of towns and counties had by the 1830s become clearly subordinate to the almost unlimited power of state legislatures. "In America," he said, "the legislature of each state is faced by no power capable of resisting it. Nothing can check its progress, neither privileges, nor local immunities, nor personal influence, nor even the authority of reason, for it represents the majority. . . . So its own will sets the sole limits to its action."[32]

One prominent instrument of legislative power was the act of incorpo-

---

30 Madison's "Vices of the Political System," April 1787, in *The Papers of James Madison,* vol. 9, ed. Robert A. Rutland (Chicago: University of Chicago Press, 1975), 351–2.
31 Tocqueville, *Democracy in America,* 156–8.   32 Ibid., 89.

ration, by which the legislature formally made a community—or, in other instances a group of associated individuals—into a "body politic" with the capacity to sue and be sued and to exercise limited powers of self-government. Between 1776 and 1789, state legislatures granted charters to some twenty previously unincorporated cities, more than doubling the number of cities or "boroughs" that had been incorporated by the Crown before independence and scattering them through sections of the South and Northeast that had no chartered cities in the colonial period. That development awoke controversy—indeed, city government became a major source of debate during the last quarter of the eighteenth century[33]—because corporations were traditionally understood as aristocratic remnants of the feudal past whose chartered privilege of self-government made them *imperia in imperio,* governments within a government, isolated from the authority of the community as a whole, and so from the supervisory power of legislatures. But the proponents of corporations, inspired by the constitution-writing of their time, redesigned corporate charters to meet those objections. They eliminated all "closed" or self-perpetuating institutions, establishing elected governments instead (often with generous voting requirements), took care to avoid concentrating legislative, executive, and judiciary powers in the same hands, and made charters subject to renewal or revision by legislatures, whose superior power was thereby firmly established.[34]

Even the relatively advanced "open" or elective corporations of the colonial past, such as that of New York City, hesitated to act as "independent republics" with powers and privileges sealed off from those of the sovereign people. Soon after the revolutionary war, New York City began turning to the state legislature first to authorize the raising of taxes, then to approve the exercise even of powers granted by the colonial charter and confirmed by the state constitution of 1777. It sought, as Henrik Hartog argues, "to depoliticize its position as a privileged local government . . . and make its actions appear to emanate from the power of the

---

[33] Jon C. Teaford, *The Municipal Revolution in America: Origins of Modern Urban Government, 1650–1825* (Chicago: University of Chicago Press, 1975), 67 and passim. Teaford's findings conflict with the more common assumption, stated by Daniels in *Town and County,* that "the American Revolution produced . . . very few pleas for changes in government beneath the colony level" (p. 8). On the growth of corporations, see Pauline Maier, "The Revolutionary Origin of the American Corporation," *William and Mary Quarterly* 50 (1993): 51–84, esp. 58–64.

[34] Ibid. and Hendrik Hartog, *Public Property and Private Power: The Corporation of the City of New York in American Law, 1730–1870* (Chapel Hill: University of North Carolina Press, 1983).

state legislature." It could at first do so with more gain than loss, since the legislature readily agreed to bills that were "invariably drafted by city employees." But, beginning in 1857, New York's Republican legislature, in part to capture patronage from the traditionally Democratic rulers of New York City, began to create state-controlled metropolitan service districts that assumed powers previously exercised by the city's Common Council. New York's Democratic mayor Fernando Wood challenged the right of the state to take control of the police, citing a provision in the city's charter allowing it to create a watch, but the Court of Appeals ruled that the legislature could rearrange local government in whatever way suited its purposes. To decide otherwise, it said, would undercut the legislature's sovereignty. Almost unwittingly, though perhaps necessarily, the city had yielded what autonomy it once had; it became as vulnerable to legislative interference as unchartered towns and counties.[35]

State legislatures further extended their power in the late eighteenth and early nineteenth centuries by creating corporations to build roads and bridges, improve waterways, found schools, establish banks or manufactories, and perform other public-service tasks. All such corporations received the right to function as a "body politic" with defined powers of self-government, to function in law as a person with the ability to sue and be sued, and to persist after the lifetimes of their founding members. (More controversial attributes, such as limited liability, came later.) At relatively little cost, therefore, legislatures could enlist private energies in providing services that in many cases the state itself might otherwise perform. Corporate charters, which bore a clear resemblance to the constitutions that created state and federal governments, defined the governance or managerial structures of the organizations they sanctioned, limited their legitimate functions and the assets they could accumulate, and, particularly after the Supreme Court's decision in the Dartmouth College case (1819), explicitly reserved the legislatures' right to revoke or revise their terms. As such, through most of the nineteenth century, even profit-seeking corporations were in some measure subordinate units of government, carefully subjected to the authority of state legislatures. These corporations were part of a "compound republic" whose structure remained radically different from the French "monist" or centralized model famil-

[35] Maier, "Revolutionary Origin," 63–4, and Hartog, *Public Property,* passim, with quotations at 101 and 98, and see also 237–8. The story of the New York conflict is told in detail by James F. Richardson, *The New York Police: Colonial Times to 1901* (New York: Oxford University Press, 1970), ch. 4, 82–108.

iar to Tocqueville. The United States became instead a "pluralist" state in which "the state is conceived of as a 'plurality of corporations.'"[36]

In a state so structured, the extension of state legislative power and decentralized administration in Tocqueville's use of the term could coexist. As late as 1857, Theodore Sedgwick could still insist—like Tocqueville two decades earlier—that "American freedom is based on the idea of local action, localized power, local sovereignty," and that the American system of government sought, "as far as safely possible, to strip the central authority of influence, and to distribute its functions among local agents and bodies."[37] It was not the government but the American people that energized the system—a people, Tocqueville noted, who were "forever forming associations" of a "thousand different types" to perform an immense variety of useful functions. He underestimated the extent to which the state encouraged such associations by the process of incorporation, but not their impact in relieving government of direct responsibility for founding schools, building and maintaining roads or bridges, and other public works. The inhabitants of the United States, Tocqueville said, "care about each of their country's interests as if it were their own," and saw so intimate a bond between general prosperity and private happiness that they worked "for the good of the state, not only from duty or from

[36] Maier, "Revolutionary Origin," esp. 80 on the Dartmouth decision and 83 on the "pluralist" nature of the American state. The requirement of public service for incorporation persisted into the late nineteenth century; even Justice Joseph Story's decision in the Dartmouth College case defined some corporations as "private" only because their assets came from private sources, and so in no way affected the pervasive expectation that they serve a public purpose. See Kent Newmyer, "Justice Joseph Story's Doctrine of 'Public and Private Corporations' and the Rise of the American Business Corporation," *DePaul Law Review* 25 (1976): 825–41, esp. 832–5, and Mauro Calise, "The Corporate Sea-Change: How Modern American Corporations Succeeded Where Ancient European Corporations Failed," unpublished paper presented at a conference on "Private Governments, Public Choices" at Trent, Italy, June 10–12, 1992.

The privatization of corporations seems to have been the result of states competing for the business of incorporation, which generated fees sufficiently large in the aggregate that, in some cases, they obviated the need for other taxes. In short, the more severe restrictions and regulations that states included among the terms of incorporation fell victim as other states such as Delaware became more permissive, forcing states such as Massachusetts to follow suit or see all its major corporations organized under the laws of other states. That process seems to have occurred mainly in the late nineteenth and early twentieth centuries, although its beginnings can be seen earlier. It should perhaps also be noted that the power to incorporate has remained on the state level because it was not among the powers granted to the federal government under the Constitution of 1787, probably because members of the constitutional convention feared that its inclusion would make ratification of the Constitution substantially more difficult.

[37] Theodore Sedgwick, *A Treatise on the Rules Which Govern the Interpretation and Application of Statutory and Constitutional Law* (New York: V. S. Voorhies, 1857), 460, cited in Hartog, *Public Property and Private Power*, 206, note 4.

pride, but . . . from greed." Americans also saw government as their responsibility, not that of some distant bureaucrat, which explained for Tocqueville what he called their "irritating patriotism": An American felt compelled to defend his country from all criticism because "it is not only his country which is attacked . . . but himself." In the end, he concluded, the people's readiness to add their efforts to those of public officials made possible the accomplishment of far more than even the most energetic centrally administered state could achieve. But how could one account for that extraordinary civic activism, that pervasive personal involvement in the community's welfare? For Tocqueville it was a direct consequence—indeed, the single most important consequence—of the widespread participation in government that administrative decentralization demanded. "The most powerful way, and perhaps the only remaining way, in which to interest men in their country's fate," he said, "is to make them take a share in its government."[38]

Tocqueville's argument here is, I think, more tenable than a generation ago, when scholars emphasized the elitist character of early American local government. To be sure, colonial America was nowhere a democracy in the modern sense. Membership in the gentry was a prerequisite for positions on Virginia's county courts. In New England, the same selectmen, or others with the same family names—those that connoted rank and respectability—were returned to office year after year, and sometimes governed for decades without substantial interference from town meetings.[39] But the increasing administrative demands on counties and towns caused a dramatic expansion in the number of men who held an office of some sort. Tocqueville reported that a New England town had nineteen "main officials," most of whom were paid "so that poorer citizens can devote their time to them without loss," but that figure probably understated by a significant amount the number of people who exercised authority on the local level. Already at the end of the colonial period, Hartford, Connecticut, with a population of about 5,000, elected 76 town officers; Norwich, with a population of 7,000, elected 116; and Farmington, with a population of 5,600 and a large land mass to govern, elected a full 206.[40] These

---

[38] Tocqueville, *Democracy in America*, 513–20, 236–7, and also 93–5.

[39] Charles Sydnor, *American Revolutionaries in the Making: Political Practices in Washington's Virginia* (New York: Collier Books, 1965 [originally published in 1952 as *Gentlemen Freeholders*]); Kenneth A. Lockridge and Alan Kreider, "The Evolution of Massachusetts Town Government, 1640–1740," *William and Mary Quarterly* 23 (1966): 549–74.

[40] Tocqueville, *Democracy in America*, 66; Daniels, "Local Government in Colonial Connecticut," 59, 60–1.

were not just selectmen but constables, surveyors of highways, fence or chimney viewers, leather sealers, surveyors, listers or rate makers or tithingmen, branders, "key keepers," or jurymen of one sort or another. Since such offices rotated from man to man far more than those that manifested high social rank and conferred prestige, it seems likely that a substantial part of the white male population held office at some time. Similarly, in Maryland the justices of the peace who made up the county court were assisted by paid sheriffs, coroners, and clerks, and also by a mass of unpaid local officers and jurors. "Wide participation was a necessity if the burdens of office and jury duty were to be spread," and as a result, according to Lois Carr, "most county householders" participated in government in the late seventeenth century. The participation level may have declined somewhat as the population grew, but civic activism remained substantial. "Every man who contributed [public service] made his stake in, and support of community order visible to himself and to others," notes Carr, and so "strengthened the authority of government." There is some evidence, in fact, that persons holding lesser offices became more assertive over time. In Maryland, for example, grand jurors not only decided whether a sufficient case existed to try persons accused of crimes, but issued statements on the general state and needs of their communities, sometimes even criticizing local justices.[41]

The vitality of eighteenth-century local life seems, in fact, to have survived the massive economic and social transformations of the nineteenth century. As Americans gradually left behind the towns and villages of their rural past and became an urban people, their civic activism found new expressions in the neighborhoods that together constituted the country's burgeoning cities. Within urban neighborhoods, again, a matrix of churches, clubs, and other associations linked people together and enlisted their energies in serving the needs and promoting the improvement of their communities. All politics were then in fact local: City councilors represented neighborhood constituencies, and political parties formed coalitions that crossed religious, class, and ethnic divisions in battles for votes fought on the ward level. Not everyone could hold public office, but those who did came from a range of social ranks. Jamaica Plain, for example, one of Boston's several neighborhoods, regularly elected lower white-collar and blue-collar workers, including a butcher and a fish merchant,

---

[41] Carr, "Local Government in Colonial Maryland," in Daniels, *Town and County,* 72–110, esp. 76, 89–90. Grand juries elsewhere acted much like those in Maryland; see Richard D. Younger, *The People's Panel: The Grand Jury in the United States, 1634–1941* (Providence: Brown University Press, 1963).

to the local Common Council in the 1890s and early 1900s. Jamaica Plain sent a similarly diverse set of representatives to the state legislature. Public office was not a prerogative of the privileged.[42]

Some disadvantages followed from what Tocqueville was willing to call the Americans' excessive localism. However powerful the early-nineteenth-century American state remained in terms of the amount it accomplished, the forces that drove it were "less well regulated, less enlightened, and less wise" than where administration as well as government was centralized, and "those little details of social regulations which make life smooth and comfortable" were relatively neglected.[43] And it was from a felt need for more efficient local governments than the cumbersome institutions designed to realize post-revolutionary ideas of the separation of powers—governments that could better provide paved streets, public transportation, electric lighting systems, and other similar services—that Progressive reformers of the late nineteenth and twentieth centuries undertook the reform of municipal government. In short, the local governments that gained power in the seventeenth century in the interest of better administration lost it two centuries later when it came to seem that more and better government services could be provided from the center. The reformers were also tired of having authority exercised by the "wrong" people ("Are we not weary of voting for men," one asked, "whom we would not trust in our business to hold any position whatever?") and of the corruption that traditional urban democracy seemed to foster. They sought to "transcend the sordidness of political parochialism" and to apply "universal principles of administration" unaffected by the social or cultural differences that distinguished one city or one neighborhood from another—which meant, of course, taking power from the population in general and giving it to the educated middle class. The "coarse elements" that had ruled in times past and their "blunders" were no longer tolerable.

Progressivism brought massive changes to the government of American cities and towns: Henceforth, some communities were managed professionally by businesslike city managers or city commissions. In others, charters were changed to establish strong mayors with city councils cho-

---

[42] For a particularly fine analysis of one urban neighborhood that relates its history to the larger story of social and political change, see Alexander von Hoffman, *Local Attachments: The Making of an American Urban Neighborhood, 1850–1920* (Baltimore: Johns Hopkins University Press, 1994), esp. 207–9 on officeholders.

[43] Tocqueville, *Democracy in America*, 92.

sen in at-large elections to minimize the influence of neighborhoods. It was as if Tocqueville's scenario, with the forces of "enlightenment" suppressing the embarrassments of localism, was at last being played out on the American stage. Occasionally, in fact, the proponents of local democracy cited Tocqueville in what turned out to be a losing battle against a modern form of "improvement" that put its faith not in the energies of the people but in the expertise of professionals exercising centralized authority.[44]

The forces of change were not, however, confined to a handful of reformers. Early American localism was the product of a specific historical context—one in which the primitive state of transportation and communications made central authority difficult to exercise, where fear of power overshadowed the advantages of efficient administration, and where communal rights were valued more highly than individual rights. The self-governing communities of colonial and post-revolutionary New England and the Chesapeake were, moreover, not chance collections of individuals, but corporate bodies bound together by a strong sense of common interests and identity. Such men might act on behalf of a larger public interest, but they assumed no necessary obligations to the interests or rights of outsiders or of persons who violated their norms. Problems necessarily arose when communities' conceptions of their self-interest conflicted with the claims of others. The heightened dedication to civil rights in the twentieth century therefore logically led to a further corrosion of local power, as Martha Derthick argues in Chapter 5 of this volume. In short, a complex transformation of both circumstances and values undermined localist America. Then the locus of authority moved toward the center—not gradually, but quite suddenly over the past century.

If Tocqueville's historical understanding of the original relationship of towns and counties to colonial and, later, state governments was incorrect—if there his New England teachers misled him—his grasp of the broader problem of maintaining vital local governments in a modern "civilized" state remains, in retrospect, remarkably insightful. He had, after all, seized upon Sparks's historical theories because they offered an explanation for the bizarre persistence of a strong tradition of local self-government in the United States. The origin of that phenomenon proba-

---

[44] Ibid., esp. 223–7, and ch. 7 passim; on citations of Tocqueville, see Roger Lane, *Policing the City: Boston, 1822–1885* (Cambridge, Mass.: Harvard University Press, 1967), 153, 218. See also James Weinstein, "Organized Business and the City Commission and Manager Movements," *Journal of Southern History* 28 (1962): 166–82.

bly lay in the dynamics of colonial life and in the colonists' English political traditions rather than in a priority of local to central government within one region of the country, which meant that strong local governments were established early on not only in New England, but through the greater part of British North America—and by a process more similar than different from place to place. The persistence of that tradition was, however, of more immediate practical significance than how it began, and Tocqueville not only noticed the vitality of American local government but sensed from the first its far-reaching significance. His observation that Americans were actively involved in the development and government of their country into the nineteenth century was surely correct, and his depiction of the perils faced by local self-government stands confirmed by events that occurred long after his lifetime. If anything, the fact that American towns and counties had been created and granted power by central governments served to enhance those perils—a government that gave power in one historical moment might well try to reclaim it in another—and to make the continuing strength of local government all the more striking.

Moreover, if (as Tocqueville argued) administrative structures have implications beyond government alone—if they shape the political culture of a people—the undercutting of local power in the late nineteenth and early twentieth centuries perhaps caused or contributed to one of the most puzzling attributes of modern American politics. It might, in short, explain the persistent civic malaise of the late twentieth century, the widespread sense of individual detachment from government that contrasts so dramatically with the vibrant democracy Tocqueville observed—and that threatens to provoke yet another major restructuring of the American republic.[45]

---

[45] See, for example, Wilfred M. McClay, "A More Perfect Union? Toward a New Federalism," *Commentary* 100 (Sept. 1995): 28–33.

4

Localism, political parties, and civic virtue

SIDNEY M. MILKIS

INTRODUCTION: POLITICAL PARTIES AND LOCAL SELF-GOVERNMENT

It has become routine for scholars and pundits to declare that a crisis of citizenship plagues contemporary American political life.[1] This chapter is intended to shed light on the relationship between the people and their government by revisiting the origins and history of political parties. Political parties were formed in the early part of the nineteenth century as a means of engaging the attention of ordinary citizens, and with localistic foundations that were critical for the maintenance of an engaged citizenry. As Barry Karl has noted, "local government and community control," supported by the Constitution's federal structure and decentralized political parties, "remain at the heart of the most intuitive conceptions of American democracy, even though they may also represent bastions of political corruption and locally condoned injustice."[2] Yet economic and political dynamics have transformed the United States from a decentralized republic to a mass democracy in which the principles and political associations that sustained civic attachments have been weakened.

The weak foundation of political engagement in the United States is not new, of course; indeed, it prompts us to revisit long-standing issues about the limited attention to civic virtue in the American Constitution—

---

[1] For the most widely discussed take on the crisis of citizenship in the United States, see Robert Putnam, "Tuning In, Tuning Out: The Strange Disappearance of Social Capital in America," *PS,* vol. 28 (December 1995): 664–83. For a carefully researched account of the contemporary state of civic participation in the United States, see *Voice and Equality: Civic Voluntarism in American Politics* (Cambridge, Mass.: Harvard University Press, 1995).

[2] Barry Karl, *The Uneasy State: The United States from 1915 to 1945* (Chicago: University of Chicago Press, 1983), 236, 238.

an "extended republic" that attempts to employ institutional arrangements and the constructive use of interests to compensate for the defects
of better motives in political life. The American tradition of local self-
government, which preceded and was only partly modified by the "more
perfect Union" formed in 1787, played a critical part in relating the private order to the public life of the United States. As Alexis de Tocqueville
observed in the 1830s, this tradition went well beyond the legal division
between the national and state governments and left considerable discretion to counties and townships. The vitality of townships and counties depended on the well-founded idea in the United States that "each man
[was] the best judge of his own interest and best able to satisfy his private
needs." The practice of leaving townships and counties in charge of their
"special interests," in turn, cultivated civic attachments by giving each individual "the same feeling for his country as one has for one's family."
Happily, Tocqueville concluded, "a sort of selfishness makes [the individ-
ual] care for the state."[3]

As Pauline Maier has shown, the "municipal spirit" admired so by
Tocqueville thrived into nineteenth-century urban America. By the end of
the nineteenth century, however, the fabric of civic attachments had been
loosened by the emergence of laissez-faire capitalism, which celebrated
economic opportunity and industrial development to the detriment of local community. The Progressive Movement that arose to challenge industrial capitalism sought to create a national citizenship, to transfer "our
sense of security in ourselves as citizens . . . from the state and local governments where it originated to the federal government."[4] In truth, Progressive reformers were ambivalent about using the federal government
to reform society and the economy. But they hoped to free state and local
governments from what they took to be the parochial, often corrupt influence of political parties. Attempting to reform government by establishing a system of direct popular rule on a national scale, Progressive
democracy further corroded Americans' vital contact between the populace in local communities and the national government.

The weakening of civic attachments in the United States points to the
limited yet essential role that political parties have played in organizing
the work of American constitutional government. As Wilson Carey

[3] Alexis de Tocqueville, *Democracy in America,* ed. J. P. Mayer (Garden City, N.Y.: Doubleday, 1969), 68, 82, 95.
[4] Karl, *The Uneasy State,* 238.

McWilliams has observed, "In the Constitution of the United States, political parties are like a scandal in polite society; they are alluded to but not discussed."[5] Indeed, James Madison's famous discussion of "factions" in *Federalist* No. 10 reveals the Framers' hope that the division and separation of powers, operating within a large commercial society, would transform vital party dialogue and conflict into muted competition among a multitude of diverse interests. The "Constitution-Against-Parties," as Richard Hofstadter calls it, embodied the Framers' fears that the "civic virtues" cultivated by local communities and militant political associations were but local prejudices that threatened to degenerate into anarchy—or, worse, into majority tyranny.[6]

Nevertheless, political parties would find a critical, if uneasy, place in American government. As formed during the first three decades of the nineteenth century, they reflected the concerns first expressed by the Anti-Federalists, and later revised by Thomas Jefferson, that the Constitution provided inadequately for the cultivation of an active and competent citizenry. Like Tocqueville, the Anti-Federalists and their Jeffersonian descendants viewed the states and localities as schools of American democracy. But they were more concerned than Tocqueville seemed to be that the original Constitution provided inadequate support for provincial institutions.

Political parties embodied Anti-Federalist principles.[7] Forged on the anvil of Jeffersonian democracy, political parties were conceived as bulwarks of decentralization—as localized political associations that could provide a vital link between constitutional offices, especially the executive, and the people. They would do so by balancing state and local communities, championed by the Anti-Federalists, and the national government, strengthened by the Constitution of 1787.

Significantly, Madison, the principal architect of the "Constitution-Against-Parties," became a defender of parties and local self-government during the critical partisan battles between the Republicans and the Federalists. Alexander Hamilton's success as secretary of the treasury in the Washington administration in strengthening the executive led Madison to rethink his understanding of republican government. By the early 1790s,

[5] Wilson Carey McWilliams, "Parties as Civic Associations," in *Party Renewal in America,* ed. Gerald M. Pomper (New York: Praeger, 1980), 51.

[6] Richard Hofstadter, *The Idea of a Party System* (Berkeley: University of California Press, 1969), 40–121.

[7] Wilson Carey McWilliams, "The Anti-Federalists, Representation, and Party," *Northwestern University Law Review* 84 (Fall 1989): 12–38.

Jefferson and Madison had become committed to a party program of government decentralization, which renewed the conflicts that had divided the Federalists and Anti-Federalists—and, consequently, gave birth to the American party system.

To be sure, those who played the leading parts in legitimizing and building parties—in making them part of the "living Constitution" by the 1830s—were not "anti-federalists." Even the Jacksonians, who embraced a more militant states'-rights position than their Jeffersonian forebears, supported the idea that the Constitution beheld "a more perfect Union." Jacksonian parties, in fact, found their strength principally in the political combat of presidential elections—a battleground that encouraged partisans to overlook their differences in the interest of victory. But the "critics" of the original Constitution, so to speak, feared that its institutional arrangements tended toward "consolidation," undermining the foundation of local self-government, which they sought to strengthen as the sentinels of liberty in American constitutional democracy. The Jeffersonians and Jacksonians sought a remedy for this political disease in partisan principles and practices that celebrated the decentralization of power.

Given the constitutional and political difficulties involved in establishing a national programmatic, let alone a social democratic party in the United States, Progressives looked to revive the national character of the original Constitution as an agent of reform. Progressive democracy glimpsed a national community, in which new political institutions such as the popular primary, initiative, and referendum would forge a direct link between public opinion and government representatives. Progressives hoped, as Herbert Croly put it, "to give democratic meaning and purpose to the Hamiltonian tradition and method." Progressive democracy rested on the possibility of creating a "modern," independent executive that might become, as Theodore Roosevelt put it, "the steward of the public welfare."[8]

Progressive democracy came into its own with the New Deal. Yet the expansion of the central government's power that followed from the New Deal realignment did not result in the formation of the national state that Progressive reformers such as Croly had anticipated, one that established national regulations and welfare programs that were expressions of a

---

[8] Herbert Croly, *The Promise of American Life* (New York: Macmillan, 1909; Dutton, 1963). The phrase, "steward of the public welfare" comes from Roosevelt's 1909 "New Nationalism" address, given in Osawatomie, Kansas. See *The Works of Theodore Roosevelt* (New York: Scribner's, 1926), vol. 17, 349.

shared understanding of principles; rather, the reconstituted executive was hitched to a plebiscitary politics that exposed the fragile sense of citizenship in American political life.[9] In the final analysis, the limits of Progressivism—the danger of resurrecting Hamiltonian nationalism—point to the limits of the original Constitution, the "Madisonian system" that Madison himself came to view as defective.

LOCALIZED PARTIES AND CONSTITUTIONAL REFORM

"Many factors have influenced the historical development of federalism," states a report of the Advisory Commission on Intergovernmental Relations. "Among the most important of these was the decentralized, nondisciplined party system which, the historical record suggests, had a significant decentralizing influence on intergovernmental relations by providing an often powerful institutional link between local, state, and national offices."[10] The decentralizing influence of political parties in the United States does not reflect simply the federal structure of the Constitution. Rather, the origins and organizing principles of American political parties yielded a highly mobilized, highly competitive, locally oriented democracy that subordinated the powers of the national government to the prerogatives of the states and localities. As V. O. Key explained in 1964, "Federalism in our formal governmental machinery includes a national element independent of the states, but in our party organization the independent and national element is missing. Party structure is more nearly *confederative* than *federal* in nature."[11]

The confederative form of parties seemed to defy the "more perfect Union" created by the Constitution of 1787. Indeed, even though the early development of party organizations emerged with the arousal of national electoral followings for presidential candidates, these political associations were shaped by institutions such as the nominating convention and the patronage system, which centered power in states and localities. As McWilliams has written, "Traditional American party organization paralleled Anti-Federalist ideas of representation."[12] That the traditional

---

[9] I make this argument in *The President and the Parties: The Transformation of the American Party System Since the New Deal* (New York: Oxford University Press, 1993).

[10] Advisory Commission on Intergovernmental Relations, *The Transformation of American Politics: Implications for Federalism* (Washington, D.C., 1986), 45.

[11] V. O. Key, Jr., *Politics, Parties, and Pressure Groups* (New York: Crowell, 1964), 334 (my emphasis).

[12] McWilliams, "The Anti-Federalists, Representation, and Party," 36.

party was rooted in the local community was no accident; nor was it merely a pragmatic adjustment to political events. The persistent, confederate form of political parties stemmed from their creation as agents of constitutional reform. Political parties, in fact, were founded as part of a program to modify the original Constitution so that it would conform in practice to many of the principles of Anti-Federalism. These political associations served the purposes of those who shared the Anti-Federalist commitment to local self-government but joined Jefferson in accepting the Constitution as a working document, hoping to shape it by amendment, interpretation, and practice.[13]

Ironically, one of the leaders of this revisionist project was James Madison, who played a critical part in writing and ratifying the Constitution. Madison's statements about property and majority rule at the time of the Constitution gave no hint that he saw the need for strong political associations to cultivate an active and competent citizenry. To the contrary, he celebrated the Constitution for the way it separated the cup of power from the lips of the people. In the normal course of events, the majority would be indifferent (if not avowedly hostile) to the rights of property, and all too likely to carry out "wicked projects" that sought to distribute property equally—and thus to deny individuals the fruits of their own labor. Writing as "Publius," Madison argued in *The Federalist Papers* that the control of the majority lies in "enlarging the orbit" in which critical political relationships and associations form, so that a majority will necessarily be composed of diverse and narrow factions that are unlikely to agree about much or for long. As Madison wrote in a letter to Jefferson in October 1787—an extraordinary postmortem on the Constitutional Convention—"Divide et impera, the reprobated axiom of tyranny, is under certain qualifications, the only policy, by which a republic can be administered on just principles."[14] Or, as Madison put it somewhat more delicately in *Federalist* No. 51, "In the extended republic of the United States, and among the great variety of interests, parties, and sects which it embraces, a coalition of a majority of the whole could seldom take place on any other principles than those of justice and the general good."[15] Within this scheme of government, the states and localities were

---

[13] Wilson Carey McWilliams, "Democracy and Citizen: Community, Dignity, and the Crisis of Contemporary Politics in America," in *How Democratic Is the Constitution?* ed. Robert Goldwin and William A. Schambra (Washington, D.C.: American Enterprise Institute, 1981), 91.

[14] James Madison to Thomas Jefferson, October 24, 1787, in *Writings of James Madison,* ed. Gaillard Hunt (New York: G. P. Putnam's, 1904), vol. 5, 31.

[15] Alexander Hamilton, James Madison, and John Jay, *The Federalist Papers* (New York: New American Library, 1961), 325.

to play an important role, but they would be transformed from the principal sites of political authority into mere interests, which added to the variety and diversity of factionalism. The state legislatures would defend "local interests," Hamilton observed, and could be relied on "to erect barriers against the encroachments of the national authorities."[16]

Given their collaboration on *The Federalist Papers,* and given Madison's brilliant efforts to create a new national regime capable of remedying the "mortal diseases of popular government," Hamilton had good reason to believe that Madison would support his efforts as secretary of the treasury in the Washington administration to seize the governing initiative. Yet by the winter of 1791–92, Madison was becoming the philosophical and congressional leader of an opposition group that would soon harden into the Jeffersonian Republican party, a group Hamilton and his political allies dismissed derisively as representing a recrudescence of *Anti-Federalism*.

Hamilton's program required a liberal—"elastic"—interpretation of the national government's authority, and some discretion for the judiciary in drawing the boundary between state and national power, that anticipated a significant extension of executive power. The power of the more decentralizing institutions—Congress and the state governments—was necessarily subordinated in this enterprise. More than the policies themselves, Hamilton's interpretation of the Constitution persuaded Madison that he had underestimated the warnings of the Anti-Federalists that the original constitutional design portended a unitary system that would destroy the delicate balance beheld in his understanding of Federalism. In the aftermath of Washington's Neutrality Proclamation of 1793—issued without consulting Congress—Madison wrote a letter to Jefferson in June 1793 expressing a far less sanguine view of the Constitution than he had expressed in *The Federalist Papers*. "I must own my surprise that such a prerogative should have been exercised," he stated. "Perhaps I may have not attended to some parts of the Constitution with sufficient care, or may have misapprehended its meaning."[17]

As revealed by Madison's essays in the *National Gazette,* which were written during the critical period of partisan maneuvers between 1791 and 1792, this recognition of the inadequate safeguards of the separation of powers in the original Constitution encouraged him to reformulate the arguments of *Federalist* No. 10: Whereas Madison originally feared that

---

[16] *Federalist* No. 85, 526.
[17] James Madison to Thomas Jefferson, June 13, 1793, in *Writings of James Madison*, vol. 6, 131.

the security of liberty would be violated by a majority faction bent on a misconceived notion of economic justice, requiring institutional arrangements that divided and muted the voice of the people, his concern about Hamilton's program focused on the need to arouse a "common sentiment" among the states against government consolidation—a task that informed the creation of the Republican party.[18]

As such, Madison—the chief architect of the "Constitution-Against-Parties"—played a leading role in founding the first majority party. This popular party was dedicated to strengthening the decentralizing institutions of the Constitution—the legislature and the states—against the encroachments of national administrative power. In *The Federalist Papers,* Madison defended the Constitution's strengthening of the national government as necessary to "break and control the violence of faction." His revised understanding of government and society championed *political* centralization—that is, a consolidation of public opinion under the banner of the Republican party—as a way of defending state and local interests against *governmental* centralization. Combining political centralization and governmental decentralization, Madison argued, was the "proper object" to unite former Anti-Federalists—"those who are most jealously attached to the separate authority reserved to the states"—and the more ardent Republicans of the Federalists—"those who may be more inclined to contemplate the people of America in light of one nation":

Let the former continue to watch against every encroachment, which might lead to a gradual consolidation of the states into one government. Let the latter employ their utmost zeal, by eradicating local prejudices and mistaken rivalships, to consolidate the affairs of the states into one harmonious interest; and let it be the patriotic study of all, to maintain the various authorities established by our complicated system, each with its respective constitutional sphere; and to erect over the whole, one paramount Empire of reason, benevolence, and brotherly affection.[19]

After the election of 1800, Madison was committed to a doctrine, later set forth by Jefferson's first inaugural address, that celebrated "the state governments in all their rights as the most competent administra-

[18] This discussion draws on two essays that have called attention to Madison's party papers, and to the importance of the debate about party government. See James Piereson, "Party Government," *The Political Science Reviewer* 12 (Fall 1982): 2–52; and Harry Jaffa, "A Phoenix from the Ashes: The Death of James Madison's Constitution (Killed by James Madison) and the Birth of Party Government," prepared for delivery at the Annual Meeting of the American Political Science Association, Washington, D.C., 1977.
[19] "Consolidation," *National Gazette,* December 5, 1791, in *Writings of James Madison,* vol. 6, 68–9.

tions for our domestic concerns and the surest bulwarks against anti-republican tendencies."[20] Madison's alliance with Jefferson helped to re-vitalize a tradition dedicated to local self-government, thus insuring that Federalism—the interplay between one nation and many local communities—would be a central feature in the dynamic of American constitutional government.

"Out of this original clash" between the Federalists and the Republicans, James Piereson has written, "there developed in America the tension between party politics, on the one hand, and governmental centralization and bureaucracy, on the other."[21] Similarly, the emergence of open party conflict altered the Constitution, which was now joined to a doctrine of local self-government. But Jefferson and Madison were dedicated to transforming government, not necessarily to establishing a permanent, formal, two-party system. Indeed, the complete triumph of the Republicans over their Federalist rivals, ushering in the so-called Era of Good Feelings, appeared to restore the nonpartisan character of the Constitution, albeit on terms set by the "Revolution of 1800." In truth, party politics was replaced by narrow factionalism. The national party structure formed by the Republicans had broken down by the presidential election of 1824, in which the choice of the Republican congressional caucus, William Crawford of Georgia, finished third in electoral votes behind Andrew Jackson of Tennessee and John Quincy Adams of Massachusetts, both of whom had been nominated by their state legislatures.

After the 1824 election, the task of transforming party politics into a formal institution fell to such militant Republicans as Martin Van Buren and Thomas Ritchie, who began to defend political parties as indispensable allies of local democracy. The outcome of this election, in which John Quincy Adams was selected by the House of Representatives, even though Jackson had more popular and electoral votes, persuaded Jacksonian reformers that the Constitution's vulnerability to centralized administration had not been corrected by Jeffersonian democracy. With the weakening of the national party structure, Van Buren lamented, a system of personal and local factions displaced the "common sentiment" that had upheld republican principles, thus favoring champions of "consolidation." Indeed, the spectacle of a fragmented and apathetic electorate allowing the House to select the neo-Federalist Adams as president revealed

[20] Thomas Jefferson, "First Inaugural Address," March 4, 1801, in *The Portable Thomas Jefferson,* ed. Merill D. Peterson (New York: Viking Press, 1975), 293.
[21] Piereson, "Party Government," 51.

the need to establish political parties as permanent institutions.[22] The Jacksonian ambition to make partisanship part of the "living Constitution" abetted the rise of the Democratic party, which organized voters on the basis of principles that were militantly decentralizing—as was the very process of party politics they established.

Jacksonian democracy established the "confederate" form of political organization that would endure until the twentieth century. The Jeffersonian emphasis on political centralization comported with national parties, which rested on the nomination of presidential tickets by the congressional caucus. As this national structure weakened, state party organizations emerged as key actors in national as well as state and local politics. The Jacksonian political reforms institutionalized this political devolution. With the collapse of "King Caucus" after 1824, presidential tickets were nominated by national conventions, which were dominated by state party organizations. "The proponents of the convention system in the Democratic party, Van Buren being foremost among them, thought of the convention as merely a substitute for the caucus in which instructions would continue to be handed out from Washington," James Ceaser has written. "But they soon discovered the federalizing influence of the new institution, an influence that exceeded even their own republican principle of limiting the powers of the Washington establishment."[23]

That the decentralizing thrust of their movement sometimes went further than Jacksonian leaders preferred is not in doubt; however, the Jacksonian political philosophy, rooted in the understanding that "consolidation" was a chronic problem, encouraged a much bolder assault on national institutions and programs than the Jeffersonians had undertaken. After his election in 1828, Jackson withdrew the federal government from the realm of internal improvements. Military power, especially the army, was kept to a minimum. Jackson's fiscal policy was to hold down

---

[22] Martin Van Buren, *Inquiry into the Origin and Course of Political Parties in the United States* (New York: Hudson & Houghton, 1867), 4–6. The controversy stirred by the 1824 election was further aroused by its aftermath: Adams's selection of Henry Clay, who orchestrated the victory in the House, as secretary of state; and the president's first State of the Union address, which proposed an active role for the federal government in society and the economy. In the face of these developments, Jefferson endorsed Van Buren's plan to reintroduce party competition. Responding to Van Buren's concern that Adams and his political allies were but disguised Federalists, Jefferson wrote in a letter of June 29, 1824, "Tories are tories still, by whatever name they may be called." *The Writings of Thomas Jefferson*, ed. Paul Leicester Ford (New York: Putnam's, 1899), vol. 10, 316. For an excellent discussion of Van Buren and the critical part he played in renewing party competition, see James Ceaser, *Presidential Selection: Theory and Development* (Princeton, N.J.: Princeton University Press, 1979), chap. 3.

[23] Ceaser, *Presidential Selection*, 149.

expenditures. Most significant, the Bank of the United States, which Jeffersonians had learned to live with, was dismantled; its deposits were reinvested in selected state banks. As such, the strengthening of the presidency during Jackson's stay in the White House, as Marvin Meyers has written, "mobilized the powers of government for what was essentially a dismantling operation."[24]

In light of the ardent Jacksonian commitment to constraining national power, the political decentralization brought by the revitalized party system could hardly have been unanticipated—or unwanted. As Jackson pointed out in his veto of legislation that would have renewed the national bank's charter, Democrats believed that the "true strength" of the Union consisted "in leaving individuals and States as much as possible to themselves—in making itself felt, not in its power, but in its beneficence; not in its control, but in its protection; not in binding the States more closely to the center, but leaving each to move unobstructed in its proper orbit."[25] Viewed through the lens of contemporary mass democracy, this dismantling operation might appear to serve a radical concept of individualism. In fact, the Jacksonian assault on the national government was intended to preserve the integrity of local communities, which were thought to be the home of popular collective action—that is, of collective assertions against the rich and powerful who threatened the economic and political independence of the democratic individual.[26]

So dominant had this doctrine of local self-government become by the end of Jackson's presidency that even the Whig opposition led by Adams and Henry Clay, dedicated to expanding the economic and social responsibilities of the national government, imitated the Jacksonian brand of national politics. By 1840, the Whigs subscribed to Jacksonian democracy, shaped by the convention system and widely disbursed patronage appointments, which held the national counsels of power accountable to the states and localities. In part, the Whigs' acceptance of Jacksonian politics was strategic—an acceptance of popular campaigns and practices so as to avoid the fate of the Federalists. Just as significant, however, the Whigs, no less than Democrats, appreciated the importance of local self-government to the tradition of popular rule in the United States. Massachusetts Whig statesman Edward Everett voiced this understanding in his review of Tocqueville's *Democracy in America,* in which he praised

[24] Marvin Meyers, *The Jacksonian Persuasion: Politics and Belief* (Stanford, Calif.: Stanford University Press, 1957), 28.
[25] Andrew Jackson, "Veto Message," July 10, *Messages and Papers of the Presidents,* ed. James D. Richardson (New York: Bureau of National Literature, 1897), vol. 3, 1153.
[26] Robert H. Wiebe, *Self-Rule* (Chicago: University of Chicago Press, 1995), 28.

Tocqueville's recognition of New England town meetings as the "primary schools" of liberty. "On the whole," Everett wrote in hearty agreement, "no element of American liberty is more essential than the unobtrusive, humble, domestic, municipal organization. Everything is done by the neighbors; by the people, whose interest and comfort are to be promoted. It is the curse of *centralization,* that it puts power into the hands of those who know not Joseph."[27]

The Democrats and Whigs were national organizations, but they celebrated a national idea that comported with a deep and abiding respect for localized politics and governance. Indeed, the Jacksonian theory of governance was not one of states rights per se, but a defense of local community. To be sure, Democrats believed that local rights were best guaranteed in national politics by states' rights. As Tocqueville recognized, however, the power of state governments was challenged by reformist aspirations that sought to devolve power to counties and townships.[28] New York Governor Horatio Seymour proclaimed this doctrine of local self-government in a widely distributed July 4th oration of 1856, delivered in Springfield, Massachusetts. "The democratic theory takes away control from central points and distributes it to the various localities that are most interested in its wise and honest exercise," he observed. "It keeps at every man's home the greatest share of political power that concerns him individually. It yields it to the remoter legislative bodies in diminishing proportions as they recede from the direct influence and action of the people." Such a system of local self-government, Seymour instructed, was not based on a naive view of "the people's wisdom and patriotism"; rather, it was dedicated to the proposition that republican government rested on right opinion, which was nurtured by "the great theory of local self-government" and the parties that made it effective:

This system [of local self-government] not only secures good government for each locality; but it also brings home to each individual a sense of his rights and responsibilities; it elevates his character as a man; he is taught self-reliance; he learns

---

27 Tocqueville, *Democracy in America,* 63; Edward Everett, "On the *Democracy in America,* Alexis de Tocqueville," *North American Review* 43 (July 1836): 197–9 (emphasis in original).

28 Tocqueville noted that the townships and municipal life were strongest in New England, but everywhere, even in the South, he detected the gravitational pull of local self-government: "County and township are not constituted everywhere in the same way, but one can say that the organization of township and county in the United States everywhere depends on the same idea, viz. that each man is the best judge of his own interest and the best able to satisfy his private needs. So township and county are responsible for their special interests. The state rules but does not administer. One finds exceptions to that principle, but no contradictory principle." Tocqueville, *Democracy in America,* 82.

that the performance of his duty as a citizen, is the best corrective for the evils of society, and is not led to place a vague, unfounded dependence upon legislative wisdom and inspirations. The principle of local and distributed jurisdiction, not only makes good Government, but also makes good manhood.[29]

Seymour's defense of local self-government was not empty rhetoric. The decentralizing spirit of Jacksonian democracy influenced reform not only at the national level, but also in the states. By the 1840s, constitutional reform had spread to most of the states, including most of those in the South, and it had devolved considerable power from the state capitals to the counties and townships. In New York, for example, the constitutional convention of 1846 created small electoral districts to give better representation to local patches of opinion, made elective offices of most state and local positions (hitherto appointed by either the governor or legislature), and decentralized patronage. Before these changes, Democratic reformer Jabez Hammond wrote, the "central power [of the state] reached every county, and was felt by every town in the state. The convention of 1846 [has] wholly annihilated this terrible power."[30]

Such action did not go unchallenged. As Ceaser suggests, many Democratic leaders, including Van Buren, were somewhat taken aback by the radical devolution loosed by Jacksonian democracy. At the New York constitutional convention of 1821, in fact, Van Buren had opposed the direct election of justices of the peace, powerful officials whose patronage he thought essential to the New York Democratic party's dominance. When taunted by his political enemy, DeWitt Clinton, for not trusting the people, Van Buren replied that direct popular election would give the opposition minority faction in New York control over as many as half of the state's justices of the peace. More penetratingly, Van Buren believed that the Democratic party had the special function of protecting the principle "first formally avowed by Rousseau that the right to exercise sovereignty belongs inalienably to the people."[31] Subjecting all offices to direct election, Van Buren argued, favored wealthy figures of reputation, such as

---

[29] Governor Horatio Seymour, "The Democratic Theory of Government," July 4, 1856, in *Seymour and Blair: Their Lives and Services,* ed. David G. Croly (New York: Richardson, 1868), 49, 52.

[30] Jabez D. Hammond, *Life and Times of Silas Wright* (Syracuse, N.Y.: Hall and Dickson, 1848), 670. For an overview of constitutional reform in the states during the Jacksonian era, see George P. Parkinson, Jr., *Antebellum State Constitution-Making: Retention, Circumvention, Revision,* unpublished Ph.D. dissertation, Department of History, University of Wisconsin, 1972.

[31] Van Buren, *Political Parties in the United States,* 11; *Reports of the Proceedings of the New York Constitutional Convention, 1821* (New York: Da Capo Press, 1970), 341, 353–4. For an excellent discussion of Van Buren's struggle to balance party organization

Clinton; majority rule and the rights of the average citizen required the
support of a disciplined state party organization that could exercise firm
control over public opinion and government action. The humble members of society—the farmers, the mechanics, the laborers—stood in need
"of an extraneous force to secure harmony in their ranks."[32] Thus, as
John Casais has written, "While it possessed a legislative majority, the
[New York Democratic party] would rule, protecting the common man
from his own enemies, and, in a Rousseauan way, from his own folly."[33]

The Anglo-American devotion to provincial liberties, as Tocqueville
observed, would not easily abide such a centralized instrument of the
"general will." Indeed, Van Buren's party suffered the consequences for
challenging the sovereignty of local opinion in the state elections of 1824,
which returned Clinton and his allies to power. Two years later, an
amendment was added to the 1821 Constitution giving "the people in
their several towns, at their annual elections," the power to choose justices of the peace.[34] Thereafter, Van Buren's ideal of a rigorously disciplined, united party as a guide to public opinion had to be modified, ac-
quiescing to popular aspirations for the direct election of local officials.
The Regency, as the New York Democratic party was known, led the fight
at the 1846 state convention for reforms that subjected all judicial offices
to popular election. At the same time, this self-effacement enabled the
Democratic party to endure as an important intermediary between government and society—to remain an essential "extraneous means to secure
harmony" in the ranks of the people.

The Whig press charged that Jacksonian reforms went too far, invest-
ing "a revolutionary, fickle and radical spirit in politics" that undermined

and direct election of local officials, see John A. Casais, *The New York State Constitutional Convention and Its Aftermath,* unpublished Ph.D. dissertation, Department of
History, Columbia University, 1970, especially chap. 9.

[32] Van Buren, *Political Parties in the United States,* 5.

[33] Casais, *The New York State Constitutional Convention,* 295. Whether Van Buren truly
understood Rousseau is debatable; but clearly, he viewed the party system as a corrective
to what he understood to be the Constitution's inadequate regard for self-government.
As such, I would take issue with Ceaser's observation that Van Buren and his allies were
"less concerned with . . . abstract considerations of democratic theory than with certain
immediate problems in the presidential selection process." Ceaser, *Presidential Selection,*
132. Like Madison in the 1790s, Van Buren was struggling to find an institutional solution to the original Constitution's failure to resist the centralizing ambitions of those like
Hamilton who hoped to transform a regime of checks and balances into an administrative republic.

[34] "Amendments to the Constitution of 1821, Ratified September, 1826," in *The Federal
and State Constitutions,* ed. Francis Newton Thorpe (Washington, D.C.: U.S. Government Printing Office, 1909), vol. 5, 2651.

the republican character of the Constitution. "Our judges are to be chosen directly by the people!" lamented the *American Review,* a Whig journal, in the wake of New York's 1846 constitutional convention. "And that serene and elevated region, which the winds and waves of political excitement have, till this time, respected, is to be thrown open to their utmost violence."[35]

Tocqueville shared the Whig concerns about the popular, decentralizing thrust of the Democratic party. Although he admired the Americans' "taste for local freedom," considering it a critical corrective to their excessive attention to private matters, Tocqueville feared that Jacksonian democracy might make it impossible for the national government to attend to those few, critical matters "important enough to attract its attention." He praised American democracy for achieving government centralization, which involved the government in such matters as foreign policy and national commerce, even as it avoided administrative centralization, which involved the national government in "secondary concerns" better left to states and localities. And yet, militant Jacksonian reformers would destroy this balance between government centralization and administrative decentralization. Jackson himself, according to Tocqueville, was a popular, not strong, leader—"the majority's slave"—who threatened to deprive the federal government of the limited government centralization without which a nation could not "live, much less prosper." In attacking the Bank of the United States, he merely flattered the "provincial jealousies" and "*decentralizing* passions" that had brought him to power.[36]

But Jacksonian Democrats defended the political reforms of the 1830s and 1840s as necessary to prevent the consolidation that they considered a threat to constitutional government in the United States. Jackson was no slave of the majority, they claimed. Indeed, there was no popular demand to kill the bank; Jackson, through the medium of the party organization and press, convinced the people that this relic of Hamiltonian nationalism was not only bad public policy but also unconstitutional. Moreover, as his stand against John Calhoun in the nullification crisis of 1832 revealed, Jackson's commitment to devolution had its limits. As argued by a review of *Democracy in America* that appeared in the Jacksonian press (the author was John O'Sullivan), the president did not "shrink from responsibility; on the contrary . . . by the freedom and firmness with

---

[35] "Responsibility of the Ballot Box; With an Illustration," *The American Review,* November 1846: 440.

[36] Tocqueville, *Democracy in America,* 262–76; 392–3 (emphasis in original).

which he used his legislative veto, and asserted his right to act upon the Constitution, as he understood it, [he] developed the energies of government in a point where they had been previously dormant, and thus left it more efficient than he found it."[37] What Tocqueville did not appreciate, Jackson's Senate ally Thomas Hart Benton alleged in his memoirs, was that the president's attack on the bank was rooted in Jeffersonian principles, and that it meant "going back to the constitution and the foundation of party on principle."[38] The renewal of party conflict did not weaken federal authority, but linked it vitally with the public.

Whereas Tocqueville feared that the American celebration of local self-government might become excessive, corroding representative institutions and making even the most limited objectives of government centralization profoundly difficult, the Jacksonians viewed it as a fragile obstacle to Hamiltonian nationalism, made dangerously seductive by the Whigs. Indeed, political culture in the United States might not have been as hostile to centralized administration as Tocqueville claimed. The honor that most Americans accorded the commercial spirit demanded in some sense a national state that would cultivate economic integration and protect interstate commerce from local government interference. Tocqueville underestimated, his Jacksonian critics charged, how far the Constitution of 1787 proscribed popular rule—how the Constitution might foster, if shaped by Federalist or Whig doctrine, a national state that would protect vested commercial interests at the expense of equal opportunity.

To be sure, the Jacksonians did not see themselves as dishonoring the free enterprise system—they were not civic republicans. Rather, they denied that free enterprise, properly understood, was linked to energetic government. Jacksonian Democrats hoped to unleash the commercial spirit from government-created monopolies, such as the national bank. Only then would commercialism conform to a "natural-rights" republicanism whose clarion call of "equal rights to all and special privileges to none" promised political and economic independence to the productive "bone and sinew" of the country. This independence required local self-government—a deep and abiding effort, as Governor Seymour put it, "to distribute each particular power to those who have the greatest interest in its wise and faithful exercise."[39]

[37] John O'Sullivan, "European Views of Democracy—Number II. (M. De Tocqueville)," *United States Magazine and Democratic Review* 8 (July 1838): 355.
[38] Thomas Hart Benton, *Thirty Years' View; or, A History of the Working of the American Government for Thirty Years, from 1820 to 1850* (New York: Appleton, 1854), 224.
[39] Seymour, "The Democratic Theory of Government," 51.

PROGRESSIVISM, THE STATE, AND DIRECT DEMOCRACY

The confederate form of party organization that was legitimized during the Jacksonian era endured well into the twentieth century. Even the rise of the Republican party during the 1850s as a result of the slavery controversy, and the subsequent decline of the Whigs, did not alter the essential characteristics of the party system in the United States. These characteristics—decentralized organization and hostility to centralization of power—ultimately short-circuited the efforts of radical Republicans to complete their program of Reconstruction.

In truth, like their Whig forebears, Republicans were diffident in their opposition to the Democratic doctrine of local self-government. Senator Stephen Douglas justified northern Democrats' defense of "popular sovereignty" in the territories on the basis of this theory of government, proclaiming in his 1858 debates with Abraham Lincoln that government in the United States was "formed on the principle of diversity in the local institutions and laws, and not on that of uniformity." "Each locality," Douglas argued, "having different interests, a different climate and different surroundings, required different local laws, local policy and local institutions, adapted to the wants of the locality."[40] To Republicans, this marked the triumph of petty particularism over the principles of the Declaration of Independence, rightly understood. Still, Lincoln pledged not to interfere with slavery where it was already established—a promise he reiterated in his first inaugural address, in which he disavowed "any purpose, directly or indirectly, to interfere with the institution of slavery in the states where it exists."[41] Given their tepid opposition to local self-government, Republicans saw little purpose in dismantling the localized party system; rather, to the dismay of Progressive reformers such as Herbert Croly, they more or less took "over the system of partisan organization and discipline originated by the Jacksonian Democrats." As Croly would put it in *Progressive Democracy,* this party system "bestowed upon the divided Federal government a certain unity of control, while at the same time it prevented increased efficiency of the Federal system from being obnoxious to local interests."[42]

---

[40] *The Lincoln-Douglas Debates of 1858,* ed. Robert W. Johannsen (New York: Oxford University Press, 1965), 126–7. On the Democratic ideology and its support of local self-government, see Bruce Collins, "The Ideology of the Ante-bellum Northern Democrats," *American Studies* II, no. 1: 102–21.

[41] *Messages and Papers of the Presidents,* ed. James D. Richardson (New York: Bureau of National Literature, 1897), vol. 7, 3206.

[42] Herbert Croly, *Progressive Democracy* (New York: Macmillan, 1914), 99, 347.

Not surprisingly, Progressives viewed the decentralized party system as an obstacle to their programmatic ambitions. Their reform zeal aimed, above all else, at the concentration of wealth, specifically at the giant trusts—which, according to reformers, constituted uncontrolled and irresponsible units of power in American society. These industrial combinations created the perception that opportunity had become less equal in the United States, that growing corporate power threatened the freedom of individuals to earn a living. This threat to equal opportunity posed a severe challenge to the doctrine of local self-government, as reformers had good reasons to believe that the great business interests—represented by newly formed associations such as the National Civic Federation—had captured and corrupted state legislatures and local officials for their own profit. Party leaders—both Democrats and Republicans—were viewed as irresponsible "bosses" who did the bidding of "special interests."

Progressives saw little possibility of converting the existing party machinery into an instrument for the realization of their national program. Dedicated to Jeffersonian principles, political parties in the United States were wedded to constitutional arrangements that impeded the expansion of national administrative power in the name of the people's economic welfare. The origins and organizing principles of the American party system established that system as a force against the creation of a "modern state." The Progressive reformers' commitment to building such a state—that is, to the creation of a national political power with expansive programmatic responsibilities—meant that the party system had to be weakened or reconstructed. As Karl has noted, the Progressive party campaign of 1912 was as much "an attack on the whole concept of political parties as it was an effort to create a single party whose doctrinal clarity and moral purity would represent the true interest of the nation as a whole."[43]

The Progressive party campaign represented a critical historical moment in the transformation of the United States from a decentralized republic to a mass democracy. "While fully admitting that the transition may not be as abrupt as it seems," Croly wrote in the wake of the 1912 election, "we have apparently been witnessing during the past year or two the end of one epoch and the beginning of another." Political scientists and historians have tended to confirm Croly's belief that the 1912 election was a barometer of fundamental changes taking place during the

---

[43] Karl, *The Uneasy State,* 234–5.

Progressive Era. "In several respects, the election of 1912 was the first 'modern' presidential contest in American history," Arthur Link and Richard McCormick wrote in 1983. "The use of direct primaries, the challenge to traditional party loyalties, the candidates' issue orientation, and the prevalence of interest-group political activities all make the election of 1912 look more like 1980 than that of 1896."[44]

Although a number of works attribute importance to the changes brought by the Progressive Era, scholars continue to disagree significantly about the character of these changes and their legacy for twentieth-century American politics. Indeed, for the past quarter century, the scholarly effort to define Progressivism or to identify principles and organizational forms of the Progressive Movement has been under full-scale attack. Peter Filene has argued, in fact, that the Progressive Movement is an intellectual construct—a mere semantic that never existed.[45] Although not going this far, Daniel Rogers acknowledges that "the trouble with comprehending 'progressivism' as a list of beliefs is that progressives did not share a common creed or a string of common values." This era, he suggests, exemplified a new fragmented and issue-oriented politics, in which often contradictory reform movements sought to capitalize on the declining influence of traditional party control over politics and government. After all, Rogers notes, "those whom historians had labelled progressives shared no common party or organization."[46]

There was a Progressive party, of course, but its brief (albeit significant) existence underscores the powerful centrifugal forces of progressive democracy. With the celebrated former president Theodore Roosevelt as its candidate, the Bull Moose party won 27.4 percent of the popular vote and eighty-eight electoral votes from six states in 1912. This was extraordinary for a third party; in fact, no third-party candidate for the presidency before or since has received so large a percentage of the popular vote or as many electoral votes as did Roosevelt. Despite its remarkable showing in 1912, however, the Progressive party was forlorn four years later, its fate inseparable from the dynamic leader who embodied its cause. At the end of the day, it had brought about neither an ongoing multiparty system nor a fundamental party transformation, pitting progressives against con-

---

[44] Arthur S. Link and Richard L. McCormick, *Progressivism* (Arlington Heights, Ill.: Harlan Davidson, 1983), 43–4.
[45] Peter Filene, "An Obituary for the Progressive Movement," *American Quarterly* 22 (1970): 20–34.
[46] Daniel T. Rogers, "In Search of Progressivism," *Reviews of American History* (December 1982): 114–23.

servatives, for which many participants in the Bull Moose campaign had expressed hope.

Arguably, however, the Progressive party lies at the very heart of fundamental changes in American politics—changes that were initially, if only partially, negotiated during the Progressive Era.[47] The personal quality of Roosevelt's campaign was part and parcel of these changes, but they went much deeper than his desire to regain political mastery. The Progressive party, with its leader-centered organization, accommodated and embodied an array of reformers—insurgent Republican officeholders, disaffected Democrats, crusading journalists, academics, social workers, and other activists—who hoped that the new party coalition would realize their common goal of expanding the responsibilities of the federal government and making it more responsive to the economic, social, and political demands of the people.

The Progressives' pledge to rescue the government from the throes of corporate capitalism resembled the Jacksonian hatred of the "monster bank." In truth, however, most Progressives were avowedly hostile to Jacksonian democracy, which Croly branded "pioneer democracy." As Martin Shefter has written:

> For each of the major institutional reforms in the Jacksonian era, the Progressives sponsored an equal and opposite reform. The Jacksonians had increased the number of executive offices subject to popular election; the Progressives sought to reduce that number and to create the position of chief executive through such reforms as the short ballot and the strong mayor plan of municipal government. . . . The Jacksonians extended the franchise; the Progressives contracted it through registration, literacy, and citizenship requirements. The Jacksonians established party conventions to nominate candidates for elective office; the Progressives replaced them with primary elections. The Jacksonians created a hierarchical structure of party committees to manage the electorate; the Progressives sought to destroy these party organizations or at least render their tasks more difficult through such reforms as the nonpartisan municipal government, and the separation of local, state, and national elections. Finally, the Jacksonians established a party press and accorded influence to the political editor; the Progressive movement was linked to the emergence of a self-consciously independent press (magazines as well as newspapers) and with muckraking journalists.[48]

---

47 For a more complete discussion of the Progressive party and its legacy, see Sidney M. Milkis and Daniel J. Tichenor, "'Direct Democracy' and Social Justice: The Progressive Party Campaign of 1912," *Studies in American Political Development* 8 (Fall 1994): 282–340.

48 Martin Shefter, "Party, Bureaucracy, and Political Change in the United States," in *Political Parties: Development and Decay,* ed. Louis Maisel and Joseph Cooper (Beverly Hills, Calif.: Sage, 1978), 232. Also see Eisenach, *The Lost Promise of Progressivism,* chaps. 1 and 4.

Still, the profound shift in regime norms and practices represented by Progressivism did not entail a straightforward evolution from party to administrative politics. Indeed, the Progressive party crusade was badly crippled by fundamental disagreements among its supporters over issues that betrayed an acute sensitivity, if not attachment, to the commitment in the country to local self-government. The party was deeply divided over civil rights, leading to bitter struggles at the Progressive party convention over delegate-selection rules and the platform that turned on whether the party should confront the shame of Jim Crow. In the end it did not, acknowledging the right of states and localities to resolve the matter of race relations. Moreover, Progressive delegates waged an enervating struggle at the party convention over whether the appropriate method to tame the trusts was through an interstate trade commission with considerable administrative discretion or through a militant antitrust policy. New Nationalists, led by Roosevelt, prevailed; they pledged the party to regulate, rather than attempt to dismantle, corporate power. However, this disagreement carried over to the general election: The Democrats, under the tutelage of their presidential candidate Woodrow Wilson and his adviser Louis Brandeis, embraced a New Freedom version of Progressive reform, which emphasized antitrust measures and state regulations as an alternative to the expansion of national administrative power.

The split between New Nationalism and New Freedom Progressives cut to the very core of the modern state that, ostensibly, the programmatic initiatives touted by Progressives anticipated. The Progressive program, presupposing a more activist national government, "foreshadowed administrative aggrandizement," Croly acknowledged. Yet Progressives could not agree on how administrative power should be used; indeed, the conflict between New Nationalism and New Freedom Progressives revealed that many reformers were profoundly uneasy about the prospect of expanding national administrative power. Woodrow Wilson expressed this concern in a series of lectures he delivered at Columbia University in 1908:

Moral and social questions originally left to the several States for settlement can be drawn into the field of federal authority only at the expense of the self-dependence and efficiency of the several communities of which our complex body politic is made up. Paternal morals, morals enforced by judgment and choices of the central authority at Washington, do not and cannot create vital moral habits or methods of life unless sustained by local opinion and purpose, local prejudice and convenience,—unless supported by local convenience and interest; and only communities capable of taking care of themselves will, taken together, constitute a nation capable of vital action and control.[49]

The reluctance of many Progressive reformers to embrace centralized administration did not necessarily represent a commitment to local self-government, at least as it was then practiced in the United States. But it did reveal a desire to find nonbureaucratic and noncentralized solutions to the ills that plagued the political economy—to achieve, in Tocqueville's words, governmental, but not administrative, centralization. Achieving such a balance involved, in part, building on measures such as the Sherman Act, enacted in 1890, that would rely on competition and law, rather than administrative tribunals, to curb the abuses of big business. Just as significant, Progressives believed that reforming the political economy had to go hand in hand with political changes that would invest in the people more power to elect officials and to govern. Ultimately, the Progressive hope for sustaining self-government in the United States depended on transmuting local self-government into direct rule by the people, who would not have to suffer the interference of political associations and institutions. "Truly, the voice of the people is the voice of God," wrote a Progressive journalist in the early part of the twentieth century; "but that means the voice of the *whole* people."[50]

Just as surely as the Progressive schism over the appropriate methods to reform the political economy betrayed fundamental disagreements in its ranks, so its program of direct government elicited a shared sense of endeavor. The one doctrine that unified the disparate strands of the Progressive party was its advocacy of "pure democracy," including support for measures such as the universal use of the direct primary, the initiative, referendum, and recall, and an easier method to amend the Constitution. Above all, the measures of direct government espoused by Roosevelt marked the Progressive party campaign as militantly reformist. "These _____ measures have been more widely discussed, more bitterly condemned, and more loyally praised than almost any other measures connected with the whole progressive movement," wrote Benjamin Park Dewitt.[51] Yet Roosevelt did not flinch in the face of this controversy. Sens-

[49] Woodrow Wilson, "Constitutional Government in the United States," in *The Papers of Woodrow Wilson,* ed. Arthur S. Link (Princeton, N.J.: Princeton University Press, 1974), vol. 18, 197–8.
[50] William Hemstreet, "Theory and Practice of the New Primary Law," *The Arena* 28, no. 6 (December 1902): 592 (emphasis in original).
[51] Benjamin Park Dewitt, *The Progressive Movement* (Seattle: University of Washington Press, 1915), 215.

ing that popular rule was the glue that held together the movement he sought to lead, his defense of it became bolder throughout 1912. Indeed, toward the end of September, Roosevelt announced that he "would go even further than the Progressive Platform," applying the recall "to everybody, including the president." TR "stands upon the bald doctrine of unrestricted majority rule," *The Nation* responded. "But it is just against the dangers threatened, by such majority rule, in those crises that try the temper of nations, that the safeguard of constitutional government as the outgrowth of the ages of experience has been erected."[52]

The more extreme measures of the program of direct democracy, such as the right of people to recall judicial decisions, alarmed not only conservatives (such as incumbent Republican president William Howard Taft) but also TR's Progressive rivals in the Democratic and Republican parties (such as William Jennings Bryan, Robert LaFollette, and Woodrow Wilson). Yet Roosevelt's campaign resonated with the American people. It stirred enthusiasm—indeed, a remarkable religiosity—that put on the defensive those Democrats and Republicans who attacked the Progressive party's program as too radical. Wilson was nominated and elected, in fact, not only because of his "anti-statism," but also because he was nearly as enthusiastic as Roosevelt in bowing to the court of public opinion. "What these critics never understood," John Dewey wrote in his penetrating eulogy of TR, "was the admiring affection and unbounded faith with which the American people repaid one who never spoke save to make them sharers in his ideas and to appeal to them as final judges."[53]

Although their faith in public opinion distinguished them from their Jeffersonian and Jacksonian forebears, Progressives' celebration of the rights of the people resonated with the public at a time when industrial capitalism and urbanization threatened the integrity of local and state governments. The Progressive defense of direct rule by the people, in fact, capitalized on the commitment to popular sovereignty in the tradition of local self-government—which, as we have shown, coexisted uneasily with strong local and state party organizations. Arguably, the seeds of the celebration of the whole people, unmediated by either local institutions or political associations, were present in the constitutional reforms of the

[52] "Let the People Rule," *The Nation*, September 26, 1912: 276–7. *The Nation* article referred to a speech Roosevelt gave in Phoenix, Arizona. TR also spoke of his willingness to have the recall extended to the presidency in a speech in Denver, Colorado. See "Roosevelt Favors the Recall of the President," *New York Times*, September 20, 1912: 1.

[53] John Dewey, "Theodore Roosevelt," in *John Dewey: The Middle Works, 1899–1924*, ed. Jo Ann Boydston (Carbondale: Southern Illinois University Press, 1982), vol. 2, 146.

Jacksonian era, resisted by Van Buren, that provided for the direct popular election of state and local judges. The assault on judicial patronage
during the Jacksonian era was frequently linked with a broader challenge
to representation itself.[54] Indeed, one early Progressive tract that defended direct government made this connection explicitly between the nineteenth-century concept of self-government and the Progressive idea of
democracy:

> Direct legislation is law-enacting by the electors themselves as distinguished from
> law-enacting by representatives or by some aristocratic body, or by a single ruler,
> such as the king, emperor, or czar. In small communities this is accomplished by
> electors meeting together voting on every law or ordinance by which they are to
> be governed. This is done in New England town meetings. . . . In communities too
> widespread or too numerous for the voters to meet together and decide on the
> laws by which they are to be governed, Direct Legislation is accomplished by the
> use of imperative petitions, through what is known as the Initiative and Referen-
> dum.[55]

In effect, Progressives hoped that the election or polling district, organizing the voter's immediate neighborhood, would replace the small village meeting as a source of civic involvement. But Progressive measures
such as the initiative, referendum, and direct primary did not benefit from
"the power of meeting" that was so central to Tocqueville's celebration of
the New England town meeting; nor did these measures support the
strong party organizations that Van Buren considered an imperative force
to secure harmony in the ranks of the people. Rather, Progressives dedicated themselves to political forms and associations that freed individuals
from provincial concerns and partisan organizations in order to prepare
them for participation in a more enlightened government. Progressives
preferred public opinion to localized parties, as one ardent reformer put
it, "for the people are patriotic, they do not expect offices, they cannot be
bribed, they are disinterested, they have an unbiased judgement and they
are yet sound to the core."[56]

In condemning Progressive reformers for lacking a coherent set of

---

[54] As Jacksonian historian George Bancroft put it, "They who deny the right of instruction,
deify the will of the representative, or temporary agent, and refusing to the people the
right of a paramount judgement, surrender the government for the time to the arbitrary
caprice, the desperate ambition, the bigotry or the selfishness of the individual." Bancroft, "An Oration Delivered before the Democracy of Springfield and Neighboring
Towns," July 4, 1836. Reprinted in Leon Stein and Philip Taft, *Labor Politics: Collected
Pamphlets*, vol. 1 (New York: Arno Press, 1971), 4.
[55] Eltweed Pomeroy, "Needed Political Reforms: Direct Legislation; Or, the Initiative and
the Referendum, and the Recall," *The Arena* 28, no. 6 (November 1902): 465–6.
[56] Hemstreet, "New Primary Law," 592.

principles, contemporary scholars point to the apparent contradiction between the Progressives' celebration of direct democracy and their hope to achieve more disinterested government, which seemed to demand a powerful and independent national bureaucracy. But Progressives believed that the expansion of social-welfare provisions and "pure democracy" were inextricably linked. Reforms such as the direct primary, as well as the initiative and referendum, were designed to overthrow the localized two-party system in the United States, built on Jeffersonian and Jacksonian principles, which bestowed on the divided federal government a certain unity of control; at the same time, the two-party system restrained programmatic ambition and prevented the development of a stable and energetic administration of social policy. By the same token, the triumph of "progressive" over "pioneer" democracy would put the American people directly in touch with the councils of power, thus strengthening the demand for government support; this triumph would also allow—indeed, it would require—administrative agencies to play their proper role in the realization of Progressive social-welfare policy.

In the final analysis, the Progressive faith in public opinion can be viewed as a compromise with the fear of a centralized state in the United States—a willingness on the part of the most nationalist of reformers to accommodate these fears, even as they sought to strengthen national administrative power. As the zealous new nationalist, Croly, wrote in *Progressive Democracy*, many well-meaning social democrats in England or France, as well as the United States, favored the formation of a national programmatic party to bring about social and economic reform. Such devotees of a permanent social democratic party disdained direct popular government, Croly pointed out, because they expected that, at least in the near future, direct popular government, dependent on the vagaries of public opinion, would increase the difficulty of securing the adoption of many items in a desirable social program. Herein they were right, Croly acknowledged. But reformers of this sort attached too much importance to the accomplishment and maintenance of specific results, and not enough to the permanent social welfare of democracy.

An authoritative representative government, particularly one which is associated with inherited leadership and a strong party system, carries with it an enormous prestige. It is frequently in a position either to ignore, to circumvent or to wear down popular opposition. But a social program purchased at such a price is not worth what it costs.[57]

[57] Croly, *Progressive Democracy*, 281–2.

The Progressive party dedicated itself to expanding the national government's responsibility to secure the economic welfare of the individual; at the same time, it stood for the proposition that any program of social control, social insurance, and standardization of industry could not be adopted until it was well digested by public opinion. There was no hope in the United States—where centralized administration was a cardinal vice—that the people would grant legitimacy to a welfare state that was not attuned to the preferences, even biases, of public opinion. The popularity of the direct primary in the United States, Croly noted, revealed how centralized and disciplined national parties went against the looser grain of American politics. To the extent that government became committed to a democratic program that was essentially social in character, the American people would find intolerable a two-party system that stood between popular will and government machinery. As prominent social reformer Jane Addams noted in a speech she gave at the Second Annual Lincoln Day dinner of the Progressive party in 1914, a fundamental principle of Progressivism was that a welfare state could not be created in the United States "unless the power of direct legislation is placed in the hands of the people, in order that these changes may come, not as the centralized government [has] given them, from above down, but may come from the people up; that the people shall be the directing and controlling factors in this legislation."[58]

The short-lived existence of the Progressive party, then, is not attributable simply to its dependence on TR's candidate-centered campaign, or even to the fundamental disagreements over race and trusts that divided its leaders. In large measure, it followed from the almost hopeless task of reconciling loyalty to the Progressive ideal with loyalty to a particular organization. Indeed, in the celebration of political reforms such as the direct primary, recall, initiative, and referendum, the Progressive party was a *party to end party politics*. The direct primary subordinated parties as collective organizations with a past and a future to the personal ambitions of candidates and the issues of the moment; just as significant, measures such as the initiative, the referendum, and recall presupposed an ongoing dialogue between representatives and their constituents about issues that denied parties their traditional responsibility to shape public opinion. "The logic of the progressive democratic principle was self de-

---

[58] Jane Addams, "Social Justice Through National Action," speech delivered at the Second Annual Lincoln Day Dinner of the Progressive party, New York City, February 12, 1914. Printed ms. located in Jane Addams Papers, File 136, Reel #42.

structive," Croly predicted. "Just in so far as a progressive political program is carried out, progressive social democracy will cease to need a national political party as an instrument."[59] Progressive democracy would reach its fulfillment in an alliance between public opinion and the autonomous political executive, now freed from the constraints of localized party organizations and practices.

Viewed in this way, the Progressive idea of democracy was not a radical rejection of the American constitutional tradition, but an effort to restore it—to free it from political machines that paralleled Anti-Federalist principles. Whereas the Articles of Confederation read, "We the undersigned delegates of the States," the Preamble to the Constitution of 1787 was declared by "We, the People." The change to "We, the People," claimed Theodore Gilman at a Progressive party rally in Yonkers, New York, "was made at the Federal Convention with the full understanding of the meaning and effect of the new form of words," signifying that the new Constitution represented the aspirations of one sovereign people to create a "more perfect Union."[60] Political parties had preempted this original design, shifting power to states and localities in the service of "local self-government." Jeffersonian and Jacksonian reforms were necessary in the nineteenth century to thwart the "aristocratic" pretensions of the Federalists, but the problems thrown up by the Industrial Revolution demanded that Progressives revisit the potential for national democracy in the original Constitution. As Croly put it, "the nationalism of Hamilton with all its aristocratic leaning, was more democratic, because more constructively social, than the indiscriminate individualism of Jefferson."[61] Just as the original theory of the electoral college had been abandoned after the Revolution of 1800, closing the space between presidential politics and popular choice, so Gilman claimed, "the people now propose to come into closer touch with their representatives by the abolition of the machine, and the substitution thereafter of the direct primary, the initiative, referendum, and recall. This is all one logical and irresistible movement in one direction, having as its object the restoration of our form of government to its original pu-

---

[59] Croly, *Progressive Democracy*, 336.
[60] Theodore Gilman, "The Progressive Party Comes Not to Destroy, But to Fulfill, the Constitution," address delivered at a public rally in Yonkers, New York, September 27, 1912. Progressive Party Publications, 1912–1916, Theodore Roosevelt Collection, Harvard University, Cambridge, Mass., 4.
[61] Croly, *Progressive Democracy*, 54–5.

rity and ideal perfection, as a government under the control of 'We, the people,' who formed it."[62]

The Progressive party's brief but significant existence anticipated a shift in which a political order defined by the differences between Democrats and Republicans gave way to one defined by differences between Progressives and conservatives. Before the 1912 election, one belonged to a party as one belonged to a family or church—and national politics was held accountable to state and local party leaders. Progressivism was advanced in 1912 in a way that began to weaken party loyalties; thereafter, the individual's relationship to the nation's capital and an expanding federal power rivaled his ties to party and place. This shift, one might say, was ratified by Woodrow Wilson's move toward positions and policies that accepted national administrative power. Most significant, Wilson eventually supported the idea of a regulatory commission with broad responsibilities for overseeing business practices, resulting in the creation of the Federal Trade Commission in 1915.[63]

To be sure, as the "return to normalcy" of the 1920s showed, this did not signal the triumph of New Nationalism. But it did mean that localized parties were no longer the principal agents of democracy, and that the alliance between decentralization and democracy was gradually weakened in favor a relationship between the individual and the "state." The advance of the idea and institutions of Progressive democracy invariably followed. With the celebration of public opinion spawned by the Progressive party campaign of 1912, even conservatives like Calvin Coolidge could hardly resist going to the public.[64] The "confederate" party system would endure as an important institution until the 1970s, yet it would never again be a bulwark of local self-government—"a wall of separation" be-

---

[62] Gilman, "The Progressive Party Comes Not to Destroy, but to Fulfill, the Constitution," 5–6.

[63] Wilson's acceptance of many elements of the Progressive platform was duly acknowledged by social reformers, many of whom supported his reelection in 1916. In October 1916, eleven of the original nineteen members of the 1912 Progressive party platform committee issued a statement endorsing Wilson on the grounds that he had signed into law all or part of twenty-two of the thirty-three planks of the 1912 platform. "Progressive Voice Raised for Wilson," *New York Times,* November 1, 1916.

[64] Robert LaFollette's 1924 Progressive party campaign, which captured 16 percent of the popular vote, was further evidence that Progressivism did not go into hibernation during the 1920s. Indeed, LaFollette's campaign, lacking any semblance of a party organization, advanced the Progressive concept of direct democracy. That LaFollette received such an impressive vote, despite a booming economy and a popular incumbent president, testified to the growing fragility of the two-party system. See Kenneth Campbell, *The Progressive Movement of 1924,* Ph.D. dissertation, Columbia University, 1947.

tween one national community and many communities at the state and local levels.[65]

CONCLUSION

Progressive democracy came into its own with the New Deal realignment. As John Dewey saw so clearly, Progressivism could have a profound effect on the American polity insofar as it could be transformed into a new liberal tradition—one that did not celebrate a rugged individualism that abhorred state interference with private property, but instead emphasized a new concept of individualism that viewed the state as a guarantor of social and economic welfare. In his influential *Liberalism and Social Action,* a book he dedicated to Jane Addams, Dewey wrote, "these new liberals fostered the idea that the state has the responsibility for creating institutions under which individuals can effectively realize the potentialities that are theirs."[66]

Although the hope of many social reformers that the Progressive party would serve as an instrument for unifying disparate advocacy groups and causes came unraveled, Dewey's celebration of a new conception of liberalism underscores the important ties between the Progressive party of 1912 and the New Deal's programmatic and institutional aspirations. Indeed, the New Deal realignment marks the consolidation of changes begun by the Progressive campaign of 1912. The so-called purge campaign and other partisan practices during the New Deal period suggest a project to create a national programmatic two-party system. The system of party responsibility, Franklin Roosevelt argued, "required that one of its parties be the liberal party and the other be the conservative party."[67] Ultimately, however, Roosevelt and his New Deal allies, some of whom were erstwhile Bull Moosers, took actions and pursued procedural reforms that would extend the personal and nonpartisan responsibility of the president to the detriment of collective and partisan responsibility. Like his cousin TR, FDR conceived of a party program as an assault on party politics, but he presided over a full-scale realignment—the first in American history to place an independent executive at the heart of its approach to politics and government. Understood within the context of the Progres-

---

[65] See, for example, Michael E. McGerr, *The Decline of Popular Politics: The American North, 1865–1828* (New York: Oxford University Press, 1986).
[66] John Dewey, *Liberalism and Social Action* (New York: G. P. Putnam, 1935), 26.
[67] Franklin D. Roosevelt, *Public Papers and Addresses,* ed. Samuel I. Rosenman (New York: Random House, 1938–50), vol. 7, xxviii–xxxii.

sive tradition, the New Deal is appropriately viewed as the completion of a realignment that makes future *partisan* realignments unnecessary. As the important Brownlow Committee report put it, "Our national will must be expressed not merely in a brief, exultant moment of electoral decision, but in persistent, determined, competent administration of what the nation has decided to do."[68]

The expansion of national administrative power that followed the New Deal realignment did not result in the form of national state that Progressive reformers like Croly and Dewey had hoped for—one that established regulation and social-welfare policy that could be expressions of national unity and commitment. Indeed, the hallmark of administrative politics in the United States is the virtual absence of a state that can impose its will on the economy and society. The limits of administrative centralization in the American context were revealed clearly enough by the fact that strong opposition to the growth of the central government continued to have force in American politics, especially during times of frenetic government activism. The Great Society, which represented an effort to expand and radicalize the New Deal, as well as the culmination of the Progressive assault on the two-party system, was widely perceived as "excessive statism," giving rise to a movement that would pose hard challenges to liberal reforms. With Ronald Reagan's ascent to the White House, it seemed, "government was not the solution to our problems; government was the problem."[69]

The "Reagan Revolution" did not mark a revival of local self-government, however. The Reagan administration became committed to programmatic innovations in defense and foreign policy that required expanding, rather than rolling back, the national government's responsibilities. Furthermore, the moral imperatives of the modern conservative movement, which Reagan identified as that movement's most fundamental calling, are animated by a missionary zeal that seems to want to abol-

[68] *Report of the President's Committee on Administrative Management* (Washington, D.C.: U.S. Government Printing Office, 1937), 53. The President's Committee on Administrative Management, headed by Louis Brownlow, played a central role in the planning and politics of New Deal institutions. Charles Merriam, an influential advisor to TR in 1912, was an important member of this committee. I am not taking issue here with Otis Graham's argument that many Progressives opposed the New Deal. See Graham, *An Encore for Reform: The Old Progressives and the New Deal* (New York: Oxford University Press, 1967). It is the case, however, that the New Deal political program was very much inspired by TR's Bull Moose campaign. On the link between Progressivism and the New Deal, see Milkis, *The President and the Parties,* especially chap. 2.
[69] Alonzo Hamby, *Liberalism and Its Challengers: FDR to Reagan* (New York: Oxford University Press, 1985), especially chap. 6 and epilogue.

ish, rather than restore, the distinction between state and society. The spectacle of Patrick Buchanan, who challenged President George Bush in the 1992 Republican primaries, speaking at the GOP national convention in Houston before a prime-time television audience while Ronald Reagan waited offstage until after 11 P.M. was striking evidence of just how powerful New Right fundamentalist groups had become in the party. Buchanan likened his party's quarrels with liberalism to a "religious war," a dark tale that testified to the decrepitude of the Reagan Revolution. Conservatives, it seemed, did not want to dismantle the state forged on the New Deal realignment; instead, they desired to put it to new uses—fighting enemies abroad, protecting the domestic economy, and preserving "family values."

Notwithstanding the continuing expansion of national administrative power, our current politics does not confidently presume the existence of a national state. As Karl has argued, Americans continue to abhor national administrative power even as they embrace it. The surprising Republican victories in the 1994 elections, in which the GOP achieved majority control of the House and Senate for the first time in forty years, testified to growing public concern with "big government" and its cumbersome regulatory structures. Significantly, the Republicans achieved this dramatic victory after running a national ideological campaign that promised to fulfill the failed promise of the Reagan Revolution—to get government off the backs of the American people.[70] Even so, the public's persistent commitment to middle-class entitlements such as Social Security and Medicare and its strong support for regulatory initiatives dedicated to environmental and consumer protection makes the revival of local self-government unlikely.[71]

In truth, Americans have formed a love-hate relationship with the national state, a profound ambivalence that seeks refuge in Progressive

[70] David Shribman, "Contract on the New Deal," *Boston Globe*, October 1, 1995: A35.
[71] In fact, even conservative Republicans remain profoundly ambivalent about whether the appropriate path to reform is "devolution" or a national conservative policy. With respect to reforming Aid to Families with Dependent Children, for example, the party's campaign document, the so-called Republican Contract with America, proposed to expand the flexibility of the states, allowing them to design their own work programs and to determine who participated in these work programs. As Melissa Buis has shown, however, the Personal Responsibility and Work Opportunity Reconciliation Act of 1996, although giving states more discretion to tailor their individual welfare programs, imposes important new national standards to determine eligibility, to attack illegitimacy and teen pregnancy, and to establish work requirements. See C. Melissa Buis, "Devolution Then and Now: Redefining the Federal Role in Welfare Policy," paper presented to the Northeastern Political Science Association Annual Meeting, Boston, Mass., 1996.

democracy—the *direct* form of democracy Americans have adopted to ease their anxiety about the expansion of national administrative power. Unwilling to embrace or reject the state, we have increasingly sought to give the "people" more control over it. Consequently, "pure" democracy has evolved, or degenerated, into a plebiscitary form of politics that mocks the Progressive concept of "enlightened administration" and exposes citizens to the sort of public figures who will exploit their impatience with the difficult tasks involved in sustaining a healthy democracy. As the shifting fortunes of Bill Clinton's two terms as president have dramatically illustrated, Progressive democracy has freed the executive from party politics, only to enslave it to a demanding and fractious public.

The displacement of localized parties by Progressive democracy has not meant the end of party conflict. The erosion of old-style partisan politics has allowed a more national and issue-oriented party system to develop, one that is more compatible with the "nationalized" electorate created by Progressive reforms and the mass media. But the emergence of more centralized parties has strengthened the national party organizations and allowed for more partisan discipline in Congress, only to weaken further partisan loyalties in the electorate. Increasingly, parties seem to be "centralized bureaucracies," writes Wilson Carey McWilliams, "less mediators *between* rulers and ruled than a *part* of the government tier."[72]

The insurgency of H. Ross Perot in the 1992 presidential campaign, the most significant assault on the two-party system since TR's Bull Moose campaign, revealed at once the triumph and disappointment of Progressive democracy. TR's campaign foretold not only the emergence of an active and expansive national government but also presidential campaigns conducted less by parties than by individual candidates. Perot's campaign suggested just how far presidential politics had been emancipated from the constraints of party. Disdaining the importunities of those interested in party renewal that he form a third party, Perot launched his campaign without the formality of a nominating convention; his supporters were summoned to Armageddon on *Larry King Live.* Just as significant, the broad appeal of Perot's call for electronic town meetings as a principal vehicle to solve the nation's political and economic problems testifies to the resonance of simple-minded notions of direct democracy—

72 Wilson Carey McWilliams, "Two-Tier Politics and the Problem of Public Policy," in *The New Politics of Public Policy,* ed. Marc K. Landy and Martin A. Levin (Baltimore: Johns Hopkins University Press, 1995), 275 (emphasis in the original). See also A. James Reichley, "Party Politics in a Federal Polity," in *Challenges to Party Government,* ed. John Kenneth White and Jerome Mileur (Carbondale: Southern Illinois University Press, 1992); and Milkis, *The President and the Parties,* chaps. 10–12.

and to the threat this politics of instant gratification poses to constitutional forms. Although Perot's personal popularity had abated four years later, the direct plebiscitary politics he championed did not. Indeed, President Clinton and his Republican challenger, Robert Dole, openly imitated Perot's personalistic politics, even as they exploited campaign funds—so-called soft money—that, ostensibly, were designated for party-building activities. With Perot's politics, if not Perot himself, still having strong support in the nation as the country approached the millennium, the Progressive idea of "direct government" might be destined to play a more important part in American political life.[73]

Just as political parties were formed to make constitutional government in the United States safe for democracy—to ameliorate the Constitution's insufficient attention to the cultivation of an active and competent citizenry—so the weakening of political parties has exposed the fragile sense of citizenship in American political life. Progressive reformers recognized the possibility that dismantling the parties would breed an apathetic public susceptible to plebiscitary appeals; it was in this very respect that TR's dominant presence posed the greatest challenge to Progressive ideals. But they believed that this risk had to be taken, lest government remain impotent in the face of the major changes taking place in the economy and society. "[The democratic principle] has been kept warm and vigorous in the hearts of the people, but in both the Democratic and Republican organizations it has become so encumbered with party machinery and loaded with the ball and chain of obsolete governmental dogmas that it has ceased to find expression in the Government through either of these organizations," wrote an enthusiastic supporter of Theodore Roosevelt's Progressive party campaign. "Both parties are verbose in declaring for a government by the people, but the power of the people is so diluted through an indirect choice of officials, a division of powers of government under the Constitution, and an irresponsible party government wholly outside the Constitution, that it largely disappears

---

[73] Scot Lehigh, "Right Idea, Wrong Leader? Third Party Favored By Many, but Perot Presents a Problem." *Boston Globe*, October 1, 1995: A33. On the cultural and institutional factors that cultivate "outsiderism" in contemporary politics, see James W. Ceaser and Andrew Busch, *Losing to Win: The 1996 Elections and American Politics* (Lanham, Md.: Rowman and Littlefield, 1997), especially chap. 6. Perot's promise in 1996 to subordinate his personal ambitions to a collective organization—the Reform Party—was not kept; indeed, as Ceaser and Busch point out, the Reform Party's nomination process "only served to accentuate [Perot's] control and to deepen the split between those who were primarily Perot supporters and those who wanted to depersonalize" the movement he represented (112). On the uses and abuses of "soft money," see Anthony Corrado, "Financing the 1996 Elections," in *The Election of 1996: Reports and Interpretations,* ed. Gerald M. Pomper (Chatham, N.J.: Chatham, 1997).

before it is applied to the actual making and administration of the laws."[74] In the event that the people failed to participate in progressive democracy, some reformers suggested, they should be, so to speak, forced to be free. "The people will *not* go to the primaries; that is settled," declared an editorial in the Progressive journal *The Arena*. "If they will not do it voluntarily they should be compelled by law to do it and deposit there a ballot, and also at the general election, even though a blank, under the penalty of disenfranchisement and fine."[75]

There was no prospect, however, that the American people, dedicated above all to individualism, could be forced to be free. As Tocqueville understood, civic attachments in modern commercial republics would have to rely largely on associations and practices that encouraged long-term self-interest—"self-interest, rightly understood."[76]

In a sense, the wayward path of Progressivism takes us back to the beginning. Despairing of the constraints the Revolution of 1800 threatened to impose on the national government, Hamilton urged in an 1802 letter to James A. Bayard that there be "a systematic and persevering endeavor to establish the future of a great empire on foundations much firmer than have yet to be devised." Hoping to strengthen the "frail" system the Constitution proved to be in the hands of the Jeffersonians, Hamilton expressed approval of a proposal then before the House of Representatives to reform the electoral college by providing for discrimination between candidates for the presidency and vice presidency, as well as having electors chosen by the people under the direction of Congress. Hamilton supported the popular election of electors, for he regarded as "sound principle, to let the Federal government rest as much as possible on the shoulders of the people, and as little as possible on those of the State Legislatures."[77] In Hamilton's view, a strong executive, linked directly to the support of the people, could become the linchpin of an "administrative republic." The dominance of executive leadership in the formulation and carrying out of policy was essential to resist the deterioration of republican government.[78]

---

[74] Miles Poindexter, "Why I Am for Roosevelt," *North American Review* (1912): 473.
[75] Hemstreet, "New Primary Law," 589–90 (emphasis in the original).
[76] Tocqueville, *Democracy in America*, 525–8.
[77] Alexander Hamilton to James Bayard, April 6, 1802, *The Papers of Alexander Hamilton* (New York: Columbia University Press, 1977), vol. 25, 587–9.
[78] Harvey Flaumenhaft, "Hamilton's Administrative Republic and the American Presidency," in Joseph M. Bessette and Jeffrey Tulis, *The Presidency in the Constitutional Order* (Baton Rouge: Louisiana State University Press, 1981).

Such a view was considered mischievous by the more ardent defenders of popular rule among the Founders, such as Jefferson and Madison, as well as their Jacksonian successors, who believed that republican government required more support for local self-government than could be found in the original Constitution. This constitutional defect required political parties, which might arouse a common sentiment against "consolidation." Progressive reformers understood that the development of a more purposeful national government meant loosening the hold of traditional parties on the loyalties and voting habits of citizens. But they failed to appreciate the purpose these parties served as effective channels for democratic participation.[79] Political parties, which embodied the principle of local self-government, were critical agents in counteracting the tendency of citizens to shut themselves up in a limited circle of domestic concerns beyond the reach of broader public causes. By enticing Americans into neighborhood organizations and patronage practices outside their tiny private orbits, traditional party organizations helped to show individuals the connection between their private interests and their public concerns. Similarly, highly decentralized party structures insured that national campaigns and controversies focused on the partisan activities of townships, wards, and cities, thus cultivating a delicate balance between local and national community.[80] Drawn into political associations by the promise of social, economic, and political advantage, Americans might also learn the art of cooperation and form attachments to government institutions. As Tocqueville put it in a nice turn of phrase,

---

[79] Jane Addams was highly critical of machine politics in Chicago; at the same time, she warned her fellow reformers that the ward bosses ruled in spite of their vices because they practiced "simple kindness" in the community day in and day out. "[I]f we discover that men of low ideals and corrupt practice are forming popular political standards simply because such men stand by and for and with the people, then nothing remains but to obtain a like sense of identification before we can modify ethical standards." Addams, "Why the Ward Boss Rules," *The Outlook*, April 2, 1898, reprinted in William L. Riordan, *Plunkitt of Tammany Hall*, ed. Terrence J. McDonald (Boston: Bedford Books, 1994), 122.

[80] See McGerr, *The Decline of Popular Politics*, especially chap. 2. McGerr argues that the promise of entertainment, no less than petty favors, drew Americans to local party organizations. Presidential campaigns, in particular, were occasions for "spectacular partisan displays" in communities that made elections highly emotional episodes. Still, McGerr insists, spectacular displays were not simply a matter of entertainment or emotional identification with a party: "[Nineteenth] century campaigns tied parades and fireworks to long expositions of issues on the stump and in the press. In a sense, the excitement of partisan display could lure men into dealing with complex issues such as slavery. Popular politics fused thought and emotion in a single style accessible to all—a rich unity of reason and passion that would be alien to Americans in the twentieth century" (p. 41).

"Public spirit in the Union is . . . only a summing up of provincial patriotism."[81]

Still, we must not allow the present discontents of the American people
to blind us to the shortcomings of the nineteenth-century polity. Certainly, there was no "golden age" of parties. Progressive reformers had good
reasons for viewing political parties and the provincial liberties they upheld as an obstacle to economic, racial, and political justice. The resurrec-
tion of the Hamiltonian nationalism that they favored, which required
weakening the political parties, yielded a stronger executive that became
the principal agent for undertaking domestic and international responsibilities that all decent commercial republics must assume. The nobility of
the modern presidency comes from, to use Woodrow Wilson's phrase, its
"extraordinary isolation," which provides great opportunity for presidents to leave their mark on the nation, even as it subjects them to a
volatile mass democracy that makes popular and enduring achievement
unlikely.[82] Examining the rise and decline of local self-government in the
United States demands that we come to terms with a legacy that yields a
more active and better-equipped national state—the national resolve to
tackle problems such as forced segregation at home and communism
abroad—but one without adequate means of common deliberation and
public judgment—the very practices that nurture a civic culture.

---

[81] Tocqueville, *Democracy in America,* 162. Although Tocqueville criticized political parties in the United States for being relatively indifferent to broad moral questions and dedicated to the personal ambitions of their members, he also suggested that they might be
considered valuable political associations, as "great free schools to which all citizens
come to be taught the general theory of association." See esp. pp. 189–95, 509–13, and
520–24.

[82] Wilson describes the "extraordinary isolation" of the president in "Constitutional Government in the United States," 114–15.

5

How many communities?

The evolution of American federalism

MARTHA DERTHICK

Everyone who knows anything about American government knows that it is federal. Asked what that means, most people say that functions are divided between one national government and many state governments. Politically sophisticated people may add that the governments are constituted independently of one another. Their respective functions are constitutionally defined and therefore cannot be altered by ordinary legislation.

This is, however, not the only (or the most interesting) way to conceive of federalism. In this chapter, I borrow an idea from the late Martin Diamond and speak of federalism as an arrangement that is chosen by people who are unable to decide whether to be one community or many. He put the point as follows:

The distinguishing characteristic of federalism is the peculiar ambivalence of the ends men seek to make it serve. The ambivalence is quite literal: Federalism is always an arrangement pointed in two contrary directions or aimed at securing two contrary ends. One end is always found in the reason why the member units do not simply consolidate themselves into one large unitary country; the other end is always found in the reason why the member units do not choose to remain simply small, wholly autonomous countries. The natural tendency of any political community, whether large or small, is to completeness, to the perfection of its autonomy. Federalism is the effort deliberately to modify that tendency. Hence any given federal structure is always the institutional expression of the contradiction or tension between the particular reasons the member units have for remain-

The author wishes to thank the White Burkett Miller Center of the University of Virginia for financial support, and Michael Lacey, Sidney Milkis, Clarence Stone, and Richard Valelly for their comments.

ing small and autonomous but not wholly, and large and consolidated but not quite.[1]

Federalism involves, then, a choice about how many communities to be, which is not merely a matter of legal arrangements, but one of the most fundamental political questions. I am assuming that "communities" take the form of "polities." Polities have institutions through which people define the objectives of their collective life, whether through deliberation—the democratic ideal—or through a struggle among power-holders, which is always in greater or lesser degree the reality. Polities make and enforce laws, raise taxes, and provide public goods and services.

I will argue that Americans chose originally—in the late eighteenth and early nineteenth centuries—to be both one great nation and many relatively quite small, local communities. Beginning with the states as a base, the core polities of their federation, Americans moved paradoxically both to centralize and to decentralize. They opted for nationalism *and* localism.

For some time, national and local political development progressed simultaneously, without serious tension (even if national development was challenging the states). Indeed, the most eminent social commentators on the United States, from Alexis de Tocqueville to David Potter, have argued that local mores helped to sustain national patriotism—in the nineteenth century, the two were mutually reinforcing.[2]

Eventually, however, tension was bound to develop. In the Progressive Era, the New Deal, and then more purposefully during the rights revolution of the 1950s and 1960s, national power was employed in such a way as to reduce the place of the local polity in American life. In pursuing the choice to be one great nation, Americans steadily abandoned their historic localism—but not without reluctance and regret.

After sketching out original choices about political communities, I will describe the strongly nationalizing effects of twentieth-century reforms, then conclude by asking where America stands today with the how-many-communities question that lies at the heart of its federalism.

---

[1] "The Ends of Federalism" in *As Far as Republican Principles Will Admit: Essays by Martin Diamond,* ed. William A. Schambra (Washington, D.C.: American Enterprise Institute, 1992), 145.

[2] Alexis de Tocqueville, *Democracy in America,* ed. J. P. Mayer (Doubleday Anchor Books, 1969); David M. Potter, "Social Cohesion and the Crisis of Law," in *American Law and the Constitutional Order: Historical Perspectives,* ed. Lawrence M. Friedman and Harry N. Scheiber (Harvard University Press, 1978), 420–34 (reprinted from *History and American Society: Essays of David M. Potter* [Oxford University Press, 1973], 390–418).

ORIGINAL CHOICES

Americans' choice to be one great nation must be one of the best-documented political decisions ever made. It is manifest principally in two events: the framing and ratification of the Constitution in 1787–89; and the Civil War, with associated constitutional amendments, in 1861–68.

There was, of course, much more to it than that. The establishment of a national judiciary through Congress's enactment of 1789 and John Marshall's three decades of leadership was crucial. Had the Supreme Court not successfully asserted its role as constitutional interpreter and its superiority to state courts, there would have been no great nation. Crucial, too, was the early establishment of the practice of a loose, expansive interpretation of the Constitution, manifested in the creation of the national bank and Marshall's sweeping, pregnant defense of it in *McCulloch v. Maryland*. Less generally recognized, but hardly less important, was the early failure of the Senate to develop as a "peripheralizing institution," in William Riker's phrase. Because state legislatures could not enforce instructions upon them, senators did not become spokesmen for the interests of state governments.[3] Neither in the Senate nor outside it were state governments per se able to concert their actions vis-à-vis the national government. When state legislatures generally declined in 1798–99 to endorse the Virginia and Kentucky resolutions, they set a pattern of inaction and non-cooperation that augured well for nation-building. Finally, one should note the prompt emergence—beginning with Washington—of the president as a heroic leader and unifying symbol, the development of the presidential election as the central political ritual of the American people, and the development of rival political parties whose prime objective was the capture of that office.

The choice for localism is quite obscure by comparison, and more diffuse in time. That it could be made at all depended on the fact that the states, though on balance losers in 1787–89, nonetheless emerged from the framing intact, with powerful claims to be vigorous polities themselves—"commonwealths," no less, some of them proclaimed. The principle on which American federalism was founded, which even leading nationalists accepted, was embodied in the Tenth Amendment: The national government had only those powers delegated to it, all else remaining with the states and the people. The states were the fundamental polities, pos-

---

[3] William Riker, "The Senate and American Federalism," *American Political Science Review* 49 (1955): 452–69.

sessing residual functions. They would presumably be the place of first resort when there was a need for domestic government. The burden of proof would rest on those who claimed jurisdiction for the national government.

But if states were in principle the core polities, they did not for long enjoy as such the confidence of the people. Constitutional revisions occurring periodically in the nineteenth and early twentieth centuries curbed the powers of their legislatures and limited the frequency and duration of legislative sessions.[4] As of the mid-1930s, only five state legislatures met annually. All of the rest met every two years except for that of Alabama, which met every four.[5] Although local governments enjoyed no legal independence—and, in the case of big cities, were frequently the object of intervention—they benefited from these restrictions and the state governments' lethargy. They became the residual domestic governments of the American federal system. "Our local areas are not *governed*" Woodrow Wilson wrote in the late nineteenth century. "They act for themselves. . . . The large freedom of action and broad scope of function given to local authorities is the distinguishing characteristic of the American system of government."[6] County and municipal debt, at $800 million in 1880, was three and a half times that of the states.[7]

Among the restrictions placed on state legislatures were some that reserved to the populace decisions about the creation and definition of units of local government. Following the lead of the Massachusetts constitutional convention of 1820, the local referendum spread to all parts of the country in connection with legislation affecting the forms, organizations, powers, and procedures of local government. It became common for state constitutions to forbid legislatures to enact measures to incorporate villages and cities, to define the boundaries of counties or divide them into townships, to locate county seats or change county names, or to alter the forms of local government without the consent of the people of the localities affected.[8] This meant that Americans were allowed to create and de-

---

[4] On the elaboration of state constitutions as "the people's law," see Herbert Croly, *Progressive Democracy* (Macmillan, 1914), chap. 12, esp. 260.

[5] William Seal Carpenter and Paul Tutt Stafford, *State and Local Government in the United States* (F. S. Crofts, 1936), 41–3.

[6] Woodrow Wilson, *The State*, rev. ed. (D. C. Heath, 1898), 501, 506. Generally on the restriction of the powers of state legislatures, see Arthur N. Holcombe, *State Government in the United States* (Macmillan, 1926), chap. 5, and Howard Lee McBain, *The Law and Practice of Municipal Home Rule* (Columbia University Press, 1916).

[7] *American Almanac and Treasury of Facts, Statistical, Financial, and Political, for the Year 1886* (The American News Company, 1886), 305.

[8] Holcombe, *State Government*, 133–4. See also Alfred Zantzinger Reed, *The Territorial Basis of Government under the State Constitutions*, Columbia University, Studies in History, Economics and Public Law, vol. 40, no. 3 (1911), 54–6.

fine their small-scale governing communities for themselves.[9] That nine-teenth-century Americans cared very much about such decisions is sug-gested, for example, by the fact that in the Midwest people fought pitched battles—sometimes resulting in loss of life—over where the county seat was to be located.[10]

Americans at the local level were also enabled to choose their own leaders. Jon C. Teaford has shown how the municipal corporation, upon being transplanted to the colonies and subjected to revolutionary influ-ences, became republican. No longer a closed, self-perpetuating body, its officers were popularly elected and served fixed terms.[11] As the nineteenth century progressed, state constitutions were amended to provide for pop-ular election of local officials where it did not already prevail. County governments in particular became more democratic as judges, sheriffs, and justices of the peace were made subject to election. At least in princi-ple, the change was significant especially in the South, where oligarchical county courts had controlled local government.[12]

Hand in hand with their becoming more democratic, counties also be-came much more numerous. The increase, between the time of the Revo-lution and the early twentieth century, was from 12 to 61 in New York, 12 to 67 in Pennsylvania, 34 to 97 in North Carolina, and 8 to 146 in Georgia. Americans had come to treat counties, even, as institutions of lo-cal self-government (and entitled as such to representation in state legisla-tures), rather than as administrative subdivisions of the state, serving the convenience of the state governments.[13]

Over time, local governments and their electorates gained more pow-er to tax—another crucial element of the formal founding of local self-government. At least in New York, early municipal charters, following the precedents of English borough charters, conferred on municipal cor-

---

[9] For contemporary observations on the significance of this fact, see Gregory R. Weiher, *The Fractured Metropolis: Political Fragmentation and Metropolitan Segregation* (State University of New York Press, 1991); Jon C. Teaford, *City and Suburb: The Political Fragmentation of Metropolitan America, 1850–1970* (Johns Hopkins University Press, 1979); Gary J. Miller, *Cities by Contract: The Politics of Incorporation* (MIT Press, 1981); and *Local Government Reform and Reorganization,* ed. Arthur B. Gunlicks (Ken-nikat Press, 1981).

[10] James A. Schellenberg, *Conflict Between Communities: American County Seat Wars* (Paragon House, 1987).

[11] *The Municipal Revolution in America* (University of Chicago Press, 1975), esp. chap. 5.

[12] Charles S. Sydnor, *The Development of Southern Sectionalism, 1819–1848* (Louisiana State University Press, 1948), chap. 12, and Fletcher M. Green, *Constitutional Develop-ment in the South Atlantic States, 1776–1860* (University of North Carolina Press, 1930, and W. W. Norton, 1966).

[13] Reed, *Territorial Basis,* 237.

porations no power of taxation. When the colonial legislature authorized the cities to levy taxes, those authorizations were at first only for limited amounts necessary for specific purposes, and the tax laws had to be reenacted from year to year. Early in the nineteenth century, however, these special laws gave way to general authorizations, and new city charters conferred on municipal corporations the authority to levy taxes.[14] Having been lodged in local governments, decisions about taxing, spending, and borrowing then became susceptible to further decentralization to local electorates. State legislatures that had been made subject to constitutional limits on taxing and borrowing sometimes reacted by prescribing referenda to check the powers of local governments.[15] Eventually, it became common for state constitutions to limit the amount of tax that could be levied by local governments without popular approval in a referendum.

Resting on such foundations, local governments became for most Americans most of the time the most important domestic governments. As the twentieth century began, they administered and overwhelmingly financed schools—as agents of socialization, the most important domestic public institutions. They predominated in the administration and finance of poor relief. They administered and overwhelmingly financed road construction. They financed and were responsible for police protection. At the opening of the twentieth century, local governments were raising more revenue and doing more spending than the federal and state governments combined. The bedrock of American domestic government was local.

To be sure, state governments retained a larger role than simple figures on revenue and expenditure might seem to indicate. Their courts created the framework of law within which American capitalism developed, family relations were structured, and the holding and transfer of real property took place. Their legislatures had promoted and subsidized economic development with measures for the construction of roads, canals, and reclamation works. They created penitentiaries, almshouses, orphan asylums, and reformatories in the early nineteenth century, in what one scholar has called "the discovery of the asylum."[16] Local governments were legally their creatures, and what local governments did was done under the authorization or command of state law. This gave local powers a contingent character. Whatever state constitutional conventions and

[14] John A. Fairlie, *The Centralization of Administration in New York State* (AMS Press, 1969; reprint of Columbia University Press edition, 1898), 186.
[15] Holcombe, *State Government*, 134.
[16] David J. Rothman, *The Discovery of the Asylum: Social Order and Disorder in the New Republic* (Little, Brown, 1971).

legislatures gave, they could withdraw. On the other hand, the states' supervision of local governments' activity was initially minimal. As late as 1890, the median size of state departments of education was two persons, including the state superintendent.[17] Moreover, even where state governments had been most active—in regard to economic development—they tended over the course of the nineteenth century to become less so.[18]

In sum, the American choice—insofar as choice was made consciously through the medium of government—was for one large political community and many small ones.

THE EROSION OF LOCALISM IN
THE PROGRESSIVE AND NEW DEAL ERAS

The bedrock of local government was deeper and firmer than the preceding discussion implies, because it was constituted of custom as well as consciously decentralizing choices. The bedrock functions—roads, poor relief, police, schools—developed at the local level originally. Before they were carried out by local governments, they were provided privately or not at all.

Although state laws mandating such functions sometimes were filled early in the nineteenth century with exhortation and command, state governments lacked organizations and practical means with which to supervise local governments and enforce instructions. Thus, Massachusetts law in the late 1820s prescribed in considerable detail the duty of towns to support schools, specifying the subjects to be taught, the number of teachers per household, the qualifications of teachers, and the moral content of their instruction (they should teach "the principles of piety, justice, and a sacred regard to truth, love to their country, humanity and universal benevolence, sobriety, industry and frugality, chastity, moderation and temperance, and those other virtues which are the ornament of human society, and the basis upon which the republican Constitution is struc-

---

[17] Michael W. Kirst, *Who Controls Our Schools? American Values in Conflict* (Stanford Alumni Association, 1984), 27.

[18] In a monograph on political development in New York between 1800 and 1860, L. Ray Gunn writes that beginning about 1840, public involvement in the economy began to contract. Mercantilist regulations disappeared from the statute books. Gunn also documents the shift of power from state to local governing institutions, arguing that delegation of authority to local governments invigorated them, county boards of supervisors especially. L. Ray Gunn, *The Decline of Authority: Public Economic Policy and Political Development in New York State, 1800–1860* (Cornell University Press, 1988), 1, 199–200.

tured"). Towns were obliged to create school committees, which were enjoined to visit the schools and to report to the secretary of the commonwealth how many schools they maintained and what they spent. He was to furnish them with a blank form on which to report these returns.[19] That appears to have been the extent of state supervision.

As urbanization progressed later in the century, the states of the Northeast—Massachusetts and New York especially—began creating agencies with powers at least of information-gathering and advice, and sometimes more formal oversight. The professions were beginning to develop and find a toehold in state governments. The new agencies took the form of individual offices or multimember boards of varying sizes—state commissioners or superintendents of instruction, boards of charities, boards of public health, and so forth. States to the west then followed the lead of Massachusetts and New York.[20]

One turn-of-the century sign of the states' growing role was a change in spending ratios. Whereas local governments spent 14 times as much on education as the states did in 1902 and 43 times as much on roads, by 1913 these ratios had fallen to 9 to 1 and 15 to 1, respectively. State-level centralization proceeded, however, in halting fashion, affecting states and functions unevenly and not very deeply. State-level administrative centralization became penetrating and widespread only when national action caused it to.

In intergovernmental relations, national action in the Progressive and New Deal periods took the form principally of grants-in-aid with conditions attached. The conditions suited both the administrative convenience of the federal government and the ideology of Progressive reform, one strand of which was marked by the pursuit of efficiency and expertise. Two bedrock functions in particular were affected: roads, for which federal aid began in 1916, following the introduction of the automobile, and poor relief, for which federal aid was enacted in 1935 in response to the Great Depression.

---

[19] *Town Officer: Or, Laws of Massachusetts Relative to the Duties of Municipal Officers,* 2d ed. (Dorr and Howland, 1829), 177–85.

[20] This development is documented in a series of studies done at Columbia University at the turn of the century: Fairlie, *Centralization;* Robert H. Whitten, *Public Administration in Massachusetts: The Relation of Central to Local Activity* (1898); Samuel P. Orth, *The Centralization of Administration in Ohio* (1903); Harold Martin Bowman, *The Administration of Iowa: A Study in Centralization* (1903); and William A. Rawles, *Centralizing Tendencies in the Administration of Indiana* (1903). All appeared in the series Studies in History, Economics and Public Law, edited by the political science faculty at Columbia, and were reprinted by AMS Press (New York) in 1968 and 1969.

Grant-in-aid conditions were above all delocalizing—quite deliberately so. The county, one eminent professional social worker declared, was the "dark continent" of American public administration.[21] State governments were to be prodded and helped in a modernizing, civilizing mission. They were required to match federal grants with state funds, to secure statewide uniformity in program operations, to create agencies that would be responsible to the federal administration for meeting statewide standards, and to create merit systems of personnel administration.

When federal highway aid began in 1916, sixteen states had "no highway department worthy of the name."[22] Federal law did not initially require the creation of state highway departments, but within five years it was amended to do so. The U.S. Bureau of Public Roads suspended grants to Arkansas in 1923, Kansas in 1925, and Maine in 1929 "until the personnel of the State Highway Department . . . shall be so changed that this [agency] can have . . . confidence in the organization as a whole."[23] By 1922, the ratio of local-to-state spending for roads had dropped to 3 to 1, a change in nine years so precipitous that it must be attributable in substantial measure to the introduction of federal aid. The growth of state authority continued thereafter. In 1962, a student of highway policy succinctly summarized the change:

> In 1920 the local units of government occupied a dominant position in the overall highway picture. Approximately 70 per cent of all road work was undertaken by the political subdivisions of the states. Today over three quarters of the highway funds are channeled through state authorities. In short, the roles of the two levels of government in highway affairs have been reversed.[24]

Similarly, when federal grants for public assistance were enacted in 1935, local responsibility for that function was still entrenched. Although most states had enacted laws for aid to widowed mothers and the aged, these were not necessarily backed with state funds, and they were not always mandatory for local governments. Only half of the counties in the country that were authorized to give mothers' aid were actually doing so as of 1934. In only ten states were old-age assistance laws in effect

---

[21] Cited in Martha Derthick, *The Influence of Federal Grants: Public Assistance in Massachusetts* (Harvard University Press, 1970), 20.

[22] Philip H. Burch, Jr., *Highway Revenue and Expenditure Policy in the United States* (Rutgers University Press, 1962), 213.

[23] Jane Perry Clark, *The Rise of a New Federalism* (Columbia University Press, 1938), 193, 203.

[24] Burch, *Highway Revenue*, 81.

statewide. Administrative structures were likewise varied and haphazard, for state welfare agencies had developed unevenly. Responsibility for administration rested predominantly at the county level, with boards of commissioners or judges. Only twelve states had set up county welfare agencies.[25]

The Social Security Act required state financial participation and mandatory statewide operation, which the Social Security Board, as the federal administering agency, chose to interpret as a requirement for statewide *uniformity*. Beginning in 1946, the board successfully pressured states to establish statewide standards of need and assistance, so that benefits would no longer vary among local places.[26] The ratio of local-to-state spending for assistance—5 to 1 in 1932—dropped to 1.3 to 1 in 1942. By 1952, state spending surpassed local spending.

The federal requirement that a single state agency administer assistance or supervise administration of it contributed to the formation and strengthening of state welfare departments. Federal law also fostered the professionalization of welfare agencies after amendments to the Social Security Act in 1939 authorized the Social Security Board to require the establishment of merit systems. As attachments of welfare workers to a profession grew with federal encouragement, attachments to place weakened; professionalization meant delocalization.

Although merit-system requirements did not extend to all federally aided agencies, a companion measure—the prohibition of partisan activity by state and local employees—did. This was enacted in 1940 as an amendment to the Hatch Act, and upheld by the Supreme Court in *Oklahoma v. Civil Service Commission* (1947)—a case involving the federal government's decision to withhold highway grant funds in order to secure removal of a state highway commissioner who was also chairman of the state Democratic party. Breaking the ties of state and local employees to state and local parties was crucial to the twentieth-century project of rationalizing state and local administrative structures and making them responsive to national leadership.[27]

Scholarship on the New Deal has generally stressed the extent to which

---

[25] *Social Security in America* (Social Security Board, 1937), chaps. 8, 13, 14, and 19.

[26] Derthick, *Federal Grants,* 72–3.

[27] For a detailed account of the federal effort in one state's welfare program, see Derthick, *Federal Grants,* esp. chaps. 5 and 7. For a summary of the federal impact on state and local personnel systems generally, see Albert H. Aronson, "State and Local Personnel Administration," in U.S. Civil Service Commission, *Biography of an Ideal: A History of the Federal Civil Service* (U.S. Government Printing Office, 1974), 127–59. When the Social Security Act was passed, only nine states had civil service systems. Federal requirements

it honored the traditional prerogatives of the states, accommodating the institutions of American federalism.[28] It is true that few purely national agencies were created; those that *were* often found that the price of acceptance—if not survival—was to make adjustments at the grass roots. However, this interpretation overlooks the recasting that federal action achieved in state-local relations. Eroding slowly and steadily in any case, the bedrock of localism did so much faster when federal grant programs were brought to bear.

Still, as the New Deal came to an end with World War II, much of the bedrock had barely been affected. Nothing that occurred before mid-century diminished the localism of police departments or, crucially, of schools. Neither function had been the beneficiary (or victim) of federal aid. The ratio of local-to-state spending for education, though tending to fall throughout the century, was 5 to 1 in 1942, at a time when state spending on roads had passed local spending. In one important respect, the bedrock had actually been strengthened. As urbanization progressed, state legislatures authorized zoning and land-use regulation by local governments. These functions had considerable potential for defining the socioeconomic character of the local place, and thereby shaping community identities.

THE RIGHTS REVOLUTION: THE ASSAULT ON LOCALISM

In the first half of the twentieth century, the national government's direct challenge to localism had been relatively confined. It concentrated on administrative structures in functions where grants-in-aid gave the federal government an entree and a stake. Also, it was spearheaded by professional administrators, and though they benefited from the strength of centralizing coalitions in regard to road construction and poor relief, their independent power was modest. Congress did not always give them the statutory authority they sought for state-level reforms.

The rights revolution brought an attack of greater scope, depth, and legitimacy, officially led as it was by the nation's highest court. It also had far greater mobilizing power. As political goals, efficiency and expertise did not excite large numbers of people. Equality excited many more. Besides, egalitarianism is the greater enemy of federalism. It exalts the au-

and advice contributed to their extension within and among the states. *Oklahoma v. Civil Service Commission* appears at 330 U.S. 127.
[28] For example, Philip Selznick, *TVA and the Grass Roots: A Study in the Sociology of Formal Organizations* (Harper & Row, 1966).

tonomous individual, whereas federalism, in honoring communities, implies acceptance of distinctions among and even within them. When the
Warren Court met the bedrock of localism, an epic contest occurred.

I will focus on the Warren Court for economy's sake, recognizing nevertheless that the modern rights revolution depended critically on constitutional and statutory foundations laid in the wake of the Civil War; that
it had a morally potent social basis in the protest activity of African-
Americans; that even conceived of as the work of the national government, it was not the work of the Supreme Court alone, but was in due
course embraced by Congress; and that even as the work of the judiciary,
it did not begin with Warren. The Court's project of incorporating Bill of
Rights guarantees into the Fourteenth Amendment dates at least to *Wolf
v. Colorado* (1949) in regard to criminal procedures and to *Gitlow v.
New York* (1925) in regard to speech. As of the Warren Era, however, the
Court was very much in the lead, and it acted with a consciousness of the
consequences for federalism.

Without articulating a philosophy of federalism, the Court nonetheless
had a consistent attitude—born, apparently, of its struggle to achieve
Southern school desegregation. It did not trust state and local governments. John Marshall Harlan, a sitting justice who dissented from some
of the Court's leading decisions, detected a "fundamental shift" in its approach to federal-state relationships as compared with its predecessors.
"This shift," he wrote, "must be recognized as involving something more
than mere differences among judges as to where the line should be drawn
between state and federal authority in particular cases arising under the
Fourteenth Amendment. It reflects, I believe, at bottom a distrust in the
capabilities of the federal system to meet the needs of American society."[29]

The most fundamental of the Court's challenges to localism were its
reapportionment decisions. These were the decisions of which Warren
himself was most proud, and the Court's critics most critical. "There is no
better example of the Court's egalitarianism," Robert Bork observed, and
"its disregard for the Constitution in whose name it spoke than the legislative reapportionment cases."[30]

The challenge to localism was twofold. It lay in the Court's rejection of
the local polity as an entity meriting representation in the state legislature,

[29] *Mr. Justice Jackson: Four Lectures in His Honor* (Columbia University Press, 1969), 60.
[30] Robert Bork, *The Tempting of America: The Political Seduction of the Law* (Free Press, 1990), 84. On Warren's estimate of the importance of reapportionment, see Archibald Cox, *The Court and the Constitution* (Houghton Mifflin, 1987), 290.

and secondly in its indifference to claims that the people of the states were entitled to devise their own representative arrangements. The Court laid down a doctrinaire rule—one person, one (equally weighted) vote—for which there was no warrant in custom or the Constitution. As Justice Potter Stewart wrote, citing Justice Felix Frankfurter before him, this "was not the colonial system, it was not the system chosen for the national government by the Constitution, it was not the system exclusively or even predominantly practiced by the States at the time of adoption of the Fourteenth Amendment, it is not predominantly practiced by the States today."

The upper houses of state legislatures, analogous to the U.S. Senate, had typically represented units of local government—usually counties—even though this sacrificed strict proportionality to population. In *Reynolds v. Sims,* the Court rejected the federal analogy as "inapposite and irrelevant" because the national choice had been a political compromise (as if that made it illegitimate!) and because counties, cities, and other local subdivisions, unlike the states, had never had any claim to be sovereign entities. In a companion case, *Lucas v. Forty-Fourth General Assembly,* the Court majority struck down a Colorado apportionment that had been approved by the state's voters in a referendum, including majorities in every political subdivision. Colorado's voters had rejected a plan to apportion both legislative houses on the basis of population. The Court ruled that they had no right to depart from its prescribed standard.

It was not just what the Court did in these cases, but the grounds on which it chose to do it, that showed disdain for federalism and locality. Even some of the Court's critics concede that malapportionment was severe enough in some states to warrant a federal judicial remedy. But whereas the Court grounded its holding on the equal-protection clause—equal numbers of persons must have an equal number of legislative representatives—it might have supplied a remedy (and honored federalism nonetheless) by relying instead on the clause that guarantees each state a republican form of government. This dead letter, ignored since the mid-nineteenth century, might have been given life and logically applied to cases in which the state legislatures' failure to enact reapportionments violated their own state constitutions and thwarted government by majorities.[31] Such an approach would have been less likely to culminate in the

---

[31] This argument is made by Bork, *The Tempting of America,* 85–6.

Court's prescribing a "sixth-grade arithmetic" rule as a straitjacket on the states.[32]

In the wake of the reapportionment decisions, social entities defined by space—local communities—are often sacrificed. Legislative districting has been turned into an arcane exercise for computers, consultants, and constitutional lawyers, along with the usual array of incumbents trying to save their seats or party politicians trying to protect or gain majorities. District lines now cut arbitrarily through local places that once would have been respected as such and represented intact.

The Warren Court's other leading decisions came in those areas of local government activity—police, schools—that had earlier been least subject to nationalizing influences. One of the Court's great projects was the reform of state criminal law, which entailed the steady incorporation of Bill of Rights guarantees into the Fourteenth Amendment. Another, even more deeply challenging to local mores, was school desegregation.

Among the many decisions on criminal law, the most important for local government was *Miranda v. Arizona,* which spelled out "a fairly complete code of behavior" for local police to follow when they were interrogating suspects. The Court ruled that the prosecution could not use as evidence in a criminal case a statement resulting from police interrogation of a person in custody unless he had been warned of his right not to be questioned, of the danger that any statement might be used against him, and of his right to have a lawyer present—either his own choice or one appointed at public expense. Moreover, these rights, even though waived initially, could be invoked at any time.[33]

The relatively obscure but profoundly important case of *Monroe v. Pape* (1960) also arose out of police conduct, although it had much broader ramifications. By expanding the use of one long-standing provision of federal civil rights law, *Monroe v. Pape* transformed the relations of the federal judiciary with state and local governments. Since 1871, the law had authorized suits against persons acting "under color of state law" who deprived anyone of a right secured by the U.S. Constitution or laws. In *Monroe,* the Court held that this law—section 1983 of Title 42 of

---

[32] The phrase was used by Justices Clark and Stewart in dissent in the *Lucas* (Colorado) case, objecting to the majority's "uncritical, simplistic, and heavy-handed application of sixth-grade arithmetic."

[33] David Fellman, "The Nationalization of American Civil Liberties," in *Essays on the Constitution of the United States,* ed. M. Judd Harmon (Kennikat Press, 1978), 56; Archibald Cox, *The Warren Court: Constitutional Decision as an Instrument of Reform* (Harvard University Press, 1968), 84.

the U.S. Code—would apply even though there had been no showing that the offending activities had been authorized or encouraged by state law. The Court further held that the federal constitutional remedy was immediately available as a front-line remedy; it was not a backstop available only after efforts to get a remedy in state courts had been exhausted. The plaintiff could begin by coming into a federal court and claiming a constitutional violation.

Previously, the relation between citizens and state and local governments had been governed by the large body of state tort law, administrative law, and criminal law. These rules were now superseded by federal constitutional rules, and federal courts were turned into supervisors of the whole of state and local government conduct. Thousands of cases began to be filed annually under section 1983.[34]

In regard to schools, the Court laid down its constitutional principle in *Brown v. Board of Education* in 1954—"separate educational facilities are inherently unequal"—and then, in a rare burst of practicality, acknowledged a year later in *Brown II* that full implementation "may require solution of varied local school problems." School authorities had primary responsibility for solving these problems. Courts would have to consider whether their implementation was sufficient. Because of "their proximity to local conditions," district courts would bear this burden primarily. The Supreme Court said that in fashioning their decrees, lower courts should be guided by the principles of equity—a specialized legal term meaning that they would have a great deal of freedom. The lower courts might consider "problems related to administration, arising from the physical condition of the school plant, the school transportation system, personnel, revision of school districts and attendance areas . . . and revision of local laws and regulations which may be necessary in solving the foregoing problems."[35]

There followed an extraordinary chapter in the nation's experience, as federal district courts struggled to realize racial integration. Faced with prolonged and inventive Southern resistance, federal courts ultimately endorsed drastically intrusive remedies. The key case was *Swann v. Charlotte-Mecklenburg Board of Education* (1971), in which the Supreme

---

[34] On the uses of Section 1983, see Paul M. Bator, "Some Thoughts on Applied Federalism," *Harvard Journal of Law and Public Policy* 6 (1982): 51–9; Daan Braveman, *Protecting Constitutional Freedoms: A Role for the Federal Courts* (Greenwood Press, 1989); and "Section 1983 and Federalism," *Harvard Law Review* 1133 (1977). *Monroe v. Pape* is at 365 U.S. 167 (1960).

[35] 347 U.S. 483 and 349 U.S. 294.

Court approved a plan for the massive busing of students as well as a system of attendance zones marked by "frank—and sometimes drastic—gerrymandering." The Court observed that the remedy for segregation may be "administratively awkward, inconvenient and even bizarre in some situations . . . but all awkwardness and inconvenience cannot be avoided."[36]

Each city in which desegregation suits were filed produced its own story. Federal district judges on the front lines of the federal system took charge of local schools and sought to reconcile national ideals with local realities, sometimes at considerable risk to their safety. Charlotte, North Carolina, where busing got its start, made a success of it.[37] In Boston, busing was a disaster, breeding neighborhood violence and white flight.[38] A study of school desegregation for the period 1968–80 found that as of 1980, the eleven states of the South had the lowest level of segregation of any region.[39] Southern schools had been reconstructed.

The Supreme Court gave leadership to the nation in this effort, and inspiration to the civil rights movement, but ultimately it needed the kind of help that only Congress could give. The Civil Rights Act of 1964 prohibited racial discrimination in the administration of federal grants-in-aid, and the Elementary and Secondary Education Act of 1965 authorized federal grants to elementary and secondary schools, giving the federal government enormous leverage over Southern schools. They badly needed the federal money, and stood to get a large part of it because it was designated for poor children. When the combined authority of all three branches of the federal government was brought to bear against the South after 1964, progress toward desegregation came swiftly.[40]

One subsequent instance of collaboration between Congress and the Warren Court needs to be noted. Like reapportionment, voting rights

[36] 402 U.S. 1.
[37] Arthur S. Hayes, "As Others Scale Back on School Integration, Charlotte Presses On," *Wall Street Journal*, May 8, 1991, A1; Davison M. Douglas, *Reading, Writing, and Race: The Desegregation of the Charlotte Schools* (University of North Carolina Press, 1995).
[38] J. Anthony Lukas, *Common Ground* (Vintage Books, 1986); Ronald P. Formisano, *Boston Against Busing: Race, Class and Ethnicity in the 1960s and 1970s* (University of North Carolina Press, 1991). For an excellent general account of the effort at school desegregation, see David J. Armor, *Forced Justice: School Desegregation and the Law* (Oxford University Press, 1995).
[39] Gary Orfield, *Public School Desegregation in the United States, 1968–1980* (Joint Center for Political Studies, 1983).
[40] For an excellent account, see Gary Orfield, *The Reconstruction of Southern Education: The Schools and the 1964 Civil Rights Act* (Wiley-Interscience, 1969).

produced a challenge to localism that was arguably more fundamental than that of school desegregation.

School desegregation got more publicity than any other action of the court, and it affected the daily lives of ordinary people more deeply. The spectacle of federal judges deciding the most mundane details of local school administration, as in Boston, while ethnic neighborhoods turned into battle zones caused even the most ardent liberals to ponder whether the power of national judges was being appropriately employed.[41] Precisely because it addressed social structure, school desegregation would ultimately expose the limits of judicial power. It would be settled by the people themselves. They would achieve racial harmony or not, live and go to school where they could and would. Federal judges would not dictate such choices for them.

Far different was the policy issue that arose from the Voting Rights Act of 1965. As interpreted by the Supreme Court and administered by the Department of Justice, this legislation, like reapportionment decisions, addressed who and what was to be represented in American legislatures, and who was to have power to define the spatial boundaries and governmental structures of local communities. It led to unprecedented measures of national intrusion.

Two parts of the act have had potent implications for localism.

The first is section 5, which prohibits the implementation of any changes affecting voting in certain state and local (mainly Southern) jurisdictions without the approval of the attorney general or a special three-judge federal district court in the District of Columbia. The Supreme Court construed this provision to extend far beyond mere changes in laws affecting the acts of voting or running for office. Consequently, proposed annexations, redistricting plans, shifts from district to at-large representation, and changes in the location of polling places must be precleared. From 1965 to 1991, the Department of Justice reviewed 188,048 changes and objected to more than 2,000 of them.[42]

The second significant part is section 2, as amended in 1982. It prohibits electoral practices resulting in "less opportunity [for minority citizens] . . . to participate in the political process and to elect representatives

---

[41] Lukas, *Common Ground*, chap. 29.
[42] Drew S. Days III, "Section 5 and the Role of the Justice Department" and Timothy G. O'Rourke, "The 1982 Amendments and the Voting Rights Paradox," in *Controversies in Minority Voting: The Voting Rights Act in Perspective*, ed. Bernard Grofman and Chandler Davidson (Brookings Institution, 1992), 53–4 and 86–7.

of their choice." It has elicited approximately 225 lawsuits per year attacking local representative structures. Both in response to such suits and in anticipation of them, there has been a widespread shift at the local level from at-large to district representation for county, city, and town councils and school boards.[43] Whereas the Voting Rights Act originally targeted the seven states of the Old Confederacy for the purpose of enfranchising Southern blacks, it is now being used to secure proportional representation for racial and linguistic minorities across the country. To achieve this, local electoral arrangements are made to yield to national decision.

THE AFTERMATH: THE STATES AS "WINNERS" IN THE NATIONAL-LOCAL CLASH

The Warren Court made deep inroads on localism, but if local government was changed in the course of this conflict, so was the Court. The election in 1969 of Richard Nixon, who ran for the presidency in part by running against the Court, brought a change in its composition. Warren Burger replaced Earl Warren as chief justice in 1969. Of greater long-run importance for federalism, William H. Rehnquist and Lewis F. Powell were named in 1972. Powell was a former chairman of the Richmond school board, and Rehnquist had been active in Arizona politics. Both were judicial conservatives with ingrained respect for local custom. The reconstituted Court recoiled from the recasting of local institutions.[44]

As one sign of this change, the Court moderated its position on state legislative reapportionment to acknowledge the legitimacy of representation for local communities. In *Mahan v. Howell* (1973), it held a 16.4 percent deviation from population equality in the lower house of the Virginia legislature to be justified by "the State's policy of maintaining the integrity of political subdivision lines." And, in *Brown v. Thomson* (1983), it upheld an apportionment plan of Wyoming's House of Representatives that allowed an average deviation of 16 percent and a maximum deviation of 89 percent, noting that "Wyoming's constitutional policy—followed since statehood—of using counties as representative districts and

[43] O'Rourke, "1982 Amendments," 88–9, and Laughlin McDonald, "The 1982 Amendments of Section 2 and Minority Representation," in Grofman and Davidson, *Controversies*, 66–74.
[44] On Rehnquist's commitment to federalism, see Sue Davis, *Justice Rehnquist and the Constitution* (Princeton University Press, 1989).

ensuring that each county has one representative is supported by substantial and legitimate state concerns."[45]

More telling signs came in cases dealing with school finance (*San Antonio v. Rodriguez*, 1973), school desegregation (*Milliken v. Bradley*, 1974), and exclusionary zoning (*Warth v. Seldin*, 1975). In each of these, the more conservative Court confronted the bedrock of localism and drew back.

In the school-finance case, Demetrio Rodriguez and others had brought a class action on behalf of schoolchildren who were members of poor families residing in school districts with low property-tax bases. They claimed that the Texas system's reliance on local property taxation favored the more affluent; further, they said, the Texas system violated equal-protection requirements because of substantial interdistrict disparities in per-pupil expenditures, which resulted primarily from differences in the value of assessable property. Texas had a state-funded program designed to provide a basic minimum education in every school, but it did not eliminate interdistrict disparities in expenditures nor compensate fully for disparities in assessable property.[46]

Justice Powell, writing for a five-justice majority, rejected the attempt of the plaintiffs to apply equal-protection analysis to the case, and deferred to state and local governments with a statement of judicial modesty in stark contrast to the posture and rhetoric of the Warren Court:

We find this a particularly inappropriate case in which to subject state action to strict judicial scrutiny. The present case . . . involves the most persistent and difficult questions of educational policy, [an] area in which this Court's lack of specialized knowledge and experience counsels against premature interference with the informed judgments made at the state and local levels.

After noting the uncertainty of scholars about the effect of expenditures on pupil achievement and also the unsettled condition of state-local relations in education, Powell continued:

The ultimate wisdom as to these and related problems of education is not likely to be defined for all time even by the scholars who now so earnestly debate the issues. In such circumstances the judiciary is well advised to refrain from interposing on the States inflexible constitutional restraints that could circumscribe or handicap the continued research and experimentation so vital to finding even partial solutions to educational problems and to keeping abreast of ever changing conditions.

[45] 410 U.S. 315 and 462 U.S. 835.   [46] 411 U.S. 1.

The Texas plan of school finance, Powell found, was not the result of "hurried, ill-conceived legislation," nor did it purposefully discriminate against any group or class.

In its essential characteristics the Texas plan for financing public education reflects what many educators for a half century have thought was an enlightened approach to a problem for which there is no perfect solution. We are unwilling to assume for ourselves a level of wisdom superior to that of legislators, scholars, and educational authorities in 49 States, especially where the alternatives proposed are only recently conceived and nowhere tested.

In *Milliken v. Bradley,* one sees the same reluctance to disrupt the long-standing arrangements of local government, and an even more explicit statement in their defense.

The crucial issue in this case was whether a federal court could order a multidistrict, metropolitan area-wide remedy for central-city school segregation. A district court, besides ordering the Detroit school board to formulate a desegregation plan for the city, had ordered state officials to submit desegregation plans encompassing the three-county metropolitan area, despite the fact that the eighty-five school districts in these three counties were not parties to the suit—nor was there any claim that they had committed constitutional violations. The district judge, contending that "school districts are simply matters of political convenience and may not be used to deny constitutional rights," appointed a panel to submit a desegregation plan including fifty-three of the eighty-five suburban school districts plus Detroit. He had also ordered the Detroit school board to acquire at least 295 buses for the purpose of transporting students to and from outlying districts. (The decision in *Swann* had endorsed massive busing, but all the busing occurred within a single school district.)

The Supreme Court invalidated this plan. Burger, like Powell before him in the *Rodriguez* case, wrote for a five-justice majority. Boundary lines might be bridged, he said, where there had been a constitutional violation calling for interdistrict relief, but:

the notion that school district lines may be casually ignored or treated as a mere administrative convenience is contrary to the history of public education in our country. No single tradition in public education is more deeply rooted than local control over the operation of schools; local autonomy has long been thought essential both to the maintenance of community concern and support for public schools and to the quality of the educational process.

Noting that the plan would in effect consolidate fifty-four districts into a vast new super-district, the opinion asked rhetorically what would happen as a result—to the status and authority of popularly elected school boards, to financing arrangements, and so forth. Perhaps such operational questions would be resolved by the district court, but the Supreme Court majority rejected that idea:

It is obvious from the scope of the inter-district remedy itself that absent a complete restructuring of the laws of Michigan relating to school districts the District Court will become first, a *de facto* "legislative authority" to resolve these complex questions, and then the "school superintendent" for the entire area. This is a task which few, if any, judges are qualified to perform and one which would deprive the people of control of schools through their elected representatives.[47]

In *Warth v. Seldin,* individuals and organizations in Rochester had sued the adjacent town of Penfield and members of its zoning, planning, and town boards, claiming that Penfield's zoning ordinance excluded low- and moderate-income persons—a violation of federal constitutional and statutory rights.

Powell, writing again for a five-justice majority, denied standing. While most of the opinion deals with that issue, there is more than a hint of the new majority's reluctance yet again to supplant state and local governments and to tamper with the established institutions of localism. Without standing requirements, Powell wrote, "the courts would be called upon to decide abstract questions of wide public significance even though other governmental institutions may be more competent to address the questions." And, in a footnote, he added: "We also note that zoning laws and their provisions, long considered essential to effective urban planning, are peculiarly within the province of state and local legislative authorities. . . . Citizens dissatisfied with provisions of such laws need not overlook the availability of the normal democratic process."[48]

The result of the Supreme Court's newfound restraint was not, however, that the issues presented in these cases languished. Rather, they were deflected to state governments, most particularly courts, some of which seized them with a will that had presumably been fed by the Warren Court's example. All across the country, state supreme courts have acted

---

[47] 418 U.S. 717. For a scholarly account of the Detroit case, see Eleanor P. Wolf, *Trial and Error: The Detroit School Segregation Case* (Wayne State University Press, 1981).
[48] *Constitutional Law,* 11th ed., ed. Gerald Gunther (Foundation Press, 1985), 1559–64.

on suits for equalization or adequacy of school finance, while a smaller number have attacked exclusionary zoning and considered interdistrict remedies for racial imbalance in the schools. As of 1994, education-finance systems had been overturned by courts in more than a dozen states, including California and Texas.[49] In California, which pioneered this movement, statewide equalization of per-pupil spending has been achieved. On exclusionary zoning, Pennsylvania's supreme court was the first to act, with a relatively cautious ruling in the late 1970s.[50] New Jersey's supreme court has gone furthest, with two rulings (1975 and 1983) in *Southern Burlington County NAACP v. Township of Mount Laurel.* The second, coming after the first had brought no response from the state legislature or local governments, imposed numerical fair shares of low-income housing on local places. In response, the state legislature passed the Fair Housing Act of 1985, which incorporated much of the judicial decree in statutory form. Zoning has ceased to be a local function in New Jersey.[51]

Seeking to build on the success of state-level constitutional cases in school finance, the National Association for the Advancement of Colored People in 1989 brought suit in a Connecticut court to compel racial de-segregation of public schools in the city of Hartford and its suburban districts. A similar suit also developed in New Jersey.[52] In 1996, the Connecticut Supreme Court ruled in *Sheff v. O'Neill* that racial segregation in Hartford's schools violated the state constitution; the court called on the

---

[49] Kenneth K. Wong, "State Reform in Education Finance: Territorial and Social Strategies," *Publius* (Summer 1991): 125, contains a summary of action up to that point. For an analysis of the litigation strategies employed, see William E. Thro, "Judicial Analysis During the Third Wave of School Finance Litigation: The Massachusetts Decision as a Model," *Boston College Law Review* 35 (May 1994): 597–617.

[50] Peter J. Galie, "Social Services and Egalitarian Activism," in *Human Rights in the States: New Directions in Constitutional Policymaking,* ed. Stanley H. Friedelbaum (Greenwood Press, 1988), 108–9. The initial decision came in 1977. In a subsequent case (*Fernley v. Board of Supervisors,* 1985), the court struck down an exclusionary ordinance with a finding that any ordinance that totally excludes a legitimate use will be regarded with "circumspection, and therefore, must bear a substantial relationship to a stated public purpose."

[51] Galie, "Social Services," 109–10. See also Richard F. Babcock and Charles L. Siemon, *The Zoning Game Revisited* (Lincoln Institute of Land Policy, 1985), 207–33, for a case study, "*Mount Laurel II:* Après Nous le Déluge."

[52] Armor, *Forced Justice,* 3, 60–61, 83; Elizabeth P. McCaughey, "Can Courts Order School Integration Across Town Lines?" *Wall Street Journal,* October 28, 1992, A19. In July 1996, Connecticut's supreme court ruled 4 to 3 that segregation of black children in central-city schools, even if not enforced by law, violated the state constitution. "Hartford Court Bars Imbalance in the Schools," *New York Times,* July 10, 1996, A1.

state legislature to remedy the racial discrepancy between central-city and suburban schools.[53]

All of this action (and much more) has led numerous scholars to re-mark on the revival of state constitutional law, which is just one manifes-tation of the post-1960s renaissance of state governments in general.[54] At the heart of this renaissance is expansion of the states' role in education. Schools—the most durably local of the bedrock institutions—were very much changed by centralizing forces in the 1970s.

State spending for schools began to exceed local spending in the mid-1970s and continued to gain thereafter.[55] Federal aid, introduced on a large scale in the mid-1960s, may have given impetus to the change, but that is less clear in the case of education than it was for welfare and high-ways several decades earlier. If centralizing influences emanated from the national government above, some also rose from below, in the form of re-sistance from local property taxpayers to bearing the rising costs of edu-cation. Possibly the two forces were linked. Per-pupil spending more than doubled between 1960 and 1980, responding in part to national man-dates such as that to provide a "free and appropriate education for all handicapped children." Taxpayer resistance to school-spending measures rose in the late 1970s, and the passage of Proposition 13 in California in 1978 marked the start of a multistate property taxpayers' revolt. As states assumed a larger share of school costs, they did so with revenues from other sources: income and sales taxes.

Federal grants-in-aid and the rights revolution reached local schools as companions, so the effects of the two are hard to sort out. Grants to schools in the 1960s and 1970s, designated for the poor and the handi-capped, were driven by the aim of substantive equality, and placed less emphasis on centralizing the state-and-local administrative structure than was true earlier in the century. Indeed, showing the liberals' want of con-fidence in state governments at this time, one title of the Elementary and Secondary Education Act of 1965 created a grant program administered directly to local districts for the development of "supplemental educa-

---

[53] "Hartford Court Bars Imbalance in the Schools," *New York Times*, July 10, 1996, A1, B6.

[54] See, among many sources, G. Alan Tarr and Mary Cornelia Aldis Porter, *State Supreme Courts in State and Nation* (Yale University Press, 1988), and *State Constitutional Law: Cases and Materials* (Advisory Commission on Intergovernmental Relations, 1988).

[55] Kenneth K. Wong, "Fiscal Support for Education in American States: The 'Parity-to-Dominance' View Examined," *American Journal of Education* (August 1989): 329–57.

tional centers." These were conceived of in Washington as a means to outflank the state educational agencies, which were presumed to be stagnant and conservative.[56]

Nevertheless, the introduction of federal aid did a great deal to change state education agencies. If they stagnated after 1965, it was not for lack of federal money. The act of that year and its subsequent amendments required them to approve local projects requesting federal funds for educational innovation and education for disadvantaged, handicapped, bilingual, and migrant children. One percent of the money in such programs was earmarked for state administration. Also, one title of the 1965 act provided general support for state education agencies, giving priority to planning and evaluation. From these sources, state agencies underwent a sizable expansion between 1964 and 1970. As of 1972, three-fourths of the staff members in such agencies had been in their jobs for less than three years. Seventy percent of the funding for the Texas agency, for example, was coming from the federal government.[57]

Federal court decisions in many areas—not just racial segregation, but also education for the handicapped, bilingual education, and due-process guarantees for individual students and teachers—elaborated statutes and the Constitution so as to weave an intricate web of restriction around the daily conduct of local administrators. Michael Kirst has captured the change, writing from experience as president of California's board of education as well as a professor of education. There had been a time—he called it a "golden era" from 1920 to 1950—when the local superintendent could set an agenda and shape decisions. No more: "Now, the local superintendent and administrative staff have become mostly reactive, as they try to juggle diverse and changing coalitions formed around different issues and operating across different levels of government." No longer can students be expelled without due process, meaning lengthy hearings with carefully defined procedures.[58]

Grants-in-aid were just one means of national influence, and they did not grow very much, in contrast with the earlier pattern of federal spending for welfare and highways. Federal aid reached 10 percent of school spending in 1970 but began to fall in the early 1980s and stood at less than 7 percent in 1987. (Federal aid for law enforcement, which had been

---

[56] Hugh Davis Graham, *The Uncertain Triumph: Federal Education Policy in the Kennedy and Johnson Years* (University of North Carolina Press, 1984), 153–5. I am indebted to Andrew Busch for calling my attention to this point.

[57] Kirst, *Who Controls Our Schools?* 98–9.   [58] Ibid., 11–12, 38.

enacted in the mid-1960s more or less simultaneously with the break-through on schools, temporarily collapsed altogether in the early 1980s.)[59] Ironically, in regard to schools, federal *retrenchment* may eventually have increased pressure on the states to spend, coming as it did after federal action had fostered organization and heightened expectations among a number of constituencies—the beneficiaries of federal mandates.

Despite two centuries of national development, states remain the central polities of the United States in form. Under some conditions and for some functions, form becomes fact. The states are the "default setting" of the American federal system. To the extent that other levels of government lack the resources to act—authority, revenue, willpower, political consensus, institutional capacity—the states have the job. Although there are today no important barriers in constitutional doctrine to Congress's doing whatever it wants vis-à-vis the states—and taking from them whatever functions it wants to take—political will, purpose, revenue, and a practical policy choice are often lacking. Similarly, there are limits on what the Supreme Court is willing to decree at the states' expense—limits set not just by precedents and members' beliefs about what constitutes wise policy, but also by their estimate of a national court's capacity to govern a very large, diverse, and divided country. The states retain a vitality born of the limits of national institutions' capacity—limits that the Warren Court's clash with the bedrock of localism helped to reveal. The national government did not seize control of the schools, nor did local governments maintain control of them. Neither possessed the resources that would have been required to do so. The states, possessors above all of clear constitutional authority, picked up the pieces, and began to pay more of the costs. The result, as Kirst shrewdly observes, is not so much centralization as fragmentation. Everyone and no one is in charge of the schools.[60]

TODAY'S CHOICES

To borrow once again from Diamond, the history I have sketched is that of the national political community's struggle to attain "completeness . . . the perfection of its autonomy." Resistance came from a set of deeply

[59] Thomas E. Cronin, Tania Z. Cronin, and Michael E. Milakovich, *U.S. v. Crime in the Streets* (Indiana University Press, 1981).
[60] See also John Kincaid, "Is Education Too Intergovernmental?" *Intergovernmental Perspective* (Winter 1992): 28–34.

rooted local institutions that were themselves not mere historical accidents. They were shielded by the original choice of federalism, embraced by nineteenth-century America, and slowly given up to central authority, both state and national.

To argue that communities have been shaped by deliberate choices is not to deny that other forces shape them as well. If localism lacks vitality in modern America, that is not because it was killed by the Warren Court, still less by technicians crusading for civil-service reform from within the Social Security Board in the 1930s. Both did their part, especially the Court, but the nation's numerous wars and rise to great-power status did more, both to enlarge the claim of the national government on public resources and to stimulate the geographic and social mobility of the populace. Economic development brought specialization and interdependence, creating national and international markets and exposing local economies to forces far beyond their power to control. Urbanization was followed by suburbanization, and the separation of place of work and place of residence. Transportation and communication technologies changed in ways that helped integrate the national society while attenuating local ones. If World War II assaulted the local place metaphorically, the interstate highway system assaulted it literally with concrete, while federally sponsored urban renewal gutted its physical core, not always replacing what it destroyed. The many acts with which the national government directly attacked localism, such as *Reynolds v. Sims* and the later-model Voting Rights Act, were compounded by many more that did not have that purpose, but produced that effect as an inescapable by-product of the exercise of national power.

Facing the fact that American federalism has steadily grown more centralized, we tend to attribute the change to the influence of such (presumably uncontrollable) forces and to overlook the extent to which choices steadily present themselves nonetheless.

There are, as a leading example, the debates currently raging over the schools—localism's last bastion, only recently breached. Egalitarians attack what remains of local distinction with measures for equalization of per-pupil spending. They would erase the effects of interlocal differences in taxable wealth, denying people one of the most compelling reasons for attachment both to schools that excel and to the places in which they excel. On the other hand, libertarians—the proponents of the more extreme forms of choice—would enable parents to select whatever schools they prefer, public or private, freeing them from the obligation to support the public schools in the place where they live. Policy choices about schools are choices as well about the nature and function of local communities, to which schools have been central, even defining.

There is also the question of whether the formation of private communities should be encouraged or discouraged. Private substitutes for public local governments have proliferated since the 1960s. There were about 150,000 community associations in the United States as of the early 1990s, helping to administer the lives and property of one of every eight Americans—32 million people. In the fifty largest metropolitan areas, 50 percent or more of new-home sales are in "common-interest developments" or CIDs, as privately run communities have come to be called. In the metropolitan area of Washington, D.C., the figure is around 80 percent.[61]

The impetus for the formation of CIDs comes partly from developers, who, because of dwindling supplies of land, are under pressure to develop with greater density and who gain from putting playgrounds, pools, and tennis courts on commonly owned land. It also comes from financially pressed local governments that lack the capacity to supply services to large new developments, and therefore welcome proposals that promise to relieve them of this burden.

Although some CID associations are confined to responsibility for a single building, the vast majority administer territory as well as a building. They levy fees that are in effect taxes, and they provide a variety of services, such as roads, bus routes, TV stations, security forces, parks, and swimming pools. Some of them are walled. Although most are associated with new developments, others have become established in older settings. St. Louis is laced with privately owned streets, complete with gatehouses.

Analysts of these quasi-governments disagree about their implications for citizenship. They may be merely one more organized place in which Americans engage in "political" activity, arguing over how to define their shared interests. Even if most CID residents are apathetic, the figures on participation are impressive: About 750,000 persons serve on the boards

---

[61] Mitchell Pacelle, "Not in Your Backyard, Say Community Panels in Suburban Enclaves," *Wall Street Journal*, September 21, 1994; *Common Interest Communities: Private Governments and the Public Interest*, ed. Stephen E. Barton and Carol J. Silverman (Institute of Governmental Studies, 1994); Evan McKenzie, *Privatopia: Homeowner Associations and the Rise of Residential Private Government* (Yale University Press, 1994); Robert Jay Dilger, *Neighborhood Politics: Residential Community Associations in American Governance* (New York University Press, 1993).

of directors. Dissident homeowners, chafing under restrictions about pets, alterations to their dwellings, and the like, resort to legal actions, counter-organization, and vocal assertions of their rights. All of this looks like normal American politics; we have merely invented a new setting in which to practice it.

On the other hand, what is at issue here, even more precisely and narrowly than usual, are rights and responsibilities associated with the ownership of real property. These are thoroughly private-regarding places. Maintenance and protection of private property, to the exclusion of more encompassing purposes, unite (and divide) the members of a CID. While exclusive, property-centered private community associations multiply, local public places continue to come under attack for not being inclusive enough. In the summer of 1991, President Bush's Advisory Commission on Regulatory Barriers to Affordable Housing (the Kemp Commission) recommended a series of federal actions that would compel local jurisdictions to relax restrictions on construction of low-cost housing. It proposed denial of federal housing assistance to state or local governments that failed to reduce regulatory barriers, and denial of tax-exempt status to state and local bonds issued to finance housing construction in such jurisdictions.[62]

Such policy proposals and choices raise in turn a series of larger, underlying questions: How important is it to the well-being of society that spatially defined communities be sustained? Are they entitled to primacy, or may race under some circumstances supplant place, as it has come to do in the ideological framework of the Voting Rights Act? How important is it that spatial communities have a general-purpose public character? If they are to have a public character, to what extent, to what ends, and with what instruments should higher levels of government regulate their capacity to define themselves as communities? May federal judges impose taxes on states and localities (the issue raised in 1990 in the Kansas City school desegregation case, *Missouri v. Jenkins*)? Should any autonomy remain to the local place in an America that increasingly searches for equality, including interjurisdictional equality? Should any autonomy be restored to the local place in an America that laments the

---

[62] *"Not In My Back Yard": Removing Barriers to Affordable Housing* (U.S. Department of Housing and Urban Development, 1991); Michael H. Schill, "The Federal Role in Reducing Regulatory Barriers to Affordable Housing in the Suburbs," *Journal of Law and Politics* (Summer 1992): 703–30. For a scholarly critique of exclusionary practices, see Michael N. Danielson, *The Politics of Exclusion* (Columbia University Press, 1976).

loss of a sense of community, fears for personal safety, and worries about the alienation of citizens from politics?

Underpinning any answers to such questions are a series of value judgments and facts that political theory and behavioral social science ought to be able to help clarify. They ought to be able to illuminate the value and social function of the small-scale public place, and weigh the differences in the citizen's relation to places of different scale. The starting point for any such effort today, as for 150 years, is Tocqueville's argument for the importance of decentralization in democracies—not just of the execution of centrally framed laws, but of deliberation and lawmaking in matters of daily consequence to ordinary citizens.[63]

What Tocqueville sought to decentralize, according to Martin Diamond's interpretation, were "the daily things, the intra-regime things, that make up the vast bulk of a government's business—the little things, immensely interesting to most men . . . which may be done safely and salutarily by the locality in whatever way it chooses, because the doing of them affects the whole not at all or only insignificantly."[64] Yet in a society where a high-school teacher's refusal to wear a tie can rise to the level of a constitutional question, it is hard to see what can be safeguarded to the local citizen who might have the time, taste, or temperament to participate in the labor of democratic governance.[65]

[63] For recent empirical attempts by social scientists to come to grips with the contemporary value and meaning of small-scale communities, see, for example, Jane J. Mansbridge, *Beyond Adversary Democracy* (University of Chicago Press, 1983); Harold A. McDougall, *Black Baltimore: A New Theory of Community* (Temple University Press, 1993).
[64] "The Ends of Federalism," in *As Far as Republican Principles Will Admit: Essays by Martin Diamond*, ed. William A. Schambra (AEI Press, 1992), 156.
[65] Richard S. Vacca and H. C. Hudgins, Jr., *Liability of School Officials and Administrators for Civil Rights Torts* (Michie, 1982), 117–30. This source explains (p. 117) that "over the years the notion of people expressing themselves (speaking out) through their mode of dress and attire (including hair style) has developed . . . into an acceptable concept of constitutional law."

6

Local practice in transition

From government to governance

KATHRYN M. DOHERTY AND CLARENCE N. STONE

The importance of local "place" in American politics is indisputable. Despite constraints inherent in the federal system, American localities have significant powers to shape land use, as well as to provide important services to citizens. Although local governments are the legal creatures of the various state governments, their creation has always been "bottom up"— a product of local activity. Rarely has there been legislative opposition to, or central supervision of, local incorporation.[1]

This bottom-up tradition of local-government formation has left the United States with a unique pattern of public authority. There are today a massive number and variety of local governments in the United States with overlapping jurisdictions and no obvious rationale in overall organization. Although this bottom-up pattern holds appeal for some advocates of self-government, others have a less favorable view of the results. Rather than serving as an instrument of popular democracy, local governments (some critics suggest) have developed in such a way that those individuals with market power have been able to buy into the class character of associations they desire and obtain the mix of services they want and can afford.[2]

By this account, the spatial dimension of American politics and the "bias of localism"[3] are key factors in explaining the economic exclusion and racial segregation that have been, and continue to be, a major prod-

---

[1] Jon Teaford, *Unheralded Triumph* (Baltimore: Johns Hopkins University Press, 1979); Gregory Weiher, *The Fractured Metropolis: Political Fragmentation and Metropolitan Segregation* (Albany: State University of New York Press, 1991).
[2] Gary Miller, *Cities by Contract: The Politics of Municipal Incorporation* (Cambridge, Mass.: MIT Press, 1981).
[3] Margaret Weir, "The Politics of Urban Racial Isolation in Europe and America" (Washington, D.C.: Brookings Institution, 1992).

uct of the arrangement and workings of American local institutions.[4] As population spreads beyond the urban core, local incorporation is often driven by a desire to avoid annexation and minimize taxes. Indeed, some might conclude that local government impairs rather than advances the development of democratic virtue.

Criticisms notwithstanding, one must still acknowledge that, because of their proximity to the everyday life of citizens, local governments hold the best hope for engaging citizens in self-governance; that local institutions have the *potential* for being places of reinvigorated participation, citizenship, and community; and, that, in a country increasingly disillusioned and dissatisfied with politics, this potential needs to be explored. That is the task this chapter takes on.

Exploring the potential for local self-governance takes us along two distinct paths. One is an examination of the trends—particularly an increased reliance on privatist practices—that have emerged along with the growth of disenchantment with government. The second is a consideration of how local self-governance might be reinvigorated without turning away from governing institutions and public space. This second path leads us to question reliance on market mechanisms as a means of self-governance and directs greater attention to the link between government and civil society. We suggest that the process of governance is broader than the formal institutions of government, and that self-governance can be strengthened by paying heed to this broader process.

Our approach puts us at odds with those who attribute a decline of citizenship and self-governance in American politics to meddlesome incursions into areas once deemed purely private. Some see the centralizing force of the national government as the key to the poor condition of American political and community life. The decline in morality and the decay of "traditional" values are said to be attributable, in good part, to government intrusion into, and disruption of, private arrangements—where many virtues are thought to be cultivated.

But not all that is encouraged in the private sector is virtuous. The force of the private market in a high-pressure materialist society is at least as likely as government to be responsible for eroding social norms—as

[4] Michael N. Danielson, *The Politics of Exclusion* (New York: Columbia University Press, 1976); Douglas S. Massey and Nancy A. Denton, *American Apartheid: Segregation and the Making of the Underclass* (Cambridge, Mass.: Harvard University Press, 1993); Nancy Burns, *The Formation of American Local Governments: Private Values in Public Institutions* (New York: Oxford University Press, 1994).

well as the bonds of community and political life. And though it may not be the government's role to restore moral virtues, the case can be made that government cannot be indifferent to fostering good citizenship in the form of *political* virtue—the capacity of those with diverse interests to work together in establishing and pursuing their common well-being. Yet such virtue may be something not readily accomplished through private arrangements and small, "pietistic" communities.

Moreover, we cannot ignore the fact that government and market do not operate in separate and independent domains. The forces that propel American localities toward privatism, defense of neighborhood "character," and protection of property values are not without consequences. For example, discontent with public safety and public education—both central issues in the well-being of local communities—is now at a high level. And though it is increasingly clear that these problems cannot be solved on the national level, it is also the case that, on the local level, building more prisons and retreating into private schools and communities with walls and private security guards are strategies with large political, financial, and social costs.[5]

So even though the centralizing tendencies of the national government have a potential to undermine the development of political virtue, we might ponder the potential of local governments as well. Are there ways in which local governments make it harder for political virtue to thrive? How well do local "places" nurture a capacity for diverse interests to pursue their common well-being? If we take the need for political virtue seriously, then it may be necessary to consider more than a devolution of power from federal to state and local authorities to redress the decline in American politics. There may instead need to be a more fundamental rethinking of our conception of community and self-governance. While affirming the importance of maintaining a local sense of "place," we must move from asking "How many communities?" to the more fundamental question of "What kind of community?"

As we examine some basic trends in U.S. local government, it is worth keeping the following questions in mind:

What are the hopes for republican government if our local political institutions are highly fragmented, unequal, and incomprehensible to citizens?

---

[5] Private security is one of the fastest-growing and largest occupations in the United States. It now outspends public law enforcement by 73 percent, according to Miles Corwin, "Guns For Hire," *Los Angeles Times* (November 28, 1993).

What is the value of self-governance if politics is seen by citizens as not worth participating in?

Finally, what alternative vision of citizenship and community might sustain the needs of a large, diverse, interdependent, and democratic polity?

LOCAL GOVERNMENT TRENDS

If "place" gives important meaning to citizenship and self-governance, then the changes local governments are undergoing invite thought. At the same time that localities are responsible for some of the most important citizen concerns, these governmental units are also becoming increasingly fragmented, fiscally strained, and subject to broad public disenchantment.

Fragmentation: decline of general-purpose local government. As Table 6.1 shows, the United States has almost 87,000 units of local government. In addition to the more than 39,000 county, municipal, and town governments in the country, local government is further subdivided into more than 33,000 "special districts"—independent, special-purpose governmental units with substantial administrative and fiscal discretion. Almost half of these special-purpose districts, created to respond to needs that range from transportation and utilities to public safety, have independent property-taxing power. The existence of more than 14,000 independent school districts further fragments local government authority in the United States.[6]

The term "fragmented" is an appropriate description for local government in the United States not only because there are so many governmental units, but also because these units are complex, overlapping, and widely disparate in scope and services. Of the more than 3,000 counties in the nation, just 174 of them account for 54 percent of the entire population served by county governments. California and Texas each have more than 1,000 school districts, representing 15 percent of all school districts in the country. The growth of special districts, as well, varies substantially from state to state, with only a weak relationship to population size. Nine states account for more than half of all special-district governments.[7] Only one-third of special districts serve areas with the same bounda-

---

[6] U.S. Bureau of the Census, *Census of Governments* (Washington, D.C.: U.S. Government Printing Office, 1992).

[7] Ibid. Those states are California, Colorado, Illinois, Kansas, Missouri, Nebraska, Pennsylvania, Texas, and Washington.

Table 6.1. *Number of local governments in the United States*

	1952	1962	1972	1982	1992
Counties	3,052	3,043	3,044	3,041	3,043
Municipalities	16,807	18,000	18,517	19,076	19,296
Towns/townships	17,202	17,142	16,991	16,734	16,666
School districts	67,355	34,678	15,781	14,851	14,556
Special districts	12,340	18,323	23,885	28,078	33,131
Total	116,756	91,186	78,218	81,780	86,692

Source: U.S. Bureau of the Census, *Census of Local Governments* (1992)

ries as some other institution of local government. To make the picture even more complex, the last U.S. census counted more than 9,000 inter-county governments with jurisdictions spanning two or more counties.[8]

These arrangements have consequences for the capacity of local governments to serve as sites of *self*-government. As a result of their fragmented structure, Nancy Burns argues, local government institutions are exceedingly difficult to locate and hold accountable. It is almost impossible for citizens to figure out the boundaries of the multitude of districts in which they reside. Furthermore, "simply living in one of these districts . . . does not qualify an American citizen to participate in the district's politics." If special districts have elections at all—and many of them do not—a voter turnout of 2 to 5 percent is considered remarkable.[9]

Splintering authority and coherence in American local government even further is the proliferation of districts that have become known as "private" or "shadow" governments.[10] An alternative to public authority, these common-interest communities have been set up by developers and homeowners, using private associations to provide goods and services exclusively to member property owners. In 1992, more than 150,000 such private associations existed, and developers of almost all new housing built in metropolitan areas are following this model.[11] What

---

[8] Ibid.

[9] Burns, *American Local Governments*, 12.

[10] Stanley Scott, "The Homes Association: Will 'Private Government' Serve the Public Interest?" in *Common Interest Communities: Private Government and the Public Interest,* ed. Stephen Barton and Carol Silverman (Berkeley: Institute for Governmental Studies Press, 1994); Joel Garreau, *Edge City: Life on the New Frontier* (New York: Doubleday, 1988); Evan McKenzie, *Privatopia: Homeowner Associations and the Rise of Residential Private Government* (New Haven: Yale University Press, 1994).

[11] *Community Associations Factbook,* ed. Clifford Treese (Alexandria, Va.: Community Associations Institute, 1993).

is particularly significant about these private governments is that, in order to attract an enlarged tax base while shedding some service-delivery responsibilities, local governments often willingly abdicate portions of their public authority.

Local taxing power itself has become increasingly splintered to serve the needs of particular groups. Forty-four states allow localities to use tax-increment financing for development projects, reserving the proceeds from increases in property values to pay off project bonds directly, without becoming part of the general tax base.[12] Another strain on local taxes as a source of general revenue is the creation of business-improvement districts, or BIDs. In 1992, there were an estimated 33,000 such districts.[13] Within a BID, property owners in a given area agree to tax themselves at a higher rate for enhanced services—typically, heavier policing. Here again, the funds raised do not become a part of the general revenue of the locality; instead, they are earmarked for the services agreed upon by a group of property owners.

Corporations are also creating special districts that limit the discretion of local public authorities. In one example, a south Florida government gave the Blockbuster Corporation the right to create a 2,500-acre special-purpose government. The corporation has the power to tax, issue bonds, and condemn land—all the authority of a local government but presided over by a board of five persons elected by a single landowner.[14]

Such trends call into question romantic notions of local government as modest, accessible, and the natural locus for democratic participation and the development of virtuous citizens.

Fiscal conditions: financial constraints on localities. Despite the structural fragmentation described above, local governments in the United States retain substantial service-delivery responsibility in important areas, as well as a considerable tax-revenue base. In contrast to a country such as France, where 99 percent of all revenue is collected and approximately 85

[12] Fred Allen Forgey, "Tax Increment Financing: Equity, Effectiveness and Efficiency," *Municipal Yearbook*, 1993.

[13] Figure cited in James Krohe, Jr., "Bunker Metropolis: Private Governments Can Deliver Good Service—for a Price," *Chicago Enterprise* 8:2 (September 1993).

[14] John E. Peterson, "The Blossoming of Micro-Governments," *Governing* (October 1994). For a detailed study of corporate private governments see Richard Foglesong, "Taming the Mouse: Orlando and Walt Disney World" (unpublished paper). Foglesong charts the development of Disney's governmental arm, the Reedy Creek Improvement District (RCID), and the immense powers and immunities that the city of Orlando and the state of Florida have granted this "fiefdom."

percent of all expenditures are made by the national government, U.S. local governments receive only 33 percent of their revenue from the states and the federal government. In education, for example, U.S. local governments finance 45 percent of schooling, as compared with France and Italy, where localities provide about 14 and 16 percent of education funds, respectively.[15]

Despite this relative fiscal autonomy, the discretion of local governments in the United States is severely constrained. Local governments lack substantial autonomy in part because state governments grant them only limited powers. State governments also subject localities to "unfunded" mandates—state directives, unaccompanied by revenue, with which localities must comply.[16] This is occurring at the same time that general financial assistance from the federal government to localities is declining. Transfers to localities from the federal government have been falling for the past twenty years. From 1980 to 1992, for example, the percentage of state and local government finances secured annually from the federal government dropped from more than 18 percent to 13 percent. Thus, state and local governments have had to pick up more of the financial burden for delivering local services.

But revenues collected on the local government level are becoming more constrained as well. Income from local property tax—the major source of public school funding—fell as a percentage of local tax revenue from 82 percent in 1975 to 75 percent in 1991.[17] At the same time, a number of states experienced "tax revolt," with referenda and initiatives aimed at radically limiting property taxes as a source of revenue. Yet these revolts have often been unaccompanied by plans for full revenue replacement.[18]

Significantly, these fiscal strains are developing as increasing numbers of localities, including those in the suburbs, find themselves facing the same kinds of social crises once thought to be characteristic only of big cities. Crime, drugs, unemployment, and education top the list of suburban neighborhood concerns—all problems whose solutions fall heavily upon local governments.

---

[15] Center for Education Research and Innovations, *Education at a Glance: OECD Indicators* (Paris: OECD, 1995).

[16] It has been estimated that anywhere from 20 to 80 percent of local budgets is spent complying with state and federal mandates each year. See Forgey, "Tax Increment Financing."

[17] *Statistical Abstract of the United States, 1994.*

[18] Penelope Lemov, "Taxes: The Struggle for Balance," *Governing* (August 1994).

Metropolitan governance: not on the agenda. Despite pervasive problems, fragmentation allows wide fiscal disparities, greatly uneven social responsibilities, and large differences in the problem-solving capacities of American localities. As Gary Miller points out, for a market-like "choice of jurisdictions" to work, inequality is a *necessary* condition.[19] Further, as metropolitan areas have become more fragmented geographically, so have they by race and income. The city of Atlanta, for example, is home to 40 percent of the poor children in its metropolitan region, but only 14 percent of the area's total population. For Baltimore, figures indicate that the city contains 31 percent of the metropolitan population, and an overwhelming 71 percent of the children who are poor.

For those who thought the disorders of the racially and economically segregated central cities could be left behind, findings suggest otherwise.[20] A recent study in *The Economist* concludes that "cities and suburbs stand or fall together." When the central city declines, so does the economic growth of its suburbs and the region in general.[21]

Neal Peirce's city reports make the case that for American cities to survive they must "have strong physical infrastructures; they must develop capable work forces; they must avoid social dissension and the expense of large impoverished populations."[22] His advice suggests that the wide gulf between rich and poor and the fiscal disparities between inner cities and outer suburbs in the United States cannot be sustained without serious negative consequences. Such observations signal a call for the creation of effective systems of governance for metropolitan areas.

As indicated earlier, however, most current local political boundaries are highly arbitrary; they can hamper everything from law enforcement to economic development. Police operate within the borders of their own local government units; the perpetrators of crime do not. Similarly, traffic flows without regard to local government boundaries. But regional transportation policy is a sometimes affair, resting on tenuous and limited

---

[19] Miller, *Cities by Contract.*

[20] Committee for Economic Development, *Rebuilding Inner-City Communities: A New Approach to the Nation's Urban Crisis* (New York: CED, 1995).

[21] Richard Voith, "City and Suburban Growth: Substitutes or Complements?" *Business Review* (Philadelphia: Federal Reserve Bank, 1992). See also Larry Ledebur and William Barnes, "Metropolitan Disparities and Economic Growth," *Research Report on America's Cities* (Washington D.C.: National League of Cities, 1992); Edward Hill, Harold Wolman, and Coit Ford, "Can Suburbs Survive without Their Central Cities?" *Urban Affairs Review* 31 (1995); and H. V. Savitch, "Straw Men, Red Herrings, . . . and Suburban Dependency," *Urban Affairs Review* 31 (1995).

[22] Neal Peirce, *Citistates: How Urban America Can Prosper in a Competitive World* (Washington, D.C.: Seven Locks Press, 1993).

agreements between otherwise independent units of local government. Though a metropolitan area is an economic region, taxes are rarely collected on that basis. Instead, we have intraregional competition over revenue sources. A disjointed approach to economic development is often the side effect.

In spite of the many problems of fragmentation, inequity, and inefficiency, local-government consolidation or metropolitan government is largely a nonissue. Even as federal policy calls for shifting greater responsibility to state and local government, the fragmented governance structure of metropolitan areas is taken as a given. Yet the significance of the issue of metropolitan fragmentation is unlikely to subside in importance any time in the near future. Whereas many central cities in the United States have lost residents, and a large regional migration is taking place out of the old industrial cities of the North, many metropolitan areas and cities continue to grow. People may, in their idle fantasies, prefer small towns, but concrete reality is different. In 1970, 68.6 percent of the population lived in metropolitan areas. By 1992, this figure had reached 79.7 percent.[23]

Within the larger population shifts, Americans choose medium-sized cities. Table 6.2 indicates population loss for both the largest and smallest localities in the country. Between 1960 and 1990, the greatest gain was in cities between 50,000 and 250,000 residents in size. Nor can suburbs themselves be considered small, countryside alternatives to the city any longer. They have grown and taken on a scope of activity that invites labeling them as a new form of city.[24] Thus, whether or not people are "locals" by nature, the forces of modernity—technology, transportation, and communication—place us in communities of complex interdependence. For better or worse, "modern life has become urban life."[25]

[23] According to the 1990 U.S. census, 197.7 million Americans live in metropolitan areas; U.S. Bureau of the Census, *Statistical Brief*, April 1994. See also Harlow A. Hyde, "Slow Death in the Great Plains," *Atlantic Monthly* (June 1997): 42–5. Underlining the decline of small towns, Hyde cites evidence from the 1990 census indicating that almost 300 counties in six Midwest states have seen barely 1 percent of the nation's births.

[24] Robert Fishman, *Bourgeois Utopias: The Rise and Fall of Suburbia* (New York: Basic Books, 1987); Garreau, *Edge City*.

[25] Wilson, this volume. Interestingly, and contrary to some claims in this book, Robert Putnam, in his studies of social capital, found that although the level of social trust on the part of citizens in the largest U.S. cities is slightly lower than the social trust in the smallest towns, overall there is no significant relationship between the *size* of place and the *level of social trust* among residents. Neither did he find a relationship between social trust and size of government. See Robert Putnam, "Tuning In, Tuning Out: The Strange Disappearance of Social Capital in America," *PS: Political Science and Politics* 27 (1995).

Table 6.2. *Residents of incorporated areas
by population size*

	1960	1990
500,000 and over	24.7%	19.6%
250,000–499,999	9.3%	9.3%
100,000–249,999	9.8%	12.5%
50,000–99,999	10.8%	13.9%
25,000–49,999	11.0%	13.0%
under 25,000	34.6%	31.7%

Source: Statistical Abstract of the United States, 1995.

Citizen disconnect: Declining confidence and trust. Local government fragmentation may be a serious impediment to coherent local governance; it may work to "blur" citizens' "sense of place."[26] But any discussion of the trends and prospects for local self-government must also take into account the discontent, cynicism, and alienation that citizens feel toward the American political system in general. Although it is arguable that Americans have always been cynical and distrustful of government, recent statistics are striking.

The trend in citizen disconnection from government is well documented. The low level of voter turnout in the United States has been described as a "sickness eating away at American democracy."[27] Since 1960, the number of eligible voters who turn out for presidential elections has declined by twelve percentage points—from more than 62 percent to barely 50 percent in recent years. Turnout in off-year elections is consistently below 40 percent.[28] Turnout in local elections has been even lower, ranging in general between 10 and 30 percent.[29]

Despite greater democratization through the extension of universal suffrage, the political incorporation of women and minorities into the American political system, and the explosion in the number of interest groups, Americans seem not to be optimistic about the promise of poli-

[26] Weiher, *Fractured Metropolis,* 48.
[27] Jeffrey M. Berry, Kent E. Portney, and Ken Thomson, *The Rebirth of Urban Democracy* (Washington, D.C.: Brookings Institution, 1993).
[28] *Statistical Abstract of the United States, 1994.*
[29] James MacGregor Burns, J. W. Peltason, and Thomas E. Cronin, *Government by the People* (New York: Prentice Hall, 1987).

tics. Less than 20 percent of Americans report confidence in political organizations or organizations that lobby for a cause.[30]

Confidence in government institutions is down as well. An indicator of their low standing is the erosion of confidence in Congress. Recent polls show that only 15 percent of Americans expressed much confidence in Congress in 1994.[31] Members of Congress rate below all but used-car salesmen in honesty and ethics.[32] But before such findings are assumed to be evidence of the negative consequences of a strong national government, one would do well to heed evidence showing that Americans have the same malaise, distrust, and disdain for state and local government that they do for Congress and the federal government. Only 20 percent of Americans express a great deal of confidence in state governments. And though it is often assumed that local government is the most connected to the people, in a recent survey only 23 percent of Americans professed a great deal of confidence in *local* governments.[33] Merely 9 percent of Americans rate the honesty and ethical standards of members of Congress as high, but state and local officials do not fare a great deal better; they are rated as quite honest and ethical by only 12 and 18 percent of citizens, respectively.[34]

Trust is declining not only in government and politics. Americans also express distrust of professionals and experts, as well as lower trust in one another. Less than 50 percent of Americans consider the honesty and ethics of policemen and doctors as high—and fewer than 20 percent have confidence in the honesty and ethics of lawyers, union leaders, and reporters.

Despite romantic visions of local "place" where citizenship and friendship flourish, some suggest that the lives of Americans are increasingly isolated and lonely.[35] In an oft-quoted study, Robert Putnam claims that Americans are "bowling alone"—their membership in bowling leagues, PTAs, clubs, and other social and civic organizations is in substantial de-

---

[30] Independent Sector, *Annual Report of the Independent Sector* (Washington, D.C., 1994).
[31] Ibid.   [32] *Gallup Monthly Report,* October 1994.
[33] Independent Sector, *Annual Report of the Independent Sector.* A recent survey indicates that when asked which level of government should run programs for minorities, welfare, air and water quality, public education, and law enforcement, local governments were chosen as the most appropriate only in the case of law enforcement. For all other programs, state governments and the federal government were favored. See "Scaling Down the American Dream," *Washington Post* (April 19, 1995); "Enemy, Thy Name Is Neighbor: Local Leaders Are Latest Targets of Voters' Growing Mistrust," *Washington Post* (June 27, 1996).
[34] *Gallup Monthly Report,* October 1994.
[35] Ray Oldenburg, *The Great Good Place* (New York: Paragon House, 1989).

cline.[36] People socialize less and less with their neighbors. Compared with 1960, when 58 percent of Americans thought that most people could be trusted, by 1993 only 38 percent thought most people could be trusted.[37]

These trends in citizen alienation from politics and from one another are consequential to any discussion of the status of democratic self-government in the United States. Why is there such dramatic citizen disconnect with *all* levels of government and politics in the United States? We suggest a number of possibilities.

In the first place, many recent polls and studies find that Americans do not feel they have a stake or a voice in politics; this realm, they believe, is fundamentally out of public control.[38] In one recent poll, 68 percent of Americans said that they believed public officials do not care much about what they think.[39] Given such sentiments, it is no surprise, for example, that despite citizens' power to vote elected representatives out of office, 62 percent of Americans report that they support term limits.[40]

Citizens also seem to view government workers as increasingly unresponsive and ineffective. Beginning in the nineteenth century and continuing well into the twentieth, reformers sought institutional changes that would elevate the technical competence of public employees. But by 1968, on the heels of civil disorder around the nation, the Kerner Commission concluded that such "good government" reforms were a source of disconnection between citizens and government. The report stated that although "a merit system and professionalized civil service has made the cities more businesslike, . . . it has also tended to depersonalize government and isolate the individual." The commission warned that a widening "gulf in communications between local government and residents"—along with red tape, administrative complexity, and anger at government's failure to solve problems—was a danger for a democratic society.[41] More than twenty-five years later, polls of American citizens

---

[36] Robert D. Putnam, "Bowling Alone," *Journal of Democracy* (January 1995).
[37] Eric Uslaner, "Faith, Hope, and Charity," unpublished paper, Department of Government and Politics, University of Maryland, College Park, 1995.
[38] See Harwood Group, "A View from Main Street America," a report prepared for the Kettering Foundation, 1991.
[39] Henry J. Kaiser Family Foundation, "Why Don't Americans Trust the Government?" (Washington, D.C.: *Washington Post*/Kaiser Family Foundation/Harvard University Survey Project, 1996).
[40] *Gallup Monthly Report*, December 1994.
[41] Kerner Commission, *Report of the National Advisory Commission on Civil Disorders* (Washington, D.C., 1968), 148–9.

find that the problem continues. Bureaucracy is seen as the government's greatest impediment.[42]

The list of citizen complaints is long. The public today perceives government as inefficient, inflexible, and irresponsible with taxpayer money. Politicians are often seen as posturing rather than governing. Campaigns seem to be reduced to ten-second sound bites and negative character attacks. Despite recurring efforts at reform, money remains central to the political game. A massive professionalized and bureaucratized elite of "expert" problem-solvers, even on the local level, bypasses public deliberation and seems indifferent to citizens, further removing them from the governing process. Even more, popular perception holds that government intervention has actually made problems worse. When asked what effect government has had on opportunities for future generations and for a person who wants to get ahead through hard work, 75 percent of Americans answered that government has made things worse.[43]

Also disheartening to many is the style of contemporary American politics. As Hugh Heclo describes the "post-modern" era of policymaking, it is crusading rather than problem-solving, fundamentally confrontational, and with no overarching norms. Activists seem self-righteous and largely detached from the broader public. Battling over unfulfilled rights and policy disputes, "activists are likely to begin with presumptions, not of good faith bargaining in search of an agreement, but of confrontation with adversaries who are hostile to one's cause."[44] Politicians and pundits engage in polarized debate and rhetoric as well; they often seem to be in search of a divisive message. Given these grievances, the withdrawal from government by the American people may not be the product of apathy, "but a retreat from government that is seen as ineffective, intrusive in the wrong places, and insufficiently concerned with nurturing civic responsibility."[45]

Achieving "self-governance" in the United States, then, is a challenge greater than simply shifting power from the national level to local governments. Although many of the feelings of citizen discontent are directed toward the federal government, the confidence in, and promise of, local

---

[42] Guy Gugliotta, "Scaling Down the American Dream," *Washington Post* (April 19, 1995): A21.

[43] *Gallup Monthly Report,* October 1994.

[44] Hugh Heclo, "The Sixties' False Dawn: Awakenings, Movements and Post-Modern Policymaking," a paper presented at the conference *Integrating the Sixties: The Origins, Structures, and Legacy of Public Policy in a Turbulent Decade* (Washington, D.C.: Woodrow Wilson International Center for Scholars, 1995), 34.

[45] E. J. Dionne, "Back to Citizenship," *Washington Post* (January 24, 1991): A17.

political institutions as a wellspring for citizenship and flourishing political virtue is in question as well. As the above evidence illustrates, local government is becoming more fragmented, fiscally strained, removed from the public eye, and constrained by lack of trust and deep citizen disaffection with the political process.

REFORM STRATEGIES

Reinventing Government: *The market model*

One response to these trends has been a call to "reinvent" government— to create more effective, efficient, and flexible governing institutions. Vice President Al Gore released a report in 1993 whose title gets right to the point: "From Red Tape to Results: Creating a Government That Works Better and Costs Less." As the report states, "We need a federal government that treats its taxpayers as if they were customers. . . . The central issue we face is not *what* government does, but *how* it works."[46]

These themes are evident in *Reinventing Government,* where authors David Osbourne and Ted Gaebler use the term "entrepreneurial government" to describe the reform model. The reinvention strategy emphasizes competition between service providers, redefinition of clients as "customers," streamlined administration, decentralized authority, and a preference for market mechanisms of governance over public bureaucracy.[47]

This theme of reinventing government has had appeal in a great many states and localities. A survey of budget officers confirms that many governments are focusing reforms in this direction. Twenty-eight state agencies report targeting "customer" preferences as a high priority; twenty states report involvement in privatizing services.[48]

Cities such as Indianapolis and Phoenix have become leaders—and, to some, models—of the reinvention movement. A privatization plan in Phoenix forces city agencies to compete with private providers for contracts. Pay increases for city employees are tied to the city's growth in revenue. Indianapolis's program of "municipal federalism" has decentral-

---

[46] Albert Gore, *The Gore Report on Reinventing Government: Creating a Government That Works Better and Costs Less* (Washington, D.C.: National Council on Excellence in Government, 1993).

[47] David Osbourne and Ted Gaebler, *Reinventing Government* (New York: Penguin Books, 1993).

[48] Alliance for Redesigning Government, "NASBO Reports on State Management Innovations," *The Public Innovator* 32 (July 13, 1995).

ized power to neighborhood associations to contract for their own local-improvement services.[49] Department heads of local governments are given more autonomy, allowing them to spend money as they see fit and carry over savings from one budget year to the next.[50] Even the traditional, patronage-based, machine city of Chicago has privatized the city traffic court along with a number of other services.[51]

In education, school vouchers are high on the agenda for a number of elected officials. Some advocate turning over public schools to private management firms. Companies like Education Alternatives Inc. (EAI) and the Edison Project pledge to take the money already spent per pupil in a school district, change the curricula, streamline the bureaucracy, and contract out various services. With the money saved, these companies promise high-tech equipment and improved student performance—all while still turning a profit.[52]

Reinvention strategies recognize that self-government cannot be furthered if government itself is incapable of functioning effectively. Yet much of the approach does not question the basic relationship between government and citizens. Of the many market-oriented proposals for governmental reform, some warn that "pleading for these changes because they will restore American faith in government is at best a sales strategy. If we take it too seriously, it is sure to disappoint us in the long run."[53] Inefficiency is far from the whole explanation for citizen discontent with politics and government.[54] As one community organizer in Baltimore explained it, "Politicians . . . don't do anything to teach people how to be citizens. They teach them how to be consumers. You want something, you go to the organization. . . . But you are not a citizen. You don't know how to do it yourself."[55]

Such comments indicate good reasons, then, to be cautious about the

[49] Roger B. Parks, "Neighborhood Empowerment: Can It Happen? Does It Matter?" paper presented at the Annual Meeting of the Urban Affairs Associations, New York, 1996.
[50] Robert Gurwitt, "Entrepreneurial Government: The Morning After," *Governing* (May 1994).
[51] Charles Mahtesian, "Taking Chicago Private," *Governing* (June 1994).
[52] Although school choice and privatization have received much enthusiastic talk in the past few years, attempts to implement such ideas have met with much resistance. Baltimore dropped its contract with EAI in 1995. After years of controversy and a scaled-back plan that was originally slated to build 1,000 private schools in the next fifteen years, the Edison Project has begun in only *four* U.S. public schools. See "A Flicker of Grander Plans, Edison Project Underway at Four Schools," *Washington Post* (October 21, 1995): A3.
[53] Alan Ehrenhalt, *Governing* (November 1993).
[54] Gurwitt, "Entrepreneurial Government."
[55] Joe Coffey, quoted in Matthew Crenson, *Neighborhood Politics* (Cambridge, Mass.: Harvard University Press, 1983).

"entrepreneurial" approach to self-government. Some advocates of reinvention assume that these reforms are just alternative methods of service delivery and "contracting out." But the trends may have far-reaching consequences for our conception, and the future shape, of local government in the United States. In some instances, reforms have replaced the authority of localities with "consumer choice" arrangements. Perhaps unthinkingly, many local governments have been in the process of abdicating authority to private interests—returning tax dollars to communities that hire private police forces, allowing the creation of special tax districts, and surrendering zoning and land-use powers to corporations and developers. Such market-modeled arrangements are often posed as an *alternative* to government.[56]

But we might be wary of a reform philosophy based on disdain for (and rejection of) governing institutions. In fact, some studies show that successful "choice" reforms have been sustained only under the strong leadership and intervention of government.[57] And critics declare that although the entrepreneurial approach to reinvention may lead to some improvement in service-delivery efficiency, it may also remove decision-making even farther from the public eye and democratic process.[58] Furthermore, versions of reinventing government that conceptualize the citizen's relationship with government simply as that of a consumer seem unlikely to restore social trust, broaden social identities, and cultivate "small-place virtues" in local communities.[59] The "citizen as consumer" metaphor is atomistic and fails to place value on restoring political virtue or any attempt to pursue collective identity and community interests. As Jeffrey Henig suggests, not only must private and public institutions be evaluated for their service-delivery capacity, but "we need to focus on the differences between private and public institutions and processes as *vehicles for deliberation, debate and decision-making.*"[60]

If this is the case, more than merely "new managerialism"[61] is required to reinvent local self-governance. The challenge is also to break the *im-*

---

[56] See John E. Chubb and Terry M. Moe, *Politics, Markets and America's Schools* (Washington, D.C.: Brookings Institution, 1989).

[57] Jeffrey Henig, *Rethinking School Choice: The Limits of the Market Metaphor* (Princeton: Princeton University Press, 1993).

[58] See Robert Gurwitt, "Entrepreneurial Government." His report on Visalia, California, indicates that although city manager Ted Gaebler made it "a holy site" of reinvention in the 1980s, the reinvention movement in that city is now dead. Citizens questioned whether Visalia had become more interested in entrepreneurship than in governing.

[59] The phrase is Wilson's, this volume.

[60] Henig, *Rethinking School Choice*, xiii.

[61] Robin Hambleton and Paul Hoggett, "Rethinking Consumerism in Public Services," *Consumer Policy Review* 3:2 (April 1993): 103–11.

personal relationship between citizens and government, to make politics more coherent, and to give citizens in the United States the tools and the forums to participate in governing in a way that has consequences. It involves rethinking the relationship between government and citizens on all levels. Is citizenship mainly a form of consumption—the citizen as a "selector" of services? Or is it about being a member of a self-governing political community?

CITIZEN INVOLVEMENT: THE VOLUNTARY SECTOR

Some would have us conclude that attempts to *reconnect* citizens with governing institutions are futile. In one view, Americans are too self-absorbed to participate in politics.[62] They want to be left alone to pursue their own private interests, and they desire little more if public services are delivered efficiently.

Yet if it is not simply rhetoric that democratic life is important—and that local community is the essence of that life—then there must be something more to what it means to live in a self-governing political community. Indeed, there is much evidence to suggest that, under the proper conditions, citizens are willing to participate in the public life of their communities.

A look at the voluntary activities of citizens offers testimony. Although disconnected from government, and despite having a low level of "political" participation, American citizens *are* involved in their communities.[63] Even with recent declines due to economic insecurity and uncertainty, the participation of Americans in voluntarism and charity work remains impressive.

Three-quarters of all American households reported contributions to charitable organizations in 1994. More than 89 million American adults volunteered in 1993, giving an estimated 19.5 billion hours of service.[64]

Where there is trust, citizens are more connected and involved. This is the logic behind the concept of "social capital."[65] And, as it turns out,

---

[62] Thomas R. Dye and Harmon Ziegler, *The Irony of Democracy: An Uncommon Introduction to American Politics* (North Scituate, Mass.: Duxbury Press, 1978).

[63] Sidney Verba, Kay Lehman Schlozman, and Henry Brady, *Voice and Equality: Civic Voluntarism in American Politics* (Cambridge, Mass.: Harvard University Press, 1995).

[64] Independent Sector, *Annual Report of the Independent Sector*, 1994. Independent Sector also reports that most voluntarism and charitable giving—24.1 percent—is related to religious affiliation. Only a little more than 3 percent of respondents indicated voluntary participation in "political" organizations and activities.

[65] James S. Coleman, *Foundations of Social Theory* (Cambridge, Mass.: Harvard University Press, 1990); Robert Putnam, *Making Democracy Work: Civic Traditions in Modern Italy* (Princeton: Princeton University Press, 1993).

Americans are relatively confident about the trustworthiness of charities and nonprofit organizations. Almost 70 percent of Americans believe that charities are honest institutions.[66] Interestingly, citizens see their community involvement as explicitly *not* politics, which carries a connotation of "morally unsavory" activities.[67] Community involvement is about solving problems, whereas politics, as one woman phrased it, "is about rules, laws, policies [and] has nothing to do with why I am involved in my community."[68] David Mathews, president of the Kettering Foundation, points out that Americans "have lost that broader sense of politics that goes beyond what governments do."[69]

These observations might lead us, then, to embrace the workings of the voluntary sector as a *replacement* for governmental action. Certainly, turning to the voluntary sector to provide services and to build trusting relationships that involve citizens in their communities is a noble sentiment. But this should not lead us to conclude, as some do, that the voluntary sector can stand alone as a viable *alternative* to government.[70] Although the voluntary sector can sometimes mobilize an intensity of purpose and commitment that governmental agencies rarely elicit,[71] this sector is no panacea.[72] Nonprofit and other voluntary organizations have limited resources, are vulnerable to paternalism and particularism, and can serve only a limited number of recipients.[73]

Research has also shown that the efforts of the voluntary sector are not evenly spread. First, people tend to volunteer within their own social stratum. Voluntarism tends to be sporadic—few participate over the long term or donate their time to work with the poor.[74] For example, approximately 60 percent of volunteers in education work with students in sub-

---

[66] Independent Sector, *Annual Report of the Independent Sector,* 1994.

[67] Robert N. Bellah et al., *Habits of the Heart: Individualism and Commitment in American Life* (New York: Harper and Row, 1985).

[68] Harwood Group, *Citizens and Politics: A View from Main Street,* a report prepared for the Kettering Foundation (Bethesda, Md.: Harwood Group, 1991), 49.

[69] David Mathews, *Politics for People: Finding a Responsible Public Voice* (Chicago: University of Illinois Press, 1994).

[70] Steven Rathgeb Smith and Michael Lipsky, *Nonprofits for Hire: The Welfare State in the Age of Contracting* (Cambridge, Mass.: Harvard University Press, 1993).

[71] Anthony S. Bryk, Valerie E. Lee, and Peter Holland, *Catholic Schools and the Common Good* (Cambridge, Mass.: Harvard University Press, 1993).

[72] See Steven Rathgeb Smith, "Community Organizations and Local Government," paper presented at the annual meeting of the Association of Public Policy Analysis and Management, November 1995, on the crucial role government plays in sustaining local community problem-solving coalitions.

[73] Lester Salamon, *Partners in Public Service* (Baltimore: Johns Hopkins University Press, 1995).

[74] Dale Russakoff, "Looking for Help to Even Some of Society's Odds," *Washington Post,* (April 26, 1997), A1, A10.

urban schools, whereas only 28 percent of voluntary partnerships are in urban schools.[75] The Carnegie Corporation reports that affluent neighborhoods have three times as many activities available for children as do poor neighborhoods. Thus dependence on the voluntary sector does not guarantee that help will go to those who need it most.[76]

Financially, it is unlikely that voluntary associations could take on the burdens of becoming an alternative to government. First, approximately 30 percent of nonprofit budgets nationwide come from the government.[77] And while some suggest that cuts in government spending and taxes would fuel charitable giving, a recent economic report estimates that each dollar the government cuts from the nonprofit sector will likely result in only a nickel increase in donations from the public.[78] Thus government may be necessary to compensate not only for market failures but for "voluntary failures" as well.[79]

PARTNERSHIPS: CITIZEN-GOVERNMENT COOPERATION

Some romanticize the voluntary sector, attributing great—and unrealistic—capacity to it. The limits described above illustrate why the voluntary sector cannot stand alone. The limitations of both the market and the voluntary sectors strongly suggest the need for reform strategies that will reconnect citizens with governing institutions and with one another. As we turn away from viewing citizens as consumers and government as an entrepreneur to a vision of citizens and government as partners in problem-solving, we can see that there are other reinvention strategies.

An alternative vision of reform focuses on building political virtue and community through partnerships. Less publicized than "entrepreneurial government," partnerships have nevertheless acquired a growing role in local government.[80] This strategy aims at improving citizens' capacity for

[75] National Association of Partners in Education (NAPE), *National School District Partnership Survey* (November 1991).
[76] Carnegie Corporation of New York, *Matter of Time: Risk and Opportunity in the Non-School Hours,* report of the Task Force on Youth Development and Community Programs (Woodlawn, Md.: Wolk Press, 1992).
[77] Independent Sector, *Annual Report of the Independent Sector, 1994.*
[78] Richard Steinberg, "What the Numbers Say," *Advancing Philanthropy,* National Association of Fund-Raising Executives (Summer 1995).
[79] Lester M. Salamon, "Of Market Failure, Voluntary Failure, and Third-Party Government: Toward a Theory of Government-Nonprofit Relations in the Modern Welfare State," *Journal of Voluntary Action Research* 16 (January 1987): 29–49.
[80] There are a great number of innovative partnership activities in addition to those discussed here. For some examples, see United States Conference of Mayors, "U.S. Cities' Public/Private Partnerships," prepared by the National Center for the Revitalization of Central Cities at the University of New Orleans, 1995.

collective action with an emphasis on citizen enablement through participation. Partnership suggests that the *self-service* (of market-type reforms) is not *self-government*. Self-government really means that citizens are involved in *governing*, not just *choosing*, and that citizens have a stake and a role in the process. As one activist put it, "If there is to be genuine participatory politics, there must be opportunities for ordinary citizens to initiate action about matters that are important to their interests."[81] This vision of governance, then, calls for a reinvigoration of civil society.

A reform agenda focused on partnership acknowledges first that government—even effective, streamlined government—cannot work alone. Government in the United States can command neither the authority and the resources nor, in many cases, the flexibility to solve the complex social problems that communities face today. Many have also come to realize that these problems fail to fit the neat, independent, bureaucratic boundaries of government agencies. Isolating problems and assigning their solutions to separate bureaucratic professionals increasingly ends in frustration.[82] Programs that work offer a "broad spectrum of services," cross "traditional professional and bureaucratic boundaries," and are "fundamentally flexible."[83]

This conception of governance recognizes that community support and citizen input are essential for most problem-solving efforts. Partnerships between local governments and communities have the capacity to harness citizen energy in a way that government does not, either acting alone or acting through contracts with businesses. By eliciting the support and knowledge of local communities, partnerships may be a way to reinvest the term "self-government" with meaning by attaching to citizenship real tasks of solving problems and engaging in "public work."[84] Further, partnerships between government and voluntary organizations might help to repair citizens' sense of disconnection from government—and restore social trust in one another.

---

[81] Ernesto J. Cortes, "Reweaving the Fabric: The Iron Rule and the IAF Strategy for Power and Politics," in *Interwoven Strategies,* ed. Henry Cisneros (New York: W. W. Norton, 1993).

[82] Paul Florin and Abraham Wandersman, "An Introduction to Citizen Participation, Voluntary Organizations and Community Development," *American Journal of Community Psychology* 18:1 (1990).

[83] Lisbeth Schorr, *Within Our Reach: Breaking the Cycle of Disadvantage* (New York: Doubleday, 1988).

[84] Harry C. Boyte, "Beyond Deliberation: Citizenship as Public Work," paper presented at the PEGS Conference Citizen Competence and the Design of Democratic Institutions, Washington, D.C., 1995.

Skeptics might question the workability of the partnership idea. Is it just a nice-sounding ideal, bound to fade away after a few short-lived experiments? Or do partnerships represent a realistic vision in the broad scheme of "reinvention"? The test of durability is time, but for the present we can see that partnerships have established a firm beachhead in several policy arenas.

For example, the movement toward community-based policing acknowledges that police cannot do their jobs without the assistance of citizens and neighborhood groups. Police departments can no longer take a paternalistic attitude toward crime and the protection of the community. Thus, community policing involves decentralizing authority, but also eliciting cooperation and two-way communication between police and members of local communities. Community policing programs in Portland, Seattle, Newark, and many other communities have shifted police officers from behind their desks and out of their cars to create city foot patrols—part of an effort to commit "the city's resources to the day-to-day work of building ongoing relationships between police and neighborhood residents."[85]

As an alternative to hiring private security patrols, this approach "encourages people to see themselves as *co-responsible* for maintaining order, and as *co-producers* of order with the police."[86] Community policing has been hailed by many communities as a success—not just in older central cities like Jersey City, but also in places as varied as St. Petersburg, Florida; suburban Montgomery County, Maryland; and Fort Bend, Indiana. One foundation study reports that violent crimes have dropped by 15 percent in areas with community policing,[87] and a variety of organizations (including the U.S. Department of Justice) are strong advocates. The push toward rethinking the relationship between citizens and police is likely to continue, as the Community Policing Consortium in Washington, D.C., reports that more than 7,000 police agencies received grants from the 1994 Crime Bill to implement community-policing programs.[88]

---

[85] Cortes, "Reweaving the Fabric," 315.

[86] Michael Taylor, "Good Government: On Hierarchy, Social Capital and the Limitations of Rational Choice Theory," *Journal of Political Philosophy* (1995).

[87] Milton Eisenhower Foundation, *The State of Families* (Milwaukee: Family Services, 1995).

[88] This is not to suggest that community policing is without resistance. In many places, community policing remains an "add-on" for selected neighborhoods rather than a means whereby whole departments are transformed. Lawrence Sherman, a criminal-justice expert at the University of Maryland, also suggests that some of the greatest resistance to community policing comes from police officers, whose training can be at odds

In the realm of housing policy, community-based advocacy has "infused the policy debate with a number of new and alternative means of providing . . . affordable and quality housing."[89] The use of nonprofit community-development corporations (CDCs) to provide housing has increased dramatically since the early 1980s, when federal assistance was severely cut. By 1991, there were an estimated 2,000 CDCs in the United States, providing (according to some estimates) 30,000 to 45,000 units of housing per year.[90]

Instead of depending on market forces and private production of low-income housing, CDCs represent partnerships between local governments and nonprofit, community-based organizations, which are committed to a broad approach to affordable housing. CDCs have also made a number of efforts to link federal agencies such as Housing and Urban Development (HUD) to community groups that combine efforts to build lower-cost housing with efforts to provide work for high-risk youth. In addition, CDCs have made efforts toward resident management of public housing so that, in the same way as community policing, citizens can actively participate in problem-solving initiatives.[91]

Partnership has become an important trend in education as well. The National Association for Partners in Education reports that partnerships among schools, businesses, and voluntary organizations in the United States have more than doubled in the past ten years; the association estimates there are 200,000 nationally.[92] Where public education was once thought to be a "rational enterprise" run by "dispassionate professionals,"[93] there are now a number of initiatives, such as school-based management, that attempt to bring parents, teachers, staff, and community representatives into closer involvement in schools (not to mention the

---

with (and make them resistant to) the kinds of changes required by a reworking of the relationship between citizens and police. See "The Mixed Success of Community Policing," *Washington Post* (October 31, 1995): C1.

[89] Edward G. Goetz, *Shelter Burden: Local Politics and Progressive Housing Policy* (Philadelphia: Temple University Press, 1993), 36.

[90] Avis Vidal, *Rebuilding Communities: A National Study of Urban CDCs* (New York: CDC Research Center, 1992); Goetz, *Shelter Burden.*

[91] The record of CDCs is mixed. Though underutilized and inadequately supported, CDCs have been instructive in their recognition of the interconnectedness of community life. See Robert Halpern, *Rebuilding the Inner City* (New York: Columbia University Press, 1995).

[92] NAPE, *Partnership Survey,* 1991.

[93] Edward B. Fiske, *Smart Schools, Smart Kids: Why Do Some Schools Work?* (New York: Simon & Schuster, 1991).

day-to-day process of education).[94] Federal, state, and local authorities have encouraged various forms of parental involvement in education, both to improve student performance and to make the school the center of local community-building.[95]

Linking the voluntary and nonprofit sector with government can help reconnect citizens to politics and to one another, giving them a stake and a voice in their political community. Partnerships may also compensate for the weaknesses in governmental service provision while building community capacity for self-reliance and social capital. Such shared decision-making and partnership does not *assure* success. Its significance, as one observer explains, "lies not in what it guarantees but in what it makes possible."[96] Partnerships between the government and civil society can add flexibility to the way government and communities respond to challenges. Partnerships may also bolster the comprehensive approaches that many advocate to solving social problems, which would be very difficult to sustain by either government or voluntary efforts alone.[97] Under the conditions of partnership, reform can be locally controlled, it can elicit citizen participation, and it can be given catalytic direction by government—federal, state, or local.[98] In this vision, government can help nurture and sustain what are often well-intentioned but frail problem-solving activities on the part of citizens while decreasing dependence on government and highly specialized experts.[99]

Rather than simply changing the managerial style of government, or putting the instruments of democratic control in the hands of the marketplace, reforms of this kind include strategies to enable civil society and to

---

[94] See especially James Comer, *School Power* (New York: Free Press, 1980); Fiske, *Smart Schools;* Larry Martz, *Making Schools Better* (New York: Times Books, 1992); and Deborah Meier, *The Power of Their Ideas* (Boston: Beacon Press, 1995).

[95] For more community-building and partnership strategies, see Committee for Economic Development, "Rebuilding Inner City Communities."

[96] Fiske, *Smart Schools*, 61.

[97] Robin Garr, *Reinvesting in America* (New York: Addison-Wesley, 1994).

[98] For more on how a strengthened civil society demands a multilevel commitment from government in support of local initiatives, see "To Restore Civility to Government, Local Efforts Are Necessary," *Nation's Cities Weekly* (March 18, 1996). See also *Public Policy for Democracy,* ed. Helen Ingram and Steven Rathgeb Smith (Washington, D.C.: Brookings Institution, 1993) on the impact of government policy on citizenship and democracy, and how policy plays a role in engaging citizens in the process of self-government.

[99] The "Project for American Renewal," for example, is a collection of legislation that would "use federal funds and taxes to help communities mobilize private efforts to meet social needs." According to the author, Senator Dan Coats, "relimiting" government is not a sufficient strategy for restoring a strong civil society. See "Coats Seeks to Warm GOP Image Through 'Poverty Tax Credit' Plan," *Washington Post* (February 26, 1996).

give meaning to notions of "self" government and political community. In Michael Taylor's terms, partnerships in policing, education, and the like can strengthen both vertical social capital—the relationship of mutual trust between the government and the community—and horizontal social capital—improving the levels of social trust within communities.

GOVERNMENT VS. GOVERNANCE

To appreciate the role of civil society, it is helpful to distinguish between government and governance. In any community, the formal institutions of local government are easy to identify. They levy taxes, employ civil servants to provide services, and maintain a degree of order. Yet the governance of the community is more than the operations of the agencies and institutions of government. Services and maintaining order actually rest on the combined efforts and cooperation of governmental and non-governmental actors.

Genuine governance also includes what Selznick calls "critical decisions."[100] This is the process by which the problems and challenges of the community are considered, and the capacity of the community to respond is assessed—and, where there is a need, bolstered. This is the ideal. In reality, local governance in this broad sense is weak, elusive, and piecemeal.

The bottom-up tradition of local-government creation has involved little reflection and deliberation about what a political community is or should be. James Q. Wilson's essay in this volume points to the expansion of individualistic claims as a force detrimental to "fragile communal institutions." He warns of the pernicious potential of the federal government in this vein. But if communities are being pulled apart, it is as likely to be happening from the bottom up as from the top down. Fragile community institutions are likely to be damaged as much or more by market competition, privatization, and fragmentation as by exertions of authority by the central government. The rise of private residential communities, for example, might be construed as a move to rebuild "community." More often than not, however, residents and developers are making self-interested calculations about the protection of private (property) values.

Such weakness in local governance is particularly regrettable at a time when social responsibilities are in the process of being reallocated among the various sectors of community life, and the various sectors themselves

---

[100] Philip Selznick, *Leadership in Administration* (New York: Harper & Row, 1957).

are being joined and disjoined in new ways. When disenchantment with government is at such a high level, the temptation is strong for those who can afford it to abandon public institutions—and withdraw to market-created "private" places.

Markets and the logic of market-style reforms applied to politics, however, do not function in isolation from the workings of government; in turn, they have consequences for the social institutions of civil society. In an era in which markets and entrepreneurialism are widely and uncritically celebrated, we would be well-advised to be leery of the consequences of expanding market arrangements deeply into community life. Just as governmental authority, unwisely employed, can supplant mutual assistance, so can market mechanisms. Indeed, market transactions, if anything, may accentuate the tendency toward immediate concerns, and they do so to the point of isolating households from the kinds of shared concerns and activities on which community is built.

Reliance on the market as the panacea for societal problems is not the only simplification that beckons to the unsuspecting. In an era in which it is fashionable to talk about downsizing government, it is also wise not to exaggerate what the voluntary sector can do by itself. As we have seen, much of the support for the voluntary sector comes from government payments and grants. A voluntary sector working in partnership with government and business can accomplish much more than it could operating alone.[101]

Civic capacity: Cross-sector collaboration

The "big picture" question—perhaps the central question about local governance—is one of how the various sectors of government, market, and civil society can be linked in response to problems and challenges. We suggest the concept of "civic capacity" as the term to describe this phenomenon—mobilizing the business and voluntary sectors to act in conjunction with government on behalf of community problem-solving. To use this capacity is to engage people in governance.

Creating and using civic capacity builds on the idea of citizen-government partnerships presented earlier in this chapter, but it also includes a level of coordination, inclusiveness, and comprehensive strategizing that may not necessarily be present in isolated partnerships or

---

[101] Garr, *Reinvesting in America.*

voluntary activities. In this vein, there are some significant, though limited, initiatives worth noting.

For example, Mayor Freeman Bosley of St. Louis showed that local governments could become a catalyst for community-building. St. Louis is one of a growing number of communities that has put federal money into creating projects like Community Education Centers, housed within elementary schools. The plan is to use the school as a locus for bringing people together, coordinating social services, offering encouragement and instruction in such matters as parenting and family-enrichment programs, and providing a forum for discussing neighborhood problems.[102] Such centers have the potential to enhance not only the ability of neighborhoods to respond to their problems but also their capacity to work with other sectors of the community.

In Baltimore, Mayor Kurt Schmoke has provided support for initiatives started by others by contributing resources to neighborhood-based activities. He has responded with strong support for Sandtown-Winchester, a comprehensive effort in community revitalization, even though the project began in the voluntary sector before Schmoke took office.[103] Again there is a potential for civic-capacity building.

In Chicago, Mayor Harold Washington convened a broad coalition of business executives, parents, community representatives, and professional educators to focus on community issues. This coalition, called the Education Summit, became a key step in Chicago's move toward far-reaching school reform.[104] Similarly, in 1991, the mayor's office in the city of New Orleans rallied a local summit—including public- and private-school officials, parents, businesses, police, and health- and job-training agencies—to lay the groundwork for collaboration between public and private agencies in creating a comprehensive strategy for linking education and social services for the city's youth.[105]

---

[102] St. Louis Board of Education, "Report on Community Education for the City of St. Louis" (St. Louis, Mo., 1993); Lana Stein, "Education Reform and Civic Capacity," site report on St. Louis, Missouri, for Civic Capacity and Urban Education Project.

[103] Marion E. Orr, *Black Political Incorporation, Phase Two: The Cases of Baltimore and Detroit*, Ph.D. dissertation, University of Maryland, College Park, 1992.

[104] Kenneth K. Wong and Sharon Rollow, "A Case Study of the Recent Chicago School Reform," *Administrator's Notebook* 34:5 (1990); Alfred G. Hess, Jr., "Restructuring the Chicago Schools," in *Education Reform in the '90s*, ed. Chester Finn and Theodore Rebarber (New York: Macmillan, 1992).

[105] James R. Garvin and Alma H. Young, "Resource Issues: A Case Study from New Orleans," in *The Politics of Linking Schools and Social Services*, ed. Louis Adler and Sid Gardner (Washington, D.C.: Falmer Press, 1993).

Although examples of such broad-based cooperation are far from routine, they show that it is possible for otherwise disconnected capabilities in a community to coalesce around a shared concern. These illustrations also suggest that government can become a catalyst for improving self-governing capacities and sowing the seeds of dedication to community purpose. Given the level of voluntary activity in the nation and citizens' expressed interest in community involvement, this seems like an achievable goal—albeit not an easy one.

As demonstrated above, some current urban-policy initiatives are directed at building inclusive partnerships. Community policing has surfaced as a response to public-safety problems. Site-based management and parent involvement have emerged as education reforms. In both areas, these are policy initiatives that call for cross-sector collaboration. They are based on the realization that a need exists to enlist the community sector of civil society in meeting broad social responsibilities.[106]

Consider again community policing and public safety. Effective policing and a high level of security at home and in the streets require citizen cooperation. This cooperation takes two forms. One is lessening the task to be done through a high level of compliance with the law and a low level of antagonistic relations among people. The other is contributing actively to law enforcement—that is, citizens serving as an arm of surveillance, reporting on potentially illegal activities, and providing support such as evidence to police and testimony in courts.

Much the same could be said about enlisting civil society in schooling. Families can provide learning readiness. The family and peer group serve as a source of aspirations. The business and employment world is a fount of potential opportunities and cues about how to make it into the mainstream economy.

As an element of governance, civic capacity is the process by which various sectors come together to respond to community needs. Civic capacity is typically underdeveloped and social capital is in short supply. Yet various policy initiatives signal an awareness that cross-sector coopera-

---

[106] As public discourse reexamines the role of government, we should be mindful of the many ways in which government, *at all levels,* can enhance or diminish the role of civil society. As one illustration, the state of New Jersey has established and used a procedure by which the state can take over and direct local school systems that are performing badly. This process includes no place for active civil society. By contrast, the state of Maryland has established a procedure for poorly performing schools mandating that such a school shall reconstitute itself. This process of reconstitution calls for the active involvement of parents and the community.

tion would be highly useful in responding to a range of social needs. Necessity is, however, not always the mother of invention. Most localities lack institutional arrangements whereby civic capacity could be developed and expanded beyond the kind of loose and informal personal networks that any community has. The now-popular market-based reform strategies do little or nothing to acknowledge or remedy this condition. As a result, fragmentation not only characterizes the formal structure of local government in the United States, it also characterizes the relationship between and within various sectors of community life.[107]

WHAT KIND OF LOCAL POLITICAL COMMUNITY?

We have suggested that the genuine self-governance of a community would rest on governing institutions that are effective, open to citizen involvement, and conducive to cooperative problem-solving among government, business, and civil society. These arrangements, in turn, may encourage the attributes of good citizenship associated with local self-governance.

But how are local polities to be defined in order to best promote those goals? The bottom-up formation of American localities has occurred with little serious thought to this question. Yet the answer is central to understanding what it means to be a self-governing political community.

An effective self-governing political community may require, along with a closer link between government and civil society, a reinvigorated and more enlarged vision of an active community than proponents of "reinventing" government have identified. If this is the case, the logic of the American system of local self-government is limited in a number of ways. First, it is confined by practices that have elevated the role of professionals and experts in governance, thus downplaying the role of citizens and leading to the isolation and fragmentation of problem-solving into functional specialization rather than to general local governments.

Furthermore, the most prominent institutional legacies on the local-government landscape today may not be those built by mayors and other elected officials, but special-purpose districts—structures that make political leadership more, not less, difficult by the kind of functional splinter-

---

[107] Particularly instructive is the experience of foundations that have sought to promote broad collaboration. See, for example, Annie E. Casey Foundation, "The Path of Most Resistance: Reflections on Lessons Learned from New Futures" (Baltimore: Annie E. Casey, 1995), and the lessons that foundation learned about the challenges of coordinating a comprehensive reform initiative.

ing they accentuate. Contributing to the march toward further fragmentation, these structures are now joined by special tax districts and, outside the formal sphere of government altogether, the growth of private homeowner associations. Each of these represents a spinning of responsibilities away from general local government.

The vision of local self-government in this country has also been limited by the dominance of the market mentality and our bottom-up tradition of local-government formation. That and an ideology of unchecked individualism suggest that the amount of "community" we have is only as much as we can buy into. Community-building is thus based heavily on economic and racial calculations—and a strategy of keeping out "unwanteds." But such communities seem incompatible with political virtue, and such a conception of local polities creates a "civility" that can only be a facade. As Robert Reich described the trend of the "secession of the successful":

> If generosity and solidarity end at the borders of our common property values, then [we] can be virtuous citizens at little cost. . . . It has become possible to maintain a preferred self image of generosity toward, and solidarity with one's own "community" without owing any responsibility to "them" in another community.[108]

The alternative to "exit" from racially and economically diverse political communities is "voice."[109] But effective self-government in the United States has also been limited by a refusal to use diversity as an asset to democratic life. Instead, we have been quite successful in this country at isolating and (in the bottom-up tradition) sorting by race and class—often in the name of preserving communities with "shared culture and common experiences."[110]

Romanticism about small, homogeneous communities aside, there is no escaping the fact that we live in a diverse society. In cities such as New York, Los Angeles, Jersey City, and San Antonio, well over 40 percent of the population speaks languages other than English at home. In Miami, the number is 73 percent. Attempting to create small, homogeneous, and "pietistic" communities may be a short-sighted strategy as we move into the twenty-first century. As Norton Long suggests, "if diverse city inhabi-

---

[108] Robert Reich, *Tales of a New America* (New York: Times Books, 1987), 278.
[109] Albert O. Hirschman, *Exit, Voice and Loyalty* (Cambridge, Mass.: Harvard University Press, 1970).
[110] Wilson, this volume.

tants are not seen as a potential asset to governing—they will almost certainly become liabilities."[111]

Dealing with diversity may also be a "realistic good."[112] It is much more difficult to achieve collective action among diverse people with differing particular interests. Why, then, make the effort? Why not simply go with what is easiest to do? The answer has to do with effectiveness and a tradition that traces back at least to Aristotle. Just as a group can envision and accomplish aims that an individual cannot, so diverse groups can envision and accomplish aims that a homogeneous group cannot. The capacity for these larger aims is what Aristotle meant by the political character of humankind. One of these aims is social peace, and social peace is unalterably a political "good," not a consumer commodity.[113]

Different groups can add creativity to the political process because of the different resources they bring to the political table. "Resource exchange" can strengthen a community's problem-solving capacity.[114] Such a conception of a political community moves beyond what Benjamin Barber describes as "thin democracy"—an understanding of politics only as "self-interested bargaining"—to politics that makes an effort to bring disconnected capacities and visions into the decision-making process.[115] As Bernard Crick explains, "diversity of resources and interests is itself the education which is necessary for politics."[116]

Ideally, participation in a diverse political community may be valuable for its "educative" role, and for the belief that it will bring citizens to a common ground, not to mention a recognition of their common interests and goals.[117] Politics, by this account, transforms people.[118] And by participating in politics with people who have different points of view, citizens can learn democratic virtues. As J. S. Mill puts it, an individual who participates in politics is forced to "weigh interests not his own; to be

[111] Norton Long, *The Unwalled City* (New York: Basic Books, 1972).
[112] Bernard Crick, *In Defence of Politics,* second ed. (Middlesex, England: Penguin Books, 1982).
[113] Ibid.
[114] Seymour Sarason, *Parental Involvement and the Political Principle* (San Francisco: Jossey-Bass, 1995).
[115] Benjamin Barber, *Strong Democracy: Participatory Politics for a New Age* (Berkeley: University of California Press, 1984).
[116] Crick, *In Defence of Politics,* 142.
[117] Jane Mansbridge, *Beyond Adversary Democracy* (New York: Basic Books, 1980); Barber, *Strong Democracy;* Stephen L. Elkin, *City and Regime in the American Republic* (Chicago: University of Chicago Press, 1987).
[118] Samuel Bowles and Herbert Gintis, *Democracy and Capitalism* (New York: Basic Books, 1986).

guided, in case of conflicting claims, by another rule than his private par-
tialities."[119]

Diversity, tolerance, and community-government partnership may not
be the path of least resistance or conflict. According to Crick, "the more
one is involved in relationships with others, the more conflicts of interest,
or of character and circumstance will arise."[120] But it may be just this citizen involvement in relationships with one another and with governing
institutions—a reassertion of politics as the interaction of citizens rather
than clients or customers—that is the key to self-governance, political
virtue, and a realistic vision of how greater social trust, political participation, and social problem-solving can be achieved in local political communities.

CONCLUSION

The desire for community does not automatically focus on local government. Still, local polities are central to community life and may hold the
best hope for reinvesting political virtue and community with meaning.
They are responsible for matters that citizens care about deeply, particularly public safety and the education of their children. They are also involved in the provision of affordable housing and a variety of other social
services. So the response to many basic needs rests heavily on local governments in the United States.

At the same time, America's tradition of mistrusting public authority is
at work locally as well as at higher levels. This mistrust is evident not only
in recent attitude surveys, but also in a long-standing reluctance to re-
structure local government to accord with the regional and metropolitan
character of modern life. Even though people no longer work, shop, and
live their lives within a small geographic domain, they meet their overlapping needs mainly by increasing the number and reach of special districts,
not by expanding the boundaries or responsibilities of general local government. Consequently, local place is blurred, and metropolitan areas are
fragmented into a myriad of local jurisdictions.

In theory, government in America may be about how an interdependent people discuss and act on shared problems. In actuality, public authority, especially at the local level, is heavily infused with private values
and calculations about private advantage. The continuation of metropol-

---

[119] J. S. Mill, 1862   [120] Crick, *In Defence of Politics*, 24.

itan fragmentation is not a simple matter of adhering to an abstract ideology about limited government. It is a means for creating life-style enclaves, protecting property values, and harboring economic advantages in an uncertain world. The local-government experience is testimony to how difficult it is to establish and maintain effective public authority in a highly diverse, mobile, and changing society. The "private" in Warner's "private city"[121] has moved over the metropolitan landscape, taking shape in suburban fragmentation, fiscal disparity, special districts, and the spread of "gated" communities.

With rising disaffection from government, there is little inclination to enlarge the sphere of public authority and seek ways to make it work more effectively through such measures as consolidation and reorganization. Pundits increasingly use the term "citizen empowerment," but it is an ill-defined phrase, often equated with consumer choice rather than a citizenry's capacity for collective action. Thus some see empowerment as a process outside government—a process whereby the wants of the individual citizen will be protected from governmental rules and institutions. At the same time, others recognize that citizenship is not atomistic, that people face problems and achieve satisfactions in association with one another. There is, after all, an ancient tradition that a people are free only to the extent that they can act together.

These two contrasting views of empowerment—consumer choice versus partnership and a capacity for collective action—have standing in the literature on reinventing government. Both present themselves as alternatives to governance by career politicians who preside over professionally staffed public bureaucracies. In a society in which market activity is pervasive, consumer choice offers ease of promotion. It also reinforces an already established pattern of economically segmented living, and it renders citizenship into a matter of interacting with others from the same income level.

As the nineteenth century was coming to a close, government was being reinvented to provide the modern democratic state with a technical capacity to govern in the modern world. Today, something even more basic seems to be at issue. The search for alternatives to conventional politics and government points to a reexamination of the nature and role of civil society.

Civil society is not an aggregation of private consumers, bent on buy-

[121] Sam Bass Warner, *The Private City* (Philadelphia: University of Pennsylvania Press, 1968).

ing what they want and can afford. Indeed, it is less about consumption than production. Civil society contains a network of voluntary and nonprofit organizations as well as families and informal bonds, capable of contributing to common problem-solving and the maintenance of order.[122] Civil society therefore represents a capacity to promote social cooperation and can appropriately be deemed a potential contributor to self-governance.

If we make a distinction between conventional politics, centered on career politicians and professional administrators, and genuine politics—the ordering of the community to achieve social cooperation in pursuit of community aims—we can see that conventional politics is largely inattentive to civil society as a contributor to governance, whereas genuine politics is heavily concerned with civil society. Because the word "politics" has acquired such negative connotations, alternative phrases such as "civic leadership" and "civic capacity" have come to the forefront as ways of addressing the concerns of genuine politics. Under whatever name, genuine politics survives.

Still, civil society should not be romanticized as a benevolent and spontaneous expression of the human spirit. The institutions and practices of civil society are unevenly developed and can deteriorate as well as progress. They can also be narrow and exclusive if not linked to broad and inclusive community activities. If developed and linked appropriately, however, institutions of society can operate to transcend local-government boundaries, drawing people out of their economically segmented places of residence into the wider life of the metropolitan community. Local self-government would rest on a more solid foundation if communities developed an institutionally based means for taking stock of civil society and its ability to contribute to community problem-solving.

---

[122] See Joshua Cohen and Joel Rogers, "Secondary Associations and Democratic Governance," *Politics and Society* 20 (1992) for a discussion of "associational democracy" and how social groups can, under certain conditions, play a central role in public reasoning and successful governance.

III

The place of locality in current policy choice

7

The ideo-logics of urban land-use politics

ALAN A. ALTSHULER

I: THE ARGUMENT IN BRIEF

The centralizing forces highlighted by Derthick and others in this volume have encountered unusually successful resistance in the field of land-use policy. The rights and social regulatory revolutions, growing fiscal dependence on higher-level governments, and demands within urban areas themselves for services requiring metropolitan scale have all had significant impacts over the past half century. When all is said and done, though, localities remain the most significant public actors in shaping urban land use. My purposes in this chapter are to explain why and to portray the contours of contemporary debate about whether the land-use policy system is in need of fundamental reform, and if so how.

As for why: I argue that the resilience of localism in the field of land-use policy rests primarily on three pillars: the continuing view of land use as mainly an arena of private ownership and initiative, the predominant judgment of property owners that their interests are best served by local control, and the prosaic fact that land-use regulation is cheap.

As for the contours of debate: I shall argue that American land-use conflict is organized around two competing ideologies, one emphasizing communal values and the benefits of government intervention on their behalf, the other emphasizing individualistic values and the benefits of reliance on free markets. Within this framework, it is useful to distinguish three broad normative positions:

1. Greater centralization would be desirable.
2. The existing pattern, which combines local primacy in development permitting with highly varied organizational patterns for other purposes, is preferable to any likely alternative.

3. Government should reduce its role in favor of greater reliance on private
   market forces.

By and large, centralizing critics perceive a need for better instruments
to pursue egalitarian, environmental, or regional development objectives.
Privatizing critics seek greater insulation for private-property owners
against government regulation and the elimination of governmental impediments to the expression of market forces in land. In practice, champions of these opposing "reform" positions often find themselves defending
the status quo—as preferable, at least, to reform in the wrong direction.
This position of the status quo as the backup choice of even its most severe critics—who seem fairly evenly balanced in contemporary American
politics—is one of its greatest survival assets.

I concentrate here primarily on controversies about centralizing reform versus the status quo. The case for privatizing reform will loom constantly in the background, however, because it is ever on the minds of
those who advocate the other two positions.

The remainder of this chapter is organized as follows: Because there is
no consensual definition of the term "land-use policy," I seek to make my
own usage clear in section II. Section III provides a brief summary of key
themes that have emerged from recent scholarship on urban land-use politics. Section IV introduces the term "ideo-logic," arguing that most land-
use conflict is organized around ideologies that, in turn, are rooted in the
contrasting "logics" of public and free-market institutions in American
life. Section V examines ways in which the existing land-use policy system, characterized by nothing so much as fragmentation, enables propertied interests to combine (some would say cherry-pick among) elements
of the public and private ideo-logics in ways that serve their own interests.

Section VI addresses the question: Why has resistance to centralization
in the land-use arena been a good deal more successful than in another
arena of traditional (and often fiercely defended) local primacy, K–12 education? Section VII focuses on three specific cleavages between arguments for centralization on the one hand and local primacy or privatization on the other. Sections VIII and IX zero in on two sets of centralizing
arguments, emphasizing respectively the aims of managerial effectiveness
and of constraining private-sector tendencies toward inequality. Section
X considers the most promising institutional reform of a centralizing nature that has come along in recent decades, state growth management,

asking why its progress currently seems stalled and how (if at all) it promises to alter the dominant value orientations of land-use policy.

In the concluding section I argue that the existing land-use policy system works well for most purposes, but that its systemic bias, magnifying private market tendencies toward inequality and segregation, constitutes a profound moral flaw. Because many people consider this attribute one of the system's most attractive features, major change is unlikely in the near term. It represents a gross violation of the nation's public ideo-logic, however, so there is no likelihood, either, that pressures for reform will significantly abate.

II: THE SCOPE OF LAND-USE POLICY: TWO DEFINITIONS

Viewed narrowly, land use is among the most localized of policy arenas in urban America. It is, furthermore, among those most firmly in the hands of general-purpose local governments. In this narrow definition, land-use policy includes developing permitting (which I define to include zoning, subdivision, and building-occupancy regulation), property taxation, and the provision of local infrastructure.

Viewed broadly, on the other hand, collective land-use services are provided by all levels of American government, and increasingly as well by private associations of property owners. This broad definition includes the development, operation, and regulation of all common-use infrastructure (a term broad enough to include publicly owned expressways and privately owned electric power systems), whether serving one locality or many; all tax and regulatory policies bearing significantly on real property; and the government-like activities of private associations of property owners, at least insofar as these are undertaken to protect or enhance members' property values.

Following most students of land-use policy, I shall concentrate in this chapter on the narrow definition, and particularly its regulatory component. Land-use authority as so defined is a limited instrument. It does not enable local governments to command private actors or higher-level governments to invest within their boundaries. Nor is it invariably sufficient to block developments of importance to their residents.[1] In general, however, local land-use authority, combined with prevailing norms against development activity by higher-level governments in the face of local op-

[1] Michael N. Danielson and Jameson W. Doig, *New York: The Politics of Regional Development* (Berkeley: University of California Press, 1982), chap. 4.

position, provides an effective buffer against unwanted development activities within the boundaries of any general-purpose local government. Development regulation and real-estate taxation are among the powers that local residents most have in mind, furthermore, when they act to incorporate new suburbs and resist calls for metropolitan government.[2]

III: PATTERNS, TRENDS, PERSPECTIVES

Politics involves, most notably, interests, institutional arrangements, and normative beliefs (values). Students of urban politics have concentrated in recent decades overwhelmingly on the first and second elements of this triad. I shall emphasize the third, with particular attention to the issue of land-use regulation and to the value choices embodied in choices among institutional arrangements. Before proceeding, however, permit me to note several key points about patterns of interest aggregation and conflict in the land-use arena.

Localities vary widely in their land-use objectives. Numerous recent studies have effectively documented the primacy of prodevelopment coalitions in central cities, particularly in those with a recent history of economic decline or recession.[3] By contrast, antidevelopment forces tend to predominate in many residential suburbs, particularly those with mainly affluent residents. The residents of such jurisdictions commonly prefer to concentrate on amenity at home while earning their keep a reasonable commute away.[4]

Across this entire spectrum, conflict has intensified in recent decades between those who view land as a factor of production, to be transformed in pursuit of profit (for example, developers and industrialists) and those who view it as an element of nature or consumption, to be preserved and

---

2 Gary Miller, *Cities by Contract* (Cambridge, Mass.: MIT Press, 1981), chaps. 3–5; Nancy Burns, *The Formation of American Local Governments* (New York: Oxford University Press, 1994), 19–21, 41; Paul Kantor, *The Dependent City Revisited* (Boulder, Colo.: Westview Press, 1995), 161–75; John R. Logan and Harvey L. Molotch, *Urban Fortunes* (Berkeley: University of California Press, 1987), 181–99.

3 Logan and Molotch, *Urban Fortunes*, chaps. 3, 5, and 6; Kantor, *Dependent City*, chaps. 5–7; Clarence N. Stone, "Summing Up: Urban Regimes, Development Policy, and Political Arrangements," in *The Politics of Urban Development*, ed. Clarence N. Stone and Heywood T. Sanders (Lawrence: University Press of Kansas, 1987), 269–90; Alan DiGaetano, "Urban Political Regime Formation: A Study in Contrast," *Journal of Urban Affairs* (1989): 261–81; I. S. Rubin and H. L. Rubin, "Economic Development Incentives: The Poor (Cities) Pay More," *Urban Affairs Quarterly* (September 1987): 37–62; Robyne S. Turner, "Growth Politics and Downtown Development," *Urban Affairs Quarterly* (September 1992): 3–21.

4 Paul Peterson, *City Limits* (Chicago: University of Chicago Press, 1981), 30–2; Logan and Molotch, *Urban Fortunes*, 187–92; Danielson and Doig, *New York*, 79–94.

enjoyed as it is (for example, environmentalists and neighborhood residents). John R. Logan and Harvey Molotch usefully label this the conflict between exchange and use values in land, and I follow their example below.[5]

Additional contributing factors to the intensification of land-use conflict in recent years have included major federal aid cutbacks, state aid stagnation, and antitax pressures at the local level. Consequences of these trends have included more intense scrutiny of the net local fiscal consequences of any proposed development and a growing tendency for localities to impose exactions as conditions of building permits—that is, requirements for developers themselves to finance some of the infrastructure and public-service requirements generated by their projects.[6]

In arriving at its decisions, the typical locality ignores regional impacts. Regional authorities and agencies of higher-level governments as well often act with negligible regard for consequences outside the scope of their narrow mission definitions.[7] How do the activities of all these uncoordinated entities cumulate over time, and at regional scale?

Responses to this question fall into two diametrically opposed categories. According to the first, the overall pattern is one of surface incoherence and policy drift, yet also of deep-seated, perverse "mobilization of bias."[8] What one perceives at first glance is apparently hopeless fragmentation, an inability to make deliberate choices about urban form, and paralysis in the face of such critical issues as segregation, the growing inequality between rich and poor, and urban sprawl. A deeper analysis reveals, however, that the system serves a number of powerful interests extremely well. Most notably, it provides partisans of racial-class homogeneity at the neighborhood level with great protection, while ensuring investor dominance, frequently to the detriment of communal values, at regional scale. (Even if some localities opt out, major investors can nearly always find localities eager to compete for their favor.) The current favored reforms of those who advance this interpretation are state growth management, state judicial action to override exclusionary local land-use regulation, and in some cases metropolitan government.

Responses in the second category, by contrast, highlight key strengths

[5] Logan and Molotch, *Urban Fortunes*, 1–2, 17–31.

[6] Alan Altshuler and Jose A. Gomez-Ibanez, *Regulation for Revenue: The Political Economy of Land Use Exactions* (Washington, D.C.: Brookings Institution Press, 1994), chaps. 2 and 6.

[7] See Danielson and Doig, *New York*, 67–109, 154–62.

[8] The term "mobilization of bias" was coined by E. E. Schattschneider in *The Semi-Sovereign People* (New York: Holt, Rinehart, and Winston, 1960).

of the existing system, particularly its responsiveness and flexibility. The system is responsive in that local decision-makers are easily accessible to ordinary citizens and acutely sensitive to their concerns. It is flexible in that higher-level authorities can provide finely nuanced answers when, from time to time, they conclude that urgent problems require centralizing measures. While centralizing authority to deal with such issues as mass transit and regional water supply, for example, they can encourage greater neighborhood participation in local planning and zoning. In considering just how to centralize, moreover, they can choose among such options as encouraging localities to cooperate, creating regional authorities, or transferring authority to higher-level governments (county, state, or federal). If certain objectives have proven difficult to realize over the years (racial integration and control of urban form, for example), the primary explanation in this view is weakness of political support rather than institutional rigidity. The ability of the system to adapt when public support is clear has been demonstrated again and again, in areas as diverse as environmental protection, waste management, and expressway development. If change is difficult without such support, that is merely evidence of democracy at work.

IV: IDEO-LOGICS IN CONFLICT

Roger Friedland and Robert R. Alford have written that each major institution in contemporary society (for example, the family) has a distinctive logic—that is, a set of "organizing principles . . . available for organizations and individuals to elaborate." For example: "The institutional logic of capitalism is accumulation and the commodification of human activity. . . . That of democracy is participation and the extension of popular control over human activity. . . ." Modern social and political conflict, they observe, often has to do with selecting the institutional logic to prevail in specific policy arenas and circumstances. Ought health care, for example, to be regulated in accord with market or state criteria? What roles, if any, ought the logics of family and church be accorded in education?[9]

I speak of "ideo-" rather than "institutional" logics because my con-

---

[9] Roger Friedland and Robert R. Alford, "Bringing Society Back In: Symbols, Practices, and Institutional Contradictions," in *The New Institutionalism in Organizational Analysis*, ed. Walter W. Powell and Paul J. Dimaggio (Chicago: University of Chicago Press, 1991), 232–63, esp. 248 and 256. Students of public management commonly speak of such conflict as contending over "the face of the issue." Is the regulation of TV marketing to children, for example, predominantly an issue of child protection or of civil liberties?

cern is to spotlight those elements most pertinent to political combat and mobilization—which have the character of ideology as well as institutional orientation.[10] The basic Friedland-Alford proposition, however—that social conflict often revolves around the question of which institutional domain ought to be recognized as holding primary jurisdiction (and therefore which "ideo-logic" ought to prevail)—is central to the argument presented here.

As I read it, the overarching conflict in urban land-use politics is between two sharply disparate ideo-logics, one dominant in the public sector, the other in the private economy. The former highlights such communal values as equality, integration, and democracy, and provides a rationale for frequent government intervention to correct market failures. The latter stresses individual freedom to own property and choose one's associates, the efficiency of market allocation, and the perverse effects of big government.[11]

To be more precise: In the public sector, one is normally entitled to services on the basis of need, expressed demand, or residence rather than the amount of revenue contributed; and discrimination on the basis of such characteristics as race, creed, gender, or disability is generally forbidden.[12] By contrast, the private ideo-logic stresses the benefits of letting incomes and services be allocated in the marketplace, and of government non-intervention with respect to matters of personal association (the membership practices of private clubs, for example). The public ideo-logic venerates community decision-making and the procedures of democracy, whereas the private ideo-logic venerates individual decision-making and the procedures of market interaction. The public ideo-logic,

[10] I employ the term "ideology" to denote an integrated set of ideas—beliefs, values, behavioral norms, and generic action priorities—serving to portray a desirable set of social arrangements and to provide supportive arguments on which partisans can draw.

    For a useful discussion of key ideologies that have influenced state and local governance in American history, see Charles R. Adrian and Michael R. Fine, *State and Local Politics* (Chicago: Lyceum and Nelson-Hall, 1991), chap. 2. The theme conspicuously missing from this discussion, however, is the twentieth-century ideology of democratic reform, oriented toward the purification of democratic institutions (e.g., by civil-service and campaign-finance reform) and the perfection of mechanisms by which citizens can control government (e.g., the primary and referendum, sunshine and citizen-participation requirements, citizen-suit provisions). This ideology has arguably had a greater impact on twentieth-century American politics at every level of government than any other. See James A. Morone, *The Democratic Wish* (New York: Basic Books, 1990), introduction and chaps. 3 and 8.

[11] See Daniel Bell, *The Cultural Contradictions of Capitalism* (New York: Basic Books, 1978), 251–82, for an excellent general discussion of these contrasting value sets.

[12] See, for example, Aaron Wildavsky, *Speaking Truth to Power* (Boston: Little, Brown, 1979), chap. 15.

finally, stresses the communal interest in natural resources (for example, land), even where they are privately owned, because the externalities of use decisions—that is, effects on parties other than the immediate buyers and sellers—are often highly significant. The private ideo-logic, by contrast, views property ownership as a fundamental human right, defines it expansively, and maintains that compensation should be paid whenever governments impose regulations that impair market value.

In specific political controversies, these two ideo-logics are typically associated with groups in conflict. More generally, however, they coexist in the minds of voters, who typically consider each applicable in its place. It follows that the most important decision to be made about a specific issue is often whether to classify it as public or private. Nowhere is this more true than in the field of land use, where most ownership and investment is private, but where claims of communal interest are intense—and, indeed, are commonly made even by property owners against one another.

Needless to say, policymakers often blend elements of these two ideo-logics in practice—for example, in authorizing zoning boards to strive for both property-value enhancement and environmental protection. And institutions often stray from their organizing principles in practice, as witness the long history of blatant racial discrimination by public bodies.[13] Additionally, there are significant tensions *within* each of these ideo-logics. Two elements of the private ideo-logic, for example, are the right of homeowners to undertake collective action against change (via private covenants or public zoning) and the right of investors to develop their land with minimal concern for side-effects. Similarly, two elements of the public ideo-logic are the high valuation placed on small-scale, grass-roots democracy and on governmental capacity to realize broad societal objectives even where this requires large scale—for example, to regulate air quality.

V: OBTAINING THE BEST OF BOTH IDEO-LOGICS: THREE STRATEGIES

Propertied interests in the modern metropolis, ranging from homeowners to great corporations, have a problem. Their first instinct is to argue that land use is essentially private, that government should leave them alone to

[13] See Evan McKenzie, *Privatopia: Homeowner Associations and the Rise of Residential Private Government* (New Haven, Conn.: Yale University Press, 1994), 62–8.

enjoy and exploit their property as they will. But they are also eager for a wide variety of collective services, some of which (such as zoning to protect property values) are even regulatory. In seeking these collective services, they risk strengthening the view that land use is an arena in which the public ideo-logic should apply.

This danger cannot be entirely averted. In its complexity, however, the land-use policy system affords an array of mix-and-match opportunities, enabling those with wealth and influence often to secure the best (for themselves) of both ideo-logics at once. Most notably, it presents few barriers to the incorporation of newly developing enclaves and independent localities; it is open to the substitution of private governance by groups of property owners for significant components of traditional public governance; and it is adept at meeting the supralocal service demands of corporate and homeowner interests while minimizing impacts on local regulatory prerogatives.

The ease and ubiquity of local incorporation in small, homogeneous jurisdictions has long been one of the most salient features of U.S. urban governance. Its significance lies in the fact that the egalitarian norms of American public life are generally held to apply only within the bounds of specific jurisdictions. If, on the one hand, a responsibility is defined as federal (for example, social security and national parks), the norms dictate equal treatment of all Americans or preference for those in greatest need. If, on the other hand, it is defined as local (for example, admission to public schools and local recreational facilities), the norms apply only locally.

Stated another way, local incorporation enables groups of urban residents, and particularly the more affluent among them, to import major elements of the private ideo-logic into the public sector. They can exercise public land-use authority to exclude people who might make redistributive claims upon them, and they can procure collective services almost as if from a private association of like-minded members. Not quite, of course. No community is entirely homogeneous. But local residents can rest comfortably in the knowledge that egalitarian norms are operative only within the narrow community they have created.

To the extent that governmental responsibilities within a region are thus diffused, the pattern of public action viewed regionally will be supportive of segregation and inequality—even if actions within each locality are integrationist and egalitarian. This is not just possible, of course. It is the American norm.

The second method noted above, private governance, displays these characteristics in even more accentuated form. More than 30 million Americans now live in private-interest communities (governed in significant part by private-property owner associations), including about 4 million who live in physically gated communities.[14] By all accounts, their number is growing rapidly.[15] These organizations, generally authorized by deed covenants at the time of original development, typically provide a wide variety of collective services—including land use and design regulation far more intrusive than would normally be legal if carried out by a public entity.[16] Private-property associations are typically exempt from other strictures on governmental action as well. For example, they often bar outsiders (except those specifically invited by residents) from their streets. This movement toward private governance is evident in the business sector as well. More than a thousand business-improvement districts (BIDs) have been created in recent years to provide collective services over and above those available from government agencies.[17]

Many observers of this movement toward private-association responsibility for the provision of collective services worry that it will sap member support for government-provided services, on which most residents and enterprises still depend, thereby sharply accentuating the overall pattern of urban inequality. The standard defense, of course, is that associa-

---

[14] Timothy Egan, "Many Seek Security in Private Condominiums," *New York Times* (September 3, 1995): 1, 22. These associations now have their own trade group, the Community Associations Institute (CAI) of Alexandria, Virginia. CAI is the source of Egan's numbers. The *Los Angeles Times* reported in 1990 that 54 percent of Southern California home shoppers said they wanted a gated, walled community. Cited in Edward J. Blakely and Mary Gail Snyder, *Fortress America: Gated and Walled Communities in the United States* (Cambridge, Mass.: Lincoln Institute of Land Policy, 1994), 8. See also McKenzie, *Privatopia*, 12.

[15] See David J. Kennedy, "Residential Associations as State Actors," *Yale Law Journal* (December 1995): 761–93. Kennedy reports that the number of homeowners' associations known to the Community Associations Institute rose from about 500 in 1962 to 150,000 in 1992 (764–5). Since reporting is voluntary, he adds, these figures are clearly underestimates.

[16] In Houston this system substitutes entirely for public zoning. See Robert D. Thomas and Richard W. Murray, *Progrowth Politics: Change and Governance in Houston* (Berkeley: IGS Press, Institute of Government Studies, University of California, Berkeley, 1991), chap. 12.

[17] The nation's best-known business improvement district is New York City's Grand Central Partnership. In New York State, at least, such districts operate under state charter. It takes a majority vote of the affected businesses to form one, but thereafter they have the power to levy mandatory assessments—in effect, to tax. See Thomas J. Lueck, "Business Improvement Districts Grow at Price of Accountability," *New York Times* (November 20, 1994): 1, 46; and Heather McDonald, "BIDs Really Work," *City Journal* (Spring 1996): 29–42.

tion members are just exercising self-reliance in the face of government service inadequacies beyond their control.[18]

Local government incorporation and private governance are, it bears mention, complementary rather than substitute strategies. The members of private-property associations have at least three reasons to seek public incorporation or to become firmly ensconced in accommodating localities. First, most associations provide only a narrow range of services. Second, without local incorporation there is always the danger of annexation by adjacent municipalities or inclusion within county service jurisdictions. Third, incorporated localities are eligible for many types of intergovernmental aid that are not available to private associations.

Finally, a word on regional issues. The greatest challenge to local and property-owner primacy in urban land-use politics stems from the obvious supralocal scale of many urban problems and public-service demands. When business groups become convinced that expressway or airport improvements would be good for the regional economy, or homeowner groups become persuaded that environmental regulation (mainly of corporations) would benefit health, amenity, and their property values, their commitments to classifying land use as private and to local primacy in the public sector often prove elastic.

So there *has* been considerable centralization in the land-use arena (broadly defined) over the past half century. The nation's main-line transportation, housing finance, and environmental regulatory systems are almost entirely products of federal and state action, for example, and most metropolitan areas today have regional transit, airport, water-supply, and sewage authorities. Policymakers have generally crafted new supralocal missions narrowly, however, and assigned them to specialized functional agencies, thereby responding to urgent demands seriatim while striving to guard against drift toward broad-gauge regional government. In most cases, furthermore, by statute or political norm, they have preserved the most valued jewel in the local land-use crown—the capacity to veto unwanted development.

One way of thinking about these mix-and-match opportunities is that they represent "loopholes" in the public ideo-logic, enabling propertied interests perversely to carry their private-sector privileges with them into the public sector. An alternative view, however, is that the dichotomy be-

---

[18] Ibid., 31–2, 41.

tween the public and private ideo-logics is so stark that most Americans long to soften it. In this view, the system's openness to mix-and-match arrangements is among its greatest strengths. Regardless of one's normative judgment, it is difficult to escape the conclusion that this feature of the existing land-use policy system is an important source of its political resiliency.

VI: RESISTANCE TO CENTRALIZATION: LAND USE AND EDUCATION COMPARED

The desire for opportunities to obtain collective services without triggering redistributive claims, I have argued, appears to be an extremely powerful motivator in U.S. urban politics. If this were the only factor that entered into decision-making about governmental structure, all public functions would be performed locally. This is manifestly not the case. So the question remains: Why have pressures for centralization had so much less effect in the field of land-use regulation than in most others? A comparison with the field of K–12 education may be instructive.

Land use and education are often paired as the two policy arenas in which pressures for local control are most intense. Both are—to use a term coined by Oliver Williams—characterized by high "lifestyle impact."[19] In Williams's definition, a public function is high in lifestyle impact to the extent that it bears heavily on patterns of human interaction and socialization—for example, by influencing the population mix of neighborhoods and schools.[20] Urban residents are most resistant to the centralization of functions with high lifestyle impact. When forced by circumstances beyond their control, moreover, to consider inter-local cooperation in the performance of such functions, they seek partners with similar socioeconomic profiles.[21] By contrast, such programs as utility regulation, sewage treatment, and highway transportation, though vital,

---

[19] Oliver Williams, *Metropolitan Political Analysis* (New York: Free Press, 1971), 88–93.

[20] "Zoning and schools are two prime local policy areas which affect the socialization of children and the casual associations centered around the domicile. To a lesser extent, other civic policies, such as those which pertain to libraries, recreation programs, cultural programs, and certain aspects of police and health programs, also partake of these qualities" (Williams, *Metropolitan Political Analysis*, 89). Williams goes on to note that some other services have lifestyle significance in selected communities—fire protection, for example, in those with volunteer departments.

[21] Willis D. Hawley, "On Understanding Metropolitan Political Integration," in *Theoretical Perspectives on Urban Politics*, ed. Willis Hawley and Michael Lipsky (Englewood Cliffs, N.J.: Prentice Hall, 1976), 119–24.

have few obvious social interaction effects, and there is far greater receptivity to their centralization.[22]

Despite these similarities, the structure of educational governance has proven far more susceptible to pressures for centralization over the past half century than that of land-use regulatory governance. The number of general-purpose local governments—the usual repository of land-use authority—has been roughly constant since 1940, but the number of local school districts has contracted by 87 percent.[23] Though the remaining local school districts are still the frontline vehicles of educational service delivery, they have been subjected to increasingly pervasive state and federal policy guidance.[24] Such oversight of local land-use regulation remains sporadic and weak.

What accounts for these sharp differences? One cannot be sure, but the following factors stand out as prime candidates:

1. From a political (even if not an economic) standpoint, education is a quintessential public function. That is, there is near-universal agreement in modern America that children have a right to education without charge, that governments are obligated to provide it (or arrange for its provision), and that this public obligation overrides even the prerogatives of parents, who may in some cases resist having their children educated.[25] Two implications follow: that government bears responsibility for the success of the whole enterprise, rather than merely for guarding against

---

[22] "Assuming no outside interventions, policy areas which are perceived as neutral with respect to controlling social access may be centralized; policy areas which are perceived as controlling social access will remain decentralized" (Williams, *Metropolitan Political Analysis,* 93).

[23] The peak period of school-district consolidation was 1939–40 to 1970–1, when the number of districts contracted by 85 percent, from 117,108 to 17,995. As of 1992–3 the count stood at 15,025. *Digest of Educational Statistics,* U.S. Department of Education, National Center for Educational Statistics, 1994.
  Meanwhile, the number of incorporated municipalities rose from 16,220 in 1942 to 19,296 in 1992. The number of nonschool special districts rose from 8,299 in 1942 to 33,131 in 1992. *Statistical Abstract of the United States 1994,* Table 460. See also Kathryn A. Foster, *The Political Economy of Special Purpose Governments* (Washington, D.C.: Georgetown University Press, 1997).

[24] David Tyack and Elizabeth Hansot, *Managers of Virtue* (New York: Basic Books, 1982), chaps. 17 and 18; Gerald Grant, *The World We Created at Hamilton High* (Cambridge, Mass.: Harvard University Press, 1988), 124–9.

[25] Education is not a pure public good in economic terms because a high proportion of the benefit accrues to the immediate service recipients, and it is very susceptible to being marketed privately. The political justification for treating it as a public good is that major benefits accrue to society as well. See E. S. Savas, *Privatization: The Key to Better Government* (Chatham House Publishers, 1987), 53; and John Donahue, *The Privatization Decision* (New York: Basic Books, 1989), 19–20.

negative side effects; and that this enterprise as a whole should be driven by public values.

Land development, by contrast, is generally considered a private-sector activity. Historically, government has concentrated on three primary roles: establishing the framework of law for market transactions; regulating private land use for the protection of owners against their neighbors; and providing certain collective services widely desired by private owners.[26] The scope of government responsibility has expanded beyond this historic core in recent decades, most notably to prohibit racial and religious discrimination, to protect the natural environment, and in a few states to reduce barriers to affordable housing.[27] But the primary responsibility for initiating land-use change remains in private hands, and government action continues to be overwhelmingly reactive rather than proactive.

It bears emphasis that the element of land-use policy that remains most decentralized is the most negative—the right to reject proposed development. The closest analogue in the education sphere is the right to exclude students who live outside the district. And this is the element of local autonomy that remains most sacrosanct—even in the face of constitutional challenges based on the fact that it precludes racial integration of the public schools.

2. Most voters spend a dozen or more years in the public education system while growing up (and again when they have children). So they are more familiar with it than any other public function, and they are deeply imbued with its ethos as an egalitarian, socially unifying institution. By contrast, most voters experience their own real property as private, and have few if any direct encounters with regulatory bodies during their entire lives. Thus it seems natural to view education as among the most public of functions, and land use as among the most private.

3. Equality is a value with many dimensions. Among these, the American public ideo-logic has always stressed equality of opportunity and equality before the law rather than equality of economic outcomes. Since

---

[26] With respect to the last item in this series, collective-service provision, it is useful to distinguish between direct government production and government activities to arrange for production by others (e.g., contracting and franchising). See also Savas, *Privatization*, chaps. 4 and 6; and Donald F. Kettl, *Sharing Power: Public Governance and Private Markets* (Washington, D.C.: Brookings Institution Press, 1993), chaps. 1, 2, and 7–9.

[27] For a brief, exemplary treatment of this evolution in one (vanguard) state, see Gerrit Knaap and Arthur C. Nelson, *The Regulated Landscape: Lessons on State Land Use Planning from Oregon* (Cambridge, Mass.: Lincoln Institute of Land Policy, 1992), 16–36.

the origin of public education, it has been generally perceived as the nation's principal instrument for the realization of equal opportunity. As such, it has gradually become recognized as a fundamental right.

Thus, while the United States lagged behind other advanced democracies in adopting most elements of the welfare state, it led the world in developing universal public education. And though the nation's income distribution is the most unequal in the developed world, the most conspicuous feature of its public education system is its leveling orientation—in the sense of emphasizing the needs of average and below-average students far more than those of gifted students.[28] Educational segregation provided the flashpoint that ignited the civil rights movement in the 1950s, and the civil rights movement in turn brought the theme of equality before the law into all aspects of education during the 1960s and 1970s—from school assignment to tracking within schools to the rights of students threatened with discipline.[29]

Although significant efforts have been made to bring about similar changes in land-use policy, they have by and large failed.[30] The connection between land-use regulation and equality of opportunity has proven too subtle to provide a focal point for mass mobilization. The land use element of immediate concern to most people is housing, and it is a commodity that all except some of the very poor obtain in the private marketplace. The great majority of Americans, furthermore, enjoy excellent housing conditions, and nearly two-thirds are members of households that own their own units.[31] So the basis for a popular movement to overturn the dominance of market perspectives on land use is lacking.

[28] See, for example, Arthur G. Powell, Eleanor Farrar, and David K. Cohen, *The Shopping Mall High School* (Boston: Houghton Mifflin, 1985), esp. chaps. 3 and 4.

[29] Tyack and Hansot, *Managers of Virtue*, 224–49; Grant, *Hamilton High*, 124–9, 144–50; John W. Meyer, "Organizational Factors Affecting Legalization in Education," in *Organizational Environments,* ed. John W. Meyer and W. Richard Scott (Beverly Hills, Calif.: Sage, 1983), 217–32.

[30] The main exceptions to this rule are as follows: Massachusetts and Connecticut have enacted antisnob zoning laws, which enable developers to appeal local refusals of development permitting to build affordable housing. California requires municipalities to provide regulatory incentives, including density bonuses, to facilitate the development of low- and moderate-cost housing. And the New Jersey Supreme Court, in a series of "Mount Laurel" decisions since 1975, has specified that each municipality's regulations must provide a "realistic opportunity for the construction of its fair share of the present and prospective need for low- and moderate-income housing." J. Barry Cullingworth, *The Political Culture of Planning* (New York: Routledge, 1993), chap. 5. The quotation, from the first Mount Laurel decision, appears on page 67.

[31] As of 1990, 64 percent of American households owned the dwelling units in which they resided. U.S. Bureau of the Census, *City and County Data Book: 1994* (Washington, D.C.: U.S. Government Printing Office, 1994), Table A: States—Housing.

4. Education is a very expensive function. Thus, localities encountering fiscal stress have had powerful incentives to seek assistance from higher levels of government. With such assistance, of course, has come increasing regulation, predominantly oriented toward egalitarian and due-process values. Moreover, as the state share of education spending has come to rival the local share in most states, the idea has gathered force that egalitarian spending norms should apply statewide rather than just within localities. The result has been a wave of litigation at the state level—some of which has already resulted in landmark rulings—to equalize school-district finances.[32] By contrast, the public costs of land-use regulation are very low,[33] so localities have felt negligible pressure to seek higher-level financial assistance.

5. Finally, the components of land-use policy, broadly defined, are much more easily separable than those of education policy. Local authority to reject new land development does not preclude the existence of similar authority at higher levels of government (based on environmental regulation, for example); state and local infrastructure agencies go about their separate activities with very limited need for interaction; and so on.

By comparison, the elements of education policy are much more tightly coupled. The purpose, after all, is to bring the elements together, in integrated fashion, for the benefit of each child. Consequently, centralized policy choices (for example, on tracking, testing, special education, and student disciplinary rights) must be blended with local choices in every classroom. When conflicts arise between the policy preferences of different levels of government, moreover, authoritative decisions about how to resolve them can be made only at the higher level. Informally, teachers and school administrators often have considerably more discretion than this would suggest, but the centralizing trend has been clear and strong.[34]

[32] The U.S. Supreme Court, by a vote of 5–4 in *San Antonio v. Rodriguez* (411 U.S. 1, 1973; 1973 U.S. LEXIS 91), rejected the contention that large variations in school spending among school districts within a state violate the U.S. Constitution. Since then, however, nineteen state supreme courts have found cause in their state constitutions to mandate school fiscal equalization, including twelve since 1989. As of 1994, litigation was pending in another seventeen states. See Deborah A. Verstegen, "The New Wave of State Finance Litigation," *Phi Delta Kappan* (November 1994): 243–50.

[33] Although the costs to regulated parties can be high, the popularity of land-use regulation is based on the widespread conviction that on balance it enhances property values. See Robert H. Nelson, *Zoning and Property Rights* (Cambridge, Mass.: MIT Press, 1977), 11–8; Christine Boyer, *Dreaming the Rational City* (Cambridge, Mass.: MIT Press, 1983), 156–69.

[34] David Cohen, "Reforming School Politics," *Harvard Education Review* (November 1978): 429–47; Tyack and Hansot, *Managers of Virtue*, 242–54; Gerald Grant, "Children's Rights and Adult Confusions," *The Public Interest* (Fall 1982): 83–99.

Only in Oregon and perhaps Florida can anything comparable be observed in the field of land-use regulation (see below).

VII: THEMES OF CRITIQUE AND REFORM

As noted previously, local primacy in the field of land-use policy faces challenges from two camps: those who favor stronger regulation and greater government centralization on one hand, and those who favor greater deference to private property rights and market forces on the other. Both challenges involve a mix of substantive and managerial arguments. Those favoring centralization emphasize communal values and the need for regional or greater scale to carry out certain missions effectively. Those preferring less government altogether emphasize the value of private ownership and the inefficiency of government relative to the market sector. Although these debates largely pit elements of the public ideo-logic against elements of the private, this is not the entire story. Advocates of local primacy and those of regionalism, for example, often differ primarily in their choices of which aspects of the public ideo-logic to stress.

The crosscurrents can get rather confusing. But in practice, urban land-use debate tends to be organized around three main cleavages: democracy versus effectiveness; equality versus market deference; and community versus private property.

The first of these cleavages pits the ideal of neighborhood-scale democracy against that of businesslike effectiveness in addressing large-scale problems. The democratic impulse as conceived in local politics is for decisions to be made by citizens assembled face-to-face.[35] Where this is not feasible, it is to maximize opportunities for citizen participation via such procedures as referenda, public hearings, citizen suits, and open-meeting requirements. The managerial impulse, on the other hand, is to professionalize government, match it in scale to the problems it confronts, and insulate it from day-to-day political pressures. Armed with evidence that urban problems can be traced to large-scale forces and interaction effects, its champions commonly press for transfers of responsibility from gener-

---

[35] Democracy need not be face to face. The distinguishing characteristic of representative democracy and bureaucratic action at the local level, however, is face-to-face interaction between officials and citizens. See Douglas Yates, *The Ungovernable City* (Cambridge, Mass.: MIT Press, 1977), 20–33, 120–45. On local direct democracy, see Jane Mansbridge, *Beyond Adversary Democracy* (Chicago: University of Chicago Press, 1980), Part II.

al-purpose local governments to quasi-autonomous regional authorities, new metropolitan governments, or higher-level governments.[36]

The egalitarian-market cleavage is about the substantive purposes of public land-use policy. Should it be driven primarily by such objectives as racial integration and the improvement of housing opportunities for the poor, or should it aim mainly to provide a favorable climate for new investment while protecting existing property values? Advocates of the former position stress that whenever public authority is invoked—to zone, for example, or to develop infrastructure, or to adjudicate disputes under property-owner covenants—public values should predominate. Advocates of the latter maintain that market deference benefits everyone. Above all, they argue, it is the surest path to prosperity—which enhances the capacity of both individuals and institutions to pursue whatever objectives they may have. It is, in this sense, value free itself, though of great value to all community members.[37]

These factual claims on behalf of market deference, it bears note, have themselves become increasingly controversial in recent decades. Critics have pointed out that growth often has negative as well as positive effects. On the micro level, it frequently produces greater traffic congestion, more crowded schools, increased pressure on open space, water shortages, and even tax increases. On the macro level, there is at most a weak correlation between rates of regional population and economic growth, on one hand, and rates of per capita income growth and unemployment decline on the other.[38] Despite these criticisms, however, the market-deference model remains politically dominant in the great majority of American localities.

The communitarian-libertarian cleavage has most fully manifested itself as a doctrinal battle in the domain of law and regulation. Its foci are the nature of property ownership, the procedures that should be followed when regulation is deemed necessary, and the circumstances in which owners are entitled to compensation.

---

[36] See Neal R. Peirce, *Citistates: How Urban America Can Prosper in a Competitive World* (Washington, D.C.: Seven Locks Press, 1993), chap. 1; David Rusk, *Cities without Suburbs* (Washington, D.C.: Woodrow Wilson Center Press, 1993), chaps. 1 and 4; Anthony Downs, *New Visions for Metropolitan America* (Washington, D.C.: Brookings Institution Press, 1994), chaps. 9 and 10; *Reshaping Government in Metropolitan Areas* (New York: Committee for Economic Development, 1970); Luther Halsey Gulick, *The Metropolitan Problem and American Ideas* (New York: Knopf, 1962).

[37] On the concept of value-free development, see Logan and Molotch, *Urban Fortunes*, 32–3.

[38] Peter K. Eisinger, *The Rise of the Entrepreneurial State* (Madison: University of Wisconsin Press, 1988), 41–9; Logan and Molotch, *Urban Fortunes*, 84–95.

In the communitarian view, land is a natural resource and owners are properly conceived as trustees—with privileges, to be sure, but also profound obligations, both to contemporaries and to future generations. It is the task of government to define these obligations and ensure that owners respect them. No definitive limits on the scope of regulation can be established, because the scope and nature of future threats cannot be foretold. Nor, for the same reason, is it wise to require regulation in accord with precise standards. So long as owners are left in physical possession of (and with some viable economic use for) their property, they should not be entitled to compensation. Government regulatory action, like change in the tax code, is a normal risk of ownership. At times, more generous compensation may be advisable from a political standpoint. To establish any broader "right" of compensation, however, would severely undermine the capacity of government to safeguard the paramount community interest in land.[39]

In the libertarian view, by contrast, land is fundamentally a market commodity. Government should, in general, limit itself to enforcing contracts and adjudicating "nuisance" disputes among property owners. Regulation in the name of broader values should be exceptional. Regulatory standards should be precise and known in advance. Most significantly, private owners should have a right to compensation for any adverse effects of such regulation on their property values.[40] Given the imprecision of real-estate appraisal and the potential for infinite amounts of litigation, most libertarians accept that compensation should in practice be available only when losses exceed some percentage. But many would set that percentage quite low. The Republicans' 1994 Contract with America, for example, specified just 10 percent, and the U.S. House of Representatives voted in 1995 to require compensation whenever a federal action reduced the value of private property by 20 percent or more.[41] This bill did not be-

[39] See William Michael Treanor, "The Original Understanding of the Takings Clause and the Political Process," *Columbia Law Review* (May 1995): 782–887. Treanor demonstrates persuasively that this was the original understanding of the takings clause, and that with very rare exceptions it has prevailed throughout American history. It is under intense current fire, however.

[40] See Richard A. Epstein, *Takings: Private Property and the Power of Eminent Domain* (Cambridge, Mass.: Harvard University Press, 1985), chaps. 17–19 and conclusion; Richard A. Epstein, *Bargaining with the State* (Princeton, N.J.: Princeton University Press, 1993), 80–9; William A. Fischel, *Regulatory Takings* (Cambridge, Mass.: Harvard University Press, 1995), chaps. 4 and 5.

[41] Treanor, "Takings Clause," 878–9; Bob Benenson, "GOP Sets the 104th Congress on New Regulatory Course," *Congressional Quarterly* (June 17, 1995): 1693–1705, esp. 1699.

come law, but the enactment of something like it remains a central objective of the conservative movement.

The remainder of this chapter focuses on the managerial and egalitarian critiques, and on the most significant reform proposal that they have stimulated in recent decades—state growth management.

VIII: THE MANAGERIAL CRITIQUE

Like the theme of market deference, that of managerial rationality purports to be value-free—purely instrumental, that is, facilitating the achievement of whatever substantive objectives the community may have. The basic values in this case are capacity and efficiency—capacity to deal with the great issues of urban life (as opposed merely to those contained within the boundaries of specific localities), and efficiency in the sense of mission accomplishment at the lowest possible cost. A further claim routinely advanced is that local government "rationalization" will enhance regional competitiveness, thereby serving the value-free objective of prosperity.[42]

Managerial critics of the existing land-use policy system commonly focus on its perverse incentives for localities to pursue "beggar thy neighbor" policies (for example, luring employers while refusing to accept housing for employees); on its incapacity to formulate or pursue a regional vision; on the need for supralocal scale to perform certain vital functions effectively; and on the policy gridlock at metropolitan scale that often flows from local government fragmentation.[43] All of these criticisms point toward the need for metropolitan government or state leadership in achieving integrated solutions to metropolitan problems.

Although appealing to good-government organizations, regional me-

---

[42] See Peirce, *Citistates*, 291–8; Rusk, *Cities without Suburbs*, 40–1; William R. Barnes and Larry C. Ledebur, *City Distress, Metropolitan Disparities, and Economic Growth* (National League of Cities, 1992); Scott Greer, *Metropolitics* (New York: Wiley, 1963), esp. 8–10. Greer labeled the three dominant themes of metropolitan reform "capitalist realism" (efficiency and economy), "fertility and the future" (economic competitiveness and growth), and "purification" (eliminate political corruption). Only the last, he found, when it was advanced in a context of recent scandal, had much capacity to offset voter fears and suspicions of proposals for governmental reorganization.

[43] *Metropolitan Politics: A Reader*, 2nd ed., ed. Michael N. Danielson (Boston: Little, Brown, 1971), 85–103, 241–59; Committee for Economic Development, *Reshaping Government*; Peirce, *Citistates*, 1–37, 291–325; Victor Jones and Donald Rothblatt, "Governance of the San Francisco Bay Area," in *Metropolitan Governance: American/Canadian Intergovernmental Perspectives*, ed. Donald N. Rothblatt and Andrew Sancton (Berkeley: IGS Press, Institute of Government Studies, University of California, Berkeley, 1993), 388–421.

dia, academics, and many business leaders, these concerns have rarely become major issues in local politics. How come? Probably not because the idea of matching governmental scale to the magnitude of problems, or of making each region more competitive economically, is in principle controversial. But these ideas have proven too abstract to serve as effective foci for political mobilization.[44] So problems associated with them tend to appear on the agenda in far more specific, concrete form—how to address a regional water shortage, or improve the regional airport, or secure funding for a new convention center.

Those seeking support for regional solutions to such problems have invariably faced intense pressure to demonstrate that their recommendations pose no threat to business, homeowner, or local government interests. Indeed, the reformers have generally found it insufficient to calm local fears. They have been unlikely to succeed in the absence of widespread, enthusiastic local support. Their primary tactics in pursuing such support have been to emphasize that new regional programs will be assigned to agencies with unambiguous economic development agendas, that they will be insulated from normal politics (via special district management or dedicated revenue streams), and that they will respect local land-use prerogatives.

These strategies have been less available, of course, to groups pursuing state or regional land-use regulation. It has occasionally been possible to recruit developer support, however, for some affordable-housing initiatives without triggering opposition from other business interests,[45] and large numbers of homeowners have frequently been responsive to calls for environmental regulation—so long as they perceive it as focused primarily on business practices. Whatever the proposed regional or statewide initiative, however, it has usually been crafted to leave local veto power over development proposals untouched.

Inequality problems, however, are often invulnerable to attack by infrastructure investment or by adding new regulatory barriers for developers to overcome. When pressure has grown to address such problems, the tendency has been to define them as purely fiscal, requiring monetary transfers, rather than directly to attack patterns of segregation and the local policies that help sustain them. This has recently occurred in the field

---

[44] Greer, *Metropolitics*, chaps. 5–8.
[45] See, for example, Charles A. Hales, "Higher Density + Certainty = Affordable Housing for Portland, Oregon," *Urban Land* (September 1991): 12–15; Knaap and Nelson, *The Regulated Landscape*, 200, 202.

of education, where litigation about state responsibility for addressing cross-district disparities has been sweeping the country. Both plaintiffs and the courts have chosen to define this issue as fiscal, despite ample evidence that student mix has a greater impact on educational outcomes than spending levels,[46] and despite concern that in selecting this approach they were leaving themselves open to the charge of reviving the "separate but equal" doctrine, once thought to have been dispatched forever by the U.S. Supreme Court in its 1954 *Brown* decision. The focus on money had considerably less potential for generating an explosive backlash, of course, than a focus on student transfers or strategies to increase residential integration.[47]

The overall capacity of localities to manage land use within their boundaries has certainly ebbed in recent decades—a victim of cumulative shifts of functional and fiscal responsibility to higher levels of government and the increasing mobility of private-investment capital. Even to carry out redevelopment initiatives covering areas of a few square blocks, localities are generally dependent on grants, loans, or direct infrastructure investments by higher-level governments, along with commitments by global corporations that lack any sentimental ties of place.[48] They are increasingly preoccupied, moreover, with reacting to the initiatives of regional, state, and federal agencies—mainly public-works initiatives during the 1950s and 1960s, and regulatory initiatives more recently.[49]

What localities have retained (with rare exceptions), however, is legal authority to block private development within their boundaries. Because their primacy is so well accepted in this domain, they have great legitimacy as well when they seek to block development initiatives by higher-level

[46] See John E. Chubb and Terry M. Moe, *Politics, Markets, and American Schools* (Washington, D.C.: Brookings Institution Press, 1990), 115–40; and Christopher Jencks et al., *Inequality* (New York: Basic Books, 1972), 93–106.
[47] The evidence is weak, it bears note, that either approach would have large effects on educational outcomes. For additional evidence on the weak effects of spending differences (over and above the studies cited in the previous footnote), see Eric A. Hanushek et al., *Making Schools Work* (Washington, D.C.: Brookings Institution Press, 1994), chap. 5.
[48] The balance, it should be noted, shifted dramatically toward reliance on private investors during the 1980s. Bernard Frieden and Lynne Sagalyn, *Downtown, Inc.* (Cambridge, Mass.: MIT Press, 1989), chap. 8. The anatomy of a much larger project, circa 1980, is laid bare in Bryan D. Jones and Lynn W. Bachelor, *The Sustaining Hand: Community Leadership and Corporate Power*, 2nd ed. (Lawrence: University Press of Kansas, 1993), chap. 6.
[49] See Altshuler and Gomez-Ibanez, *Regulation for Revenue*, 25–32; Paul Peterson, *The Price of Federalism* (Washington, D.C.: Brookings Institution Press, 1995), chap. 7; Danielson and Doig, *New York*, chaps. 4 and 5; Joseph Zimmerman, *Contemporary American Federalism* (New York: Praeger, 1992), chap. 4.

governments. Regardless of whether statutes provide for local vetoes, few public investments by regional, state, or federal agencies today go forward in the face of intense opposition by the localities most affected.[50]

Viewed at regional scale, the piecemeal adjustments of recent decades have added capacity to address many specific problems, but they have also contributed to policy incoherence and frequent paralysis. More and more agencies, weakly linked at best, are engaged in governing the same geographic space. Where problems fit neatly within their defined mandates, some of these agencies are quite effective. The system is poorly designed to address problems that cut across agency jurisdictions however, and particularly to impose broad, active visions on the evolution of urban regions.[51]

An additional impediment to dealing with the largest urban problems is that, even as the density of agencies and programs in urban space has grown, numerous procedural reforms have been adopted to enhance citizen participation—program by program, and project by project—and to protect the interests of aggrieved minorities. These further intensify the clash of narrow perspectives, and they have channeled an increasing number of disputes to the courts, where "adversarial legalism" (as Robert Kagan has termed it) rather than negotiation and compromise are the dominant behavioral norms.[52]

Frequently the outcome is policy gridlock. Growing central-city/suburban disparities cannot be addressed. Needed facilities and even housing-stock additions cannot be sited.[53] And broad efforts to shape the urban environment (for example, by curtailing urban sprawl) are considered so hopeless as scarcely to warrant the attention of serious people.

When, on occasion, proposals for broad governmental reform do receive serious consideration, their substantive goals are generally vague (because the advocates are trying to minimize controversy), and they encounter highly charged voter fears—of higher taxes, of new pressures for

[50] See Frank J. Popper, "LULUs and Their Blockage," in *Confronting Regional Challenges*, ed. Joseph DiMento and LeRoy Graymer (Cambridge, Mass.: Lincoln Institute of Land Policy, 1991), 13–30; Michael Wheeler, "Negotiating NIMBYs: Learning from the Failure of the Massachusetts Siting Law," *Yale Journal on Regulation* (1994): 241–91.

[51] Downs, *New Visions*, chaps. 7–10; Peirce, *Citistates*, 27–35; Robert C. Wood, "Metropolis against Itself," as excerpted in Danielson, *Metropolitan Politics*, 241–6. Originally published 1959.

[52] Robert Kagan, "Adversarial Legalism and American Government," *Journal of Policy Analysis and Management* (Summer 1991): 369–406.

[53] Popper, "LULUs"; John M. Bryson, Barbara C. Crosby, and Anne R. Carroll, "Fighting the Not-in-My-Backyard Syndrome in Minneapolis," *Journal of Planning Education and Research* (Fall 1991): 66–74; Danielson and Doig, *New York*, 78–96.

racial and class integration, of reduced power to veto initiatives with potential for neighborhood disruption. Most voters, nearly all of the time, seem to conclude that they are better off with a strong voice in neighborhood-scale decisions than a nearly inaudible voice in regional or statewide decisions. For those employed or otherwise deeply engaged in local affairs, the threats associated with major reorganization—to well-established channels of influence, electoral bases, and careers—are even more urgent.[54]

IX: THE EGALITARIAN CRITIQUE

Egalitarian critics of the existing land-use system wish, of course, that government would aggressively counter the private-market and social forces (including consumer tastes and prejudices) that produce urban inequality and segregation. They do not criticize the existing system merely for its passivity, however. They maintain, more provocatively, that government land-use actions significantly reinforce, and thereby magnify, these private-sector tendencies. I shall concentrate here on the latter charge, which itself has two main threads: one focused on local parochialism, the other on governmental receptivity to private "rent-seeking."[55]

As near as can be determined, local-government formation from the earliest days of American colonial history was driven in major part by the motive of excluding the poor, thereby facilitating property value increases and the maintenance of order. Nancy Burns, who has studied this phenomenon most closely, adds that the motive of racial exclusion remained highly significant as recently as the 1960s, and that by the 1980s virtually all new incorporations were driven by the motive of "walling out" pressures emanating from the wider regional community for tax increases.[56]

The central purpose of zoning, likewise, from its origins during the ear-

---

[54] See, for example, Greer, *Metropolitics,* 30–4, 74–80.

[55] Economists speak of efforts to reap private gain by influencing public policy as "rent-seeking." When such efforts are deemed to have succeeded, political scientists speak of "capture." Though their terminology refers only to effort, not success, economists tend to assume that rent-seekers dominate public policymaking. Political scientists are much more inclined to view this as an open empirical question. I prefer the open-ended alternative in each case: the political science approach, but the economics term.

On rent-seeking, see Fischel, *Regulatory Takings,* 309 and 317, and David E Mills, "Is Zoning a Negative Sum Game?" *Land Economics,* 1989, 1–12. On capture, see *The Politics of Regulation,* ed. James Q. Wilson (New York: Basic Books, 1980), chap. 10.

[56] See Burns, *Formation of American Local Governments,* chaps. 3–5. She adds that large numbers of incorporations, both of cities and special districts, have been driven by developer and citizen desires for services. Where other types of businesses have been active in incorporation movements, she concludes, their primary motive has always been to create low tax enclaves.

ly decades of the twentieth century, has been to implement exclusionary aims.[57] In its maturity, over the past several decades, it has been used with increasing refinement in most suburban jurisdictions to exclude not just the poor, but virtually any activities likely to impose net fiscal burdens on current local taxpayers or to provoke opposition from significant numbers of neighbors.[58] Cumulatively, the land-use decisions of local governments, driven by their narrow perspectives and purely self-interested motives, have sharply accentuated regional tendencies toward inequality, segregation, and shortages of affordable housing within reach of growing suburban job markets.[59]

Even professional land-use planners, who generally take pride in their long-term, comprehensive perspectives, come in for a share of this blame. The great majority of planners work for localities, after all, either as employees or consultants. And they have allowed their analytic capabilities to be employed in the perfection of exclusionary strategies.

In recent decades, illustratively, one of their proudest accomplishments has been to refine the art of fiscal-impact analysis, which has become *de rigueur* in local decision-making about new development proposals. With rare exceptions, however, the singular purpose of fiscal-impact analysis is to arm local taxpayers against the possibility that they might end up subsidizing newcomers.[60] Where the newcomers are expected to be affluent, and the solution is merely to extract payments from the developers seeking to build for them, fiscal zoning may be benign. Where the solution is to prevent new development entirely, however, or to impose development costs that render it impossible to serve lower-income people, fiscal zoning can powerfully reinforce regional tendencies toward segregation and inequality.[61]

Many reflective planners find this quite troubling. The profession's sensitivity to the problem, however, is generally a weak force in comparison with the pressures it faces to serve employer and client interests.[62]

[57] Nelson, *Property Rights*, chaps. 1 and 2; Sidney Plotkin, *Keep Out: The Struggle for Land Use Control* (Berkeley: University of California Press, 1987), chap. 3.
[58] Altshuler and Gomez-Ibanez, *Regulation for Revenue*, 32–3, 77–96; William A. Fischel, *The Economics of Zoning Laws* (Baltimore: Johns Hopkins University Press, 1985), chap. 4; Fischel, *Regulatory Takings*, 259–67; Danielson and Doig, *New York*, 77–94.
[59] Plotkin, *Keep Out*, chap. 8; Paul L. Niebanck, "Growth Controls and the Production of Inequality," in *Understanding Growth Management*, ed. David J. Brower et al. (Washington, D.C.: Urban Land Institute, 1989).
[60] Danielson and Doig, *New York*, 78–105; Altshuler and Gomez-Ibanez, *Regulation for Revenue*, chaps. 5 and 6.
[61] Downs, *New Visions*, chap. 3.
[62] Norman Krumholz and John Forester, *Making Equity Planning Work* (Philadelphia: Temple University Press, 1990), chaps. 3 and 15; Peter Marcuse, "Professional Ethics and

The argument of critics who focus on "rent-seeking" is that those with the greatest intensity and continuity of interest in any policy domain, particularly if they have access to large amounts of money, tend to dominate policy formation within it. When it comes to decisions about profit-seeking land development, this analysis predicts dominance by what Harvey Molotch has labeled "the growth machine"—developers, property owners, banks, organized construction labor, real-estate attorneys, etc.[63] These dominant groups influence appointments; they contribute to the campaigns of elected officials; they employ the best experts; they provide employment for former public officials and other influential civic actors; they find it easy to recruit support in the media; and they make sure that decision-makers are constantly exposed to their perspectives.

When it comes to decisions about consumption-oriented land uses (most notably, homes and public open spaces), this analysis leaves room for domination by groups of neighbors and even committed environmentalists—depending on their capacity for organization (normally a function of affluence, education, and, in the case of neighborhood groups, stability of occupancy) and their legal status (homeowners more than renters). The resultant pattern may include bitter conflicts among propertied interests, such as developers and groups of middle-class or affluent homeowners. But those whose interests are routinely sacrificed will be the poor. If they are further weakened politically by such factors as racial isolation, their vulnerability will be all the greater.[64]

Beyond: Values in Planning," in *Ethics in Planning,* ed. Martin Wachs (New Brunswick, N.J.: Rutgers University Press, 1985), 3–24; Elizabeth Howe and Jerome Kaufman, "The Ethics of Contemporary American Planners," in Wachs, *Ethics in Planning,* 25–50; Dennis Keating and Norman Krumholz, "Downtown Plans of the 1980s: The Case for More Equity in the 1990s," *Journal of the American Planning Association* (Spring 1991): 136–52.

[63] Harvey L. Molotch, "The City as a Growth Machine," *American Journal of Sociology* (1976): 309–30; Logan and Molotch, *Urban Fortunes,* chap. 3.

[64] Logan and Molotch, *Urban Fortunes,* chaps. 4 and 6; Plotkin, *Keep Out,* introduction and chaps. 1 and 2; *The Politics of Urban Development,* ed. Clarence N. Stone and Heywood T. Sanders (Lawrence: University Press of Kansas, 1987), chap. 14 (by Stone).
  This critique extends to many federal and state actions bearing on urban land use as well. Examples include the commitment to segregation in federal mortgage-guarantee programs well into the 1960s, the widespread use of urban-renewal funding for "Negro removal," and the tendency of interstate highway planners during the 1950s and 1960s to seek out routes occupied by the poorest and politically weakest urban residents. These actions were all responsive, of course, to local pressures. See Frieden and Sagalyn, *Downtown, Inc.,* chaps. 2–4; Gwendolyn Wright, *Building the American Dream: A Social History of Housing in America* (Cambridge, Mass.: MIT Press, 1981), 247–8. They also date from several decades ago. The main charges against the federal government (and some states) more recently have been indifference to growing central-city/suburban disparities and, more generally, fiscal withdrawal from serious engagement with urban problems. See, for example, Kantor, *Dependent City,* chap. 8; Robert Warren, "National Urban

There are, of course, exceptions to these general patterns: instances of state action to override exclusionary zoning; of local exactions and zoning regulations to bring about the production of affordable housing; of major development proposals blocked by low-income neighborhood groups; and of local rent-control programs to protect renters at the expense of landlords.[65]

These remain rare exceptions in the overall constellation of land-use policy actions, however, and the trend is toward increasing segregation by income, accompanied by widening fiscal, educational, public safety, and general amenity gaps between affluent and low-income jurisdictions. (Segregation by race, extreme to begin with, declined slightly in the 1970s but has been stable ever since.)[66] At the state and national levels, moreover, the dominant trend of recent years has been toward greater market deference (less regulation, less redistribution). In the great majority of metropolitan areas, consequently, the near-term prospects for egalitarian land-use reform appear to be dismal.

X: THE STATES AS POTENTIAL INSTRUMENTS OF MANAGERIAL AND EGALITARIAN REFORM

Recognizing that metropolitan government is highly improbable in the largest U.S. urban areas, and that states are already the main constitutional repositories of land-use authority, the champions of managerial and egalitarian values have increasingly sought to realize their aims at the state level in recent years. Most states have responded with numerous initiatives to address specific problems at metropolitan or larger scale. I shall focus here, though, on efforts to achieve two breakthroughs at the state level: first, movement beyond specific functional concerns to state leadership in the achievement of comprehensive growth management, and second, a shift in the central thrust of land-use policy from exclusionary to egalitarian orientations.

The movement for a greater state role in land-use policy first achieved prominence under the banner of state "land-use planning" during the

---

Policy and the Local State," *Urban Affairs Quarterly* (June 1990): 541–61; and Michael Stegman, "National Urban Policy Revisited," *The North Carolina Law Review* (June 1993): 1737–77.

[65] Logan and Molotch, *Urban Fortunes*, 209–28; John E. Davis, *Contested Ground: Collective Action and the Urban Neighbourhood* (Ithaca, N.Y.: Cornell University Press, 1991), chaps. 8–10.

[66] Douglas S. Massey and Nancy A. Denton, *American Apartheid: Segregation and the Making of the Underclass* (Cambridge, Mass.: Harvard University Press, 1993), chap. 3; Downs, *New Visions*, 25–6.

1970s. Nine states adopted significant state land-use legislation during this period, and a federal-aid program for such planning came within an ace of passage in 1974.[67] Most of these state programs, notably, applied only to specific, environmentally sensitive or large-scale projects deemed to be of regional impact. After a pause for recession, the issue again came to life in the mid-1980s, this time under the banner of state "growth management." Eight states adopted significant legislative initiatives between 1985 and 1992, including four of those on the earlier list.[68] With the real-estate bust of the early nineties, however, interest fell off, and despite more recent prosperity there have not been any additions to the list of growth management states since 1992. A couple of the state programs enacted during the late 1980s, moreover, are today (1998) in virtual hibernation (most notably, those in Maine and Rhode Island).

More generally, several points stand out with respect to the experience of state growth management to date:

1. Only about one-quarter of the American states, concentrated along the coasts, have so far enacted statewide growth-management legislation. This group includes just one of the seven states with populations above ten million as of 1993 (Florida) and three of the ten with populations between 5 million and 10 million (Georgia, New Jersey, and Washington).[69] Other large states have adopted strong programs covering specific subareas (such as the California coast and New York's Adirondack Park area) or land-use activities (such as surface mining in Pennsylvania), but these were responses to specific urgent problems and directly affect only a small percentage of each state's population.

2. State land-use initiatives of the 1970s had an overwhelming tilt in favor of environmental objectives, and they emerged from the decade in bad odor with business, labor, and other pro-development interests. The second wave of state land-use reform, consequently, emphasized balance

---

[67] The nine were California, Colorado, Florida, Maryland, New York, North Carolina, Oregon, Pennsylvania, and Vermont. In addition, Hawaii had adopted a land-use law in 1961. John M. DeGrove, "Growth Management and Governance," in Brower, *Growth Management;* Frank J. Popper, *The Politics of Land Use Reform* (Madison: University of Wisconsin Press, 1981), chap. 5. The federal legislation passed the Senate overwhelmingly in 1974, but failed by seven votes in the House. Plotkin, *Keep Out,* chap. 6.

[68] The states were Florida (1985); New Jersey (1986); Maine, Vermont, and Rhode Island (1988); Georgia (1989); Washington State (1990); and Maryland (1992). John M. DeGrove, *The New Frontier for Land Policy; Planning and Growth Management in the States* (Cambridge, Mass.: Lincoln Institute of Land Policy, 1992), 1–2.

[69] The 1993 population data are from *Significant Features of Fiscal Federalism 1994* (Washington, D.C.: U.S. Advisory Commission on Intergovernmental Relations [ACIR], December 1994), vol. 2, 16. These 17 states accounted in 1993 for four-fifths of the U.S. population.

between environmental and development values. The thrust was now to be on "managing" growth rather than impeding it.[70]

3. The central themes of this second wave were "consistency" (among pertinent government programs) and "concurrency" (between private-development actions and the public investments required to accommodate them).[71] Only in New Jersey, where the stimulus came from the judiciary, were egalitarian values prominent from the outset. This was not a reflection of political support for a vigorous state egalitarian role. Rather, the New Jersey Supreme Court, in a series of decisions beginning in 1975, took a uniquely strong position against exclusionary zoning and called explicitly upon the state to overcome it.[72]

4. Although the state programs vary widely, all of the "comprehensive" programs are deferential to local primacy in the domain of land-use planning and regulation. The state programs aspire to provide a framework of procedures and goals that are usually quite vague, within which localities are to remain the principal government actors.

5. One might reasonably expect that state land-use agencies would be most effective in pursuing policy consistency within state government itself. This has not been the case in practice, however. The problem is that within state government the land-use agencies are generally mice among the elephants—able to get their attention, even make them a bit nervous, but not even to dream of coordinating their actions. Nor have governors been disposed to serve as frequent arbiters. The major state agencies got that way because they had large and powerful constituencies. The state land-use agencies can seek to persuade them—ideally, along with their constituencies—but almost never are they in a position to do more.

Although a mere petitioner within state government, however, the state land-use agency generally has some sanctions or incentives at its disposal in pressing localities for consistency. It typically seeks to ensure that local plans are consistent with state goals, regional plans (if any), and the plans of neighboring localities—and, further, that each locality's permitting and investment actions are consistent with its own approved plan.[73]

---

[70] DeGrove, *Growth Management.*   [71] DeGrove, *New Frontier,* chap. 10.
[72] For good brief reviews of the Mt. Laurel decisions and their consequences in practice, see Cullingworth, *Culture of Planning,* 66–74, and Fischel, *Regulatory Takings,* 336–41. Additionally, two valuable books have recently appeared on this topic: Charles M. Haar, *Suburbs under Siege* (Princeton, N.J.: Princeton University Press, 1996), and David L. Kirp, John Dwyer, and Larry A. Rosenthal, *Our Town: Race, Housing, and the Soul of Suburbia* (New Brunswick, N.J.: Rutgers University Press, 1995).
[73] See, for example, David Luberoff, *Growth Management in New Jersey* (Cambridge, Mass.: Taubman Center for State and Local Government, Kennedy School of Government, Harvard University, 1991); Arnold M. Howitt, *Growth Management in Maine*

This is an ambitious agenda, and there are serious questions about the types of constituencies required to sustain it. It is one thing to point out inconsistencies and urge negotiation. It is quite another to arbitrate major conflicts or to press localities for adherence to state goals with which they do not sympathize. This is rarely possible even for governors. Consider the case of New Jersey Governor Jim Florio, a Democrat, who assumed office in 1990 with an impassioned commitment to statewide fiscal equalization, and who quickly secured enactment of a major tax increase to bring it about. At the end of his first two years in office, New Jersey voters returned veto-proof Republican legislative majorities. Two years later, at their first opportunity, they overwhelmingly retired Florio himself in favor of a conservative Republican who promised repeal of his tax increases—and further cuts beyond that.[74] The Florio example did not seem likely to inspire much emulation.

The central question, then, is consistency for what? Most state land-use agencies have had very weak substantive agendas, preferring to concentrate on procedure—that is, consistency for its own sake.[75] New Jersey, for example, has organized its state land-use program around the theme of voluntary "cross-acceptance" of plans across local, regional, state, and federal agency jurisdictions. The state land-use agency has been successful in bringing about vast amounts of interaction and deliberation, but it lacks authority to impose goals—or even to compel consistency among the goals arrived at locally.[76] It has had much greater success, moreover, in bringing localities than state and federal agencies to the table.[77]

Oregon's growth-management program, which began with an almost

(Cambridge, Mass.: Taubman Center for State and Local Government, Kennedy School of Government, Harvard University, 1992); Allan W. Wallis, *Growth Management in Florida* (Cambridge, Mass.: Taubman Center for State and Local Government, Kennedy School of Government, Harvard University, 1993).

[74] See Frank Luntz and Mike Dababie, "Read Our Lips: No More Florio," *Campaigns and Elections* (December 1993–January 1994): 32–3.

[75] The best discussion of why this should normally be expected is still R. Kenneth Godwin and W. Bruce Shepard, "State Land Use Policies: Winners and Losers," *Environmental Law* (1975): 703–26.

[76] Roland Anglin, "Constructing Cooperation: Instituting a State Plan for Development and Redevelopment," *Journal of Policy Analysis and Management* (Summer 1995): 433–45; Luberoff, *Growth Management in New Jersey*, 30–45.

[77] Anglin surveyed 146 participants in the New Jersey cross-acceptance process in 1992. His respondents indicated by overwhelming majorities that the state planning process had had no significant impact on the frequency or quality of state agency–local interactions, and that they did not expect the process to have any substantive policy impacts. Anglin, "Constructing Cooperation," 440–2.

purely procedural orientation in the mid-1970s, has emerged over time as the most conspicuous exception. It assigns land-use authority within the boundaries of each locality to the state Land Development and Conservation Commission (LDCC) until the commission has approved the locality's own comprehensive plan. Thereafter it provides for state review, on appeal, of local land-use actions in particular cases. The strength and specificity of these state responsibilities, combined with the heavy caseload they have generated, have led to the gradual clarification and prioritization of state goals—notably in favor of compact urban development, affordable housing, agricultural land preservation, and streamlined development permitting.[78] As it proceeded, this breathtaking shift toward state dominance in land-use policymaking provoked a series of referendum challenges in 1976, 1978, and 1982. (Additional initiatives failed to get on the ballot, for lack of sufficient signatures, in 1984 and 1986.)[79] In every case, however, the program emerged unscathed. Today, it appears firmly entrenched—if still nationally unique.[80]

Concurrency as a theme of land-use policy reform proceeds from a concern that, in communities experiencing rapid growth, the public investments required to accommodate new private development often fail to occur, or occur only after delays of many years. The consequences frequently range from water shortages to overcrowded schools to severely congested highways. States and localities can ignore these consequences for a while, but over time they tend to become vividly apparent—and to generate antigrowth backlashes.

Public concern about infrastructure deficiencies sharply intensified during the 1980s. There were several obvious reasons why. Capital spending for infrastructure purposes had been declining since the mid-1960s. The most severe cutbacks, furthermore, were in federal grants-in-aid, leaving states and localities more on their own than they had been since the early 1950s. Voter resistance to tax increases was also more in-

---

[78] Gerrit Knaap, "The Political Economy of Growth Management in Oregon: A Historical Review," *Review of Regional Studies* (Winter 1989): 43–9.
[79] Knaap and Nelson, *The Regulated Landscape*, 189.
[80] Hawaii's program, which dates from 1961 and reserves all zoning authority to the state, is even stronger than Oregon's. It functions in circumstances radically different from those of any other state, however. There are only four local governments on Hawaii, for example, and the state has a long tradition of highly centralized regulation. I have therefore followed the practice of virtually all commentators on state growth management in ignoring it. See David Callies, *Regulating Paradise: Land Use Controls in Hawaii* (Honolulu: University of Hawaii Press, 1984), and Popper, *The Politics of Land Use Reform*, 77.

tense than it had been for many years. Finally, new federal mandates for infrastructure upgrading were proliferating—for such purposes as environmental protection, safety, and accessibility by the handicapped—and the costs of many older mandates were coming home to roost.[81]

Viewed nationally, new development accounted for only a modest proportion of infrastructure need. Older, declining cities had vast needs for replacement and renovation—in some cases, more costly per capita than those facing new, rapidly growing jurisdictions. Additionally, the entire population was generating greater infrastructure demand per capita. Traffic volumes, for example, were growing due to income growth, suburban sprawl, the rapid entry of women into the labor force, and the coming of age of the baby boomers.[82] Waste-disposal investments were being driven by new environmental requirements, new industrial processes, and new fashions in consumer packaging. Inadequate capacity was most visibly an issue in rapidly growing areas, however, and it was there that the share of need attributable to new development was greatest.[83]

As concern about infrastructure shortfalls intensified, two responses materialized. First, growing localities turned increasingly to developers as a source of infrastructure financing. The instruments of choice were exactions—special cash and in-kind levies imposed as development-permit conditions. Exactions and various precursors had been around for many years, but the variety of purposes for which they were utilized, and their financial magnitude, burgeoned from the late 1970s through at least the early 1990s.[84] Their great political appeal was that they seemed "free" to current voters, who could assume that either developers or future residents and business occupants, not yet identified, would end up paying for them.

[81] Altshuler and Gomez-Ibanez, *Regulation for Revenue*, chap. 2. See also Helen F. Ladd, "Big City Finances," in *Big City Politics, Governance, and Fiscal Constraints*, ed. George E. Peterson (Washington, D.C.: Urban Institute Press, 1994), 201–69, esp. 214–26.

[82] According to the Nationwide Personal Transportation Survey (NPTS), U.S. vehicle miles of motor vehicle travel (VMT) rose 41 percent from 1983 to 1990, against a population increase of only 6 percent. Alan E. Pisarski, *Travel Behavior Issues in the 90s* (Federal Highway Administration, U.S. Department of Transportation, July 1992), 9, 10, 13; for the population growth estimate, see *Significant Features of Fiscal Federalism 1991* (Washington, D.C.: U.S. ACIR, December 1991), vol. 2, table 7. Charles Lave has recently found persuasive evidence that the NPTS overestimated travel growth (at least as measured in terms of VMT per average vehicle) by as much as a factor of two. See Lave, "What Really Is the Growth of Vehicle Usage?" *Transportation Research Record* 1520 (1996), 117–21. Even if he is right, though, travel growth exceeded population growth by more than a factor of three.

[83] Altshuler and Gomez-Ibanez, *Regulation for Revenue*, chap. 6.

[84] Ibid., chap. 3.

Exactions were generally utilized only to finance local capital needs, however, and were nearly always set at levels far below the full cost of meeting even these. In this context, growth-control advocates articulated the doctrine of concurrency—that private development should not go forward until it is certain that adequate infrastructure will be available to serve it.

The state of Florida adopted concurrency as perhaps the central feature of its state growth-management program in the mid-1980s, and its land-use debates have revolved around it ever since.[85] The central dilemma of Florida concurrency has been that neither state nor local governments have been prepared to smother growth, finance enough new infrastructure to keep up with it, or levy exactions large enough to make up the shortfall. As John DeGrove has commented, "Concurrency without money equals urban sprawl," since slack infrastructure capacity, especially to carry traffic, is more common in fringe than core areas.[86] Yet one of Florida's other key objectives has been to resist urban sprawl. Due to the grandfathering of large volumes of old development rights, and depressed real estate conditions through much of the 1990s, the internal contradictions of Florida's policy mix have not yet produced a meltdown. The state's concurrency regulations were significantly relaxed, however, in 1993, and the state's will to make concurrency a reality remains highly uncertain.[87]

To date, state growth management has been a modest force for affordable-housing construction in several states (Oregon and Florida, most noticeably), but it has not demonstrated significant capacity anywhere to take on the problems of inequality and segregation at regional scale. One's instinct is to doubt that this will change at any time in the foreseeable future. But it is also conceivable that several factors will alter this prognosis:

First, the American pattern, as discussed previously, is to observe egalitarian norms within jurisdictions, even if not across them. Insofar as the

---

[85] Thomas G. Pelham, "Adequate Public Facilities Requirements: Reflections on Florida's Concurrency System for Managing Growth," *Florida State University Law Review* (1992): 974–1052. See also Wallis, *Growth Management in Florida,* and DeGrove, *New Frontier,* 7–32, 163–4.

[86] John Koenig, "Down to the Wire in Florida: Reflections on Florida's Concurrency System for Managing Growth," *Planning* (October 1990): 4–11, esp. 8.

[87] John M. DeGrove and Dennis E. Gale, "Linking Infrastructure to Development Project Approvals: Florida's Concurrency Policy under Statewide Growth Management," conference paper, Association of Collegiate Schools of Planning, November 1994; see esp. 16–18.

jurisdiction is seen to be the state, or a region designated by the state, the same forces of law and public philosophy should come into play. The recent wave of state judicial decisions mandating statewide equalization of K–12 school expenditures, notably, followed closely on the growth of state educational spending and regulation to the point where states were generally perceived to bear central responsibility for the performance of their educational systems.[88]

Second, such aims as affordable housing and racial integration are much easier for politicians to embrace in the abstract than in the context of site-specific controversies. State policy deliberations are more likely than local to avoid site specificity. This may in some cases enable state officials to adopt regulatory standards and programs of financial aid without stirring up the fierce passions typically observed in site-specific disputes.

Third, no state is under growth pressure nearly as intense as those of its localities most in favor with developers at any moment, and every state is on balance progrowth. So local growth-control advocates, who often thrive in localities experiencing rapid growth, are likely to fare less well in state forums. Growth controls tend to be regressive in their distributional effects; they keep the supply of developed property below what the market would otherwise provide, producing windfall profits for many current owners and price or rent increases for all others who wish to locate in the community.[89] So state overrides of local growth-control tendencies, for

---

[88] The first year in which the state share exceeded the local was 1978–79. Level of government revenue shares for the support of K–12 education in selected years were as follows:

School Year	Federal	State	Local
1929–30	0.4	16.9	82.7
1949–50	2.9	39.8	57.3
1969–70	8.0	39.9	52.1
1979–80	9.8	46.8	43.4
1984–85	6.6	48.9	44.4
1989–90	6.1	47.3	46.6
1994–95	6.8	46.8	43.8

Sources: U.S. Department of Education, *Digest of Educational Statistics,* 1997, table 159; U.S. Department of Education, *State Comparisons of Education Statistics,* 1995, table 31. These figures exclude private contributions, which totaled 2.7 percent of overall spending in 1994–95.

[89] William A. Fischel, *Do Growth Controls Matter?* (Cambridge, Mass.: Lincoln Institute of Land Policy, 1990), chap. 9; Fischel, *Regulatory Takings,* 221–4; John K. Landis, "Do Growth Controls Work? A New Assessment," *Journal of the American Planning Association* (Autumn 1992): 489–508, esp. 499–501; Altshuler and Gomez-Ibanez, *Regulation for Revenue,* 134–6.

all that they may be spurred by interests with few egalitarian concerns, are likely to have net egalitarian effects. In a similar vein, legislators representing central-city, working-class suburban, and rural interests may from time to time ally in support of restrictions on exclusionary zoning by affluent suburbs.

On the other side of the coin, those few local communities with dominant coalitions of renters rather than property owners may be among the first to encounter new restraints if decisions move into state forums. In Massachusetts, for example, landlords opposed to rent control had found themselves outnumbered for many years in the cities of Boston, Brookline, and Cambridge. State legislation by voter initiative has become increasingly common in recent years, however. So the landlords, emphasizing property rights and market efficiency arguments, placed a referendum initiative forbidding local rent regulation on the 1994 statewide ballot. By this means, they prevailed. Quite apart from the merits of this decision, the general point is that shifts of responsibility to higher levels of government do not automatically strengthen egalitarian forces.[90] This is particularly true if the shifts are piecemeal, as in the Massachusetts case, and driven by those interests with the resources to mount successful referendum or legislative lobbying campaigns.

XI: CONCLUSION

Americans consider land-use issues, I have argued, within the framework of two sharply disparate ideologies: one communal and egalitarian, the other individualistic and disinclined to view inequality as a problem. In any specific controversy, one observes self-interested groups organizing their briefs around aspects of one or the other of these ideologies. So it is easy to miss the crucial fact that both enjoy near-consensual support. Americans favor both private capitalism and public communalism—each in its place. The disputes are most typically at points of interface, where consensus is lacking about which ideology ought to be ceded primary jurisdiction, or about how the claims of the two ought to be balanced.

---

[90] Virtually all economists, of course, would applaud the elimination of rent control, and add that it was even beneficial from an egalitarian standpoint; over time, rent controls, by depressing the supply of rental housing, harm more low-income people than they help. See, for example, Peter D. Salins and Gerard C. S. Mildner, *Scarcity by Design: The Legacy of New York City's Housing Policies* (Cambridge, Mass.: Harvard University Press, 1992). On the merits, I agree with this position. If one thinks about which voters prevailed, however, it is clear that the change of venue shifted power from a local-renter majority to a statewide property-owning majority.

The land-use arena is chock-full of such points. Ownership is private. Most development initiative is private. And the predominant force of tradition is toward viewing land as a market commodity. But virtually all human activities take place on land; the by-products of land use profoundly affect every aspect of the human environment; and no one is an owner everyplace she or he goes. Owners themselves, moreover, are eager for collective services, from effective zoning to good public schools. The value of urban real estate hinges critically on the quality of such services, as well as on the tax rates needed to achieve it, and on investor confidence that desirable community characteristics will remain stable or improve over time. Consequently, whether their aim is development or simply enjoyment of what they already have, owners are drawn inevitably to the public realm.

The public realm is one in which communal values predominate, however. For those well positioned in the land-use marketplace, and reluctant to trigger wide egalitarian claims, this represents a severe problem—to which local-government fragmentation is a welcome solution. The subdivision of an urban region into numerous local jurisdictions provides a means of confining the application of communal norms within small, largely homogeneous groups of residents. And it makes available to such groups an instrument of extraordinary power for the pursuit and preservation of homogeneity: land-use regulation.

Pressures have continued to build, nonetheless, for public land-use action on a wider scale. Some of these pressures (for example, to construct regional infrastructure) have come largely from property owners themselves, and are not perceived as posing serious threats of redistribution or unwanted social interaction. Insofar as decisions are piecemeal, moreover, propertied interests can generally screen out centralizing proposals with significant redistributive potential.

Less favored groups have also made centralizing proposals, however—to equalize local tax bases, for example, and to promote residential integration. Higher-level governments have frequently responded with fiscal transfers. Very rarely, though, have they adopted proposals with significant potential to increase racial or class mixing. In the context of this chapter, the most notable such reform would be to centralize land-use regulatory authority at the regional or (more likely) the state level. Some movement in this direction, generally slight, occurred in about one-quarter of the states during the 1970s and 1980s. But the predominant national pattern of local primacy in land-use regulation remains firmly entrenched.

This said, the question remains: Would state land-use assertiveness on a wide front yield better policy outcomes? In thinking about this question, I have found it vital to distinguish between broadly consensual and controversial purposes. The former include a surprisingly wide range of economic and quality-of-life objectives, ranging from prosperity and efficient transportation to clean air and water. The latter are primarily redistributive—for example, affordable housing dispersed throughout the suburbs—but not exclusively so. The aim of more compact urban development, for example, is controversial because it would require a broad shift of land-use regulatory authority to the regional or state level, for purposes about which most people are indifferent or skeptical. But it is not intrinsically redistributive.

There does not seem to be much need for organizational reform to serve the consensual purposes. The existing system is quite capable of generating centralized initiatives when business and other civic leaders become persuaded that they are desirable, or when courts determine that greater centralization is required to carry out mandates from higher levels of government. The champions of such initiatives often wish that the political system were less complex, but it is the American way to require advocates of the new to run complex gauntlets, and most of us think that this is a good thing—so long as the complexity does not degenerate into gridlock.

Where gridlock in fact prevails is with respect to the controversial purposes. Most notably, the system frustrates egalitarian initiatives and efforts to arrive at any large decisions about urban form. Additionally, it reinforces market tendencies toward racial and class homogeneity, and toward private-sector dominance in government-business interactions. This is not entirely the case, because local communities are better able to block business-sponsored development than they might be in a more centralized system.[91] By setting prodevelopment localities in competition with one another, however, the system enables even those investors who are firmly rooted in a region to set up auctions for their favor.

The Oregon experience suggests that state growth management at its best can make a significant difference with respect to these issues, and at quite modest cost in terms of the vigor of grass-roots democracy. Local action always occurs within a framework of federal and state law, and threats of appeal to higher-level courts and regulatory agencies have long been standard tactics in local land-use disputes. A statewide system like

---

[91] See, for example, Danielson and Doig, *New York*, 106–8.

Oregon's encourages wide-ranging debate, in which localities can vigorously participate, about the extent to which regional goals such as compactness, affordable housing, and open-space preservation ought to guide local decision-makers in arriving at their decisions. Additionally, because the Oregon system places great pressure on localities to respect their own plans in arriving at specific permitting decisions—they are highly vulnerable to being overturned on appeal if they do not—it shifts the balance of public deliberation marginally away from individual siting disputes and toward general policy choices. (This feature may reduce citizen involvement, it bears mention, because policy issues are both fewer and more abstract than siting disputes.)

As consensus grows that certain types of decisions should be made at statewide or regional scale, and that they should reflect policy rather than ad hoc choices, the case for applying the public ideo-logic becomes more compelling. Thus, growing state involvement in the financing and regulation of K–12 education led naturally to the current wave of judicial decisions mandating school-finance equalization, and every state that has gone through the process of formulating land-use goals has ended up highlighting some themes of equity.

Few have carried their commitment much beyond rhetoric, however. So the general tendency of the urban land-use system to magnify inequality and segregation remains firmly in place. When the issue is posed squarely, few people offer an explicit defense. The conflict with American public values is too obvious. Most of those active in urban politics are eager to preserve local land-use primacy, however, and are ready with alternative explanations of their case-by-case positions. Land-use regulation, they claim, is really about preserving neighborhoods and protecting property values rather than segregation! My town needs large-lot zoning in order to protect the purity of its groundwater! It is not politically feasible to address this issue regionally, and my community would be inviting disaster if it acted alone!

The current system of land-use governance excels in providing such escape hatches—or, to state it another way, in facilitating evasion of the issue of publicly sponsored exclusion. This is at once its greatest source of political strength and moral weakness. The former seems likely to prevent significant change in the near future. The latter guarantees that this issue will not go away.

8

Local government and environmental policy

MARC K. LANDY

> The end of a good government is to ensure the welfare of a people, and not merely to establish order in the midst of its misery.
>
> —Alexis de Tocqueville

Decentralization has become a major theme in environmental policymaking. In virtually all areas of resource and pollution policy, more decision-making autonomy is being turned over to the states and even to the localities. Because the impetus for most of this effort has come from the Republican right, the temptation is to view this development in partisan terms and to assume that decentralization is simply a smoke screen for an effort to degrade the environment—and, conversely, that environmental improvement requires recentralization. Whatever the specific motives of partisans on either side of this conflict might be, it would be a grave mistake to underestimate the deeper significance of this decentralizing phenomenon. Its import will outlast the specific partisan terms in which it has been cast.

To consider dispassionately the prospects and promise of policy decentralization, it must be rescued from its most vociferous supporters on the right wing of the Republican Party. Because those advocates are so selective in their support for decentralization—they also favor nationalizing key aspects of welfare policy and tort law, among other things—they are liable to the charge that they favor decentralization only when it serves a broader ideological agenda.[1] This chapter seeks to disentangle the issue of

---

[1] For a well-articulated example of right-wing ambivalence on the issue of decentralization, see Clint Bolick, "Local Control and Its Discontents," *The Weekly Standard* 1 (December 18, 1995): 25–8.

decentralization from that of opposition to government regulation in order to consider fairly the likely impact of decentralization on democratic
and republican practice.

POLICY MAKES POLITICS

One of the most important lessons of postwar political science, as exemplified in the writings of Theodore Lowi, Philip Selznick, and others, is
that policy makes politics.[2] The design as well as the objectives set forth
in statute and concretized in administrative regulation bring forth new
political forces and alter the power balance of existing ones. Indeed, the
landmark federal statutes passed during and after the New Deal serve as
mini-constitutions, educating citizens about the ends of government and
the appropriate means by which those ends are to be realized.[3]

Democracy in America is in a sorry state. If politics stems from policy,
then it is important to understand how policy has contributed to this political failure. If centralization of policy is partly to blame, then decentralization should form part of the solution.

To support decentralization is not to deny the wisdom of much of the
centralization of policy that occurred between 1935 and 1965. States had
proven themselves inadequate to protect blacks and industrial workers
from political oppression and economic exploitation. The Wagner Act
created a federal role in governing labor relations in order to countervail
the concentration of economic power in the hands of large corporations
that had taken place over the previous fifty years. The Civil Rights and
Voting Rights Acts of 1964 and 1965 belatedly provided the means to enforce the 14th and 15th Amendments to the Constitution, which had
been adopted almost a hundred years earlier.

The exponential increase in agricultural and industrial output that
took place after World War II made an increased federal presence in environmental regulation necessary. Air and water move; they do not respect
state lines. The vast expansion of air and water pollution that attended
the rise in output increased the likelihood that significant economic dam-

---

[2] Grant McConnell, *Private Power and American Democracy* (New York: Knopf, 1967);
Theodore Lowi, *The End of Liberalism,* second ed. (New York: Norton, 1979); Philip
Selznick, *TVA at the Grassroots* (Berkeley: University of California Press, 1949).
[3] Marc Landy, "Public Policy and Citizenship," in *Public Policy for Democracy,* ed. Helen
Ingram and Steven Rathgeb Smith (Washington, D.C.: Brookings Institution Press, 1993),
19–44.

age from pollution would spill over state boundaries. Even a narrow reading of the Constitution's commerce clause, therefore, would justify a federal regulatory role.

The point is not to decry the creation of a strong national policy apparatus, but rather to consider what might constitute its appropriate limits. Environmental laws—and the administrative apparatus created to implement and enforce them—are no longer sufficiently constrained by the simple spillover arguments that were their initial rationale. The question that has yet to be fully addressed is at what point do the harms wrought by increased policy centralization exceed its benefits?

This would seem to be a question particularly appropriate for a political scientist to ask. The serious claim that the discipline has to be a science stems less from its efforts to emulate the techniques of natural science than from its ability to detach itself from the partisanship that perhaps inevitably dominates most of political discourse. This relative impartiality should enable political scientists to recognize the problems posed by even the most praiseworthy actions. In that spirit, this chapter examines the pendulum swing from centralization to decentralization that has characterized modern environmental policy; it also considers the impact of both extremes of the pendulum's trajectory upon fundamental democratic and republican principles.

CITIZENSHIP

If policy flows centrally, so will politics. People have become more attentive to national politics in large measure because they recognize that national authorities have more control over their destinies than state and local ones do. This shift of attention has dire consequences for citizenship. Centralized politics inevitably means mass politics. The public becomes so large that it is next to impossible for the voice of an ordinary citizen to be heard. Citizenship is reduced, for the most part, to the relatively petty act of voting, an act that makes an individual just one among tens of millions. A more robust civic role is reserved only for the powerful, the very rich, and the highly celebrated.

Hypocrisy is the gift that vice gives to virtue. The frequency with which mass plebiscitary events are referred to as "town meetings" reveals the grudging admiration that practitioners of mass politics have, or feel they ought to have, for local politics. In the 1992 campaign, one candidate (Bill Clinton) conducted televised "town meetings" while another (Ross

Perot) made electronic town meetings a central plank of his platform. Both of these "gifts" illustrate the inadequacy of substituting the illusion of political involvement for the real thing.

Hypocrisy aside, the televised town meetings that President Clinton ran during his first campaign and after were hardly that. There was no serious deliberation about town issues. No collective decisions were reached. No deliberation took place. No real information was requested or elicited.[4] The meetings were instead opportunities to show that the candidate, by fielding questions from ordinary people, could "feel their pain."

Perot, for his part, sought to provide a means for direct democracy that did not rely on place. He claimed that, via computer, citizens could avoid relying on their representatives and have a direct say in policy deliberation. He presented a vision of millions of citizens commenting directly on national policy issues and conducting a nationwide policy deliberation.[5] Unfortunately, Perot's electronic town meeting failed to come to grips with the two key problems that real, geographically based town meetings cope with all the time: who gets to speak, and who is worth listening to.

Bertrand De Jouvenel labels the first of these issues "the Chairman's Problem."[6] There is really no fair answer to the question of who gets to speak, and for how long. The larger the gathering, the more difficult (and less fair) the choice involved. An "electronic town meeting" would presumably involve thousands of e-mailers. How will the "Chairman"— human *or* digital—decide which of these messages get responded to in real time? How is a deliberation that must, by definition, involve sustained give-and-take (not just message and response) be carried on? In practice, no such sustained interchange will occur. These electronic occasions will turn into yet another form of opinion poll—and an unscientific one at that.

The second problem is even more vexing: How to judge the quality and

[4] Jeffrey H. Birnbaum, "Town Hall Sessions Evolve for Clinton into Strategic Tool," *Wall Street Journal* (May 9, 1994): A9C; Ruth Marcus, "Clinton Defends Handling of Foreign Policy: All Leaders Forced to 'Back and Fill,' Town Hall Is Told," *Washington Post* (May 4, 1994): A2; David Lauter, "Town Hall Health Hearing Presents Few Cures," *Los Angeles Times* (March 13, 1993): 21.

[5] Michael Kelly, "Perot's Vision: Consensus by Computer: Electronic Town Hall Would Link Officials and Public by TV," *New York Times* (June 6, 1992): A1, A8; William Booth, "New-Age Rally Falls Prey to Familiar Bugs: Perot Conducts 'Town Hall' Meeting via Satellite Link among Six Cities, Technology Willing," *Washington Post* (May 30, 1992): A10.

[6] Bertrand De Jouvenel, "The Chairman's Problem," in *The Nature of Politics: The Collected Essays of Bertrand De Jouvenel*, ed. Dennis Hale and Marc Landy (New Brunswick, N.J.: Transaction, 1992), 108–18.

sincerity of political remarks? In local politics, one can count on knowing the person who speaks, at least by reputation. What is one to do when confronted with thousands of e-mail messages from people one does not know and has not even heard of? Because small numbers of people who share some common experience can more adequately cope with these two fundamental democratic problems, "town meetings" are best conducted live—in *towns*, not in cyberspace.

Citizenship is a mix of opportunity and obligation. It combines a voice in collective decisions with a share in the sacrifices those decisions impose. Centralizing policy and politics not only minimizes one's voice in public affairs, it reduces one's responsibilities.

In local affairs, there is frequently a close connection between enjoying a collective benefit and paying for it. In order for my children to go to a new school in my town, I will have to pay higher property taxes. At the national level, this direct relationship is frequently lost. If a toxic dump in my town is declared a federal Superfund site, it will be cleaned up free of charge. I contribute to paying for it only to the infinitesimal degree that any other federal income-tax payer does. Under such circumstances, it is rational for me to be irresponsible and demand as much cleanup as I could possibly want, rather than to consider how little cleanup would really be acceptable.

Critics of pluralism have long bemoaned the endemic irresponsibility of American government caused by the concentration of benefits in a few hands while the concomitant costs are diffused among the population as a whole. Because these critics so fear the inegalitarian aspect of decentralized government, they choose to ignore the spatial dimension of the phenomenon they decry. The disjunction between costs and benefits can take place only where the populace is so large that costs can in fact become diffuse. In small politics, both costs and benefits remain concentrated because there are too few people amongst whom to diffuse them.

Thus the centralization of policy—and the centralization of politics that results from it—robs citizens of the opportunity to participate. It also robs them of the appropriate psychological orientation to participate properly.

DECENTRALIZATION AND DEMOCRACY

It is possible to accept much of the argument made above and still oppose decentralization on democratic grounds. The great modern political-science critiques of decentralization by E. E. Shattschneider, Philip

Selznick, and Grant McConnell do not claim that mass politics produces better citizens, only that mass politics is much more democratic. These critics demonstrate that the scope of a political system introduces biases that affect the ability of the majority to rule.[7] In particular, elements of the population that are diffused widely throughout the nation will lose out in a federal system because the latter favors elements that are concentrated in particular localities. Power at the local level therefore tends to concentrate itself in the hands of economic and social elites.

This claim is true as far as it goes. But much of this critique was written before the dust had fully settled on the post–New Deal centralized policymaking machine. Therefore, these writers were unable to pursue the full logic of their argument. In fact, the nationalization of decision-making has biased the political system in several ways, not all of them so favorable to majority rule. It is not simply that popular rule at the national level has displaced the country-club crowd that ran things locally. Instead, different elites whose skills and resources are better suited to the national scene have come to exert enormous leverage in Washington. It is by no means clear whether the success of these new elites renders the current system more or less democratic than the one it displaced.

The Chairman's Problem operates at the national level with a great deal more severity than in a town meeting. Even in Washington, the day is only 24 hours long. Too many issues chase too little time. The president's desk, dominated by foreign policy, has room for only the most pressing domestic matters. In the absence of his scrutiny, the centralizing policy appetite deploys a digestive mechanism that is so complex, so specialized, and so convoluted as to render it far less accessible to the ordinary citizen than an all but the most hidebound local government.

Most real policy deliberation is conducted in administrative agencies, federal courts, and among congressional staff. Expertise and privileged access are the coins of those realms. The antipathy toward Washington that pervades the opinion polls shows that whatever scholars may think, the demos doubts that centralized politics is more democratic.

EQUALITY

Opinion polls notwithstanding, the persistent scholarly conviction concerning the inherently more democratic character of national as opposed

---

[7] See especially E. E. Schattschneider, *The Semi-sovereign People* (New York: Holt, Rinehart & Winston, 1960).

to state and local government stems from an equation of two very different ideas: equality and democracy. On the whole, it *is* fair to say that national policymaking is more egalitarian in regard to the relationship among individuals. As the later discussion of environmental policymaking will demonstrate, the tendency of national policymaking institutions to treat policy questions in terms of rights does have a powerful egalitarian bent. But democracy is about choice. As recent elections indicate, the majority has little love for using the government to redistribute wealth from the rich to the many, to create privileged access for minorities to schooling and jobs, or to do a host of other things that would provide greater equality of result.

What decentralization can provide is greater diversity. Decentralized environmental policy might well produce a more varied landscape, with some localities choosing to make great sacrifices in order to keep their environment relatively pure and others choosing to allow more pollution and congestion as the price of greater prosperity. But that landscape would also be less uniform and would therefore embody greater environmental inequalities.

GOVERNMENT AND ADMINISTRATION

The most persuasive effort to deal with the tension between uniformity and diversity remains that of Tocqueville. His theory of federalism revolves around the distinction between what he calls government and what he calls administration. Government should be centralized, administration decentralized.[8]

The government-administration distinction is crucially different from the one between policymaking and administration. The idea is *not* that the federal government should set policy and leave the execution of that policy to local governments. Instead, Tocqueville proposes that we recognize a fundamental difference between types of policy. Some policies—a very few—are so central to the liberty and well-being of all citizens that they must be determined nationally. They are too important to allow Maine to have one policy and Arizona another. Most policies, however, are essentially of a housekeeping nature. It is not crucial to the integrity of the Union that Maine and Arizona dispose of their hazardous waste in the same fashion and according to the same standards.

[8] Alexis de Tocqueville, *Democracy in America,* vol. 1 (New York: Random House, 1945), 89–101.

Since housekeeping matters *can* be decided locally, they must be. There are two reasons for this. First, it is the only way to prevent the establishment of a large centralized state, which Tocqueville considers inimical to preserving liberty. Second, it is the only way to retain sufficient tasks for citizens to enable them to learn the deliberative skills and develop the appropriate level of personal responsibility necessary to preserve their freedom.

"Administration" differs from "implementation." Even in this centralist era, most federal policies are implemented by state or local-government personnel. However, the terms under which these policies operate are very carefully and elaborately established by the federal government. State governments are not granted enough discretion to administer in Tocqueville's meaning of the word. For administration to occur, governmental objectives must remain broad, granting states and localities great latitude in how to achieve them.

Administration offers three great advantages over mere implementation. Tocqueville clearly perceived two of these. The first (and perhaps most important) is the check that local administration provides on the growth of a large and powerful national state. Setting broad policy can be done by a legislature; it does not require a vast army of apparatchiks. A small state, even one that is powerful governmentally, lacks the policing apparatus needed to successfully squelch liberty.

The second advantage is that administration is the best method for teaching citizenship. It is utopian to expect to educate citizens about matters that require a great deal of expertise or are too abstract. But citizens can come to understand the issues at stake in concrete matters that affect them directly. Also, because the number involved is small, they can participate directly and therefore learn the actual arts of governing.

The third advantage, policy integration, was not noticeable in Tocqueville's day, but it has become ever more important as government expands the range and breadth of its ambitions. Government now produces such a welter of policies that efforts to centrally administer wreak havoc on the lives of ordinary people. State and local administration provides the only opportunity to integrate disparate policy objectives and so enhance the well-being of ordinary people, rather than simply fulfilling the myriad (and often contradictory) guidelines issued by federal alphabet agencies such as DOT, USDA, EPA, HCFA, and so on. Governors and mayors are the only politically responsible executives to be found between the president and the people. They are uniquely well placed to reconcile national-policy guidelines with unique local circumstances—and to make these diverse strictures compatible with each other.

TROUBLING COROLLARIES

Tocqueville's principle for dividing responsibility has two troubling concomitants. First, the dividing line between what is appropriately viewed as government and what is administration is inevitably fuzzy and permeable. One can always find some broad principle of national significance at work in even the most mundane local chores. For example, minimum-height requirements for new police recruits would, at first glance, appear to be a purely administrative matter. However, they might serve to substantially reduce the pool of women or minority applicants.

To preserve the spirit of the government/administration distinction, it is necessary to ask not whether governmental questions are involved in administrative determinations, but rather how much they are involved—and how severe would be the loss of local decision-making autonomy—if the national government intervened to protect them. In other words, a presumption exists in favor of local administration, but it can be overcome by a strong demonstration that governmental concerns are overriding. Exclusion of whole segments of society from the police force is a very serious matter. If it was proven to be systematic and not clearly based on job requirements, it might well constitute an appropriate occasion for governmental intervention.

On the other hand, consider dress codes for high-school students. Certainly a case could be made that such codes limit free expression. But their imposition is not, per se, frivolous or capricious. The real issue is whether such expression rises to the level of a right that is worthy of government protection at the expense of the ability of localities to administer their schools as they see fit.

The second concomitant is even more troubling for those who view government as a "problem-solver." Regardless of what the objective of government is, relying on the states to administer that objective guarantees that progress will be uneven. Because this is true almost by definition, it is not an appropriate grounds for criticizing state administration. Yet the charge that some states are slower than others (and that some are dragging their heels) is in fact the most common, and seemingly the most telling, criticism made of state administration.

Here again, a serious commitment to the Tocquevillean federalist principle requires a presumption in favor of state administration. The presumption is based on the enormous value obtained by enabling each state to deliberate about how best to attain the federally mandated objective— and how best to reconcile it with other worthy goals the state is trying to attain. This would require abandoning the expectation that states will comply with governmentally imposed objectives at a more or less uniform clip. Instead, the expectation would be simply that they are moving in the right direction, albeit at different paces. Those states that flagrantly defy the objective must of course be made to suffer for their illegal action so that the principle of federal supremacy may be upheld.

LIMITED GOVERNMENT AND PROGRAMMATIC RIGHTS

The necessary adherence to these two concomitants is another way of saying that Tocqueville's principle of federalism is underpinned by a commitment to limited government, particularly at the national level. The uncomfortable aspect of limited government is the acceptance of the notion that government is not established for the purpose of righting all wrongs. This view assumes that all efforts by government to control behavior will exact a significant cost upon the body politic, and it requires a convincing demonstration that the benefits of such efforts outweigh that cost.

James Q. Wilson refers to this understanding as the "legitimacy barrier."[9] Throughout most of American history, surmounting this barrier was very difficult. It was assumed that the liberty that resulted from keeping government at arm's length was worth the inevitable injustices that would result. In particular, Tocqueville would have been troubled by the shift from the notion that rights are prepolitical—that they are essentially protections *against* governmental intrusion—to the notion that rights require governmental intervention to ensure their fulfillment.

The modern idea of a right to such things as economic security, shelter, and a safe and healthy environment requires that government develop programs and policies to secure those rights. Inherent in the idea of a right is its universal enforceability. A right does not exist if it is available in Maine but not in California. Therefore, these new kinds of rights— which Shep Melnick aptly calls "programmatic rights"—create a power-

---

[9] James Q. Wilson, "New Politics, New Elites, Old Publics," in *The New Politics of Public Policy*, ed. Marc K. Landy and Martin A. Levin (Baltimore: Johns Hopkins University Press, 1995), 250.

ful bias in favor of government centralization in order to ensure their uniform applicability.[10]

Much of the animus toward greater decentralization stems from what is taken to be the great failing of limited government: its inability to protect the rights of blacks. Lack of faith in state administration results from the failure of the Southern states to administer the Supreme Court school-desegregation decisions of the 1950s and the congressional Civil Rights Act of 1964.

One can well share the disgust at the behavior of the Southern states without leaping to the conclusion that this example undermines the validity of the Tocquevillean point of view. To the extent that the South's behavior represented defiance of federal directives, there is no disagreement at all about the need for swift and effective federal enforcement. The difficulty arises when a state adopts subtle means of undermining federal objectives while claiming to act with "all deliberate speed." But here the problem stems as much from the national government's unwillingness to adhere to the tenets of limited government as it does from the states' malfeasance.

The standard of antidiscrimination that underlay both school desegregation and the Voting Rights Act of 1965 were close in spirit to the notion of prepolitical rights guaranteed by limited government. They provided both the simplicity and the clarity that enabled the federal government to act without involving itself in the warp and woof of local school administration or state legislative districting.

Exclusion requires an overt act by government. It was only when the federal government broadened its objective to such programmatic rights as racial integration and the guarantee of electoral results commensurate with the minority percentage of the population that any effort to maintain the government/administration distinction became untenable. Those goals require subtle and complex actions *by* government; an evaluation of their efficacy, let alone their fidelity to the spirit of the law, is therefore inherently difficult and uncertain.

In any event, the sorry record of Southern states through the 1960s is hardly dispositive regarding the efficacy of decentralization in the 1990s. Black turnout in the South now exceeds that in the North. Precisely *because* enforcement of the Voting Rights Act has been so successful, it is no

---

[10] R. Shep Melnick, "The Courts, Congress and Programmatic Rights," in *Remaking American Politics*, ed. Richard A. Harris and Sidney M. Milkis (Boulder, Colo.: Westview Press, 1989), 188–212.

longer appropriate to uncritically favor centralized administration for fear of state-level racial bias.

ENVIRONMENT AND FEDERALISM

Environment is a good test of the modern-day merits of Tocquevillean federalism because it is a hard case. Air and water move. It is almost never possible to completely restrict the environmental impact of a pollutant to a local political jurisdiction. Resort to the "spillover" rationale for federal intervention is almost always plausible. If a strong argument can be made for granting local administrative discretion in this hard case, then there are likely to be many other policy domains in which greater local discretion would prove similarly beneficial.

As with any policy question, the debate about environmental policy is a derivative one. It gains its bearings from the ethical and scientific assumptions and findings the debate participants choose to invoke. For example, one's position on the Endangered Species Act will almost certainly be informed by one's answers to the following questions:

Is it morally acceptable for humans to help bring about the extinction of a species, or do other species enjoy some sort of right to exist?

Does the extinction of a species pose a threat to human well-being? If so, under what circumstances?

Should equal value be placed on the survival of all species, or are some more valuable than others?

One's ethical and scientific opinions on this subject will not only determine one's substantive policy judgments, they will also likely affect one's views about what level of government is most appropriate for addressing the issue. For example, if one concludes that species do not have a universally applicable right to exist, or that the destruction of species habitat in a distant locale will have no palpable impact on one's own physical well-being, then one is far less likely to favor centrally imposed policy remedies. If, on the other hand, one considers that species bear rights, or that the extinction of faraway species will have a significant impact on environmental quality closer to home, then one is likely to favor national, indeed global, policy remedies.

The period from 1970 to 1990 was one of environmental-policy centralization. The ethical and scientific paradigms of the period favored centralization. The current pendulum swing in favor of decentralization reflects serious ethical and scientific revision. From 1970 to the present, the dominant economic environmental paradigm has been highly receptive to decentralization. One might have expected that America's supposedly pragmatic political culture would have rendered environmental policymaking highly sensitive to the economists' invocation of a benefit-cost calculus, but such was not the case. It is only in the wake of significant ethical and scientific paradigm changes that sustained policymaking consideration has been accorded to the price of environmental protection.

THE CENTRALIST PARADIGM

The centralist spirit that dominated environmental policymaking for a generation is neatly captured by the ever-popular bumper sticker, "Think Globally—Act Locally." Whereas the command to act locally would appear to validate a decentralized approach, the prior stricture to think globally makes clear that local action is inherently tendentious; it is in the service of broader objectives that can be adequately conceptualized only on a global scale.

The essence of the centralist paradigm is a combination of political philosophy and science. The scientific metaphor that drives this paradigm is interconnectedness.[11] The world—indeed, the entire biosphere—is conceived of as a system whose parts relate to one another. Thus a perturbation anywhere in the system will have an effect on all other parts of the system. This is true not just of those parts that are closely connected, but of those whose connections are indirect and at a far remove. This system operates temporally as well as spatially. Thus events that do not have an immediate effect may well have important consequences at some time in the future.

Acid rain is an example of spatial interconnectedness. The sulfur dioxide generated by coal-fired power plants in the Midwest has been linked to the acidification of lakes hundreds of miles to the east.

Temporal interconnectedness is illustrated by the relationship that may exist between hazardous waste and certain forms of cancer. Minute quantities of toxic chemicals that have leached into the water supply may well contribute to the growth of cancerous tumors whose existence will be detected only two or three decades later.

This metaphor is neither true nor false. It is a metaphor. Adopting it

---

[11] Charles Rubin brilliantly portrays the centrality of the interconnectedness metaphor in the works of such seminal writers as Rachel Carson, Barry Commoner, and Arne Naess in *The Green Crusade: Rethinking the Roots of Environmentalism* (New York: Free Press, 1994).

encourages one to look for the interconnectedness of things, not their singularity. The power of this metaphor is amply illustrated by the issue of acid rain.

In 1980, Congress commissioned a study to provide a definitive answer to the question of the severity of the problems caused by acid rain. The National Acid Precipitation Assessment Program (NAPAP), the most lavishly funded ecological research effort in history, took ten years to complete its report, at a cost of half a billion dollars. NAPAP's findings were diffident at best. It found that only 4 percent of lakes in areas where acidification might be expected (mostly in the Northeast) had become fully acidified—that is, devoid of life. It also concluded that most of the lakes likely to become acidified had already done so.

The report found no evidence that acid rain had caused a general deterioration of Northeast forests. Only red spruce trees at high elevations seemed to be affected. Nor was there evidence of crop damage or human-health impact. On the basis of these findings, the director of the study concluded that acid rain "cannot be seen as ranking at, or even near, the top of a present-day priority list of environmental issues."[12]

This report was issued in the midst of congressional deliberation regarding the 1990 Clean Air Act. Despite having been congressionally commissioned, the report made little discernible impact either on the deliberations themselves or on their outcome. The 1990 Clean Air Act that President George Bush signed into law contained a major new acid-rain initiative estimated to cost industry $22 billion over the next ten years.[13]

Although it was hardly dispositive, the report did represent the most comprehensive impartial body of information available at the time. However incomplete its findings, its results clearly did not justify the creation of a multibillion-dollar control program.

The report's lack of impact was due to its iconoclasm. Interconnectedness had become too well-established in the public mind as a *fact*, not a metaphor, to be dislodged by a single study, no matter how massive. Stories about acid rain—including car-wash advertisements about the damage it was doing to the finish on auto bodies—had recently inundated the media. Prior to the NAPAP report, one simply did not find skeptical stories about this issue in the mass media. By the time the report was issued,

12 William K. Stevens, "Worst Fears on Acid Rain Unrealized," *New York Times* (February 20, 1990): C1, C11.
13 Ibid.

however, "everybody knew" that acid rain was a serious environmental hazard.

NATURE'S RIGHTS—HUMAN RIGHTS

Powerful as it is, the interconnectedness metaphor alone cannot fully account for the powerful centralizing thrust of environmental policy from 1970 to 1990. A strict construction of the metaphor's meaning would require all pollution and habitat destruction to cease—an impossibility by anyone's lights. Therefore, even as compelling a notion as interconnectedness cannot determine how much interference with nature to allow, how best to control that interference, and who should pay for the control effort. Those are quintessentially political decisions; they must therefore be based on values, not just facts. As the following examples demonstrate, the crucial political principle used to make the metaphor of interconnectedness meaningful in policy terms was the principle of rights.

A programmatic view of rights entered the environmental debate during the 1970s in two modes: one regarding humans, the other regarding nature. Humans were declared to have a right to a safe and healthy environment. Nature's rights were less clearly defined. They did not extend to individual plants and animals, nor to all habitats. But they *did* include the right of any species as a whole to survive, and the right of certain habitats to remain free from intrusion.

CLEAN AIR

The Clean Air Act—the most venerable and far-reaching of all modern pollution statutes—demonstrates how the centralizing thrust of interconnectedness was complemented and augmented by the declaration of a programmatic right to human health.

Before 1970, air-pollution standards were set on a state basis, with the federal role limited to that of reviewing state plans. This system had been put in place in 1967 as a result of a law whose primary author was Senator Edmund Muskie of Maine.[14] This approach was attacked by environmentalists on the grounds that it did not adequately protect environmental rights.

---

[14] For an account of Muskie's political career, see Theodore Lippman, Jr., and Donald C. Hansen, *Muskie* (New York: Norton, 1971).

In his foreword to *Vanishing Air*, published before the 1970 passage of
the Clean Air Act, Ralph Nader defines the pollution problem as the failure of the government to prosecute polluters for "harming our society's
most valued rights."[15] Clean air is a right because it is necessary for preserving humanity's essential nature: "The limits that must be imposed on
social and technological innovations are determined not by scientific
knowledge or practical know-how but by the biological and mental nature of man, which is essentially unchangeable."[16]

The Naderite appeal to human nature was echoed in congressional testimony by the Sierra Club's Michael McClosky: "The parameters of ecological health are not negotiable. Nature has its law of limits. *Absolute results ensue when certain thresholds are crossed*, whether our political and
economic institutions care to recognize them or not."[17]

Rather than defend the existing program of state initiative, Muskie
adopted the rights rhetoric. In a speech introducing his revised bill on the
Senate floor, he proclaimed the right of every American to clean air:

100 years ago the first board of health in the United States, in Massachusetts, said
this: We believe that all citizens have an inherent right to the enjoyment of pure
and uncontaminated air. . . . 100 years later it is time to write that kind of policy
into law.[18] . . . anybody in this nation ought to be able at some specific point in the
future to breathe healthy air.[19]

NAAQs

The great centralizing innovation of the 1970 Clean Air Act was the replacement of state-initiated ambient-air-quality standards with nationally
imposed standards (the National Ambient Air Quality Standards, or
NAAQs). The primary NAAQs established specific limits on the concentration of individual pollutants in the atmosphere. The shift from state to
national standard-setting was itself evidence of increased centralization,
but the stringent nature of the NAAQs magnified the import of the shift.

Standards per se do not confer rights. The NAAQs might well have

[15] John C. Esposito et al., *Vanishing Air* (New York: Pantheon, 1970), viii.
[16] Ibid., 9.
[17] "The Environmental Decade: Action Proposals for the 1970s," House Subcommittee on
Conservation and Natural Resources, Committee on Government Operations Hearings,
1970. 91st Congress, 2nd session, February 2–6; March 13; April 3. Cited in Richard
Harris and Sidney Milkis, *The Politics of Regulatory Change* (New York: Oxford University Press, 1989), 236–7.
[18] *A Legislative History of the Clean Air Act of 1970*, Senate Committee on Public Works,
Senate Debate on S. 4358, September 21, 1970; 93rd Congress, 2nd Session, 1974, 220.
[19] Ibid., 227.

been conceived in a de minimis fashion, establishing a relatively low floor above which the more ambitious states could erect higher ceilings. Instead, the NAAQs were explicitly based on the *right* of any individual, regardless of health status, not to be harmed by breathing the air. They provided a "sufficient margin of safety" so that the health of "sensitive individuals" (those with preexisting lung impairment, such as asthma) would not be harmed. The act specifically prohibits any consideration of cost in setting the standards, because the application of the utilitarian calculus inherent in a cost-benefit comparison would refute the rights-conferring status of the standards.

SIPs

At first, a strenuous effort was made to render the programmatic rights declared by the Clean Air Act compatible with Tocquevillean federalism. The 1970 Clean Air Act had taken pains to balance the "government" of the NAAQs with administrative primacy for the states. It was the states' responsibility to devise state implementation plans (SIPs) detailing how the states proposed to meet those standards within a reasonable amount of time.

In principle, at least, the standards could be met in a wide variety of ways. All polluters could be made to lower their emissions by a certain percentage. Some polluters could be shut down entirely, while those deemed vital to the state's economy could be allowed to pollute at the current rate. Various combinations of these two approaches could also be employed. SIPs therefore appeared to be administrative in the Tocquevillean sense. They fostered real civic deliberation aimed at integrating the imperative to reduce air pollution with the myriad public and private activities and programs that would have to be adapted or modified to achieve that imperative.

However, the marriage of the NAAQs (government) and the SIPs (administration) ended in divorce. Congress became increasingly frustrated with the inability of the states to establish SIPs capable of meeting the NAAQs in a timely fashion. In principle, the choice boiled down to relaxing the NAAQs or diminishing state discretion. For the Democratic majority in Congress, wedded to the rights metaphor, the choice was clear. During the 1980s, it resisted all efforts to relax the NAAQs. In 1990, with President Bush's acquiescence, it enacted a revised Clean Air Act that essentially did away with the SIPs and replaced them with detailed, legislatively determined implementation directives. These directives not only specified how and when the states should comply with the NAAQs but established severe penalties for failure to comply.

By Tocquevillean lights, the SIPs did not fail. Air-quality progress occurred almost everywhere during the 1970s and 1980s.[20] Although state efforts rarely lived up to Congress's expectations, states did, on the whole, make serious efforts to improve the air. But Congress's programmatic-rights understanding of the NAAQs made this tendentious sort of success look like failure. The states' continued inability to meet the NAAQs constituted a rights violation.[21] Therefore, steady but slow progress needed to be replaced by the sort of speedy and uniform compliance that could be achieved only by centralized administration.

SUPERFUND

Superfund was passed a decade after the Clean Air Act. By that time, the programmatic right to health had become so widely accepted that a major environmental initiative could become law without any impressive demonstration of interstate spillover. Rights had eclipsed even interconnectedness in the environmental-policy debate.

Hazardous waste sites do not move. Unless they leach into an aquifer leading to a large river or reservoir serving a distant population, their impact is almost entirely local. The initial and continuing rationale for a major federal program to clean up these sites is *not* their systemic impact, but the right of all citizens to live in an environment free of the risks the sites pose.

The initial impetus for Superfund came from a widely publicized environmental scandal. In 1978, a massive abandoned toxic-waste dump was discovered beneath a suburban upstate New York neighborhood known as Love Canal. To make the case for federal action, the EPA first had to show that this was not an isolated example. It created a task force of agency personnel whose mandate was to uncover evidence that "ticking time bombs" could be found across the land, in as many congressional

---

[20] "U.S. Air Pollution Trends 1970–1990," in *The Environmental Almanac: Compiled by the World Resources Institute* (Boston: Houghton Mifflin, 1993), 90–1.

[21] See especially R. Shep Melnick, "Pollution Deadlines and the Coalition for Failure," in *Environmental Politics: Public Costs, Private Rewards,* ed. Michael S. Greve and Fred L. Smith, Jr. (New York: Praeger, 1992), 89–103. As Melnick's work verifies, Congress rather than the courts was the primary mover in undermining the SIP process.

districts as possible. Dutifully, the task force completed its mission. Sites were found and congressional offices were so informed.[22] No similar effort went into determining how great a risk such sites might actually pose, nor under what circumstances.

Having demonstrated that this was a nationwide problem, the EPA devised a proposal designed to protect everyone's right to have it solved. Two key elements undergirded the rights approach. First, the proposal avoided the question of how much cleanup a given site should receive. To ask the question would imply that a trade-off existed between the degree of risk reduction to be achieved at a site and the amount of money spent cleaning it up. At some point, the costs of further cleanup might outweigh the benefits. Instead, the act implied that all sites would be cleaned up to a degree that guaranteed everyone's right to safety.

The revised version of Superfund, passed in 1986, reinforced and strengthened its rights-based approach. The revised Superfund protects the right to safety by establishing uniform cleanup standards. Cleanups must meet all "applicable or relevant and appropriate" state and federal environmental air- and water-quality standards.[23]

To recognize how truly ambitious this requirement is, it must be remembered that virtually all the standards deemed "applicable, relevant, and appropriate" were not written with hazardous-waste cleanup in mind. They required levels of quality that often necessitated very expensive treatment at a site that had been degraded as much as many Superfund sites were. But the new law allowed no room for asking what benefits would be obtained from spending tens of millions of dollars to restore to pristine condition a site located in the midst of other dirty and smelly industrial workplaces.[24]

The states have been heavily involved in Superfund cleanup—but as implementers, not administrators. The federal government determines which sites will be cleaned up. It then permits the states to conduct the actual cleanup, but only if they adhere to very specific federal guidelines.

---

[22] Marc Landy, Marc Roberts, and Stephen Thomas, *The Environmental Protection Agency from Clinton to Nixon: Asking the Wrong Questions* (New York: Oxford University Press, 1994), 141–2.

[23] Marc Landy and Mary Hague, "The Coalition for Waste," in *Environmental Politics: Public Costs, Private Rewards,* ed. Michael S. Greve and Fred L. Smith, Jr. (New York: Praeger, 1992), 73–5.

[24] By the early 1990s, when a series of articles entitled "What Price Cleanup?" appeared in the *New York Times,* criticism of Superfund had become commonplace. See especially the first article in the series, Keith Schneider, "New View Calls Environmental Policy Misguided," March 21, 1993.

No other country in the world has a cleanup program comparable to
Superfund. In all other industrialized countries, hazardous-waste cleanup
is treated as a mundane administrative task.[25] Where a site seems to pose
a serious danger, the local government cleans it up. Where the danger is
perceived not to be great, only the most modest ameliorative efforts—
signs, guard dogs, and so on—are taken. The U.S. program is so much
more ambitious and centralist because only here has the problem been elevated to a matter of *government*. That occurred because safety was defined as a programmatic right.

THE ARK

As Charles Mann and Mark Plummer describe in *Noah's Choice,* their excellent study of endangered species, the debate over this issue has led to the
widespread conviction that nature, too, has rights. They quote Paul and
Anne Ehrlich as claiming "that our fellow passengers on Spaceship Earth
. . . have a right to exist."[26] Mann and Plummer refer to this view as the
Noah Principle—"on moral, ethical and spiritual grounds we must preserve biodiversity above all else." They go to great lengths to document
the claim that the Endangered Species Act embodies the Noah Principle.

Like the right to environmental health, the right of species to exist has
not been fully honored. Since the enactment of the present law in 1973,
several species are believed to have become extinct; many are considered
endangered. As with clean air and hazardous waste, the most serious impact of the rights conception of endangered species has been to obviate
the possibility of decentralized administration. If every species has a right
to exist, then localities should have no real discretion when it comes to
balancing species' existence with other cherished objectives.

To protect the habitat of the American burying beetle, the Choctaw
Nation, among the poorest of all Americans, was prevented by the U.S.
Fish and Wildlife Service from building a road that would have provided
much faster and safer access to its hospital. The proposed road would
have diminished the distance some patients had to travel by as much as 50
miles.[27] This was not the *sole* habitat of this beetle. Because its endan-

[25] Thomas W. Church and Robert T. Nakamura, "Beyond Superfund: Hazardous Waste
Cleanup in Europe and the United States," *Georgetown International Environmental
Law Review* 7 (Fall 1994): 56.
[26] Charles C. Mann and Mark L. Plummer, *Noah's Choice: The Future of Endangered
Species* (New York: Knopf, 1995), 24–5.
[27] Ibid., 15–16.

gered-species designation protected it from habitat destruction, however, no meaningful deliberation could take place about the relative merits of improving Choctaw health-service delivery versus diminishing the beetle's habitat.

PERPETRATORS

A related cause of the centralization of environmental policy was the widespread perception that malfeasance by major corporations was the central obstacle to attaining environmental rights.

Because the likes of Dow, U.S. Steel, and General Motors operated on a nationwide basis, they were well defended against local and state control efforts. Only the national government could prevent these corporations from engaging in a beggar-thy-neighbor strategy toward the states in order to prevent adequate enforcement.

Indeed, the EPA's early efforts were largely devoted to bringing these major multistate polluters to heel. The first EPA administrator, William Ruckelshaus, determined that the only viable means of establishing the new agency's credibility was to engage in a series of well-publicized enforcement actions against several corporate titans.[28]

This approach had the intended effect, but it also served to reinforce the notion that environmental improvement could be achieved without public sacrifice. It instilled the idea that pollution control was mainly a police action in which "bad guys" were brought to heel. A reckoning was postponed about the role of individual consumption and dwelling and transportation patterns in causing environmental degradation.

MANDATES

The centralization of administration of environmental policy remained incomplete in one crucial respect, and this omission would play a crucial role in reversing it. None of the major environmental initiatives relied primarily on federal, as opposed to local or private, funding. The national government chose the route, but it did not pay the freight. Superfund relied on liability law to impose the bulk of cleanup costs on responsible

---

[28] Robert L. Sansom, *The New American Dream Machine: Toward a Simpler Lifestyle in an Environmental Age* (Garden City, N.Y.: Anchor Press, 1976), 24–5, 43; John Quarles, *Cleaning Up America: An Insider's View of the Environmental Protection Agency* (Boston: Houghton Mifflin, 1976), 117–18.

private parties.[29] Likewise, the federal government paid a very small percentage of the costs of air-quality improvement; these were borne mostly by those whom the government ordered to make expensive changes in capital equipment and operating procedures.

Local governments were forced to devote great amounts of money to environmental improvement because their role, unlike that of the state and federal governments, was not restricted to enforcing federally initiated rules. Rule enforcement is a relatively inexpensive task. Local governments, like their counterparts in private industry, actually operate polluting facilities—landfills, incinerators, sewage-treatment facilities, water systems, and power plants—all of which were required to make capital-intensive adjustments in order to comply with federal regulation.

The first environmental law to place heavy burdens on local government was the Clean Water Act of 1972, which demanded massive improvements in municipal sewage treatment. But unlike later laws dealing with solid waste, hazardous waste, and drinking water, the Clean Water Act allocated vast sums of money to pay for these mandated changes. These subsidies were a boon to local government, and municipal officials became enthusiastic supporters of the program. As the federal budget deficit grew, however, these subsidies were reduced; sewage treatment became yet another environmental mandate straining municipal budgets.

The rationale offered for the disjunction between centralized administration and decentralized financing of environmental policy is the economic concomitant of interconnectedness, market failure. The market fails when those who do the damage do not pay the cost of that damage. Therefore, polluting facilities (whether municipally or privately owned) that cause harm downstream should bear the burden of alleviating those harms.

However, as environmental policy developed in the 1970s and 1980s, the market-failure justification for federal government mandates weakened. The Safe Drinking Water Act, as well as Superfund, showed that the federal government was willing to impose costly requirements on localities even in the absence of impressive significant downstream effects.[30]

Of course, one could argue that no harm is entirely local; even if pollution does not travel, people do. A visitor from another jurisdiction is entitled to be protected against environmentally induced health hazards dur-

[29] Landy and Hague, "Coalition for Waste," 68–71.
[30] *The Safe Drinking Water Act,* ed. Edward J. Calabrese, Charles Gilbert, and Harris Pastides (Chelsea, Mich.: Lewis, 1989).

ing her stay. This argument has in fact been employed to defend federally mandated drinking-water standards.

At best, the travel argument would justify de minimis national standards. The drinking water one imbibes during a limited stay should not place one in peril. But the standards the federal government sets for drinking water are far more stringent than that. They are designed to put an individual who imbibes the local water regularly and over a long period of time at a risk of less than one in a million of developing cancer. Thus, in certain crucial areas of environmental policy, federal intervention flunks the market-failure test. Even where real interjurisdictional spillovers exist, only the rights rationale can explain why the costs attached to those spillovers are so high.

The more impressive rationale for the mandate approach is political, not economic. It complements the enforcement emphasis described above. The public might not have proven so amenable to rights-based environmental policy if it had clearly understood how much that approach really cost. Mandating the cleanup expenses to private industry and local government clouded the cost picture because it was now difficult to obtain a comprehensive accounting of how much was actually spent. An illusion was created that those expenditures resulted from wrongdoing and therefore did not really "count." This approach in no way reduced the price to the public; it merely meant that the cleanup costs would be paid by local tax dollars and by increases in the price of goods and services rather than by the federal income tax.

THE CATALYST

It is no accident that the first major reversal of the centralizing trend in environmental policy involved so-called "unfunded mandates"; here the illusion that environmental improvement came free of charge was most easily shattered. It is hard to prove to consumers that price increases in goods and services are indeed attributable to higher environmental compliance costs.

Although the unfunded-mandates legislation was part of the Republicans' "Contract with America," it quickly took on a bipartisan cast. Most municipal officials are Democrats. As costs skyrocketed for federally imposed mandates (many but not all of which were environmental), these officials became increasingly vocal in demanding relief.

The fuel that propelled the unfunded-mandates issue onto the congressional agenda was a study conducted by officials in Columbus, Ohio. It detailed for the first time the total financial burden of the various federally imposed mandates for one particular (but by no means atypical) municipality.[31] The staggering size of the total figure energized local officials throughout the nation. Within two years, a Democratic president signed into law a bill requiring that all nonfederal statutes specify in advance the total financial burden they will impose on local government—and that Congress specifically affirm its intention to impose those burdens. Friends and foes alike have interpreted this to mean that the future will witness a significant reduction in federal efforts to impose costs on local government in pursuit of federally determined objectives.[32]

DECENTRALIZATION

Like the centralizing trend, the decentralizing trend in environmental policy, which was spearheaded by unfunded mandates, is fueled by a combination of scientific, political, and philosophical understandings. Perhaps the most important shift in scientific understanding has been the recognition that no clear-cut thresholds exist between safe and unsafe concentrations of most pollutants in the air or water. On the whole, higher concentrations cause more human illness, whereas lower concentrations cause less.

This recognition of the *relative* nature of the relationship between pollution and disease does not dispute the interconnectedness metaphor; if anything, it reinforces it. But it does undermine the effort to marry that metaphor to a concept of rights. It demonstrates that no particular level of air or water quality offers the sort of universal protection that a right confers.

In contemporary public-policy discourse, the only readily available alternative to rights-talk is utilitarianism. If no right to environmental health is conferrable, then one is left with little choice but to calculate the costs and benefits of alternative courses of action. Over the past few decades, the profession of risk analysis has emerged to provide part of the information needed to perform a utilitarian calculation. Risk analysis attempts to discern and describe the relationship between different levels

[31] *Environmental Legislation: The Increasing Costs of Regulatory Compliance to the City of Columbus,* report of the Environmental Law Review Committee to the Mayor and City Council of the City of Columbus (Columbus, Ohio: May 13, 1991).
[32] 1995 P.L. 104–4.

and types of hazardous exposure and different probabilities of sickness and death. Armed with this information, economists can perform cost analyses to specify the costs attached to differing levels of pollution reduction.[33]

To complete the picture, economists would like to offer an assessment of the benefits to be reaped at any given concentration level. But they have been unable to do this in a convincing manner. Benefits assessment has moved beyond the crude stage of trying to assign a dollar amount to the worth of a particular life based on the amount of income that individual forgoes by dying. In that system, rich people are *prima facie* more valuable than poor people. Unfortunately, more recent and sophisticated efforts by economists remain unconvincing except to the anointed. These efforts rely on hypothetical questions about one's "willingness to pay" to save an additional life, not necessarily one's own.[34] The need to consider benefits other than reduced mortality or morbidity has led to the use of simulation and polling techniques designed to elicit opinions about the values of environmental benefits. But these methods—relying on polling and market-research tactics rife with epistemological and methodological difficulties—are of questionable value.[35]

The very dubiousness of benefits estimation makes the metaphor of risk relativity inherently decentralizing. If there is no "scientific" way to balance the costs and benefits of different levels of risk, then there is no overwhelming reason why the federal government should impose one particular risk/benefit calculation on everybody. Different communities might well choose to make different choices about how much risk to run. In recent years, the federal government has begun to acknowledge the need to encourage states and localities to engage in just this sort of deliberation by funding comparative-risk projects in several states.

---

[33] Risk analysis has become a profession of its own. Important academic centers practicing it have sprung up at several of the nation's leading universities and think tanks. A good introduction to it is Adam Finkel's *Confronting Uncertainty in Risk Management: A Guide for Decision Makers* (Washington, D.C.: Resources for the Future, 1990). A good compendium of recent applications of this mode of analysis appears in *Risk vs. Risk: Tradeoffs in Protecting Health and the Environment*, ed. John D. Graham and Jonathan Baert Wiener (Cambridge, Mass.: Harvard University Press, 1995).

[34] See especially Kip W. Viscusi, "The Dangers of Unbounded Commitments to Regulate Risk," in *Risks, Costs, and Lives Saved: Getting Better Results from Regulation*, ed. Robert W. Hahn (New York and Washington, D.C.: Oxford University Press and AEI Press, 1996).

[35] For a very useful summary of the current debate over these methods, see Paul R. Portney, "The Contingent Valuation Debate: Why Economists Should Care," *Journal of Economic Perspectives* 8 (Fall 1994): 13–17.

As early as 1984, EPA Administrator Ruckelshaus performed an experiment that presaged the current trend toward encouraging community-level risk/benefit deliberation. The EPA was required to establish an air-emissions limit for arsenic. It so happened that such a standard would affect only one plant in America, located in Tacoma, Washington. Ruckelshaus decided to actively involve the citizens of Tacoma in determining what limit to set. Public meetings were held in which citizens were presented with data about the health and employment implications of different emissions levels. The outcome was inconclusive. The Tacoma plant closed for reasons unrelated to the matter at hand. But the effort to use the federal government to spur deliberation while leaving meaningful decision-making in the hands of local citizens provides an inkling of how risk science might influence the design of decentralized policymaking in the future.[36]

BROWNFIELDS

In one policy domain at least, replacement of a right with a risk-relativity understanding has already led to a great increase in local initiative. Because Superfund requires such high levels of cleanup, it has made property in many urban manufacturing districts unusable and therefore unsalable. These are the same areas that have already experienced loss of solid, blue-collar employment due to the migration of factories to low-wage Southern rural areas and abroad. Efforts to revive these areas have frequently been stymied because would-be developers of factories and warehouses are frightened of the potentially enormous liability they would incur by becoming the owners of contaminated property.[37]

The risks posed by a site depend on three considerations: 1) how much toxic material is found at the site, and in what concentrations; 2) what pathways exist for exposing people to harm; and 3) the frequency of contact with those exposure pathways. Even if toxic concentrations are relatively high, they may pose minimal risk if the pathways of exposure are limited and the work to be done on site does not put people in contact with those pathways. Recognizing this, cities across America have rebelled against Superfund's dictum that all sites be cleaned up to the same

[36] Recounted in Landy et al., *The EPA from Clinton to Nixon.*
[37] Charles Powers, *State Brownfields Policy and Practice* (Boston: Institute for Responsible Management, 1995), 8–11.

very high standards. They are insisting that the level of cleanup be adjusted in keeping with the post-cleanup land use intended for a given site.[38]

For example, if a site is not contaminating underground drinking-water sources, then the risk involved in paving it over and building above it may be quite modest. This is especially true if it is a commercial rather than residential site, since this precludes the likelihood of 24-hour-a-day exposure and of children playing in (and possibly eating) contaminated soil. The problem posed by such a land-use-based solution is that the land use might eventually change. For example, a new owner might unwittingly put a day-care center in the basement.

Modulating cleanup levels and restrictions on use is a complex task, but it is appropriately an administrative one, not a governmental one. Geologists and hydrologists are capable of giving reasonable estimates concerning potential exposure pathways. Lawyers can devise restrictive covenants regarding permissible use that remain in place even if the property changes ownership. No implementation solution is idiot-proof, but a permanent covenant in a deed prohibiting use of the property for residential or child-care purposes is a reasonably reliable and enduring enforcement mechanism.

Local efforts to integrate cleanup and land-use policy have spread sufficiently to take on the status of a "movement"—the "Brownfields Movement." Mayors and county commissioners throughout America have lobbied their congressional representatives to remove federal restrictions on local flexibility in determining post-cleanup land use. After initially opposing such efforts, the EPA has become much more supportive; it has even gone a considerable distance toward enabling this form of local administration to flourish.[39]

"THE ENEMY IS US"

To a great extent, centralized environmental administration has become a victim of its own success. The enforcement strategy pioneered by Ruckelshaus worked. Big corporations have indeed improved their compliance

---

[38] The experience of cities and towns in 14 different states is recounted in ibid., 27–104. See also Deborah Cooney, Charles Bartsch, Jocelyn Seitzman, and Carol Andress, *Revival of Contaminated Sites: Case Studies* (Washington, D.C.: Northeast-Midwest Institute, 1992).

[39] "The Brownfields Action Agenda," USEPA, January 25, 1995.

record and now employ large staffs devoted to reconciling corporate practice with the letter and spirit of the law. Having achieved significant pollution reductions, they now enjoy much greater political credibility when they claim that further reductions would be inordinately expensive to achieve. They have succeeded in making environmental policymaking less of a morality play and more of a sober consideration about the habits of ordinary people.

A good example of this change involves water pollution. In the wake of great improvement in reducing the discharges from such large polluters as pulp mills and power plants, the most intractable remaining problems stem from so-called "non-point" sources. A "non-point" source is anyone who puts chemicals on the ground in such a way that a rainstorm will wash the chemicals into a sewer and then into a lake, stream, or river. In other words, it is every farmer who fertilizes his crops and every suburbanite who tries to get rid of crabgrass.[40]

Other examples of this new generation of diffuse environmental issues include recycling, gas-barbecue emissions, and water pollution from residential septic tanks. Although it is conceivable to attempt regulating these matters centrally, the federal government has shown no great enthusiasm for doing so. It seems to recognize that the need to subtly alter the perceptions and behaviors of masses of people requires the rapier of private, local, and perhaps state initiative—not the bazooka of federal enforcement.

EVERYTHING IS NOT EVERYTHING

Whereas one generation of ecological scientists seems to have been mesmerized by the notion of interconnectedness, more recent explorations have begun to acknowledge the equally important truth of the robustness of local environments. Individual habitats often show a remarkable ability to withstand—and recover from—external intrusions. Much of America is more heavily forested today than it was 100 years ago.[41] This is not

---

[40] John DeWitt, *Civic Environmentalism* (Washington, D.C.: Congressional Quarterly Press, 1994), 40–1.

[41] The Council on Environmental Quality reports that there were 366 million acres of forest land in the United States in 1900 and 648 million acres in 1992. Council on Environmental Quality, *Twenty-Fifth Annual Report* (Washington, D.C.: U.S. Government Printing Office, 1992), 465. Forest land more than doubled between 1900 and 1969. U.S. Bureau of the Census, *Historical Statistics of the United States* (Washington, D.C.: U.S. Government Printing Office, 1975), 433.

   Perhaps the most eloquent testimony regarding reforestation comes from Bill McKibben, a justly famous environmental writer whose book *The End of Nature* has

the result of any positive action by environmentalists or government; it is simply a result of the decline of agriculture. Once farmers cease their relentless efforts to clear their fields and keep them that way, the forest grows back. Grass and weeds breaking through the asphalt of an abandoned parking lot are powerful reminders of nature's ability to rebound.[42]

   The recognition of local robustness is not mere conservative political dogma. The following quotes come from a world-famous ecologist, Harvard's Richard Levins, who could not by any stretch of the imagination be deemed a conservative.

All things are indeed connected if we follow chains of causation through their devious twists and turns. But everything is not strongly, directly or significantly connected to everything else. The analogy between an ecosystem and an individual organism simply does not hold up. The relation between say the liver and the heart is not the same as the relation between gazelles and gnus. . . .

   The relative autonomy of linked subsystems is as important in understanding nature as their connectedness. . . . We can in fact change some things without changing others.[43]

   We are warned over and over again of the fragility of the biosphere . . . But the biosphere is remarkably robust. Ecosystems that are regularly disrupted by storms or fire or flood incorporate these disruptions into their ecology. . . . There

been praised by environmentalists and is widely read. McKibben, who continues to be an important spokesman for the environmental cause, commented extensively on the extraordinary rebound of Eastern woodlands in an April 1995 article in *Atlantic Monthly*. He began by remarking that "the reforestation of the eastern United States—thanks partly to conservationists and mostly to accident—can show the developing world how to make room for people, farming, industry and endangered species of plants and animals which have returned." McKibben recalls Timothy Dwight's journey from New York to Boston in the early nineteenth century—a distance of 240 miles, only 20 of which were forested. "Less than two centuries later, despite great increases in the state's population, 90 percent of New Hampshire is covered by forest. Vermont was 35 percent woods in 1850 and is 80 percent today, and even Massachusetts, Connecticut and Rhode Island have seen woodlands rebound to the point where they cover nearly three fifths of southern New England" (60, 63).

   McKibben then quotes Douglas MacCleery of the U.S. Forest Service: "The forest and farmland landscape of the Appalachians, *as well as many other parts of the East and South* [emphasis added], has come full circle. By the 1960s and 1970s, the pattern of forest, fields and pastures was similar to that prior to 1800, its appearance much like it must have been prior to the American Revolution" (63).

[42] The importance of natural robustness is well considered in Gregg Easterbrook's important book *A Moment on Earth: The Coming Age of Environmental Optimism* (New York: Penguin, 1995).

[43] Richard Levins, "Evolutionary Ecology Looks at Environmentalism," paper delivered at the Symposium on Science, Reason, and Modern Democracy, Michigan State University, East Lansing, Michigan, May 1, 1992, 3–6.

are quite striking examples of species returning after being locally extinct and of
forests reclaiming cleared land in New England as well as the tropics.[44] . . .
  Thus ecosystems are best understood not as harmoniously balanced wholes
but as loosely coupled semi-autonomous sub-systems.[45]

  This shift in scientific understanding threatens to deprive environmentalists of the moral high ground. If plants and animals can indeed recover
from human interventions, then new moral space is created for appreciating the ill effects of *preventing* such interventions. How many breast cancer victims would die if taxol-producing yews were *not* cut down? How
many loggers would lose their livelihood, and indeed their way of life, if
Northwest timber harvests were further restricted? As Mann and Plummer point out, the American burying beetle, once thought to exist in only
a few places, has been cropping up far more widely as ecologists take
greater pains to look for it.[46]
  Congress is reconsidering the Endangered Species Act. It is not yet
clear whether the growing perception of robustness will influence that
outcome. But in general, the decentralist implications of local robustness
are strong. By challenging the premise that everything is meaningfully in-
terconnected, decentralization undermines the strongest of all rationales
for central action, the idea of spillover. It does not deny that spillovers
may occur, but it denies the *presumption* that they occur and requires that
they be demonstrated empirically. In the absence of such proof, a presumption would exist in favor of allowing localities to govern their physical surroundings as they see fit.

TAKINGS

Revision of the scientific and ethical metaphors that dominate environmental policy has, for the most part, worked to favor local government.
But there is at least one serious exception to this rule. Much of the legal
and political opposition to the effort to create programmatic environmental rights has taken the form of reasserting another right—the right to
property. The so-called "takings" clause of the Fifth Amendment to the
Constitution states that private property shall not be taken for public use
without just compensation. Opponents of federal environmental regulation interpret any loss of property value stemming from public regulation
as constituting a taking—and therefore requiring compensation.

[44] Ibid., 9.   [45] Ibid., 10.
[46] Mann and Plummer, *Noah's Choice.*

This "anti-takings" position was incorporated into the Contract with America. It passed the House in March of 1994. If enacted, it would effectively end the use of environmental regulatory efforts, because the amount of compensation required would prove overwhelming. If a federal wetlands regulation diminished the fair-market value of someone's property by more than 10 percent, for example, the government would have to compensate the owner for that loss.[47] As of the fall of 1995 almost half the states had adopted some form of legislation to protect private-property rights in the previous five years.[48]

These political developments have been paralleled and perhaps stimulated by important Supreme Court decisions. Until recently, the takings clause had proven no serious impediment to public regulation. However, in a series of cases dating back to 1987, the Court has shown a revived interest in the concept—and a renewed willingness to use it as a rationale for constraining regulation. All these cases involved a challenge to state or local, not federal, regulation.[49]

For purposes of this chapter, the most important in this line of cases is the most recent, *Dolan v. Tigard.* Dolan challenged a decision of the Oregon Land Use Board of Appeals, which had affirmed the conditions placed by the city of Tigard, Oregon, on development of her commercial property. Dolan, the owner of a plumbing- and electric-supply store, had applied for a permit to substantially expand the store and its parking facilities and to blacktop the gravel parking lot. The city found that the expansion would significantly increase traffic congestion and (along with the paving) runoff into an adjacent creek. It therefore required Dolan to dedicate that portion of her property within the 100-year flood plain to form part of a greenway running along the creek; the greenway would provide both additional storm drainage and public access. The city also required Dolan to donate an additional 15-foot strip of land adjacent to the flood plain for a pedestrian/bicycle path intended to relieve traffic congestion in the city's central business district, in which the store was located.[50]

The Court found that these requirements violated the takings clause of

---

[47] Kirk Emerson and Charles R. Wise, "Statutory Approaches to Regulatory Takings: State Property Rights Legislation Issues and Implications for Public Administration," paper presented at the Annual Meeting of the American Political Science Association, Chicago, Illinois, August 31, 1995, 15.

[48] Ibid., 4. [49] Ibid., 2 and 3.

[50] *Dolan v. Tigard*, No. 93–518, *114 Supreme Court Reporter* (2309–2331, cited as 114 S.Ct. 2309), 1994.

the Fifth Amendment. It invoked the doctrine of "unconstitutional conditions," which states that the government may not require a person to give up a constitutional right—in this case just compensation for a public taking—in exchange for a discretionary benefit (the building permit) conferred by the government. It did not deny that preventing flooding and reducing traffic congestion were legitimate public purposes, but it determined that the degree of exaction demanded by the city from Dolan was disproportionate to the projected impact of the proposed development. In other words, the demands placed by the city seemed excessively draconian in view of the relatively small amount of damage the development would cause.

Although it rejected a "precise mathematical calculation" between the demands imposed and the need created, the Court insisted upon a "rough proportionality" between the two. It found that two aspects of Tigard's demands on Dolan were out of proportion. The Court acknowledged that the city had a legitimate interest in flood control; the city therefore had a right to insist that Dolan not build within the flood plain. But the Court also found the city's demand that Dolan donate the land to the public to be excessive, because it was unrelated to the flood-control objective.[51]

The Court likewise acknowledged that the city had an interest in decreasing traffic congestion but it rejected the demand for a pedestrian and bicycle path on the grounds that no reasonable relationship had been established between the number of additional vehicle trips the store expansion would generate and the number of trips the path would eliminate. The city had claimed only that the path "*could* offset some of the traffic demand . . . and lessen the increase in traffic congestion."

As Justice David Souter pointed out in his dissent, the crucial implications of this decision for local environmental management hinge on the word "could." "The Court only faults the city for saying that the bicycle path *could* rather than *would* offset the increased traffic from the store. . . . It appears that the Court has placed the burden of producing evidence of relationship on the city, *despite the usual rule in cases involving the police power that the government is presumed to have acted constitutionally.*" Justice Souter further pointed out that Dolan produced no proof that the path would not relieve congestion, whereas the city did provide studies showing a link between bike paths and auto-traffic reduction.[52]

This startling reversal in the burden of proof regarding use of the po-

[51] *Dolan v. Tigard*, 2319   [52] *Dolan v. Tigard*, 2330–1

lice power would appear to greatly limit the means available to local government for exerting environmental control. Although the Court explicitly rejected requiring a "precise mathematical calculation" of the relationship between added congestion from the store expansion and reduced congestion from the bike path, it seemed unwilling to settle for anything less.

Regulation, even at its most precise, is an art, not a science. It is the rare case indeed where the level of exactitude demanded by the Court can be reached. For a fee, of course, researchers can always be found who will perform studies providing the illusion of exactitude. But one would not want to accuse the Court of seeking to create added revenue for pseudo–social scientists. Elaboration of the doctrine of "rough proportionality" in future cases will determine whether it is meant as a salubrious limitation on government's temptation to load the burdens of paying for broad social benefits on just a few shoulders, or whether it is meant to limit the police power to only the most glaring examples of public nuisance.

CONCLUSION

From both ends of the political spectrum, the threat to local administration is expressed in "rights talk."[53] Property rights purport to trump nature's rights, and vice versa. Regardless of which right wins the trick, local public authority is the loser because these rights require either centrally imposed uniformity or no government intrusion at all.

Among the greatest virtues of local government is its sobriety. The city of Tigard appears to have been practicing this virtue when it sought to balance Ms. Dolan's interest in prospering with the citizenry's interest in curbing downtown congestion. Had the city resorted to "rights talk," it would have been forced to refuse her request for a building permit or accept the increased congestion caused by her store expansion. This is the immoderation that the Court—and the regulation-as-takings movement—seems to want to impose.

Local politics and government discourages the view that people are bundles of rights. Instead, it focuses debate in a manner that encourages reflection and moderation. The more the conversation can be confined spatially, the more pressure there is to behave responsibly. The person whose children cannot safely visit their friends because there are no side-

[53] Mary Ann Glendon, *Rightstalk* (New York: Free Press, 1991).

walks is the same one whose front-yard herbicides are poisoning the nearby duck pond. Although there are no guarantees, recognizing that one is simultaneously a victim and a perpetrator should encourage one to be more accommodating when responding to the demands of others and more civil when making demands of one's own.

As this chapter has taken pains to point out, not all environmental problems can be dealt with so close to home. Render unto centralized government those problems whose spillover effects require national, or indeed international, action. But as the discussion of risk relativity and local robustness shows, spillovers are neither as pervasive nor as dispositive as commonly perceived. Reduced to a bumper sticker, this chapter would read, "Think Locally—Act Locally."

9

Local self-government in education
Community, citizenship, and charter schools

GREGORY R. WEIHER AND CHRIS COOKSON

In his 1919 short-story collection *Winesburg, Ohio*, Sherwood Anderson presents a succession of "grotesques"—characters whose personalities have been distorted by the conformity and bigotry of small-town life. Small-town oppressiveness is a prominent theme in twentieth-century American literature. It contradicts another popular mythos in American culture—the small town as the wellspring of virtue. According to this view, the small town is the quiet place at the center of the storm, that place "over the river and through the woods," where folks live in white bungalows and never lock their doors at night.

There is no real paradox here, since each of these descriptions is equally applicable to small towns or, indeed, to any community. The small town, the neighborhood, the local school—each is a place where children are raised and educated, unspoken codes of courtesy and fairness are observed, meanings are attached to common experience, and rites of passage are devised. For those whose membership is unchallenged, the community will likely be recalled as a place of nurture. For those whose membership is tenuous, however, the community will be remembered as a source of big and small hurts, of implacable indifference, or cruelty.

Schools are central in this dialectic of nurture and oppression. No institutions strike an emotional nerve more directly than the local schools, which along with the church and the family, are the chief means of socializing the young. One side recalls being tormented in various ways in the local high school for being different with respect to race, creed, or national origin. The other side laments the loss of ethnic, religious, and regional distinctiveness in schools, owing to a Progressive, national conception of

The authors thank Martha Derthick, John Scott, Herb Rothschild, Joe Nogee, Rick Matland, and Mark Hinnawi for helpful comments.

education—"the one best system"—that deplores such irrational bases of association.

In U.S. public affairs, the "antilocal" position has predominated in the twentieth century. The local community and local schools have been characterized as places where the citizenship of some has been abridged and the prerogatives of others have been undeservedly broadened. Courts and legislatures have diluted the autonomy of the community, particularly over schools, in the name of greater equality and the fuller realization of citizenship for all Americans. They have determined that if community becomes a manifestation of organic[1] bases of association, it becomes oppressive. Membership based on race, gender, religion, or nationality denies "out-groups" the full enjoyment of the rights associated with citizenship, and violates the Constitution.

In keeping with the tenor of these federal interventions, the literature suggests that, rather than training democrats, local governments simply institutionalize parochial power and narrow economic interest (Burns 1994; Danielson 1976; Downs 1981, 1994; Miller 1981; Rusk 1995, 1996; Teaford 1979; Weiher 1991). Local governments are usually created by communities that want to exclude low-income or minority citizens, or by business groups seeking to manipulate public power for private gain. Zoning powers and other land-use controls are used chiefly to perpetuate ethnic and class exclusion (Downs 1981, 1994; Friedan 1979). School districts are created in preemptive strikes, keeping outside forces from imposing boundaries that would increase racial and class diversity (Weiher 1991).

The magnitude of the effort undertaken by courts and legislatures to dismantle local discriminatory structures implicitly contradicts the Jeffersonian faith that the people, when they are allowed to govern themselves in their localities, are good. In the political theories of Thomas Jefferson,

---

[1] We use the term "organic" to refer to bonds of association that are almost "biologically" transmitted, a description that will be uncontroversial regarding race and family, nearly uncontroversial regarding gender and nationality, and probably open to dispute but still useful regarding religion. Philip Selznick uses the term similarly in his discussion of Ferdinand Tonnies (Selznick 1992, 363–5; Tonnies 1963), but in some contexts exactly the opposite is intended by its use. For instance, Émile Durkheim believed there were two types of social solidarity, mechanical and organic (Durkheim, 1933). The bonds he referred to as "mechanical" characterize a historically prior order that is economically and organizationally undifferentiated and in which unity is based on symbolic experience, common socialization, etc. "Organic" solidarity characterizes an order based on contract law and the division of labor. We continue to believe that the former order is more appropriately called organic in that the bases of the social order are ascriptive, and if not exactly biologically transmitted, at least highly correlated with things that are.

John Stuart Mill, Jean Jacques Rousseau, Alexis de Tocqueville, and John Dewey, local self-government is the school in which citizens learn democratic virtues. When prescribing rules to themselves, citizens are at once free and governed by their noblest impulses. Practicing democracy makes the practitioners better democrats by forcing them to reckon with the aspirations of their fellow citizens. The result is a moral community of free, dignified, enlightened members.

Is such a community beyond hoping for? Are local communities and schools dominated by venality and bigotry, or is there redemption to be found in local self-government? Can some arrangement be found that preserves the affective influence of local communities without sanctioning meanness toward those who, while being outsiders in the organic sense, are nonetheless fellow Americans?

THE PROBLEMATIC

House Speaker Thomas "Tip" O'Neill may be longer remembered for his dictum that all politics is local than for any of his considerable accomplishments. This would not be an altogether unjust outcome. In focusing on the locality as the perennial source of civic activity, he is in good company. A long tradition in liberal political thought holds that citizen participation in the life of the local community is indispensable to the good health of democracy.

John Dewey, normally not a devotee of parochialism, found the locality to be the *only* venue in which effective community could be realized. The "great community" was to emerge through his "method of intelligence" (the use of reason, education, and communication to reach an encompassing consensus), but only insofar as it was made vital and concrete by being transmitted locally from neighbor to neighbor.

In its deepest and richest sense a community must always remain a matter of face-to-face intercourse. This is why the family and neighborhood, with all their deficiencies, have always been the chief agencies of nurture, the means by which dispositions are stably formed and ideas acquired which laid hold on the roots of character. The Great Community, in the sense of free and full intercommunication, is conceivable. But it can never possess all the qualities which mark a local community. It will do its final work in ordering the relations and enriching the experience of local associations. The invasion and partial destruction of life of the latter by outside uncontrolled agencies is the immediate source of the instability, disintegration and restlessness which characterize the present epoch. Evils which are uncritically and indiscriminately laid at the door of industrialism and democracy might, with greater intelligence, be referred to the dislocation and unsettlement of local communities. Vital and thorough attachments are bred only in the intimacy of an intercourse which is of necessity restricted in range (Dewey 1927, 211–12).

Dewey envisioned an enlightened society in which individuals would be afforded the interactions conducive to full self-realization. But this society confronts the individual as an abstraction. To have any impact, the *great* community must be manifest in the concrete affairs of the *local* community.

An important point is that Dewey recognizes the local community as an *affective* order. He says, for instance, that "a man who has not been seen in the daily relations of life may inspire admiration, emulation, servile subjection, fanatical partisanship, hero worship; *but not love and understanding*" (Dewey 1927, 213; emphasis added). Indeed, it is this affective dimension that distinguishes the term "community" from other, similar terms—"school district," "municipality," "place," "society," "group." It is like these terms insofar as it implies a collection of individuals or a determinate geographic space. But none of these terms incorporates the affective dimension that is necessary to the concept of community. Significantly, then, community cannot be achieved through contract, charter, indoctrination, or the accidental collocation of persons. Communal bonds are symbolic,[2] fraternal, and affective.

Finally, Dewey recognizes the danger as well as the potential of community, and in doing so frames the problematic that confronts any consideration of local self-government in the contemporary United States. "Is it possible for local communities to be stable without being static, progressive without being merely mobile?" he asks (ibid., 212). For it is the stability of the local community that is so attractive—the commitment to a shared and understood set of values, the context of concern and nurture, the resources for forming secure individual identities. Such stability, however, can degenerate into obdurate systems of caste and clan that nurture some only by diminishing others. When the community becomes static, we search for more progressive arrangements, loosening the traditional boundaries to include persons without regard to "tribalistic" attachments. But again, progressiveness is replaced by mere mobility when

---

[2] The role of symbols in relationship to theories of community deserves more than passing mention. Much of the concern of the science of semiology ("how things mean") is directed toward symbols as concentrations of affect. More specifically, symbols are seen as direct communications of affect that bypass rational forms of communication—and, indeed, communicate in ways that are not possible using rational discourse.

localities become so fluid that they are no longer communities at all. Such localities cease to generate the affective attachments that are the substance of community.

"STABLE WITHOUT BEING STATIC . . ."

The sense of community often grows out of a substratum of organic associations. Although we must remain open to any argument that offers hope of an alternative foundation, this connection is certainly stressed by many who have taken the communitarian side in recent debates over the ability of Liberalism to sustain adequate levels of social function and solidarity. Michael Sandel's formulation is typical:

> Can we view ourselves as independent selves, independent in the sense that our identity is never tied to our aims and attachments?
>
> I don't think we can, at least not without cost to those loyalties and convictions whose moral force consists partly in the fact that living by them is inseparable from understanding ourselves as the particular persons we are—as members of this family or community or nation or people, as bearers of that history, as citizens of this republic. Allegiances such as these are more than values I happen to have, and to hold, at a certain distance. They go beyond the obligations I voluntarily incur and the "natural duties" I owe to human beings as such. They allow that to some I owe more than justice requires or even permits, not by reason of agreements I have made but instead in virtue of those more or less enduring attachments and commitments that, taken together, partly define the person I am (Sandel 1992, 23).[3]

Even Selznick, who would obviously reject a conception of community that relied only on organic ties, recognizes their indispensability as a partial foundation. This is clear in his discussion of the "implicated self" in which he insists that individual identity, though not completely defined by inheritance, nevertheless cannot be understood apart from it. For the implicated self, obligations "arise from the continuities of socialization, selfhood, and shared experience." Whereas "bonds of family, friendship, ethnicity, and locality" (Selznick, 1992, 206) cannot entirely bind such a self, neither can its formation be imagined without them.

Community is founded on affect, not intellect. It is a function of shared belief, growing as much from the viscera as from the cerebrum, and often held in defiance of evidence. Belief is not divorced from race, family, faith,

---

[3] This passage is repeated almost verbatim in Sandel's later book, *Democracy's Discontent: America in Search of a Public Philosophy,* 14 (Sandel, 1996).

and place, but, inasmuch as these categories are used to orient experience, is an extension of them. Organic ties are essential to the vitality of community because community is an affective order, unlike municipality, school district, or state, which are only legal orders. *Places* embody all of those things we so cherish in our folklore only when they become *communities*. In this sense, the attack on organic ties of association is also an attack on community and must result in local places that fall short of our aspirations for them.

". . . PROGRESSIVE WITHOUT BEING MERELY MOBILE"

Yet the attack on gender, race, ethnicity, and other organic criteria of membership could not have been avoided without seriously impugning the value of citizenship. To cite the most obvious example, the racial segregation of American schools by law and custom, in the South and in the North, was a national scandal and an affront to the citizenship of African-Americans.

Liberal citizenship is the political manifestation of moral equality (Selznick, 1992). It is the person's claim on civil society to be accorded treatment befitting a bearer of rights and in keeping with human dignity. The actual boundaries of citizenship are always being negotiated, but citizenship cannot be sustained unless persons have access to those activities that are so conspicuous, regular, and essential that they define the social mainstream. Within these boundaries, citizenship admits of no gradations. According to classical liberal doctrine, persons who are members of a society must also be citizens (Walzer 1992, 84).

The twentieth-century attack on organic bases of membership in the name of civil rights is entirely compatible with the liberal doctrine of citizenship. It was not a perversion of American ideals foisted upon us by impostors in our midst. It was, rather, at least in its inspiration, American society calling itself to account in keeping with its own most cherished standards of justice. As Gunnar Myrdal notes, Americans were confronted with a peculiarly American dilemma (Myrdal, 1964). American majorities could not blatantly discriminate against minority groups and still claim adherence to their own liberal ideals.

This realization, however, brings us full circle, reemphasizing the unique problematic that we face in our federal political system (Derthick, this volume). The "rights revolution" was implemented from the top down, imposed on localities and states by federal institutions and supported by nationally focused elites (Wilson, this volume). As Sandel notes, it was the shift from place to nation in the American economic and political systems that resulted in a devaluing of the local place as a moral order:

Unlike the liberty of the early republic, the modern version permits—in fact even requires—concentrated power. This has to do with the universalizing logic of rights. In so far as I have a right, whether to free speech or a minimum income, its provision cannot be left to the vagaries of local preferences but must be assured at the most comprehensive level of political association. It cannot be one thing in New York and another in Alabama. As rights and entitlements expand, politics is therefore displaced from smaller forms of association and relocated at the most universal form—in our case, the nation (Sandel 1992, 27).[4]

We cherish the local community for its potential to form *affective* citizens—members of our civil society whose affection and loyalty have been secured through the nurture that can occur only in the local place. Yet the claims of a *procedural* national citizenship are inimical to the foundations of the local community. The struggle to guarantee every American the full enjoyment of the rights associated with national citizenship by purging civil activity of the taint of race, gender, faith, place, and family weakens the substratum upon which an effective local order can be built.

CITIZENSHIP, COMMUNITY, AND SCHOOLS

The tension between the affective bases of community and the universalistic, procedural claims of national citizenship is nowhere more apparent than in the local public schools. Free public schools are an American invention, and the education of the young is among the few unchallenged goods Americans will recognize. Schools are often at the epicenter of the

---

[4] Selznick offers very similar statements about the corrosive influence of nationalization on the affective bonds that sustain local community. For instance: "Particularism is diluted as the community expands. More and more people are recognized, first as fellow creatures and then as colleagues or members of the same in-group. In the modern nation-state the particularist connotations of "citizen," though far from lost, are greatly attenuated. The experience of citizenship encourages larger perspectives and undercuts primordial ties of family, tribe, religion, and locality" (Selznick 1992, 1956) and: "The programs of the welfare state are mainly designed to serve individual needs. Guided by principles of equality and personal autonomy, they display only passing concern for the integrity and well-being of groups and institutions, that is, for the spontaneous arrangements of civil society. As government moves to supplement (and replace) private ordering, the fabric of community is weakened. Kinship, religion, locality, employment, friendship, social networks, voluntary associations: all diminish in relative importance as resources for care and centers of moral obligation" (Selznick 1992, 512).

community. School events—ice-cream socials, chili suppers, athletic contests—are traditionally occasions for the community to celebrate itself. The heart of a community is never more quickly bared than when there is a suspicion of malfeasance or malignancy in the schools.

Precisely for these reasons, it is essential that the public schools nurture, protect, and enlighten *all* children. But this prescription attempts to combine two elements that are difficult to reconcile: the affective basis of community and the disinterested rationality of national citizenship. In the twentieth century, the universalistic claims of national citizenship have preoccupied policymakers. The result may be that the community no longer recognizes the public schools as its own.

THE MYTH OF LOCAL AUTONOMY OVER EDUCATION

Commentators have referred to education as one of the most local policy domains, but it is difficult to think any longer that local control predominates. In their daily actions, local educators must consult a bewildering array of federal and state regulations, including the drawing of attendance zones, the assignment of students to classes and academic tracks, student discipline, gender issues, facilities and services offered to disabled students, the hiring and firing of staff and teachers, curricula and course offerings, the allocation of resources, and the expenditure of funds. States impose further policies concerning teacher-student ratios, tax rates, accreditation, teacher qualifications, teacher salaries, and so on. Legislation in Texas putatively creates home-rule districts, but it also requires them to comply with reporting requirements and formats for the Public Education Information Management System and prohibits local interference in the following areas: educator certification and educator rights, criminal-history records, student admissions, school attendance, interdistrict or intercounty student transfers, elementary-school class sizes, the identification of low-performing campuses, high-school graduation requirements, special-education programs, bilingual-education programs, prekindergarten programs, safety in the transportation of students, the computation and distribution of state aid, extracurricular activities, health and safety standards, public-school accountability, equalized-wealth measures, bond obligation, tax rates, and purchasing. Not surprisingly, no school districts in Texas have availed themselves of the dubious autonomies these "home-rule" provisions represent.

In fact, local autonomy over schools has been greatly reduced. Even where regulations do not specifically tie the hands of local educators, the constant possibility of litigation makes them hesitant to innovate. Many of the matters of significance to parents are not under the control of local school-board members or educators. In some states, even the choice of textbooks in local districts is narrowly prescribed by a state board.

What explains this lack of local control over a policy area of supreme local concern? Obviously, localities have not always been so powerless to influence affairs in community schools. Indeed, Tyack (1974) and Link (1986) describe circumstances under which the schools were very much manifestations of their communities, and Chubb and Moe (1990) speak, albeit somewhat romantically, of an era when education

was about simple, important things that ordinary people cared about and could understand. Above all else, it centered on teaching, on how their children were to be taught and who would teach them. Because local schools were bound up with family, neighborhood, and community, and because teaching was intrinsically anchored in personal relationships and experiences, people naturally believed that they could and should be able to govern their own educational affairs. And as they proceeded—all across America, without plan or coordination—to fashion the kinds of schools they wanted for themselves and their children, the great heterogeneity of the nation came to be reflected in the diversity and autonomy of its local schools (Chubb and Moe 1990, 3).

Others have constructed excellent chronologies of the deterioration of local autonomy over education. Certain important points in this chronology deserve mention, however.

COMMON SCHOOLS AND PROGRESSIVE SCHOOLS

The Common School Movement marks a historic turn toward systematization in American education. The common schools were to be "common, not as a school for the common people—for example, the nineteenth-century Prussian *Volksschule*—but rather as a school common to all people" (Cremin 1961, 10). The common school was intended to have a homogenizing effect. "Dreading the destructive possibilities of religious, political, and class difference, [Horace Mann] sought a common value system within which diversity might flourish. His quest was for a new public philosophy, a sense of community to be shared by Americans of every background and persuasion" (ibid., 11). The goals of the common school incorporated the enduring tension in American education between the requirements of universal schooling and the unique capabilities and educational requirements of each child. As public-school enrollments grew almost exponentially through the nineteenth century, the only practical recourse was mass education, with its accompanying emphasis on standardization, efficiency, professionalization, and routine (Cremin 1961; Tyack 1977).

These contradictory impulses also beset the Progressive Movement, which was left to consolidate many of the gains first envisioned by Mann. The number of initiatives and the variety of personalities that have been placed under the Progressive umbrella defy easy generalization. Early on, substantive Progressives agreed upon a pedagogy that centered on the child rather than the subject matter, on project-oriented education that would develop an active intelligence in the learner, and on an orientation toward science as the source of educational reform. This spirit of freedom, diversity, and experiment did not carry over into the approaches of administrative reformers, however.

Convinced that there was one best system of education for urban populations, leading educators sought to discover it and implement it. They were impressed with the order and efficiency of the new technology and forms of organization they saw about them. The division of labor in the factory, the punctuality of the railroad, the chain of command and coordination in modern businesses—these aroused a sense of wonder and excitement in men and women seeking to systematize the schools. They sought to replace confused and erratic means of control with careful allocation of powers and functions within hierarchial organizations; to establish networks of communication that would convey information and directives and would provide data for planning for the future; to substitute impersonal rules for informal, individual adjudication of disputes; to regularize procedures so that they would apply uniformly to all in certain categories; and to set objective standards of admission to and performance in each role, whether superintendent or third-grader. Efficiency, rationality, continuity, precision, impartiality became watchwords of the consolidators. In short, they tried to create a more bureaucratic system (Tyack 1974, 28–9).

Many of the themes of the Common School Movement were taken up by the Progressives in the early decades of the twentieth century. In spite of their devotion to the individual child, they also embraced uniformity in education. Indeed, the emphasis on professionalism sometimes lapsed into dogma, leaving no room for shared control of the educational system (Ravitch 1983; Tyack 1974). With the founding of the Progressive Education Association, the original focus on reform was replaced by a growing orthodoxy that culminated in Life Adjustment Education in the 1940s

(Cremin 1961, 333–47; Ravitch 1983, 43–80). In spite of the diverse impulses of the early movement, the things accomplished by the Progressives—standardization of the educational program, professionalization of teaching, centralization of control in bureaucratic structures—were the fruition of initiatives first set in motion by the Common School Movement. Together, these two movements did much to construct an educational system that was impervious to nuances of place and community.

BROWN V. BOARD OF EDUCATION

Many trace the beginning of the rights revolution to *Brown v. Board of Education* in 1954, though *Brown* had its antecedents in cases such as *Shelley v. Kraemer, Sipuel v. Oklahoma, Painter v. Sweatt,* and *ex. rel. Gaines.* There is no minimizing the importance of *Brown*, both in its reversal of *Plessy v. Ferguson* and in the impetus it provided for so many decisions concerning civil rights in areas other than education. The real significance of *Brown* for local schools, however, may lie in the inconsistency of its legal reasoning. Liberalism cannot allow systematic racial segregation in schools without being tortured beyond recognition, but the grounds for schools being *integrated* are less clear. The *Brown* opinion vacillates between two standards of racial justice (Ravitch 1983). The first suggests that African-Americans have a right *not* to be singled out for distinctive treatment; the second that their rights can be insured only when they *are* treated selectively. Building upon the second precedent, U.S. policy often reflected the assumption that the mere existence of predominantly black and predominantly white schools was an affront to justice. As a consequence, decisions such as *Swann v. Charlotte-Mecklenburg Board of Education* mandated the disruption of the community basis of schools in the interest of achieving racial balance.

LEGISLATIVE INITIATIVES OF 1964 AND 1965

The Civil Rights Act of 1964 applied sanctions against discrimination to a broad array of policies in which localities and states participated chiefly as recipients of funds. It required in its Title VI that "No person . . . shall, on the ground of race, color, or national origin, be excluded from participation in, be denied the benefits of, or be subjected to discrimination under any program or activity receiving Federal financial assistance." Furthermore, policy debates at this time were influenced greatly by social-science research—an influence unwarranted by any ability to clearly isolate cause-and-effect relationships (Ravitch 1983).

In the past, the object of a housing program was to provide shelter; school aid was a matter of raising teachers' salaries or building new facilities or reducing class size; other programs, by and large, had equally explicit and measurable goals. Now, legislators and policy makers tried to stay abreast of the evolving debates among social scientists about the importance of self-esteem, of socialization skills, of community organization, and other goals that seemed unassailable yet intangible (Ravitch 1983, 161).

The combination of relying on social-science research and broadly applying federal power to define and determine the presence of discriminatory practices was no threat to local autonomy over education because the sanction—termination of federal aid—was meaningless. Federal aid had never been given to local public schools. This changed with the passage of the Elementary and Secondary Education Act in 1965. The threat of curtailing funding could now be used to insert federal scrutiny over local programs into a number of areas that had once been the exclusive province of local authorities.

SERRANO V. PRIEST

Serrano v. Priest in 1963 was the first case in which a state supreme court ruled a system of local funding of public schools unconstitutional on the grounds that it denied students the equal protection of the laws. With *Serrano* as the example, activists in a growing number of states were able to draw public-school systems and courts into intrusive debates about the nature of funding equity, the degree of equity required by state constitutions, and the funding options most likely to accomplish increased equity. Challenges to school finance arrangements have typically been based on a combination of two provisions that appear in most state constitutions: (1) a provision recognizing education as a fundamental responsibility of state government or a right of state citizens and (2) a provision guaranteeing citizens the equal protection of the laws. These challenges have resulted in the entire public-school system of Kentucky being declared unconstitutional (Bierlein 1993), as well as the closing of schools in other states while the courts, the governor, and the legislature attempted to devise alternative finance plans. In the *Edgewood v. Kirby* case in Texas, the result has been a true "Robin Hood" funding scheme: School districts can use only those local funds that are generated by the first $280,000 per pupil of assessed property valuation. Additional funds must be shared in one of several ways with less wealthy districts. Most wealthy districts choose to send the surfeit to the state capital for redistribution. Other options include annexation with a poorer district or deannexation of significant property-tax resources.

TITLE IX OF THE EDUCATION AMENDMENTS OF 1972

News programs frequently include stories about girls going out for the high school football or baseball team. In spite of these snippets, there appears to be little danger of a wholesale gender crisis in high school athletics. Girls are still very rarely found on the football team, and the girls' volleyball team remains the province of . . . girls.

There are alarming examples of the single-minded pursuit of gender equity, however. One of these has to do with a program implemented at James Madison Middle School in Prince George's County, Maryland. Under this program, the "Men of Madison," adult black males were mentors to African-American teenagers who were performing poorly in school, dropping out in large numbers, and getting in trouble with the law. Young black males aged six to eighteen—a group that constitutes about one-third of the county's students—had a grade average of D+.

The foundation of the program is a clear appeal to two of the sources of these students' identity—gender and race. The bond between mentor and student is immediate, intuitive, and symbolic. The message to the young men enrolled in the program is that other black males have succeeded by pursuing education and building careers and families. The program is compelling for these at-risk students precisely because it enlists organic sources of identity to direct their attention to their responsibilities as citizens and community members. Their particularities become, ironically enough, the means of drawing their attention to more general obligations.

The program became a casualty of the universalistic imperatives of national citizenship, however, when one parent (who evidently did not cower in the face of semantic absurdities) complained that the exclusion of her daughter from the Men of Madison constituted gender discrimination. The federal Department of Education insisted that the Men of Madison program be curtailed, and the county department of education complied (*Wall Street Journal* 1996).

THE EDUCATION FOR ALL HANDICAPPED CHILDREN ACT

Surely some measure of redress was due handicapped children and their parents when Congress passed this legislation. One of the progenitors of the law, *Pennsylvania Association of Retarded Children v. Pennsylvania,* was initiated in order to change a situation in which handicapped children could be determined uneducable by school officials without so much as a hearing or prior notification of the parents.

Nevertheless, the resulting legislation has severely curtailed the prerogatives of local educators. To give some indication of the magnitude of the intrusion, one observer notes that "from October 1981 through July 1982, some 1,100 court cases involving education were reported," 90 of which dealt with issues of educating the handicapped (Turner 1983, 8). This number includes only federal appellate-court cases. Others that were heard in federal district courts or in state courts are not included. As Turner notes, "Since its passage, implementation of P.L. 94-142 has resulted in an enormous body of regulations from the Bureau of Education for the Handicapped and from other sources. Interpretation and implementation of such regulations have produced much litigation" (Turner 1983, 9). The act requires that in return for federal funds, states must provide "free appropriate public education" for handicapped children. This standard is no more self-defining than the Necessary-and-Proper Clause of the U.S. Constitution. Consequently, whatever states and localities do in this area, they can be sure that they are always open to further challenge.

This review of centralizing developments in the history of American education is meant to be suggestive rather than exhaustive.[5] Nevertheless, one begins to wonder at the ubiquity of the observation that education is a highly decentralized policy area (see, for instance, Walzer 1980). Even though the Progressive Education Association died in 1955, the professional norms and educational practices it put in place with the assistance of university departments of education (Tyack 1974) still dictate much of what happens in American classrooms. Federal and state policies have further restricted the latitude for local input into the education of children. Polling data about schools, private-school enrollments, results of bond elections, and a growing home-schooling movement indicate that these developments may have provoked an adverse public response.

---

[5] Ascher, Fruchter, and Berne (1996, 2–5) cite a very similar list of developments leading to the alienation of the public from the public schools.

SCHISM BETWEEN THE PUBLIC AND THE COMMUNITY?

Among the prerequisites of "communal democracy" is the "moral primacy of the community over the state" (Selznick 1992, 503). This prerequisite draws heavily upon the civil-society tradition in which the community exists prior to the state. The community embodies shared moral understandings and mutually advantageous social and economic interactions. The most desired situation is congruence between community and state insofar as policies reflect these moral understandings and institutionalize advantageous relationships. On the other hand, there may be occasions when state action is inimical to the fundamental interests of the community.

When this happens, the community must reclaim its moral autonomy from the state. But what form would such a reclamation take? What are the channels in a society such as ours by which the community might exert its moral primacy? Elections might constitute one such channel. In this light, various realignments can be seen as the community reasserting itself. The community may reassert itself in other ways as well, however.

Suppose, for instance, that there were an inherent human propensity for community as we have defined the term in this chapter—(1) an affective, moral social order (2) often growing out of, though not exhausted by, organic bonds such as family, nationality, race, religion, and place and (3) associated with symbols—flags, mascots, icons, totems—that concentrate affect and transmit it in ways that are immediate and intuitive rather than discursive and rational. If there were such an inherent propensity for community, then an attack upon organic bases of association and community symbols must either provide other bases of association and symbols or invite the reemergence of old ones in new "para-public" arenas. The schools are one public institution in which the communitarian impulse has been strong. Along with land-use regulation, education is of most direct concern to localities—and has been the source of the most rancorous local controversies.[6] The community demonstrates its interest in the education of its children frequently and emotionally, whether it takes the form of black neighborhoods demanding greater control over local schools (Ravitch 1983, 1985; *Houston Chronicle* 1996) or of par-

---

[6] Oliver Williams (1968) presents a theory that identifies those local services and functions that are most central to community life-style values and over which, therefore, local control is most jealously defended.

ents demanding the dismissal of a teacher for unorthodox religious beliefs, sexual practices, or political allegiances.

The last several decades have seen frequent federal and state intrusions in local education, however. The targets of these interventions have often been organic forms of association. Obviously, these organic characteristics are not the only sources of identity, but they are among its most important sources nevertheless. By eliminating them from the explicitly sanctioned life of the schools, authorities force schools to call upon sources of identity that are more abstract. They may indeed be so abstract that students and parents are unaware of them and may no longer recognize schools as part of the community.

Perhaps as a result, enrollments are growing in private schools that *do* call upon these sources of identity—and that do so within a context of moral community. This is not to say that there has been a general increase in the percentage of students enrolled in private schools. This percentage has remained fairly steady in the postwar period, fluctuating between 10 percent in the 1970s and nearly 14 percent in the late 1950s and early 1960s. Since 1989, the percentage of students enrolled in private schools has varied from 11.0 to 11.7 percent (Table 9.1).

This aggregate stasis, however, masks a transition in the composition of private schools and their student populations. The National Center for Education Statistics (NCES) notes that "since 1970, many new Christian Schools have been established every year to serve families who wanted their children's education to be strongly founded in Christian beliefs" (1995, 1).

An inspection of the figures reported by the NCES reveals the following patterns:

- The number of Hebrew Schools increased by 43.8 percent. The number of students in Jewish schools increased by 53 percent.
- The number of schools identified as "Christian Schools International" increased by 31 percent. The number identified as "Association of Christian Schools International" increased by 7.6 percent. Although the number of conservative Christian schools decreased overall, the number of students in these schools increased slightly, perhaps indicating a consolidation of such schools in the intervening period.
- The number of Lutheran schools decreased during this period, but the number of Lutheran students increased by about five per cent—probably due mostly to the increase in Evangelical Lutheran Schools and the number of students enrolled in them.

Table 9.1. *Enrollment in educational institutions by control of institution, 1959 to 1992 (selected years)*

Year	1959	1964	1969	1974	1979	1984	1989	1990	1991	1992
Total	40,857	47,716	51,050	50,073	46,651	44,908	45,898	46,448	47,246	48,109
Private	5,675	6,300	5,500	5,000	5,000	5,700	5,355	5,232	5,199	5,375
Percent	13.9	13.2	10.7	10.0	10.7	12.7	11.7	11.3	11.0	11.2

Source: National Center for Education Statistics, *Digest of Education Statistics: 1994*, Table 3.—Enrollment in educational institutions, by level and by control of institution: 1869–70 to fall 2004.

Current growth patterns in evangelical Christian schools likely represent parents' perception that the public schools no longer defend middle-class values (as attested by both Phi Delta Kappa/Gallup and *USA Today* polling results). Such patterns are inextricably bound up with the question of community conceived as an affective, moral social order based upon organic bonds and shared symbols. Parents seek such an order in private sectarian schools when they cannot find it in the public schools.

This interpretation gains support from remarks made by private-school officials in the wake of the defeat of a Houston Independent School District bond election. In explaining the apparent paradox of the public's refusal to support school construction while private schools are experiencing a building boom, a Lutheran school principal remarked that "parents are looking for better education for their children, and the teaching of morals." The underlying dynamic was nicely captured by the example of Grace Presbyterian School:

The Grace School, run by the Grace Presbyterian Church, has grown from 230 students in 1989 to 550 students this year. The school just completed an $8 million building program, which included a new library, science labs, art rooms, classrooms and a renovated gym, said Ray Johnson, headmaster.

He said it was difficult to raise the money, but the school did it. And parents there pay from $5,200–$5,900 in yearly tuition for their children to attend the school.

Johnson said private schools continue to grow because parents want schools to be accountable. Public schools are so large, keeping them accountable is more difficult. Also parents have little control over what is taught, he said.

"If we do a good job, then our parents stay and contribute," he said. "If we do a poor job, their patience wears thin real quickly and they will leave" (Asin 1996).

The frequent defeat of bond issues for schools provides further evidence of public dissatisfaction. A National Association of School Boards survey found that one-fourth of the school districts responding (n = 85) had experienced the defeat of a bond election in the last five years (ibid.).

Other figures suggest a schism between public and community. There has always been some home schooling in the United States, often associated with insular religious denominations. The number of children schooled in the home has increased greatly in recent years, however. Estimates are that between 500,000 and 1 million children are being educated at home—about 1 to 2 percent of all students, and about 10 to 20 percent of private students (ERIC Clearinghouse on Educational Management 1995; Thomas 1994; *Education Week* no date). Whatever the precise number, it has greatly increased since the early 1980s, when the number of children educated in the home was estimated at just 15,000. In recent years, thirty-four states have made statutory changes to more easily accommodate parents who want to educate their children at home (Ramsay 1992). Furthermore, home schooling is not always an atomistic affair. Parents frequently use home-schooling curricula and aids developed and distributed by various denominations. In California, many charter schools have been created exclusively to provide such services. Home schooling gives parents great control over the values to which their children are exposed. A possible interpretation is that the home-schooling movement is a reassertion of community in the face of public forms that parents perceive as alien. According to one source,

Home schooling neither isolates children nor harms their academic growth, but approaches the true definition of education: the passing down of culture. . . . Home school parents see the family as superior to any other institution in society. . . . Schools have redefined family values and, in some cases, have ridiculed the cultural beliefs of the students and their parents. . . . Religion is a major part of the American culture, but public schools fail to take religion seriously (Jeub 1995).

Results of the annual Phi Delta Kappa/Gallup Poll of the public's attitudes toward public schools indicate a drop in approval of the public schools since 1985 (Elam and Rose 1995, Table 9.2). A similar pattern appears in Gallup Poll data on confidence in U.S. institutions (Newport and Saad 1994). In 1994, 34 percent of respondents said they had a great deal or quite a lot of confidence in public schools, down from 58 percent in 1973. Twenty-five percent reported they had very little confidence in public schools, or none at all. In receiving a 14 percent share in the high-

Table 9.2. *Grading the public schools, 1985 to 1995*

Year/ Letter Grade	95	94	93	92	91	90	89	88	87	86	85
A & B	20%	22%	19%	18%	21%	21%	22%	23%	26%	28%	27%
A	2	2	2	2	2	2	2	3	4	3	3
B	18	20	17	16	19	19	20	20	22	25	24

Source: Stanley M. Elam and Lowell C. Rose, "The 27th Annual Phi Delta Kappa/Gallup Poll of the Public's Attitudes Toward the Public Schools," *Phi Delta Kappan* 77:1, September 1995, pp. 41–60. It should be noted, however, that these figures are generated by a question which specifically refers to the *nation's* public schools. When respondents are asked about *local* public schools, or the schools that their children attend, approval ratings are much higher, and they have been stable since the mid-eighties. For instance, in 1995 41 percent of those surveyed gave the local public schools an A or B grade. Ten years earlier, the percentage was 43 percent.

est approval rating, public education was about half as highly regarded as the military and the church, and in the same range with television news, the medical system, banks, newspapers, and organized labor.

A *USA Today* poll found that a much higher percentage of respondents—75 percent—gave the public schools a grade of A or B (*USA Today* 1996). The poll, which surveyed attitudes of parents with children in public schools, produced the oft-noted result that respondents usually give higher marks to the school their own children attend than they give to public schools in general. Such results are often cited to dispute the argument that public confidence in the public schools has been shaken (Henig 1994). In spite of the high approval rating, however, 47 percent of the respondents said they would send their children to private schools if they could afford it. Nor do parents' high approval ratings for their own public schools negate the fact that approval for public schools generally has fallen precipitously in the last twenty years.

Opinion data also reveal a preference for local autonomy over public education. In the most recent Phi Delta Kappa/Gallup Poll (Elam and Rose 1995), 64 percent of respondents favored more influence for local government in determining educational programs in schools. Seventy percent of respondents would favor a change to increase local school authorities' say over how federal funds are spent; 86 percent favor recent changes that increase local input into the way federal aid-to-education funds are spent.

Significantly, 37 percent of respondents to the *USA Today* poll said they believed public schools should be more involved in teaching moral values (*USA Today* 1996). Seventy-one percent of respondents in the Phi Delta Kappa poll would favor a constitutional amendment to permit spoken prayer in public schools. A majority (55 percent), including respondents who oppose school prayer as well as those who approve, believe that the introduction of spoken prayer would improve student conduct. Eighty-one percent of the sample believed that prayers should not be basically Christian in character, with 73 percent favoring the idea of allowing Jewish, Muslim, or Hindu prayer as well.

In sum, there has been a substantial decline in levels of approval for U.S. public elementary and secondary schools. Americans believe overwhelmingly that schools should be under local control, and many feel that they should emphasize values. Responses to questions concerning school prayer indicate at least some sympathy for the recognition of students' religious attachments, though there is strong respect for religious diversity. The growth in religious private schools and their enrollments, as well as the growth in schooling in the home, is consistent with the conclusion that more parents are choosing education options that insure instruction in values and an ability to associate on the basis of organic attachments.

These are the channels through which the community might reassert its moral primacy over education. Public actions and opinion indicate dissatisfaction with the current conduct of public schooling. They may also indicate a willingness to reestablish community in para-public forms. Indeed, this outcome is predictable if growing percentages of Americans really do not see any correspondence between the things that they value and the things that are taught in public schools.

CURRENT AND PROPOSED POLICY REFORMS IN U.S. EDUCATION

Americans are indefatigable reformers of their public schools. There has rarely been a time since the inception of free public education in the United States when one slate of reforms or another has not been championed by some powerful constituency (Ravitch 1983). The reforms that currently dominate the education agenda, however, have one thing in common: They envision greater control over schools for parents and teachers, and less for centralized, professional bureaucracies. Reforms such as parental choice and charter schools would return substantial autonomy over schools to parents and communities. These reforms, at least in intent, would reverse the direction of the evolution of American education since 1830.

Parental choice has been around for some time, particularly in the form of education vouchers. Choice can have many manifestations: magnet schools, intradistrict public-school transfers, interdistrict public-school transfers, vouchers for low-income families, and a full-blown voucher system that permits students to apply education funds to any school they wish—public or private, in their district or out.

The principal advantages supposedly offered by choice plans are: (1) the increased number of education alternatives available to parents and students, particularly low-income students who are perceived to be caught in poorly performing schools, and (2) the pressure that competition puts on administrators and teachers to provide high-quality programs. For true believers in choice, the inclusion of private schools is critically important because they are taken to be better than public schools (Chubb and Moe 1990; Coleman and Hoffer 1987; Coleman, Hoffer, and Kilgore 1982) and because they are freer to supply innovative education programs that conform to the diversity of students' education requirements.

Choice plans, particularly those that incorporate private schools, are opposed by teacher groups, school administrators, civil-rights groups, and colleges of education. There are a number of fears: that money desperately needed by public schools will be diverted to private schools; that the private schools will be the beneficiaries of "creaming," leaving the public schools to educate the hard cases; that parents and students who are already advantaged will be the ones best prepared to acquire information and enroll in good schools, resulting in two-tiered, class-divided schools and society (Smith and Meier 1995). Among the most binding objections is the increased cost that a comprehensive choice plan would entail. Any student currently enrolled in a private school would become eligible for a voucher, requiring additional expenditures of millions, if not billions (Bierlein 1993, 110–13).

Other objections go to the heart of the pro-choice argument. Most evidence indicates that the private-school edge in student achievement is so small that even if public schools were reorganized to emulate private schools, the education gains would hardly justify the cost and effort (Bierlein 1993; Witte 1992; however, see Peterson and Greene 1996). Furthermore, the evidence from existing choice programs is quite equivocal about gains in achievement for students (Ascher, Fruchter, and Berne 1996; Henig 1994; Peterson and Greene 1996; Smith and Meier 1995; Witte Thorn, Pritchard, and Claibourn 1994).

In the context of this essay, perhaps the most damning injunction against choice programs is that they do nothing to strengthen ties between schools and communities. School choice is the quintessential liberal reform—individualistic and market driven. The responsibility for improving education chances is borne solely by individuals. To the extent that improvements in education institutions are made, they result from the indirect pressure of individual preferences transmitted through market mechanisms rather than direct institutional reforms carried out by visionary actors.[7] Furthermore, without state and federal deregulation, there is no guarantee that public-school administrators would be free to try new approaches that might serve students more effectively, or to take steps (such as firing poor teachers or expelling disruptive students) that would improve their programs. School-choice programs in themselves would do little to enhance community control over public schools.

Charter schools are specifically meant to return control over education decisions to local actors. They resemble choice schools in that they are required to accept applicants without regard to residence, race, or scholastic aptitude. Unlike choice schools, however, charter schools consciously incorporate much of site-based management. And unlike private schools, charter schools cannot charge tuition—they typically receive the state-wide or district-average funding for each student they enroll.

Minnesota and California pioneered charter schools. As of 1996, twenty-five states had passed enabling legislation for charter schools (U.S. Department of Education 1997), but their number is capped in many of these states. It is not unusual for enabling legislation to identify specific districts or schools to carry out pilot programs. Given the rapid passage of charter-school reforms by so many states, there is little question that charter schools have become popular with state legislators.

There is some question, however, whether legislation in all of these states actually creates charter schools. The degree of autonomy granted to what are nominally charter schools varies greatly across states. As Finn and Ravitch say, "If a state still mandates when U.S. history must be

---

[7] Ascher, Fruchter, and Berne (1996) make very similar observations: "While stressing important ideals of individual liberty and freedom, privatizers deny the capacity of either voters or politicians to move beyond self-interest to embrace forms of civic participation" (9) and "Instead of helping to improve schools through their participation, dissatisfied parents are simply to take their children elsewhere" (11).

taught, how many students must sit in each classroom, and which text-books to purchase, while imposing rigid seniority rules and tenure re-quirements, there's little point in calling an entity so regulated a 'charter school' " (Finn and Ravitch 1995; Hassel 1995a,b; Kolderie 1994, 1995; Vergari and Mintrom 1995).

We make no claim to a copyright on the term "charter school," but if it is to signify any true reform in the way public schools are run, it must denote the following things:

1. *Liberal chartering power:* The chartering power is not placed in the hands of the local school board, and local opponents hold no veto pow-er on the issuance of charters. There is no cap on the number of charter schools within the state.

2. *Deregulation:* The granting of a charter must effectively free the school in question from state regulations governing critical areas of staffing, in-struction, and resource allocation. As one source notes, states should im-pose regulations on charter schools only in the areas of health and safety, and racial discrimination.

3. *Open enrollment:* Schools created by charter must accept any student without regard to race, residence, gender, religious affiliation, aptitude, or socioeconomic status.

4. *No tuition:* Charter schools cannot charge tuition. They are compensat-ed at the per-student expenditure rate prevailing in the state or the rele-vant school district.

These would appear to be the minimal conditions for charter schools to be truly different from other public schools with regard to the goals of the charter-school movement—an ability to innovate in the interest of finding the best education techniques for students, a responsiveness to the concerns and aspirations of parents and students, and an impetus through competitive pressures to enhance the quality of educational programs.

Condition 1 is important, of course, because without some indepen-dence in chartering from entrenched education interests, charter schools will never get created—or they will be emasculated in the chartering process.

The degree of autonomy that states grant charter schools—Condition 2—is perhaps the most critical consideration. Of quintessential impor-tance here are decisions about teacher qualifications, curriculum, teach-ing methods, allocation of resources, hiring and firing, textbook adop-tion, and class sizes. Many of the states that have created putative charter schools retain control over these critical decisions. Charter schools in these states represent a symbolic concession to appease dissident elements.

Condition 3 (open enrollment) must be met for two reasons: (1) to ensure that community autonomy over schools does not become a code for invidious forms of discrimination or denial of equal educational opportunity and (2) so that the competitive impetus of the market will in fact be introduced into the educational system (that is, students living near a school should not become the captive clientele of that school).

Condition 3, combined with Condition 4 (funding), permits community control to be reconciled with citizenship in important ways. The fact that schools cannot charge tuition, but are paid the statewide/districtwide average expenditure for each pupil they recruit, invalidates challenges on the grounds of class-based funding inequities. The fact that schools must accept any applicant regardless of race, aptitude, or residence invalidates challenges on the grounds of discrimination based on the Court's suspect categories, and frees school enrollments from residential patterns that reflect discrimination. It also precludes the possibility of creaming.

Relying upon Kolderie's criteria (1994, 1995), Vergari and Mintrom classify Arizona, California, Colorado, Delaware, Massachusetts, Michigan, and Minnesota among the states with the most effective charter-school laws—that is, charter schools in these states are more likely to approximate the charter-school model.[8]

A YEARNING FOR COMMUNITY?

This essay has argued that education reform in the postwar period, with the laudable intent of insuring the full citizenship of all Americans, has shown too little concern for the bases of community that give ultimate meaning to the tradition of local self-government in America. The evidence of this imbalance is the public's skepticism about the performance of public schools, an increasing tendency to enroll children in schools that emphasize communitarian values or to educate children in the home, and a tendency to defeat school-district bond issues. These could be symp-

---

[8] The criteria that Vergari and Mintrom use to distinguish permissive laws from restrictive laws are similar to the ones we offer as the minimal conditions for the existence of true charter schools: more than one public authority to sponsor charter schools; conversions of existing schools as well as new charter schools; autonomy from the local school district; waivers of most state and local school regulations; a substantial or unlimited number of charter schools. Furthermore, both sets of criteria incorporate most of the nine attributes of the "charter schools model" presented by Mintrom and Vergari (1995, 4).

toms of many things, however. Is there any other evidence of a desire for schools that recognize organic ties and that are linked more closely to local communities?

Part of the evidence that we cite in this section is drawn from our experience as evaluators of open-enrollment charter schools in Texas. Other evidence is drawn from reports and scholarly papers describing charter schools in other states.

The early evidence in Texas, though anecdotal, strongly suggests that creating public schools based on organic communities is one of the *chief* motivations of those who apply for charters. The applications provide considerable support for this conclusion. For instance, at least four of the schools (of a total of nineteen) have been chartered by agencies affiliated with Hispanic advocacy organizations—the Association for the Advancement of Mexican Americans (AAMA), the League of United Latin American Citizens (LULAC), and the National Council of La Raza[9] (Information Referral Resource Assistance 1996; Tejano Center for Community Concerns 1996; Association for the Advancement of Mexican Americans 1996; Gulf Coast Council of La Raza 1996). One of the new charter schools (the Girls and Boys Prep Academy) was proposed specifically to institute single-gender education: "Campuses will be innovative in that they will not be the traditional coed campuses—studies indicate that in grades 6–12 there is more social interaction and disturbance between girls and boys" (Association for the Development of Academic Excellence 1996).[10]

Another sign that these schools are built around organic ties is the practice of restricting enrollment to a specific geographic catchment area. The enabling legislation, Texas Senate Bill 1, gives ambiguous guidance regarding geographic restrictions on enrollment. Though it specifies that students cannot be denied admission based on the "district the child would otherwise attend," it also mandates that applicants for charters must "describe the geographical area served by the program" (Senate of Texas 1996). Although true open-enrollment charter schools cannot deny admission to students based upon their place of residence, this ambiguity has been exploited by some of the Texas charter schools to deny admission to students living outside a self-defined catchment area. For instance,

---

[9] "La Raza" is a Spanish expression meaning "the race."
[10] The State Board of Education eventually approved the charter application to create the Girls and Boys Prep Academy, but with the stipulation that boys and girls not be segregated by classroom.

one of the schools restricts enrollment to students living in the attendance zones of two middle schools. While the school commits itself to admitting students without regard to "race, color, ethnic origin, religion, and gender," the reality is that the student population of the catchment area it has defined is 96 percent Hispanic (Tejano Center for Community Concerns 1996). There are no African-American students in the school in spite of the fact that it is located near an area of heavy black residential concentration.

Furthermore, Senate Bill 1 prescribes that students must be admitted on a "first-come, first-served" basis. Though this standard appears to be nondiscriminatory, actual student recruitment can still create application pools that are racially or ethnically skewed. A survey of Texas charter-school parents, for instance, revealed that 58 percent had heard of their children's charter school from a friend or relative. Because people tend to talk to others who are like them in terms of race, ethnicity, and socioeconomic status, this kind of word-of-mouth recruitment—coupled with a first-come, first-served admission standard—would be *expected* to produce racially, ethnically, and socially homogeneous schools.

Many of the Texas open-enrollment charter schools *do* have distinctive enrollments. Of the sixteen schools that opened in the fall of 1996, nine have enrollments that are 90 percent or more minority students. Five are more than 90 percent Hispanic, while two are more than 90 percent African-American, and two exceed the 90 percent level when African-American and Hispanic percentages are combined.

At least two of the open-enrollment charter schools in Texas are housed in churches (Genesis Schools 1996; SER—Jobs for Progress of the Texas Gulf Coast 1996). Assurances have been offered that religious symbols will be removed from the rooms in which classes actually meet. One would suspect, however, that students can hardly miss the religious significance of the structure. One of these schools held its dedication ceremony in the sanctuary of the church in which it is housed. Another school offers an optional religious service for students prior to convening classes (Medical Center Charter Schools 1996).

Available evidence is that many schools in other states are also racially distinctive (Crew 1997; U.S. Department of Education 1997; Massachusetts Department of Education 1996; Lange et al. 1996).[11] In itself, this

[11] The 1997 Department of Education report on charter schools (U.S. Department of Education 1997) has been widely anticipated as the first such report to benefit from comprehensive data collection and analysis. Its conclusions are likely to influence greatly the terms of the debate on the early implementation of charter schools. Its statement about the racial composition of these schools appears to contradict the argument that we make

finding demonstrates nothing in particular about charter schools. Traditional public schools are often racially distinctive as well. The evidence mounts, however, that many charter schools are racially distinctive *by design*. The Steele-Collins Charter School in Tallahassee, Florida, for instance, was sponsored by the Bethel African Methodist Episcopal Church. Charter schools in Florida are required to admit any student who "submits a timely application" (Crew 1997). Nevertheless, the student body of the Steele-Collins school is 80 percent African-American, and a large majority of the students are children of church members.

here. "Massachusetts, Michigan, and Minnesota charter schools stand out in that they enroll a higher percentage of students of color than the average of all public schools in their respective states. Aside from Georgia (which has only three charter schools), the average racial composition of charter schools in the other states is similar to their statewide averages" (U.S. Department of Education 1977, 4–5). The interpretation given the Department of Education report by *Education Week* is typical: "Taken as a group, charter schools reported a racial composition that roughly mirrored their respective statewide averages" (Schnaiberg 1997, 2).

The interpretation of the evidence presented in the report, however, is not so straightforward. An initial problem is that the report actually addresses only ten of the twenty-five states that have created charter schools. In Texas, for instance, the racial composition of charter schools does not mirror the statewide averages; the disparities are rather large.

A second problem is that even among the ten states addressed, the charter schools in three—Massachusetts, Michigan, and Minnesota—are identified as not having compositions similar to the statewide averages. One might reasonably conclude that the statement still pertains to a large majority of the states—seven—included in the analysis. This conclusion would be incorrect, however. The report excludes the cases of four states in which the number of charter schools is very small—Wisconsin (five charter schools), New Mexico (four), Georgia (three), and Hawaii (two). At this point, only three charter-school states remain: Arizona, Colorado, and California. Based on this evidence, the report should more accurately state that racial compositions in charter schools are roughly similar to statewide averages in three states, whereas they are dissimilar to statewide averages in another three states, and the remaining four states have too few schools to support any conclusion.

Even this statement would be misleading, however. A third problem is that statewide aggregate figures reveal nothing of what actually happens in individual schools. After all, in the aggregate, most American metropolitan areas seem integrated, but the illusion of integration quickly disappears as soon as geographic subunits are considered. Surely the individual school is the level of observation of greatest interest. The DOE does address racial patterns at the school level—after a fashion. It reports, nationally and for each state, the number of schools that fall in one of three categories: 0–20 percent Anglo, 20–80 percent Anglo, and 80–100 percent Anglo. Viewed this way, figures for charter schools diverge widely from statewide figures. For instance, California is presented in the report as one of the states in which charter-school racial and ethnic composition and statewide averages are quite comparable. However, 37 percent of charter schools in California are more than 80 percent Anglo, a category that contains only 17 percent of the state's public schools. In Arizona, 46 percent of charter schools are predominantly white, compared with 33 percent of public schools. In Colorado, 76 percent of charter schools are predominantly white, whereas only 56 percent of public schools are. The disparities are greater for Michigan, Minnesota, and Massachusetts. By this measure, *no* state examined by the report (except Hawaii, which has only two charter schools) has charter schools that approximate statewide school distributions in terms of racial composition.

The stated mission of the El Jajj Malik El Shabazz Academy in Michigan is to provide an Afrocentric curriculum. Also in Michigan, the Aisha Shule/W. E. B. DuBois Preparatory Academy emphasizes "basic skills/ independent learning with an African American focus"; the Bahwetting School integrates Native American (Ojibway) culture into the core curriculum; and the Nah Tah Wahsh Public School Academy integrates native culture and language into all subjects (*National Charter School Directory* 1996). "The mission of the Benjamin Banneker Charter School" in Cambridge, Massachusetts, "is to help minority students overcome the traditional barriers to academic success" (Massachusetts Department of Education 1996). The Johnson Urban League Charter School for Space Exploration and Technology in California serves a student body that is more than 80 percent African-American and emphasizes, among other things, "ethnic achievement" (*National Charter School Directory* 1996). Four charter schools in Arizona are sponsored by the Urban League. The American Indian Charter School is located in Oakland, California (*National Charter School Directory* 1996).

Additionally, the mission statements of many of the newly created charter schools declare their intention to "offer . . . an education . . . that will develop and strengthen students' ethical, moral, and civic values" (Massachusetts Department of Education 1996).

Again, this evidence is anecdotal, but it strongly suggests that in organizing charter schools and in choosing to send their children to them, administrators and parents are influenced by what we have called organic ties.

STRIKING THE BALANCE

We do not argue that this state of affairs is good or bad.

For one thing, this dispute will play out in many venues—not the least of which, we suspect, will be the courts.

More important, however, is the perennial tendency for race, gender, place, faith, ethnicity, and other organic characteristics to provide powerful sources of individual identity. In making much the same point (though in a more pejorative fashion), one source counsels keeping in mind the recent experience of the former Soviet Union where "events remind us that parochial and unreasonable hatreds, while they may be unfashionable, are not outdated in our enlightened age" (Henig 1994). We might also refer to the former Yugoslavia, to Rwanda, Burundi, and Zaire, to the

Kurds of Turkey and northern Iraq, and to the French separatist movement in Montreal, Quebec, to emphasize this point. Our argument is simply that we cannot choose to ignore these powerful motivating influences upon our public life. We can choose only whether we want to try to make them the foundations of healthy communities that point to more universalistic values, or whether we want them to be the ground for "parochial and unreasonable hatreds."

At this point we return to the problematic posed by Dewey. Nothing is gained if charter schools become the focus of entrenched, static communities that recognize no obligation to a greater society outside their boundaries. Many have questioned the wisdom of parental-choice schemes because they may create institutions that foreclose the discussion of ends and the search for compromise among legitimate interests that democracy requires (Ascher, Fruchter, and Berne 1996; Gutman 1987; Henig 1994).

Making government work is difficult. It especially is difficult to work through democratic procedures that invite and accept as legitimate views from disparate actors with conflicting agendas and incompatible styles. Calls for radically restructuring education through market processes appeal in part because they promise to sidestep this process. In the grand bazaar of education, families would be free to negotiate their own bargains on their own terms, paying only as much attention as they wish to the hubbub around them (Henig 1994, 23).

Another source expresses the fear that "Democratic participation, which involves individuals in a range of roles and responsibilities, is to be abandoned for narrow acts of consumerism" (Ascher, Fruchter, and Berne 1996). The potential danger of the charter-school concept is that, if not implemented carefully, it will produce balkanization rather than pluralism.

There are no surefire guarantees against this possibility, but much can be done to push the course of events in another direction. Political structures and procedures are important in this context. Schools that manifest organic ties must be created openly as the result of public discussion about the proper ends that such schools may serve, and in a way that does not explicitly exclude those who do not share those ties. Such schools do not inherently contradict the concept of a liberal, pluralist society that is serious about insuring fundamental rights.

For instance, the El Jajj Malik El Shabazz Academy, though Afrocentric in its academic orientation, enrolls a substantial percentage of white students. Its founder points out that the academy is a public school and therefore must accept any child who applies, subject to space limitations. Furthermore, she personally has no wish to exclude children simply because they are not African-American. Similarly, 20 percent of students at the Steele-Collins charter school are white, even though the school was founded by a black church. And 10 percent of students at the Benjamin Banneker charter school are projected to be white, even though the school was created to address the needs of minority students. Schools can serve primarily a particular racial, national, or cultural group without excluding students on the basis of their race, nationality, or culture. Furthermore, the white students who attend these schools will surely learn as much about diversity, pluralism, and the need for democracy as black and Hispanic students who are now consigned to traditional public schools in central cities that are, in effect, 100 percent minority.

The creation of schools such as these, however, depends greatly upon state laws and state oversight. The early implementation of charter-school legislation in many states leaves much to fear in this respect. Legislation in many states was passed on a wave of enthusiasm for charter schools. They represent an attractive alternative for legislators, who are increasingly pressured to introduce choice into public education but who shy away from controversial programs that would include private schools. The passage of charter-school laws in many states, therefore, reflects political expediency more than policy analysis.

Nor do many states have any effective mechanism in place for carrying out oversight. Often, oversight (as well as all other matters concerning charter schools) is in the hands of one person in the state department of education with little or no staff. Furthermore, even if this one person had the time, there is no mandate for oversight, no compendium of oversight procedures and goals, and no instruction as to how to proceed if a violation should be discovered.

Given the haphazard nature of much charter-school policy at the state level, it is uncertain that charter schools will fulfill their promise. As Henig (1994) points out, simply introducing market forces into education does not guarantee a salutary outcome. Deregulation and choice provide the basis for improvement, but political scientists in recent decades have demonstrated the vulnerability of policy to developments occurring during implementation. In the absence of oversight, evaluation, reporting, and discussion of outcomes in the context of broader goals, charter-school reforms are unlikely to serve the purposes that have been promised for them.

Skepticism about government leads many charter-school advocates to resist the public debate, oversight, and evaluation that we have suggested here. Having gained the ascendancy, they are proceeding full speed ahead in some states, fearing that if they pause they will be overtaken. In this headlong process, many charter schools are incorporating explicit racial, ethnic, gender, and cultural content. This is dangerous ground. Practices in charter schools sometimes presuppose outcomes to debates that have raged since the modern era in civil rights began in the late 1940s. If some charter schools come to be seen as new ethnic academies, serving a narrowly defined exclusive racial agenda—and if, worse still, they are allowed to form and exercise public power in an exclusionary fashion by an absence of regulation and oversight—the result is likely to be divisive.

RECONCILING CITIZENSHIP AND COMMUNITY

One of the purposes of this chapter has been to recognize two forces that are held in constant tension within our federal system: national citizenship and local community. Selznick expresses this as the tension between civility and piety:

The norms of civility are impersonal, rational, and inclusive, whereas piety is personal, passionate, and particularist. The conflict between these very different aspirations generates troublesome issues of morality and community. Their reconciliation is a prime object of theory and policy (Selznick 1992, 387).

There is, of course, no formulaic resolution of this contradiction. It is in the nature of a federal system that it must hold a number of contradictory forces in perpetual tension. In chapter 5 of this book, Martha Derthick notes the ambiguity that besets a federal system in terms of the number and kind of communities it will encompass. She quotes Martin Diamond's description of a federal system as an "expression of the contradiction or tension between the particular reasons the member units have for remaining small and autonomous, but not wholly, and large and consolidated, but not quite" (Diamond 1992, 145). The contradiction between community and citizenship that we have attempted to illustrate in this chapter is simply a specific instance of the inherently contradictory nature of federalist government. Local communities—affective, moral social orders identified with determinate, small places—are highly desirable components of any political system; they are even more desirable in a democracy for their ability to raise and nurture citizens, to encourage the development of healthy civic and personal identities, and to serve as intermediary objects of attachment that provide individuals with concrete ways of belonging in the more abstract national political order. To perform these functions, however, they rely on affective bonds, many of which are organic. The tendency of such bases of membership is to create outgroups as well as ingroups. They invite the violation of widely recognized citizen rights. Citizenship is another irreducible value in a federal, liberal, democratic political system. Hence any lessening of these tensions must take the form of an accommodation rather than a solution.

This conviction is reinforced by the debate between communitarians and individualists. Essays that argue for the total predominance of either rights and individualism or organic bonds and community can be discounted out of hand. By the premises we have just adduced, neither position can provide an outcome that will be acceptable in the American federal system. More interesting are those pieces that attempt to find a synthesis of rights and community (Dworkin 1992; Gauthier 1992; Gutman 1987, 1992; Selznick 1992; Taylor 1991). Although this is not the place to examine particulars, no treatment that we are aware of is completely successful in describing such a synthesis.

Thankfully, actual cases offer an infinite variety of possible gradations and accommodations that theories do not. Are there accommodations that can be reached that will allow us to enjoy simultaneously the benefits of community and citizenship?

James Q. Wilson's chapter in this volume offers a number of suggestions in this pragmatic spirit. These limited, practical references to specific types of policy offer the promise that some space can be carved out for community in ways that exact the smallest prices in terms of infringements upon citizenship.

The popularity of charter schools also provides an opportunity for restoring some balance between citizenship and community. One reason is that true charter schools place autonomy over public schools much closer to those who are most concerned with them. A second reason is that they provide new opportunities for parents to identify schools that respond to their concerns for their children. Charter schools do not represent a *deus ex machina*, however. They provide no escape from the tedious responsibility of holding disparate yet compelling goals in tension. There is nothing wrong, even in a liberal society, with schools that serve girls or boys, that are predominantly Hispanic or African-American or, for that matter, white. The way these schools acquire such identities, however, *is* critically important. If they do so through an open, democratic process of deliberation that explicitly recognizes the value of community *and* the value of citizenship, one can hope that they will fit well into our liberal society and our federal polity.

Although there are no nostrums that can permanently resolve the conflict between the claims of citizenship and community in a federal system, some room for each may be found in the conduct of practical affairs. Charter schools represent an opportunity to strike such a practical compromise. Like any reform of public institutions, they present certain dangers. But reluctance to seek those institutional forms that align community and citizenship presents equal dangers. There is no avoiding the tiring but indispensable struggle to create local communities that are "stable without being static, progressive without being merely mobile."

REFERENCES

Ascher, Carol, Norm Fruchter, and Robert Berne. 1996. *Hard Lessons: Public Schools and Privatization.* New York: Twentieth Century Fund Press.
Asin, Stefanie. 1996. "Private School Cash? No Problem." *Houston Chronicle* 95:239 (June 8, 1995): 1. Houston, Tex.: The Hearst Corporation.
Association for Development of Academic Excellence. 1996. "Application for Approval of an Open-Enrollment Charter." Austin, Tex.: Texas State Board of Education.
Association for the Advancement of Mexican Americans. 1996. "Application for Approval of an Open-Enrollment Charter." Austin, Tex.: Texas State Board of Education.
Bierlein, Louann A. 1993. *Controversial Issues in Educational Policy.* Newbury Park, Calif.: Sage Publications.
   1996. *Charter Schools: Initial Findings.* Denver, Colo.: Education Commission of the States.
Burns, Nancy. 1994. *The Formation of American Local Governments: Private Values in Public Institutions.* New York: Oxford University Press.
Chubb, John E., and Terry Moe. 1990. *Politics, Markets, and America's Schools.* Washington, D.C.: The Brookings Institution.
Coleman, James S., and Thomas Hoffer. 1987. *Public and Private High Schools.* New York: Basic Books.
Cremin, Lawrence A. 1961. *The Transformation of the School: Progressivism in American Education, 1876–1957.* New York: Alfred A. Knopf.
Danielson, Michael. 1976. *The Politics of Exclusion.* Princeton, N.J.: Princeton University Press.
Dewey, John. 1927. *The Public and Its Problems.* Chicago: The Swallow Press.
Diamond, Martin. 1992 [1973]. "The Ends of Federalism," in *As Far as Republi-*

can Principles Will Admit: Essays by Martin Diamond. Washington, D.C.: AEI Press, 145–66.

Downs, Anthony. 1981. *Neighborhoods and Urban Development.* Washington, D.C.: The Brookings Institution.

——. 1994. *New Visions for Metropolitan America.* Washington, D.C., and Cambridge, Mass.: Brookings Institution and Lincoln Institute of Land Policy.

Durkheim, Émile. 1933 [1893]. *The Division of Labor in Society.* New York: Macmillan, 130.

Dworkin, Ronald. 1992. "Liberal Community," in *Communitarianism and Individualism,* ed. Shlomo Avineri and Avner de-Shalit. Oxford: Oxford University Press, 205–24.

Education Week. No date. "Home Schooling." www.edweek.org/context/topics/home.htm.

Elam, Stanley M., and Lowell C. Rose. 1995. "The 27th Annual Phi Delta Kappa/Gallup Poll of the Public's Attitudes toward the Public Schools." *Phi Delta Kappan* 77:1 (September): 41–56.

ERIC Clearinghouse on Educational Management. 1995. "Home Schooling." *ERIC Digest 95.* Eugene, Ore.: University of Oregon.

Finn, Chester E., Jr., Louann A. Bierlein, and Bruno V. Manno. 1996. *Charter Schools in Action: A First Look.* www.edexcellence.net/issuespc/subject/charters/pewjan.html.

Finn, Chester E., Jr., and Diane Ravitch. 1995. "Charter Schools—Beware Imitations." *The Wall Street Journal* (Sept. 7, 1995), 14.

Friedan, Bernard. 1979. *The Environmental Protection Hustle.* Cambridge, Mass.: MIT Press.

Gauthier, David. 1992. "The Liberal Individual," in *Communitarianism and Individualism,* ed. Shlomo Avineri and Avner de-Shalit. Oxford: Oxford University Press, 151–64.

Genesis Schools. 1996. "Application for Approval of an Open-Enrollment Charter." Austin: Texas State Board of Education.

Glendon, Mary Ann. 1991. *Rights Talk: The Impoverishment of Political Discourse.* New York: Free Press.

Gulf Coast Council of La Raza. 1996. "Application for Approval of an Open-Enrollment Charter." Austin, Tex.: Texas State Board of Education.

Gutman, Amy. 1987. *Democratic Education.* Princeton, N.J.: Princeton University Press.

——. 1992. "Communitarian Critics of Liberalism," in *Communitarianism and Individualism,* ed. Shlomo Avineri and Avner de-Shalit. Oxford: Oxford University Press, 120–36.

Hassel, Bryan C. 1995a. "The Charter School Idea: Elements of an Effective Charter School Program." Unpublished working paper, A. Alfred Taubman

Center for State and Local Government, Kennedy School of Government, Harvard University.

1995b. "Designed to Fail? Charter School Programs and the Politics of Bureaucratic Structure." Unpublished working paper, A. Alfred Taubman Center for State and Local Government, Kennedy School of Government, Harvard University.

Henig, Jeffrey R. 1994. *Rethinking School Choice: Limits of the Market Metaphor.* Princeton, N.J.: Princeton University Press.

Houston Chronicle. 1996 (March 10). "Discouraged Blacks Forming Their Own Segregated School Districts," 5a.

Information Referral Resource Assistance, Inc. 1996. "Application for Approval of an Open-Enrollment Charter." Austin: Texas State Board of Education.

Jeub, Chris. 1995. "Why Parents Choose Home Schooling." *Educational Leadership* 52:1 (September): 50–2.

Kolderie, Ted. 1995. "Charter Schools: The New Neighborhood Schools." Action Paper. Washington, D.C.:Center for Education Reform.

1994. "The Essentials of the Charter School Strategy." St. Paul, Minn.: Center for Policy Studies.

Lange, Cheryl, Camilla Lehr, Patricia Seppanen, and Mary Sinclair. 1996 (December). *Minnesota Charter Schools Evaluation: Interim Report.* Minneapolis, Minn.: Center for Applied Research and Educational Improvement, University of Minnesota.

Link, William A. 1986. *A Hard Country and a Lonely Place: Schooling, Society, and Reform in Rural Virginia, 1870–1920.* Chapel Hill: University of North Carolina Press.

Massachusetts Department of Education. 1996. *Massachusetts Charter School Initiative.* Http://info.doe.mass.edu/cs.www/cs.indes.html.

Medical Center Charter Schools, Inc. 1996. "Application for Approval of an Open-Enrollment Charter." Austin: Texas State Board of Education.

Miller, Gary. 1984. *Cities by Contract: The Politics of Municipal Incorporation.* Cambridge, Mass.: MIT Press.

Myrdal, Gunnar. 1964. *An American Dilemma* (Twentieth Anniversary Edition). New York: McGraw-Hill.

National Center for Education Statistics. 1994. *Digest of Education Statistics 1994.* Washington, D.C.: U.S. Government Printing Office.

1995. *Private Schools in the United States: A Statistical Profile, 1990–91.* Washington, D.C.: U.S. Government Printing Office.

National Charter School Directory. 1996. Washington, D.C.: Center for Education Reform.

Newport, Frank, and Lydia Saad. 1994. "Confidence in Institutions," *The Gallup Poll Monthly* 343 (April): 5–6.

Peterson, Paul E. 1995. "The New Politics of Choice," in *Learning from the Past: What History Teaches Us about School Reform*, ed. Diane Ravitch and Maris A. Vinovskis. Baltimore: Johns Hopkins University Press, 217–40.

Ramsay, Krista. 1992. "Home Is Where the School Is," *School Administrator* 49:1 (January): 20–5.

Ravitch, Diane. 1983. *The Troubled Crusade: American Education 1945–1980*. New York: Basic Books.

1985. *The Schools We Deserve: Reflections on the Educational Crises of Our Time*. New York: Basic Books.

Rusk, David. 1995. *Cities without Suburbs* (second edition). Washington, D.C., and Baltimore, Md: Woodrow Wilson Center Press and Johns Hopkins University Press.

1996. *Baltimore Unbound: A Strategy for Regional Renewal*. Baltimore, Md.: Abell Foundation and Johns Hopkins University Press.

Sandel, Michael. 1992. "The Procedural Republic and the Unencumbered Self," in *Communitarianism and Individualism*, ed. Shlomo Avineri and Avner de-Shalit. Oxford: Oxford University Press, 12–28.

1996. *Democracy's Discontent: America in Search of a Public Philosophy*. Cambridge, Mass.: Belknap Press of Harvard University Press.

SER—Jobs for Progress of the Texas Gulf Coast, Inc. 1996. "Application for Approval of an Open-Enrollment Charter." Austin: Texas State Board of Education.

Selznick, Philip. 1992. *The Moral Commonwealth: Social Theory and the Promise of Community*. Berkeley: University of California Press.

Smith, Kevin B., and Kenneth J. Meier. 1995. *The Case Against School Choice: Politics, Markets, and Fools*. Armonk, N.Y.: M. E. Sharpe.

Taylor, Charles. 1991. *The Ethics of Authenticity*. Cambridge, Mass.: Harvard University Press.

Teaford, Jon. 1979. *City and Suburb: The Political Fragmentation of Metropolitan America, 1850–1970*. Baltimore: Johns Hopkins University Press.

Tejano Center for Community Concerns, Inc. 1996. "Application for Approval of an Open-Enrollment Charter." Austin: Texas State Board of Education.

Texas Senate. 1995. Senate Bill No. 1., Chapter 12, "Charters."

Thomas, Karen. 1994. "Learning at Home: Education Outside School Gains Respect." *USA Today* (April 6, 1994), 5d.

Tonnies, Ferdinand. 1963 [1897]. *Community and Society*. New York: Harper.

Turner, Donald G. 1983. *Legal Issues in the Education of the Handicapped*. Bloomington, Ind.: Phi Delta Kappa Educational Foundation.

Tyack, David B. 1974. *The One Best System: A History of American Urban Education*. Cambridge, Mass.: Harvard University Press.

U.S. Department of Education. 1997 (May). *A Study of Charter Schools: First Year Report*. Http://www.ed.gov/pubs/charter.

USA Today (interactive edition). 1996 (May 17). "Education Poll Gives Policy Makers Hope, Warning."

Vergari, Sandra, and Michael Mintrom. 1995. "Charter School Laws across the United States: A Policy Report." East Lansing, Mich.: Institute for Public Policy and Social Research, College of Social Science, Michigan State University.

Wall Street Journal. 1996 (January 12). "Men of Madison."

Walzer, Michael. 1980. *Radical Principles: Confessions of an Unreconstructed Democrat.* New York: Basic Books.

    1992. "Membership," in *Communitarianism and Individualism,* ed. Shlomo Avineri and Avner de-Shalit. Oxford: Oxford University Press, 65–84.

Weiher, Gregory R. 1991. *The Fractured Metropolis: Political Fragmentation and Metropolitan Segregation.* Albany: State University of New York Press.

White, Kerry A. 1997 (April 16). "Mass. Plan to Triple Number of Schools Scrutinized." *Education Week on the Web,* www.edweek.org.

Williams, Oliver P. 1968. "Life-style Values and Political Decentralization in Metropolitan Areas," in *Community Structure and Decision-making: Comparative Analyses,* ed. Terry N. Clark. San Francisco: Chandler.

Witte, John F. 1992. "Private School Versus Public School Achievement: Are There Findings that Should Affect the Educational Choice Debate?" *Economics of Education Review* 11:4: 371–94.

Witte, John F., Christopher A. Thorn, Kim M. Pritchard, and Michele Claibourn. 1994. *Fourth Year Report: Milwaukee Parental Choice Program.* Madison: University of Wisconsin, Department of Political Science, and Robert La Follette Institute of Public Affairs.

10

Net gains

The Voting Rights Act and Southern local government

RICHARD M. VALELLY

The Supreme Court—or more precisely, its regular majority in voting-rights cases (comprising Justices Kennedy, O'Connor, Rehnquist, Scalia, and Thomas)—is clearly worried about the impact of the Voting Rights Act of 1965 on state and local government.[1] Supreme Court decisions such as *Shaw v. Reno* (1993), *Miller v. Johnson* (1995), *Abrams et al. v. Johnson et al.* (1997) and *Reno, Attorney General v. Bossier Parish School Board et al.* (1997) reveal (1) overt suspicion of the Department of Justice, (2) a preference for restricting the department's role in voting-rights policymaking, (3) considerable trust in the capacity of the federal courts to guide this policy domain reasonably well, and (4) a desire to diminish the "federalism costs" (to use Court language) of national regulatory oversight of local governmental election practices.

Taking my cue from Albert O. Hirschman's widely known depiction of unnecessary pessimism in modern policy analysis, I argue that the Supreme Court's majority has misconstrued the "federalism costs" of the Voting Rights Act and its administration and implementation by the Justice Department. What has happened with Southern local government is most assuredly *not,* I argue, a case of "jeopardy": of seemingly progressive reform posing threats to existing values and rights.[2]

---

[1] For valuable help and encouragement I thank the volume's editor, Martha Derthick. The Woodrow Wilson Center graciously awarded me a guest scholarship in the summer of 1994, which enabled me to draft this chapter's earliest incarnation. Colin Apse, then on the Wilson Center's staff, provided excellent research assistance that summer. More recently, Peyton McCrary, of the Voting Section of the U.S. Department of Justice, Civil Rights Division, was very generous with his knowledge and time, reading and closely commenting on several drafts. None of the above is liable in any way for any errors of fact, interpretation, or emphasis—everything I say here is my responsibility alone.
[2] See Albert O. Hirschman, *The Rhetoric of Reaction: Perversity, Futility, Jeopardy* (Cambridge, Mass.: The Belknap Press of Harvard University Press, 1991), on the origins of the

The Court and the conservatives are not wrong to worry about "federalism costs." A large majority of the American public has strong confidence in local government, in contrast to the minority support now enjoyed by the federal government among the public.[3] Happily for this majority, what has happened in locally implementing the Voting Rights Act does not contradict the value attached by the American public to American local government; instead, it supports it. The gains in the South to what local government is about, and to the values it serves, have been substantial as a result of the process that evolved during the 1970s and 1980s.

For more than half a century, most local government in the South was "captured" government in the sense that it was disproportionately responsive to the partial interests of powerful local whites. A regional system of loosely organized one-party politics, based on white supremacist solidarity, had fundamental consequences for local government. V. O. Key, Jr., communicated these consequences well in his classic study, *Southern Politics:*

A loosely organized politics with no stable centers of power or leadership for an entire state is in one sense admirably suited for dealing with the Negro question. A pulverized politics decentralizes power to county leaders and county officials and in some areas devolution is carried even further in that public officials do not cross the plantation boundary without invitation. . . . In a granulated political structure of this kind with thousands of points of authority there is no point at which accountability can be enforced.[4]

Local government in a fundamental sense was not public, impersonal, and impartial. The Voting Rights Act has helped to rebrighten the local line between the public and the private, and this has resulted in a more desirable framework for each citizen's experience of membership in the local political community.[5] Certainly the price of that rebrightening has

---

bias for pessimism in policy analysis. See also Hirschman, "The Rhetoric of Reform," *The American Prospect* (Summer 1993): 148–52.

[3] See *Philadelphia Inquirer,* "The Public's View of Federal Powers," inset to Steven Thomas, "Reassertion of Federal Role Shifts Power Back to Where It Always Was" (October 12, 1997); page E-3 shows (on the basis of a poll for the Pew Research Center for the People & the Press) that 65 percent of the public has confidence in city and local government, 61 percent in state government, and 48 percent in the federal government.

[4] V. O. Key, Jr., with the assistance of Alexander Heard, *Southern Politics in State and Nation* (Knoxville: University of Tennessee Press, 1984 [Knopf, 1949]), 307, note 9.

[5] On the "citizenship impact" of policies, see *Public Policy for Democracy,* ed. Helen Ingram and Steven Rathgeb Smith (Washington, D.C.: Brookings Institution, 1993).

been some loss of local autonomy from national influences. But on balance it is a fair price.

Whether it has in fact been a fair price occasions strong disagreement though. The Voting Rights Act of 1965 might seem instead to have weakened Southern grass-roots democracy, and thus to have enervated citizenship at the local level. Southern local officials do not have sole custody, after all, of one of the most vital aspects of local self-government, that is, deciding what the electoral rules are. The Voting Rights Act has meant that successive congressional majorities, federal judges, a professional voting-rights bar, and the Civil Rights Division of the Justice Department have all become key players in local voting-rights policy.

However, in doing this (goes the case against the local effects of the Voting Rights Act's administration and implementation), these players have also perpetuated racial divisions by forcing local processes and outcomes into a procrustean bed of racialized categories subject to federal proscription. Furthermore, the partial loss of local custody of electoral-policy decisions has been largely to *private* actors, who have not hesitated to push beyond the legislative intent of 1965. Such organizations as the ACLU's Voting Rights Project, Common Cause, the Lawyers' Committee for Civil Rights under Law, the Leadership Conference on Civil Rights, and the NAACP-Legal Defense Fund, among others—not to mention the large foundations that aid their work—have in fact been critically important protagonists in the voting-rights policy domain. Through their monitoring of Southern local governmental decisions about electoral rules, voting-rights policy has shifted away from remedying impediments to the physical act of voting and toward questions about whether black voters can elect as many black public officials as they should be electing. The politics of black voting rights has therefore been about making black ballots count. There is nothing wrong with that per se, but these groups did not run for office. No one elected them to make public policy.

I call this claim a *regulatory-mischief view* since it concentrates on how narrow groups govern a policy domain at the expense of local government and the broader values it serves. Section I following describes this regulatory-mischief view in greater detail. The optimistic view ultimately propounded here becomes clearer through first describing its alternative. Section II lays out criticisms of the regulatory-mischief view. Section III emphasizes the Voting Rights Act's renewal of local government (this is where my optimistic case comes in). Section IV briefly concludes my contribution.

I: BUILDING FACTION IN? THE REGULATORY-MISCHIEF VIEW

Any "federalism-costs" case against the Voting Rights Act's administration and implementation runs up against the fact that with the Fifteenth Amendment the American people made an exception to whatever value they attach to local government. They did so in the weightiest and most conspicuous way provided by our polity's procedures. Nor were the people specific about how to enforce the amendment; the particular form of enforcement was left up to Congress.[6]

Still, it would be hard to argue that the people authorized rampant interest-group liberalism as *the* mechanism of "delocalization." Critics of voting rights politics have charged that liberal interest groups—recognizing the potency of Section 5—have hijacked the Voting Rights Act.[7] Because Section 5 requires local jurisdictions to "pre-clear" rules changes with the Department of Justice, voting-rights groups can enter into the regulatory process at the national level.[8] Critics have also found the 1982 amendments to the act, as well as a 1986 Supreme Court decision interpreting them, disturbing. In 1982 Congress strengthened the act to establish a tighter relationship between black voting and black officeholding. The Court's 1986 decision, *Thornburg v. Gingles,* simplified the fact-finding process for litigation under the amendment (known as Section 2 litigation). Again, interest groups were both sponsors and beneficiaries of these changes. They could now methodically pick off the many local jurisdictions that lacked black officeholders. By the 1980s, goes the case against the Voting Rights Act's local effects, interest groups effectively enveloped

---

[6] Political scientists, of course, have abandoned serious analytical use of the term "the people," but I use it here as a reminder of the special nature of democratic constitutionalism. The best brief introduction to the Fifteenth Amendment's origins is David E. Kyvig, *Explicit and Authentic Acts: Amending the U.S. Constitution, 1776–1995* (Lawrence: University Press of Kansas, 1996), 176–82.

[7] My characterization represents a sharpening of themes in Timothy G. O'Rourke, "The 1982 Amendments and the Voting Rights Paradox," and Hugh Davis Graham, "Voting Rights and the American Regulatory State," in Grofman and Davidson, *Controversies in Minority Voting,* 84–113 and 177–96. The basic work that launched critical assessment of the Voting Rights Act's evolution, and several scholarly responses, is Abigail M. Thernstrom, *Whose Votes Count? Affirmative Action and Minority Voting Rights* (Cambridge, Mass.: Harvard University Press, 1987, for the Twentieth Century Fund). See also Stephan Thernstrom and Abigail Thernstrom, *America in Black and White: One Nation, Indivisible* (New York: Simon & Schuster, 1997), chap. 16; Raymond Wolters, *Right Turn: William Bradford Reynolds, the Reagan Administration, and Black Civil Rights* (New Brunswick, N.J.: Transaction Publishers, 1996), chaps. 1–7.

[8] There is anecdotal evidence of group involvement in rule-making; see, for instance, Drew S. Days III, "Section 5 Enforcement and the Department of Justice," in Grofman and Davidson, *Controversies in Minority Voting,* 52–65, esp. 61–3.

local processes of making basic decisions about electoral rules within a central system of oversight and correction in which they predominated.

The evil said to follow from such expanded group influence is a lack of open debate (except for periodic congressional scrutiny) about how best to realize the aims of the Voting Rights Act. Absent the correcting influence of open public debate, a misunderstanding of democratic process has in turn emerged among such liberal groups as the ACLU's Voting Rights Project, Common Cause, the Lawyers' Committee for Civil Rights Under Law, the Leadership Conference on Civil Rights, and the NAACP-Legal Defense Fund. For instance, about a decade ago liberal voting-rights groups pushed for safe districting, that is, the idea that minority office-holding depended on creating legislative districts with a population at least 65 percent black. (This level was chosen because black voter registration and turnout have historically lagged behind white levels.) Critics suggested that this remedy misconceived the requirements of political equality. Equality does not mean guaranteed outcomes. The proper remedies for the losers in democratic majoritarian politics are inventive forms of coalition-building and public discussion.

II: LIMITS OF THE REGULATORY-MISCHIEF VIEW

The regulatory-mischief view thus holds that the Voting Rights Act's politics has become an interest-driven subgovernment—a voting-rights version of the way that, for instance, environmental policy is made within a system of interest groups, regulatory rule-making, and congressional committees.[9] Any responsible student of democratic politics will recognize that, if true, this would be a serious matter. Yet in key ways, the regulatory-mischief view misdescribes fundamental relationships among the Voting Rights Act, the politics of the act, and Southern local government.

Let me turn first to legal mobilization. Legal mobilization has three key elements: (1) an effort to win policy change in the courts, (2) an empowering and politicizing effect among the first-order beneficiaries of such policy change, and (3) a broadly educative effect on other institutions and actors, for example Congress or former political opponents.[10] In focusing

---

[9] On subgovernment, see Bryan D. Jones, *Reconceiving Decision-Making in Democratic Politics: Attention, Choice, and Public Policy* (Chicago: University of Chicago Press, 1994), chap. 7.

[10] The term "legal mobilization" I borrow from Michael W. McCann, *Rights at Work: Pay Equity Reform and the Politics of Legal Mobilization* (Chicago: University of Chicago Press, 1994), esp. 5–12. McCann emphasizes the first two elements of my definition. From Gerald Rosenberg's discussion of the relative efficacy of group litigation I have borrowed the third element. V. Gerald Rosenberg, *The Hollow Hope: Can Courts Bring*

on the emergence of legal mobilization in the post-1965 period, vital distinctions between the legal-mobilization account and the regulatory-mischief view will emerge. The regulatory-mischief view implies the existence of a dominant coalition of lawyers and black activists using a path-breaking law to establish a bureaucratic receivership of local governments, all the while deploying rights talk.[11] Legal mobilization, by contrast, implies that post-1965 events formed a new and often arduous phase in a long struggle to widen the inclusiveness of the American polity.

Legal mobilization for officeholding[12]

The regulatory-mischief view says little about the resistance of white Democratic party politicians, but such foot-dragging was pervasive for at least a decade and a half after the Voting Rights Act. After 1965, white Southern officials sought to dilute the ballot.[13] Reading the handwriting on the walls, many Southern state legislatures quietly but quickly recast local government with such devices as requiring local governments to adopt at-large voting. Blacks could vote, but few would hold office.

Such resistance to the Voting Rights Act transformed Southern local government into a battleground—and small wonder. The local and state offices sealed off by state legislators exercised important responsibilities. In Mississippi, for instance, county boards of supervisors levy county taxes, decide how to spend county money, direct bridge and road construction and maintenance, and appoint such boards as the welfare and planning boards. Until 1975, they also drew up jury lists for the state courts.

About Social Change? (Chicago: University of Chicago Press, 1991), esp. 25–6 discussing "extra-judicial" effects. Rosenberg, incidentally, is skeptical that legal mobilization is as effective as contentious collective action in winning policy and political change.

[11] The term "rights talk" was coined by Mary Ann Glendon in her book, *Rights Talk: The Impoverishment of Political Discourse* (New York: Free Press, 1991). For a judicious introduction to the proposition that there are pluses and minuses to rights claims in politics and policy, see Marc Landy, "Public Policy and Citizenship," in Ingram and Smith, *Public Policy for Democracy*, 19–44, esp. 27–31.

[12] A lucid—indeed, gripping—study of the "legal-mobilization" response to white legislative resistance is Parker, *Black Votes Count*. Less readable but definitive and equally full of surprises is *Quiet Revolution in the South: The Impact of the Voting Rights Act, 1965–1990*, ed. Chandler Davidson and Bernard Grofman (Princeton: Princeton University Press, 1994), chaps. 2–9. This account is based on these sources.

[13] Chandler Davidson defines vote dilution as "a process whereby election laws or practices, either singly or in concert, combine with systematic bloc voting among an identifiable group to diminish the voting strength of at least one other group. Ethnic or racial minority vote dilution is a special case, in which the voting strength of an ethnic or racial minority group is diminished or canceled out by the *bloc vote* of the majority." Chandler Davidson, "Minority Vote Dilution: An Overview," in *Minority Vote Dilution*, ed. Chandler Davidson (Washington, D.C.: Howard University Press, 1984), 4.

Other self-evidently vital elective offices are the county school board and
the county elections superintendent.

Indeed, this legislative movement to recast local government forms
part of a larger pattern. Reading the legislative and political histories of
the 1957, 1960, and 1964 Civil Rights Acts and the 1965 Voting Rights
Act would reveal a detailed inventory of state and local efforts to resist
implementation of the Fifteenth Amendment.[14]

The major "reforms" included: (1) requiring or permitting county and
municipal governments to substitute at-large voting for public office for
district-based voting; (2) requiring or permitting these governments to establish majority-voting requirements for public office, thus preventing
plurality black victory over a field of split white candidates; (3) converting elective offices to offices appointed by officials likely to have exclusively white support; and (4) reapportioning of local district lines to create white-majority voting districts.

Black out-migration from the South between the 1930s and 1950s had
drained political jurisdictions of many potential voters. Thus these lay-
ered changes were quite effective responses to both the increased black
voter registration from 1944 on and the sharp jump in black voter registration produced by the Voting Rights Act. They also blunted the potential impact of growing urban black concentrations on city officeholding.

What responses were available to civil-rights leaders? No two-party
system exercised a check on those who pressed for these legislative reforms, nor was another eruption of sustained protest comparable to the
heyday of civil-rights activity from 1961 to 1965 likely. Fortuitously,
though, official white resistance in Deep South states during the 1961–64
period attracted a new political resource: experienced white and black
non-Southern lawyers willing and able to work with local black and
white political activists and lawyers.

---

[14] See David J. Garrow, *Protest at Selma: Martin Luther King, Jr. and the Voting Rights Act
of 1965* (New Haven: Yale University Press, 1978), 6–132. From Reconstruction until
the present, white conservatives have developed many ways to resist black electoral involvement. The list includes but is not restricted to (1) *private violence* (hence the Ku
Klux Klan Act of 1870); (2) *private violence under the color of law* (proscribed by the Ku
Klux Klan Act, which in turn formed the basis for federal prosecutions of, for instance,
the Neshoba County [Mississippi] law-enforcement officers who conspired to murder
three civil-rights activists in the summer of 1964); (3) *movement building* (e.g., the Citizens Council movement that began in 1956); (4) *electoral mobilization* (e.g., the States'
Rights Party of 1948); (5) *litigation* (e.g., South Carolina's suit challenging the constitu-
tionality of the Voting Rights Act); (6) *constitution-writing* (e.g., the Mississippi Constitution of 1890); (7) *reforms of legal-electoral structures* (e.g., the establishment of white
primaries); and (8) *judicial and bureaucratic obstructionism* (e.g., great delay in the federal district courts of Alabama and Mississippi during the early 1960s after legal motions
of the United States on behalf of black voters).

The elements of the legal mobilization that eventually emerged were laid in Washington, D.C., and in Mississippi during the summer of 1963 and the "Freedom Summer" of 1964. During a White House meeting with officials of the American Bar Association and the National Bar Association in 1963, President John F. Kennedy urged the formation of a volunteer legal effort in the South; this in turn led to the establishment of the Lawyers' Committee for Civil Rights under Law (LCCR) and the LCCR's invitation to Mississippi by the National Council of Churches. Also, about 130 volunteer lawyers donated vacation time during Freedom Summer under the auspices of the Lawyers' Constitutional Defense Committee (LCDC), a consortium of legal officers from the Congress of Racial Equality, the American Civil Liberties Union, the NAACP-Legal Defense Fund, the American Jewish Congress, and the National Council of Churches.

Initially, volunteer lawyers handled the criminal cases of civil-rights workers facing local and state criminal prosecutions, but they quickly shifted into affirmative, as opposed to reactive, kinds of legal actions. They turned toward challenging antipicketing statutes and, more important, voting-rights denials. The parent organizations also opened up permanent staff offices in the black business district of Jackson.

Then, in the wake of the Mississippi legislature's thorough effort in 1966 to cordon off officeholding from black politicians, the tiny liberal wing of the Mississippi Democratic party and the larger independent party, the Mississippi Freedom Democratic Party (MFDP), forged an alliance with LCCR, LCDC, and NAACP-Legal Defense Fund lawyers in Mississippi. Together they focused on responding to the legislature's burst of electoral reform through 1) acquiring major foundation support to provide a long-run material base and 2) launching Section 5 voting-rights litigation. In doing so, they provided a model for similar combinations in Alabama and Georgia; they also reinforced a long-standing interest in combining electoral mobilization with litigation among African-American and Mexican-American organizations in Texas and other Southwestern states.[15]

By 1969, legal mobilization led to a critically important Supreme Court decision, *Allen v. State Board of Elections,* which held that such dilutive devices as at-large plans and majority-vote requirements required clearance from the Justice Department under Section 5 before they became legally effective. As shown in Table 10.1, legal mobilization was

[15] On the Southwest, see Amy Bridges, *Morning Glories: Municipal Reform in the Southwest* (Princeton: Princeton University Press, 1997).

Table 10.1. *Evolution of legal mobilization*

Date	Event	Description	Effects on voting rights activists' strategies and resources, and on perceptions and behavior of white local officials
1969	*Allen v. State Board of Elections*	The Supreme Court holds that Congress intended for the VRA to have "the broadest possible scope." Vote dilution as well as vote denial are proscribed. Challenges to local rules changes for failure to obtain Section 5 pre-clearance do not require constitutional argument.	Sharp increase in number of rules changes submitted to the Department of Justice for Section 5 pre-clearance from local and state jurisdictions "covered" by the Voting Rights Act.
1970	Renewal of VRA to 1975	Congress in effect says that the decision in *Allen* articulated congressional intent.	Legal mobilization can continue.
1973	*White v. Regester*	Supreme Court delineates wide range of circumstances that will raise an "inference of intent" (and thus be sufficient to show intent) "to deny minorities equal opportunity "to participate in the political process and to elect legislators of their choice."	Fact-finding in legal mobilization becomes more complex in exchange for what is in effect a "results" standard for showing vote dilution.
1975	Renewal of VRA to 1982, and amendment	Jurisdictions losing in court required to pay plaintiffs' costs and attorneys' fees.	Potential incentive for jurisdictions to settle with voting rights groups and plaintiffs, reducing strain on resources of voting rights legal activists.

1980	*City of Mobile v. Bolden*	Supreme Court holds that plaintiffs must directly prove intent to discriminate, vitiating *Allen* and *White.*	Potential for reversal of gains from legal mobilization. Voting rights groups turn to Congress.
1982	Congressional renewal and amendment of VRA	Congress extends pre-clearance for 25 years. Amends Section 2 of the VRA to prohibit rules that have dilutive effects regardless of intent.	Potential for Court reversal of *City of Mobile v. Bolden.*
1982	*Rogers v. Lodge*	Supreme Court accepts congressional correction in a case with facts very similar to *City of Mobile v. Bolden.*	Number of voting rights cases in federal courts increases. Number of jurisdictions removing dilutive rules more than doubles. Threat of lawsuits found by *Atlanta Constitution* survey of local Georgia officials to motivate switches to district elections.
1986	*Thornburg v. Gingles*	Supreme Court simplifies factual tests for proof of racial bloc voting among whites sufficient to cause vote dilution.	Continued correction of electoral rules and of lines of election jurisdictions.

Sources: Laughlin McDonald, "The 1982 Amendments of Section 2 and Minority Representation," in Bernard Grofman and Chandler Davidson, eds., *Controversies in Minority Voting* (Washington, D.C.: Brookings Institution Press, 1992); Frank Parker, *Black Votes Count* (Chapel Hill: University of North Carolina Press, 1990).

rather successful from then on. Not until 1980 did legal activists experience a severe crisis in the development of voting-rights law. They then turned to Congress and argued successfully for an amendment of the Voting Rights Act that would correct the Court's sudden abandonment of established principles favoring legal mobilization. In the decade following the 1982 congressional amendment of the Voting Rights Act, the Supreme Court played a key support role in legal mobilization (though now, of course, it no longer does).[16]

To put the story another way, it was a long, uncertain struggle. The original networks of legal activists had their hands full; only gradually have new networks in other states emerged. Gaining reasonably full compliance with *Allen v. State Board of Elections* at the state and local level took approximately ten years of follow-on litigation. Second, dilutive changes that preceded the Voting Rights Act were not covered by *Allen;* these have required separate litigation under the 1982 amendment to Section 2 of the act. Third, not until the mid- to late 1970s and early 1980s did local associations pushing for legal mobilization emerge in South Carolina and parts of North Carolina, and not until the early 1980s could one really find them in Virginia.

Fourth, as Table 10.2 shows, substantial rates of local black officeholding in states under complete VRA coverage are *recent*—within the last decade or so. (North Carolina is not listed because only part of it is under VRA coverage.) As one would expect from a legal-mobilization framework, the table suggests both (1) considerable delay in the emergence of significant levels of local black officeholding and (2) considerable unevenness in VRA-covered states with regard to rates of black officeholding, taking into account the percentage of the total voting-age population that is black.

Two sets of figures are displayed in Table 10.2. The set on the left (denoted as [1]) shows figures for certain categories of local officeholders only—county commissioners, members of municipal governing bodies, sheriffs, and school-board members. The set on the right (denoted as [2]) shows figures for all local elected officials—including, for instance, coroners, municipal sergeants, probate judges, and commissioners of special boards. The black voting-age population (VAP) as a percentage of the total voting-age population is displayed as a helpful benchmark. One might

---

[16] In addition to Parker, *Black Votes Count,* and Davidson and Grofman, *Quiet Revolution,* see Laughlin McDonald, "The 1982 Amendments of Section 2 and Minority Representation," in Grofman and Davidson, *Controversies in Minority Voting,* 66–84.

Table 10.2. *Change in local officeholding by African-Americans in Southern states completely covered by the Voting Rights Act*

	Total LEO's [1]	Total BLEO's [1]	BLEO's as % [1]	All LEO's [2]	All BLEO's [2]	All BLEO's as % [2]	Black VAP
AL (1974)	2634	110	4.2%	N.A.	N.A.		23%
AL (1984)	2795	241	8.6%	3125	292	9%	23%
AL (1993)	2936	605	20.6%	3237	672	20%	22.7%
GA (1974)	4077	120	2.9%	N.A.	N.A.		22.9%
GA (1984)	4209	250	5.9%	4950	276	5.6%	24%
GA (1993)	4428	459	10.3%	5760	498	8.6%	24.6%
LA (1974)	2577	141	5.5%	N.A.	N.A.		26.6%
LA (1984)	2651	374	14%	2779	425	15.3%	27%
LA (1993)	3235	511	15.8%	3362	600	17.8%	27.9%
MS (1974)	2252	190	8.4%	N.A.	N.A.		31.4%
MS (1984)	2462	296	12%	3226	410	12.7%	31%
MS (1993)	2477	546	22%	3241	708	21.8%	31.6%
SC (1974)	1961	113	5.8%	N.A.	N.A.		26.4%
SC (1984)	1817	229	12.6%	2252	242	10.7%	27%
SC (1993)	2213	407	14.5%	2602	423	16.2%	26.9%
TX (1974)	11,467	117	1%	N.A.	N.A.		11.3%
TX (1984)	12,587	183	1.5%	18,749	215	1.1%	11%
TX (1993)	12,474	438	3.5%	18,636	447	2.4%	11.2%
VA (1974)	2002	61	3%	N.A.	N.A.		16.6%
VA (1984)	1994	86	4.3%	2451	100	4%	18%
VA (1993)	1999	125	6.2%	2456	141	5.7%	17.6%

expect that over time black local elected officials (BLEOs in the table) as a percentage of total local elected officials (LEOs in the table) would rise toward black VAP (expressed as a percentage of the total VAP). Three states—Georgia, Texas, and Virginia—stand out for their relative lack of convergence.[17]

By now, a major difference between the regulatory-mischief and legal-

[17] Showing similar data for other ex-Confederate states, for Oklahoma, and for the Border States, where obstructions to black voting also emerged, is beyond this chapter's scope. These figures are imperfect; several are no more than reasonable estimates. They were derived by the author from the census of black elected officials produced by the Joint Center for Political and Economic Studies (JCPES) in Washington, D.C. It is a testament to the enduring autonomy of local government that even at this late date in American political evolution, and after more than two decades of data collection by JCPES, the *Roster* is often uncertain as to just how many local governments and local elected officials there really are. See *National Roster of Black Elected Officials,* vol. 5 (Washington, D.C.: Joint Center for Political and Economic Studies, July 1975); *Black Elected Officials: A National Roster 1984* (New York: UNIPUB/R. R. Bowker and Company, 1984, for the Joint Center for Political and Economic Studies); *Black Elected Officials: A National Roster*

mobilization views should be clear. The former view suggests a cozy arrangement for reshaping Southern local government according to certain criteria that would never pass the bar of public debate. But the merit of the latter is the clarity with which it communicates the point that enfranchisement is not just one struggle—that is, the effort to allow the physical act of voting. Enfranchisement is at least two struggles. It has also been about access to the political good of officeholding and the best ways of constructing such access.

Also, legal mobilization has involved its own kind of public debate. It is true that courts are not, strictly speaking, deliberative institutions. But decisions have been made on the basis of careful public argument and the collection and assessment by courts of a wide range of relevant information.

Bringing parties into the picture

Let me consider Voting Rights Act politics from another angle—its relationship to national party politics. Political parties always have a basic stake in how electoral institutions work, because they care about winning and retaining political offices and controlling representative institutions. Political-party leaders have preferences in such matters as reapportionment, the registration of voters, and how votes are counted. They have to be brought into any picture of voting-rights politics. Doing so also challenges the basic claims of the regulatory-mischief view.[18]

It may not be obvious, but the two major parties have an overlapping interest in protecting the regulatory framework that the act provides—although their interests overlap for different reasons, as we shall see. Neither political party, therefore, seeks deregulation. In this context, groups and judges easily seem to be the only actors governing the policy domain. They provide all the movement and action. But in the background are major but unobtrusive stakeholders in voting-rights policy: the two national parties.

Consider first the Democratic party's stake in voting rights. The Voting Rights Act has guaranteed the participation of an African-American constituency very loyal to the Democratic party, helping the Democratic par-

---

1993 (Washington, D.C.: Joint Center for Political and Economic Studies Press, 1993, by arrangement with University Press of America).

[18] On theory and evidence regarding parties having preferences over electoral institutional design, cf. Richard M. Valelly, "National Parties and Disfranchisement," in *Classifying by Race*, ed. Paul E. Peterson (Princeton: Princeton University Press, 1995), 188–216.

ty build biracial voter coalitions in the South. Although Republicans have dominated presidential elections since the 1960s, in large part because of growing strength among conservative Southern whites, Democrats have twice been able to use their strength in the South to gain unified government. This record contrasts with that of the Republican party, which has not gained unified government in more than four decades. Electoral regulation of the South has thus proved critical in giving Democrats windows of opportunity for major policy change—openings that they squandered, yes, but windows as wide as the "Reagan window" of 1981–3.[19]

As for the Republican party, the Voting Rights Act does not impede it. Instead, the act provides a framework for party-building in a region where the Republican party was weak—and associated with the putative ills of Reconstruction—for several decades. By completing the entry of black Southerners into electoral politics, the act created a crucial opening for Republicans to develop strength in the region. White Southerners have more conservative policy preferences than black Southerners. Yet the entry of black Southerners into electoral politics drove Southern Democrats to become substantially more liberal in their policy stances, affording Republicans the chance to build partisan attachments among white Southerners.[20]

More recently, national Republicans perceived the 1982 amendment to the Voting Rights Act as a chance to work with Southern legislatures to create majority-minority congressional districts. Republican strategists hoped that these new so-called safe districts would drain other districts of enough reliably Democratic black voters to increase Republican representation in the House of Representatives. Indeed, regaining control of the House was a vital strategic goal for Republicans, given the unhappy anomaly—for them, at least—of four decades of Democratic dominance there. Whether in fact the Republican strategy succeeded as intended in 1994—when Republicans regained the House with the help of the

---

[19] On windows of policymaking opportunity, cf. John T. S. Keeler, "Opening the Window for Reform: Mandates, Crises, and Extraordinary Policy-Making," *Comparative Political Studies* 25 (January 1993): 433–86.

[20] On the increased liberalism of Southern Democrats, see James M. Glaser, *Race, Campaign Politics, & the Realignment in the South* (New Haven: Yale University Press, 1996). For the consequences for the House of Representatives and the Senate, see David W. Rohde, *Parties and Leaders in the Postreform House* (Chicago: University of Chicago Press, 1991). On Southern Republicans, cf. Earl Black and Merle Black, *The Vital South: How Presidents Are Elected* (Cambridge, Mass.: Harvard University Press, 1992); Glaser, *Race, Campaign Politics;* and Donald R. Kinder and Lynn M. Sanders, *Divided by Color: Racial Politics and Democratic Ideals* (Chicago: University of Chicago Press, 1996), esp. chap. 8.

South—is sharply debated, but there is no need to settle that debate here. My point is simply that the Voting Rights Act amendment of 1982 eventually stimulated party-building efforts by Republicans.[21]

In other words, both of the major parties have important stakes in voting-rights policy, and neither has sought extensively to revise the regulatory framework established in 1965. The result? Voting-rights policy and politics look like a subsystem. Groups and lawyers affiliated with groups, most of them private or nonprofit, do almost all the work of shaping voting-rights law and policy. Government lawyers initiate only a very small percentage of cases—one estimate is 5 percent. As Gregory Caldeira puts it, "Enforcement of voting rights is . . . very much an activity of the private sector."[22] Yet if both political parties are major (if low-profile) stakeholders in the act, then voting-rights politics is not really a policy subsystem operating largely out of view.

Indeed, subgovernments are ubiquitous in American politics, for at least three reasons:

1. American political parties cannot possibly place every policy issue and domain on the national party system's agenda for electoral contestation.
2. Countervailing power in the group system is always distributed very unevenly.
3. Regulatory bureaucracy is essential to modern government.

Notwithstanding the inevitable ubiquity of subgovernments, voting-rights policymaking is not part of this universe. It comprises, in sharp

---

21 The marginal impact of this strategy—whose existence no one disputes—is open to argument. David Lublin suggests that the strategy's political repercussions have been genuinely consequential. See David Ian Lublin, "Race, Representation, and Redistricting," in Peterson, Classifying by Race, 111–25, and Lublin, The Paradox of Representation: Racial Gerrymandering and Minority Interests in Congress (Princeton: Princeton University Press, 1997). A far more skeptical view can be found in Pamela S. Karlan, "Loss and Redemption: Voting Rights at the Turn of the Century," Vanderbilt Law Review 50 (March 1997): 291–326, and Karlan, "Still Hazy After All These Years: Voting Rights in the Post-Shaw Era," Cumberland Law Review 26: 2 (1995–96): 287–312. An analysis that would also yield skepticism is J. Morgan Kousser, "Shaw v. Reno and the Real World of Redistricting and Representation," California Institute of Technology, Division of the Humanities and Social Sciences, Social Science Working Paper 915, February 1995; this work is rich with lessons about voting-rights politics since 1965. Other useful works are Michael Kelly, "Segregation Anxiety," The New Yorker (November 20, 1995): 43–54; John R. Petrocik and Scott W. Desposato, "The Partisan Consequences of Majority-Minority Redistricting in the South, 1992 and 1994," paper prepared for presentation at the Annual Meetings of the American Political Science Association, Chicago Hilton and Towers, August 31–September 3, 1995; Carol Swain, "The Future of Black Representation," The American Prospect (Fall 1995): 78–83.

22 Gregory A. Caldeira, "Litigation, Lobbying, and Voting Rights Law," in Grofman and Davidson, Controversies in Minority Voting, 230–57.

contrast, (1) legal struggle, (2) judicial governance, constrained by norms of statutory and constitutional interpretation and conducted on the basis of open, high-profile argument, and (3) the partisan use of strategic opportunities provided by the Voting Rights Act.

The regulatory-mischief view obviously provides valuable cautionary analysis, and it does so from within a rich analytical tradition.[23] But a fair-minded reading of what has happened since 1965 in Southern local government requires bringing legal mobilization and political parties into a discussion of voting-rights politics. Doing so strongly suggests that the Voting Rights Act's politics simply has not engendered democratic pathologies.

There is more, as it happens, to bring in besides legal mobilization and political parties. Let us turn to a closer focus on a cluster of three topics: (1) the character of local government, (2) enfranchisement as a two-stage process, and (3) interactions between enfranchisement and local governmental renewal.

III: THE RECONSTRUCTION OF LOCAL CITIZENSHIP AND OFFICEHOLDING

The positive case for the role of the Voting Rights Act in Southern local government hinges on appreciating (1) the value of local government in democratic theory and relatedly (2) fair access to the political good of officeholding.

Autonomous local government is a democratic resource. Its worth to democracy comes in part from simple arithmetic: Given that the ratio of local offices to numbers of citizens in a local jurisdiction is much closer to unity than it is for other governmental levels, there are more possibilities for citizens to engage in governance—and more possibilities for citizens to have some personal knowledge of those who engage in governance. More citizens will either cross (or know people who cross) the line between the public and private domains and back.

Such line-crossing can reinforce people's awareness that government is a public enterprise (at least in principle) and ought not be the creature of any group or organized interest.[24] The relatively enlarged ratio of offices

[23] A book suggesting why this is a rich analytical tradition is James A. Morone, *The Democratic Wish: Popular Participation and the Limits of American Government* (New York: Basic Books, 1990).
[24] Cf. Richard M. Valelly, "Public Policy for Reconnected Citizenship," in Ingram and Smith, *Public Policy for Democracy*, 241–66, discussion at 244.

to voters at the local level creates the possibility that—to paraphrase Aristotle—many citizens will rule and be ruled in turn.

Of course, one would not want to overstate this point about the possibilities of local government. The constant probability of citizens crossing between public and private domains will be greater if local governmental offices are vigorously contested. Yet such robust conflict may not exist. On some accounts, it is *less* likely to exist at the local level because the policy responsibilities of local governments pale in comparison with those of state governments—and particularly national government. Speaking before a county commission or a borough council is, after all, a much different "line-crossing" experience than giving congressional testimony or stepping up to the lectern to deliver an oral argument before the Supreme Court. Therefore the strength and number of moral or simply architectural reminders of being in the public domain differ at the level of county and local government.[25]

Few people, however, can give congressional testimony about social policy; many more can speak before their borough council about fire, sanitation, police, or recreational services. Relatively few people can serve in national or state office; relatively more can serve on school boards, town and city councils, and county commissions and assemblies.

Local governmental citizenship and officeholding can therefore leaven our politics with broadly diffused knowledge of government and political association. Notice, though, that the possibility for such leavening critically depends on local governments' being *public:* They and their offices cannot belong to one group and not others. Otherwise there is no "line" between the public and private domains whose crossing subtly instructs local citizens and officeholders in government and political association. For local governments to perform their leavening function, they cannot—any more than governments at other levels—be openly biased in favor of one set of people.

Southern local government during the era of Jim Crow manifestly did not fill the bill. It was *white* government—the blacker the county or town, the dimmer the line between the public and private domains.[26] This brings up the value of fair access to political office.

---

[25] Paul E. Peterson, *City Limits* (Chicago: University of Chicago Press, 1981); Steven Kelman, *Making Public Policy: A Hopeful View of American Government* (New York: Basic Books, 1987).

[26] Key, *Southern Politics in State and Nation.*

The political good of officeholding

Voting Rights Act politics is an interesting case of enfranchisement *and* officeholding among the enfranchised. But what happens when there is enfranchisement *without* officeholding? Women's suffrage in America suggests an unfortunate answer.

The Nineteenth Amendment established female suffrage nationwide; in the absence of rapid gains in female officeholding, however, it shaped the national agenda only gradually. Another critically important factor was the collapse in the amendment's aftermath of the dense infrastructure of women's suffrage organizations, leaving no associations dedicated to mobilizing women as women or to producing viable female candidates for office. Not until rates of female officeholding began to increase in the 1970s—half a century later—did a pronounced women's-issues legislative agenda emerge. Enfranchisement without officeholding and the survival of mobilizing organizations appears, on the basis of the women's suffrage case, to engender weak representation.[27]

With weak representation, there is also what I call the problem of lingering doubt: If the newly enfranchised are not fit for the responsibilities of public office why should they be fit for the other obligations and rewards of citizenship? Enfranchisement always occurs in a context of some hesitation. Invidious stereotypes long buttressed the barriers to full citizenship. Without new forms of officeholding, such stereotypes may not dissipate, tainting the well of democratic change. Thus as late as 1972, about half the electorate agreed with the statement that "Women should take care of running their homes and leave running the country up to men," and 63 percent agreed that "Most men are better suited emotion-

[27] Cf. Barbara C. Burrell, *A Woman's Place Is in the House: Campaigning for Congress in the Feminist Era* (Ann Arbor: The University of Michigan Press, 1994) and Anne Costain, *Inviting Women's Rebellion: A Political Process Interpretation of the Women's Movement* (Baltimore: Johns Hopkins University Press, 1992). For an explanation of the collapse of women's organizations after the Nineteenth Amendment, see Anna Harvey, "The Political Consequences of Suffrage Exclusion: Organizations, Institutions, and the Electoral Mobilization of Women," *Social Science History* 20 (Spring 1996): 97–132. This is not to say that the culmination in 1920 of the struggle for female suffrage had no policy effects. See Theda Skocpol, *Protecting Soldiers and Mothers: The Political Origins of Social Policy in the United States* (Cambridge, Mass.: Belknap Press of Harvard University Press, 1992), esp. part 3. See also Kristi Andersen, *After Suffrage: Women in Partisan and Electoral Politics Before the New Deal* (Chicago: University of Chicago Press, 1996). On "weak representation," see Ira Katznelson, *Black Men, White Cities: Race, Politics, and Migration in the United States, 1900–30, and Britain, 1948–68* (Chicago: University of Chicago Press, 1976), 23–8.

ally for politics than are most women." Like all survey responses, these are not unambiguously clear, and their interpretation raises new questions. But it would be hard to say that they fulfilled the expectations of those who had pushed for women's suffrage.[28]

We now have several related propositions. The first is that local government's ratio of offices to citizens makes it a potential school of democracy. Second, local government can enrich the enfranchisement process, since officeholding and the character of representation are no small matters for the quality of enfranchisement. Third, and implicit in the analysis so far, nationally sponsored enfranchisement can strengthen the democratic contributions of local government. With these propositions in mind, a comparison of the first and second Reconstruction periods is in order.

The two reconstructions of Southern local government

From 1867 to 1877, about two thousand black men served as federal, state, and local officeholders in the ex-Confederate states subject to congressional Reconstruction. They were all undoubtedly strongly Republican. In Eric Foner's survey of these officeholders, using secondary work, the U.S. Census, and the Los Angeles Genealogical Library of the Church of Jesus Christ of Latter Day Saints, he assembled a census of 1,465 officeholders. Foner omitted several hundred possible entries because the data were too sparse, but almost all of these were local officeholders. Of his sample, 78 percent were elected or appointed local officeholders. Thus the vast majority of all black officeholders were local officeholders, occupying offices as diverse as boards of education, city councils, mayoralties, county commissions, magistracies, and streetcar commissions. They were concentrated in Deep South states with majority black or significantly black populations: South Carolina, Mississippi, Louisiana, North Carolina, Alabama, and Georgia, in that order. In all, Foner found 56 kinds of local officeholding. Some 20 percent of the total were justices of the peace, 11 percent were city council members, 9 percent were county commissioners, 7 percent were registrars, 6 percent were members of boards of education, 5 percent were police officers, and 4 percent were local-elections officials.[29]

---

[28] Burrell, *A Woman's Place*, 15.
[29] This account for Reconstruction and after relies heavily on evidence (and my calculations from that evidence) in Eric Foner, *Freedom's Lawmakers: A Directory of Black Officeholders during Reconstruction* (New York: Oxford University Press, 1993), ix–xxv.

For black officeholders such as James K. Green, an Alabama state politician, their service seems to have had enormous symbolic importance:

I believe that the colored people have done well, considering all their circumstances and surroundings, as emancipation made them. I for one was entirely ignorant; I knew nothing more than to obey my master; and there were thousands of us in the same attitude . . . but the tocsin of freedom sounded and knocked at the door and we walked out like free men and met the exigencies as they grew up, and shouldered the responsibilities.[30]

From the perspective of the democratic theory sketched above, the drama of answering the "tocsin of freedom" takes on considerable meaning. Men risked their lives and livelihoods in many places, yet turnover among officeholders was high, in part to accommodate a demand for officeholding. Local black citizens had unusually high expectations of the importance of local office, bringing all manner of problems before local black officials. Local government, thanks to national intervention, was a school of democracy.

Nonetheless, most local officeholders during Reconstruction were white. What, therefore, was local democracy like in those places where white Republicans largely governed, but in a context of robust black associationalism?[31] Historian Donald Nieman has recovered the fascinating story of Washington County, Texas, midway between Houston and Austin. It is probably representative of many (if only a minority of) Southern counties.[32]

Consistent with other scholarship, Nieman shows that a vibrant black politics at the local level meant public employment for freedmen, exemplifying one of many labor-market alternatives that emerged with the col-

[30] Foner, *Freedom's Lawmakers*, s.v. James K. Green, 90–1.

[31] Here I am adding a third case to my account of enfranchisement-as-process: To the cases of enfranchisement with and without officeholding, I add enfranchisement with some officeholding in a context of robust associationalism among the enfranchised. As Anna Harvey shows in "The Political Consequences of Suffrage Exclusion," women's associations largely collapsed after the Nineteenth Amendment. Black associationalism during Reconstruction, by contrast, was vibrant, partly because no black associations existed before the Civil War amendments; thus there was no issue of negotiating the transition to a new political context, as there was for women's associations.

[32] On white officeholding, see Randolph B. Campbell, "Grass Roots Reconstruction: The Personnel of County Government in Texas, 1865–1876," *Journal of Southern History* 58 (February 1992): 99–116; Donald G. Nieman, "African Americans and the Meaning of Freedom: Washington County, Texas, as a Case Study, 1865–1886," *Chicago-Kent Law Review* 70:2 (1994): 541–82. Representativeness of Washington County discussed in e-mail message, "Washington County," Donald Nieman to Richard Valelly, July 31, 1996, hard copy in possession of author (message cited with permission of Donald Nieman).

lapse of slavery. Republican officeholders also established outdoor poor relief for black as well as white citizens. Here they innovated in a way that Democrats promptly reversed when they gained office. Rather than require residence at a county poor farm, Washington County Republicans gave monthly payments to the aged and infirm and to widows and orphans requiring help.

It is in discussing the transformation of the local criminal-justice system that Nieman breaks new ground. Between 1870 and 1876, the state district court and the county sheriff selected jurors from the registered-voter list. Rates of African-American jury service were high: About one-third of the jurors who served on 107 petit juries were black, while 40 to 50 percent of grand juries were black. Although the state legislature acted in 1876 to curb black jury service, about a quarter of both petit and grand jurors in Washington County were black until 1884—at which time Democrats violently crushed the local Republican party.

These juries consistently indicted blacks for property crimes at higher rates than for whites, but not at the punitively high rates typical of local justice where there was no African-American jury service. Evidently they did so because black property crime occurred at a higher rate. Also, for the period 1870–4, juries indicted blacks for crimes against the person at higher rates. Rates of conviction and the severity of punishment for black-on-black murder were also higher than for white-on-white murder. Black jurors were apparently determined to stop black-on-black crime; white jurors may have been more sanguine about private violence, and thus pushed for milder punishments of white-on-white murder.

Here Nieman's historiography suggests an intricate insight into the possibilities of local government. Through their determination and success in addressing black crime, black jurors constructed a new moral order in a post-Emancipation South riddled with deep conflicts over how to cope with old and new forms of violence. This may be one of the reasons why court was generally well attended by both black and white citizens. Many whites preferred malign neglect of black-on-black crime. Indeed, the local white press complained about Washington County's success in coping with black-on-black crime, finding it financially burdensome. But having constructed their own churches, schools, and communities in Emancipation's aftermath, African-American leaders and citizens clearly intended to keep those institutions as free from social disorder as they could. The case of Washington County indicates that local government during Reconstruction could be a very special school of democracy indeed.

What about the Second Reconstruction of local Southern government? No study that matches the rich depth of Nieman's is yet available. Still, the evidence so far about local black officeholding yields several conclusions.[33]

First, black officeholding is symbolically quite important. As a contemporary South Carolina official has said, "There's an inherent value in officeholding that goes far beyond picking up the garbage. A race of people who are excluded from public office will always be second class."[34]

Second, black officeholding has often stimulated black voter interest in local government (though less so in rural Deep South counties). It has also unsurprisingly led to conflicts over what black officeholders can and should do, thus heightening political factionalism among black Southern communities.

Third, although racially polarized voting persists, it is worth looking past the statistical indicators to note that fairly large numbers of whites vote for black candidates. Relatively speaking, few do; in absolute terms, however, many do.

Fourth, local services involving municipal construction and road service have become more equally distributed within local jurisdictions. More police and fire protection has been extended to black neighborhoods. But redistributing municipal or county *jobs* to blacks—other than the menial labor to which Jim Crow historically relegated them—has, not surprisingly, been much more difficult and controversial. Finally, local governments have more actively sought state or federal assistance that will benefit both black and white citizens.

On my reading, all of this counts as renewal—a rebrightening of the line between the public and private domains. It is impossible, of course, for local government to hold quite the same attraction for local citizens as it did during Reconstruction, despite the suggestion in survey results that

---

[33] The only two lengthy and systematic studies available are James W. Button, *Blacks and Social Change: Impact of the Civil Rights Movement in Southern Communities* (Princeton: Princeton University Press, 1989) and Lawrence J. Hanks, *The Struggle for Black Political Empowerment in Three Georgia Counties* (Knoxville: University of Tennessee Press, 1987). Out of the fairly well-developed journal literature, I found a recent study of a Deep South county quite worthwhile: Pildes and Donoghue, "Cumulative Voting in the United States" (which ought actually to be titled "Cumulative Voting in Chilton County, Alabama, since 1988"). An overlooked but valuable treatment that manages to make issues and debates in the scholarly literature come alive is "Hands That Picked Cotton: Black Politics in Today's Rural South," a documentary comparing local governmental electioneering and representation in rural black-belt Mississippi and small-town black-belt Louisiana; this 60-minute video, released in 1982, was directed by Alan Bell and Paul Stekler.

[34] Grofman and Davidson, *Quiet Revolution,* 16.

Americans cherish this level of government more than all others. National and state governments now do much more. Also, local voting differs. In the nineteenth century, it occurred in the open, in front of one's peers. One asked for a party ballot in plain sight of a neighbor or a former overseer. Local voting is much less stressful now, but it is also less publicly meaningful—an affair conducted at the end of a workday, in secret and in silence in a booth, somewhere in a school auditorium.

But the disappointment among black voters in the possibilities of local government speaks volumes about how they once prospectively valued—and still implicitly value—local government. White voters and local leaders often seem unhappy about the particulars of voting-rights implementation. But there is scattered survey and anecdotal evidence suggesting overall white support for how the Voting Rights Act has influenced local government. At any rate, the resistance, discomfort, and adjustment of whites to local black political influence are marks of local government's value to whites—otherwise, there would be sheer indifference.[35]

It is far from clear just how the contemporary situation will evolve. Accounts by participants in the post-1965 legal mobilization show that the overall experience was one of relative success for them. The periodization and characterization provided in Table 10.1 underscore this point. On the other hand, there is some evidence that state and local barriers to representation may now be able to survive, or even reemerge, because of the Supreme Court's hostility to race-conscious remedies for vote dilution.[36]

One hopes that such a danger is not realized. Local government can teach the arts of citizenship and government more readily to more people than other levels of government. But it must be public and socially neutral government. The reconstruction of Southern local government restores such necessary features. Given the political instruction provided by openly and publicly taming social frictions, Southern local governments may actually be *better* schools of local democracy than many non-Southern counties.

---

[35] In addition to Pildes and Donoghue, "Cumulative Voting," see Parker, *Black Votes Count*, 202–4 (though Parker finds the evidence less reassuring than others might).

[36] Worry about the future can be found in Jacqueline A. Berrien, "All Politics Are Local: The Extension of *Shaw v. Reno* to Local Election Systems," *Voting Rights Review* (Voting Rights Program of the Southern Regional Council, Summer 1997, 14–17. See also Selwyn Carter, "Justice, Section 5 Targeted: Limits on Race Cost Minority State Seats," *Voting Rights Review*, Summer 1996, 15–20. Some of the context for this worry can be explored in Saul Brenner and Harold J. Spaeth, *Stare Indecisis: The Alteration of Precedent on the Supreme Court, 1946–1992* (Cambridge: Cambridge University Press, 1995).

IV: A DEMOCRATIC AUDIT

This chapter has closely considered what would seem to be an open-and-shut view of the Voting Rights Act, namely, that it is a powerful (perhaps *too*-powerful) engine of delocalization. This view has found support among the Supreme Court's majority in voting-rights cases. If one were to imagine what might be called an audit of the Voting Rights Act's politics, the regulatory-mischief view would advise entry of such debits as private government, subsequent misunderstanding of the democratic process, and substantial federalism costs.

Yet is it clear that those items must be placed in the debit column? The major parties, as well as groups, quietly implement the Fifteenth Amendment. Also, the voting-rights policy domain is hardly shielded from public scrutiny and discussion. In fact, it is in part an arena of democratic struggle.

Through such struggle there has been a renewal of Southern local government. In this respect, the Voting Rights Act opts for *both* nationalism and localism. Local governments have to be moderately neutral and decently unbiased for them to enrich American citizenship. For more than half a century, Southern local governments did not serve the purpose; only in the last decade, really, have they again begun to do so. The truth is that the Voting Rights Act is a windfall for Southern local government. Enter into the credit column, then, the rejuvenation of a kind of local citizenship and officeholding that existed all too briefly during Reconstruction and that betokens the promise of American democratic life.

11

The people's court?

Federal judges and criminal justice

WILLIAM D. HAGEDORN AND JOHN J. DIIULIO, JR.

I: OVERVIEW

Before the late 1960s, crime was rarely on the federal agenda. Since 1968, however, Congress has passed dozens of major anticrime bills. From 1980 to 1994, it passed a new anticrime package every two years. And in various phases the federal "war on drugs" has involved an unprecedented use of the U.S. military in law enforcement.

Although Washington has become a partner of the states' in the war on crime, it is still very much a junior partner.[1] The federal role in setting, administering, and funding crime policy remains relatively minor. State and local governments spend about nine dollars on crime control for every dollar spent by the federal government. There are roughly fourteen times as many inmates in state prisons and local jails as there are in federal ones. The vast majority of law-enforcement officers are local police officers. Even the Washington, D.C., police force is under the control of a mayor, not Congress or the president. None of this is likely to change anytime soon.

As Martha Derthick has observed, how one judges federalism may well depend on where one stands in the fight "begun at the Founding and even before, about whether there should be one political community or many, and how much freedom the many communities should have to define and govern themselves."[2] Derthick is surely right. In this chapter, however, we are dealing with a major governance question—how govern-

---

[1] John J. DiIulio, Jr., Steven K. Smith, and Aaron Saiger, "The Federal Role in Crime Control," in *Crime*, ed. James Q. Wilson and Joan R. Petersilia (San Francisco: Institute for Contemporary Studies Press, 1995), chap. 19.

[2] Martha Derthick, "Up-to-Date in Kansas City: Reflections on American Federalism," *PS: Political Science and Politics* (December 1992): 675.

ment ought to handle predatory street criminals—on which the people of America's federal, state, and local communities have long been united. There is not a single American neighborhood, city, or state where most people favor policies that make it hard to detect, arrest, prosecute, convict, and incarcerate known violent and repeat street criminals. There are, to be sure, many areas of American government where one can find a large gap between persistent and widespread majority preferences and existing public policies,[3] but we argue that the size and duration of the gap with respect to criminal justice are American government's opinion-policy Grand Canyon.

Likewise, Derthick has keenly observed that much of "intergovernmental communication consists of federal courts admonishing various state and local officeholders about schools, prisons, mental-health institutions, or the conduct of police forces in enforcing criminal law."[4] In this chapter, however, we are not talking about federal judges who have made "national policy where the national legislature could not."[5] Rather, we are talking about federal judges who have diluted or derailed democratically enacted federal, state, and local anticrime policies.

There are two main areas of criminal justice in which over the last three decades federal judges have revolutionized federal-state relations and limited the ability of local communities to use government agencies as they wish in combating crime: policing and corrections.

Community policing with national standards?

In his superb single-volume history of crime and punishment in America, Lawrence M. Friedman observes that there is "an enormous literature, of praise and invective alike," about the constitutional propriety and practical consequences of post-1960 federal court decisions governing how police handle suspected criminals.[6]

For example, on June 13, 1966, by a 5–4 decision, the United States Supreme Court released its now-famous *Miranda v. Arizona* decision. The Court held that even voluntary, uncoerced confessions by a suspect in police custody would no longer be admissible as evidence, unless the po-

---

[3] "Forum: Public Opinion, Institutions, and Policy Making," *PS: Political Science & Politics* (March 1994): 538.
[4] Derthick, "Up-to-Date in Kansas City," 673.
[5] Ibid., 674.
[6] Lawrence M. Friedman, *Crime and Punishment in American History* (New York: Basic Books, 1993), 303.

lice first warned the suspect that (1) he had the right to remain silent, (2) anything he said might be used against him in court, (3) he had an immediate right to a lawyer, and (4) he could get a free lawyer if he could not afford one. Before any questioning could proceed, the suspect had expressly to waive those rights. As interpreted in subsequent federal court decisions, *Miranda* also banned any comments between police officers made in the suspect's presence that might somehow elicit an incriminating response—for example, oblique appeals to the suspect's decency, honor, or guilty conscience.

Debate continues to rage over whether *Miranda* and related federal court decisions have meant tens of thousands or millions of criminal convictions lost on legal technicalities, and whether these decisions have done more to professionalize police departments or to bureaucratize them in ways that "handcuff" street-level patrol officers and alienate them from the communities they serve.

We are in no position to settle that debate here. But in a recent essay, Robert James Bidinotto aptly reminds us that *Miranda* itself led immediately to the release of four veteran criminals whose conviction histories included robbery, rape, kidnapping, and forgery, and that it was not until 1984 that a reconstituted Supreme Court exempted police from having to "mirandize" suspects in the midst of street riots or other situations that pose "an immediate danger to the public."[7] Likewise, in a recent book, *Guilty!*, Judge Harold Rothwax calls for the repeal of *Miranda*.[8]

Also, we believe that one generally overlooked consequence of the post-*Miranda*, court-induced nationalization of policing procedures has been to hamstring the community-policing movement. Basically, community policing means that police patrol on foot as well as in cars, listen to community residents, and work with community leaders and groups. Community policing requires that police exercise greater on-the-job discretion and that they engage in highly contextualized, particularized situational problem-solving in accordance with neighborhood norms. At the same time, however, police must adhere strictly to a judicially crafted, nationally uniform codification of procedures governing virtually every phase of police-citizen and police-suspect relations.

Unavoidably, locally centered, community-oriented policing practices come into tension with nationally focused, judicially mandated policing

[7] Robert James Bidinotto, "Subverting Justice," in Bidinotto, *Criminal Justice? The Legal System vs. Individual Responsibility* (Irvington-on-Hudson, N.Y.: Foundation for Economic Education, 1994), 67–8.
[8] Harold J. Rothwax, *Guilty!: The Collapse of Criminal Justice* (New York: Random House, 1996).

standards. It is all well and good to suppose that police who engage in locally sanctioned exercises of "curbstone justice" or "aggressive tactics"
against neighborhood troublemakers, or whose mission is proactive,
community-oriented problem-solving rather than reactive, 911-style
policing, can somehow do so without running afoul of nationally prohibited (even if locally popular or demanded) treatment of suspected street
criminals and known street gangsters. But it is hard in academic theory
and virtually impossible in everyday practice to square the legal, constitutional, and operational circle of policing discretion in this way. Among
other reasons, this is why it has turned out to be so hard to get community policing out of the executive-training seminar rooms and into street-
level practice in big-city police departments, and why meaningful, non-
self-contradictory performance criteria and personnel protocols (new job
descriptions, promotion standards) for community-policing programs
have proven so difficult to devise and implement.[9]

In his chapter in this volume, James Q. Wilson refers to "the old distinction between locals and cosmopolitans." In effect, community policing is a noble and necessary effort to transcend this distinction—noble
and necessary but paradoxical and fraught with operational complexi-
ties. In the line-up of reasons for the stunted development of community
policing in America, *Miranda* and other federal court rulings that have
placed crucial decisions about police conduct beyond the reach of community norms and neighborhood preferences must be viewed as prime
suspects.

Federal judges: Sovereigns of the cellblocks?

By comparison with the vast literature on how federal courts have transformed American policing, there is little empirical research or running
commentary on the role of federal judges in determining who goes to
prison or jail, for how long, and under what conditions.[10]

---

[9] Geoffrey P. Alpert and Mark H. Moore, "Measuring Police Performance in the New Paradigm of Policing," in John J. DiIulio, Jr., et al., *Performance Measures for the Criminal
Justice System* (U.S. Bureau of Justice Statistics, 1993), 109–40; David H. Bayley, "Community Policing: A Report from the Devil's Advocate," in *Community Policing: Rhetoric
or Reality?* ed. Jack Greene and Stephen Mastrofski (New York: Praeger, 1988); David
H. Bayley, *Police for the Future* (New York: Oxford University Press, 1994); Mark H.
Moore, "Policing: Deregulating or Redefining Accountability?" in *Deregulating the Public Service: Can Government Be Improved?* ed. John J. DiIulio, Jr. (Washington, D.C.:
Brookings Institution Press, 1994), chap. 10.
[10] Still the only general treatment is *Courts, Corrections, and the Constitution: The Impact
of Judicial Intervention on Prisons and Jails*, ed. John J. DiIulio, Jr. (New York: Oxford
University Press, 1990).

Our primary purpose in this chapter, therefore, is to illustrate how it is that federal judges have come to dominate penal administration in dozens of states and localities, and to document the consequences of this nationalization of criminal justice in terms of prison conditions, financial costs, and public safety.

The crux of our argument is that the court-led nationalization of crime policy has often resulted in prison violence, skyrocketing budgets, and increased violent crime on the streets. As we see it, the facts and figures about crime and punishment in America mirror decades-old popular concerns about revolving-door justice.

We are not, however, arguing against all federal court action to uphold prisoners' constitutional rights, nor against expanding the federal role in crime control, nor in favor of block-granting federal anticrime dollars. Nor, for that matter, are we arguing against "Washington" or "big government," or in favor of documents like the Contract with America.[11]

We gladly leave to others the task of offering broad philosophical statements, historical interpretations, and empirical generalizations about American-style federalism, past, present, and future. Like most Americans, when it comes to crime and other pressing public concerns, we are acutely wary of what James Madison termed "theoretic politicians." For if we have learned anything about this country's federal system as it has operated and evolved over the last two centuries, it should be that the system secures the promises of the Constitution's preamble under certain hard-to-specify conditions better than it does under others, and that neither a general bias in favor of "devolution" and "local community" on the one hand or "centralization" and "national community" on the other fits either the predominantly pragmatic political temperament of our people or the often-wild exigencies of our domestic politics.

We begin with a review of public opinion on crime and the facts and figures behind the public's crime fears. We then discuss the evolution of federal-court interventions in state and local corrections, and spotlight the case of Philadelphia's jail system.

II: THE THIRTY-YEAR "BACKLASH"

Since the mid-1960s, a solid majority of Americans have demanded that government pursue policies that result in the detection, arrest, prosecu-

---

[11] John J. DiIulio, Jr., and Donald F. Kettl, *Fine Print: Devolution, the Contract with America, and the Administrative Realities of American Federalism* (Washington, D.C.: Brookings Institution Press, 1995).

tion, conviction, and punishment of violent and repeat criminals. For three decades, most Americans have demanded that their federal, state, and local leaders—both elected and appointed—end policies and practices that prematurely release persons who often continue to assault, rape, rob, burglarize, deal drugs, and murder. In a comprehensive review of post-1965 survey research and polling data on crime and how government should respond to it, William G. Mayer concluded:

> The conventional wisdom on this issue is that . . . public opinion became increasingly outraged by horror stories about brutal criminals set free on legal technicalities or through the ministrations of misguided social workers. And, in this case, the conventional wisdom turns out to be quite accurate. From the mid-1960's to the late 1980's, there is clear, strong evidence that American public opinion became substantially more conservative in its assessment of how to deal with crime.[12]

In his aforementioned history, Friedman writes that beginning in the 1960s a "wave of conservatism swept the country. It had its roots, perhaps, in the great fear and hatred of crime. . . . Politically speaking, crime and punishment were suddenly like an exposed nerve." Echoing the interpretations of most criminologists, he terms this rightward shift in public opinion on crime and punishment "The Age of Backlash."[13]

But if "backlash" means a sudden or violent backward whipping motion, then the metaphor fails. For rather than happening in a political instant, the get-tough march in public sentiment on crime and punishment has been steadily gathering momentum for thirty years. And rather than all the anticrime energy being concentrated in one part of the body politic, mass sentiment in favor of policies that take violent and repeat criminals off the street has manifested itself all across the country and among Americans of every race, region, and demographic description.

For example, although whites and blacks remain deeply divided over the question of whether the justice system is riddled with arrest and sentencing disparities born of racial discrimination,[14] majorities of both blacks and whites favor the death penalty for persons convicted of first-degree murder; doubt that most violent criminals can be rehabilitated; demand that juveniles who commit violent crimes be treated the same as adults; oppose the legalization of marijuana, cocaine, and other illicit drugs; believe there is too much graphic violence on television and that it

---

[12] William G. Mayer, *The Changing American Mind* (Ann Arbor: University of Michigan Press, 1992), 19–20.

[13] Friedman, *Crime and Punishment*, 305.

[14] John J. DiIulio, Jr., "White Lies about Black Crime," *The Public Interest* (Winter 1995): 30–44.

contributes to crime; strongly favor making parole more difficult; and support paying more taxes if necessary to build more prisons and put more cops on the beat.[15]

Especially on corrections policy, a more apt description of contemporary public opinion might be "The Age of the Rolling Boil." No major state or local prison-bond initiative has failed since 1970, and every voter-initiated effort to increase criminal penalties has succeeded by a wide margin. The 1994 California "three strikes and you're out" referendum is a recent and typical case in point.

The California proposal mandated prison terms of twenty-five years to life for offenders convicted of any three felony crimes. Every major news organization in the state editorialized against the measure. Prominent California-based criminologists rebuked it in the strongest terms. Top officials of the University of California system warned that "three strikes" could cripple state funding for higher education. The normally nonpartisan RAND Corporation weighed in against the referendum with a much-publicized study. RAND estimated that the law would spare Californians 340,000 serious crimes a year—crimes that the offenders would commit were they not incarcerated for their third felony conviction—but at a prohibitive cost of several billion dollars a year.[16] Even the state's leading associations of prosecutors opposed the plan, arguing instead for a more narrowly tailored measure that targeted criminals who were convicted of any three violent crimes. But voters—by nearly a 4 to 1 margin—made the proposal Section 667 of the California penal code.

Crime fears: Rational or reactionary?

As Wendy Kaminer has correctly noted, all the data indicate that "a majority of Americans favor building more prisons, despite their costs, and believe that sentencing practices are excessively lenient."[17] But Kaminer, like most commentators, insists that the crime fears that have driven voters to support the three-strikes referendum and countless other get-tough measures are rooted in irrational beliefs and a grossly exaggerated sense of how lax sentencing policies jeopardize public safety. In the words of

---

[15] U.S. Bureau of Justice Statistics (BJS), *Sourcebook of Criminal Justice Statistics, 1993* (BJS, 1993), section 2.

[16] Peter Greenwood et al., *Three Strikes and You're Out: Estimated Benefits and Costs of California's New Mandatory-Sentencing Law* (Santa Monica, Calif.: RAND, 1994).

[17] Wendy Kaminer, *It's All the Rage: Crime and Culture* (Reading, Mass.: Addison-Wesley, 1995), 179.

David Anderson, author of *Crime and the Politics of Hysteria,* "Politicians are responding to the public, which is looking to impose mild forms of torture."[18]

The charge that the public's fear of crime and its concern about revolving-door justice are more reactionary than rational is hard to square with the best available empirical data on crime and punishment in America today.

The U.S. Bureau of Justice Statistics (BJS) reports that Americans aged 12 or older experienced a total of 43.6 million crimes in 1993, including 11 million violent crimes (25 percent) and more than 32 million property crimes (75 percent).[19] There is some evidence that crime rates fell between 1992 and 1995.[20] But the BJS data and all other crime statistics make plain that Americans now suffer a great deal of crime, both in absolute terms and relative to best estimates of crime rates in the 1950s, 1960s, and 1970s.

In just about every major public-opinion survey since January 1994, crime has ranked ahead of unemployment, the deficit, environmental pollution, and other issues as the main problem facing the country today. Although nearly all Americans now feel more threatened by crime than they did in the past, urban Americans feel more threatened than suburban or rural Americans, urban blacks feel more threatened than urban whites, and central-city blacks feel more threatened than other urban blacks.[21] For example, in 1991 about 7.4 percent of all households, 16.5 percent of black households, and 22.7 percent of central-city black households identified crime as a major neighborhood problem. Between 1985 and 1991, the fraction of rural households that identified crime as a major neighborhood problem remained fairly stable, rising from 1.4 percent to 1.9 percent. But the fraction of black central-city households that did so nearly doubled, from 11.8 percent to 22.7 percent.

Likewise, a number of surveys, including one conducted by the Black Community Crusade for Children, have found that black urban children—who are far more likely than black urban adults to be murdered or victimized by many types of violent crime—ranked their top five present life concerns as follows: kids carrying guns (70 percent); violence in school (68 percent); living in a dangerous neighborhood (64 percent); in-

---

[18] Anderson, as quoted in Richard Lacayo, "The Real Hard Cell," *Time* (September 4, 1995): 31.
[19] U.S. BJS, *Criminal Victimization 1993* (BJS, May 1995).
[20] John J. DiIulio, Jr., "Time Heals," *Policy Review* (Fall 1995): 12–16.
[21] U.S. BJS, *Crime and Neighborhoods* (June 1994).

volvement with gangs (63 percent); and involvement with people who cause trouble (63 percent).[22]

Such survey findings mirror the objective risks of criminal victimization faced by Americans of given residential and racial characteristics. All of this seems perfectly rational.

Who really goes to prison?

The same is true of public perceptions of revolving-door justice. As Table 11.1 indicates, in 1994 some 5.1 million persons were under correctional supervision in America. But more than 3.65 million of them (72 percent) were *not* incarcerated. While we have been overcrowding the prisons, we have been overloading the streets. Between 1980 and 1994, the nation's state and federal prison population increased by 213 percent, but so did its parole population. Over the same period, the country's local jail population increased by 165 percent, but so did its probation population.

In 1992, more than 10 million violent crimes were committed in America. But just 641,000 of these crimes led to arrests, barely 165,000 to convictions (more than 90 percent of which were plea-bargained down from the original charges), and only 100,000 or so to prison sentences— which, on average, would end before the convict had served even half his time behind bars.[23] As Table 11.2 reveals, 47 percent of violent felons with one conviction offense, 31 percent with two offenses, and 23 percent with three offenses were not even sentenced to prison. And as Table 11.3 shows, released violent offenders in 1992 served 48 percent of their sentence behind bars (both jail credit and prison time). Even murderers spent, on average, just 5.9 years behind bars on sentences of 12.4 years.

Indeed, recent research has found that about three times as many convicted violent offenders are residing in the community as are incarcerated in prison.[24] BJS data show that 94 percent of state prisoners have committed one or more violent crimes or have served a sentence before being incarcerated or put on probation.[25] The two largest state-prisoner studies ever conducted found that state prisoners commit a median of 12 non-

[22] Black Community Crusade for Children, *Overwhelming Majority of Black Adults Fear for Children's Safety and Future* (Children's Defense Fund, May 26, 1994).

[23] BJS, *Criminal Victimization 1993* (reporting data for 1992); *Sourcebook, 1993,* 430; *Felony Sentences in State Courts, 1992* (BJS, January 1995), 4.

[24] Joan R. Petersilia, "A Crime Control Rationale for Reinvesting in Community Corrections," paper prepared for the American Society of Criminology Task Force on Community Corrections, April 1995, 8.

[25] BJS, *Survey of State Prison Inmates, 1991* (BJS, March 1993), 11.

Table 11.1. *Number of adults on probation, in jail or prison, or on parole, 1980 to 1994*

Year	Total estimated correctional population	Probation	Jail[a]	Prison	Parole
1980[b]	1,840,400	1,118,097	182,288	319,598	220,438
1985	3,011,500	1,968,712	254,986	487,583	300,203
1990	4,348,000	2,670,234	403,019	743,382	531,407
1991	4,536,200	2,729,322	424,129	792,536	590,198
1992	4,763,200	2,811,611	441,781	851,205	658,601
1993	4,943,900	2,903,160	455,500	909,186	678,100
1994	5,135,900	2,962,166	483,717	999,808	690,159
Percent change,					
1993–94	4%	2%	6%	10%	2%
1980–94	179%	165%	165%	213%	213%

Note: Some states update their counts every year. Counts for probation, prisons, and parole population are for December 31 each year. Jail-population counts are for June 30 each year. Prisoner counts are for those in custody only. Because some persons may have multiple statuses, the sum of the number of persons incarcerated or under community supervision overestimates the total correctional population.
[a]Includes convicted and unconvicted adult inmates.
[b]Jail count is estimated.
Source: U.S. Bureau of Justice Statistics, 1995.

drug felonies in the year before their imprisonment.[26] A National Bureau of Economic Research study concluded that "incarcerating one additional prisoner reduces the number of crimes by approximately 13 per year."[27] And a recent article in the *Journal of Quantitative Criminology* estimated that recently convicted criminals commit between 17 and 21 crimes a year when free.[28]

Still, some insist that prisons are teeming with petty, nonviolent, first-time offenders. Such claims are demonstrably false.[29] An analysis by the California Department of Corrections found that 88.5 percent of the 16,520 "nonviolent" offenders admitted to the prison system in 1992 were in fact repeat offenders, who averaged 4.7 prior convictions.[30]

[26] John J. DiIulio, Jr., and Anne Morrison Piehl, "Does Prison Pay?" *The Brookings Review* (Fall 1991): 28–35; Piehl and DiIulio, "Does Prison Pay? Revisited," *The Brookings Review* (Winter 1995): 21–5.
[27] Steven D. Levitt, *The Effect of Prison Population Size on Crime Rates* (Washington, D.C.: National Bureau of Economic Research, February 1995), 25.
[28] Thomas B. Marvell and Carlisle E. Moody, Jr., "Prison Population Growth and Crime Reduction," *Journal of Quantitative Criminology* 10, no. 2 (1994): 136.
[29] Charles H. Logan, "Who Really Goes to Prison?" *Federal Prisons Journal* (Summer 1991): 57–9.
[30] Data from Data Analysis Unit, California Department of Corrections, March 1, 1994.

Table 11.2. *Convicted violent felons not sentenced to prison, by number of conviction offenses, 1992*

| Most serious conviction offense | Percent of convicted felons *not* sentenced to prison for 1, 2, or 3 or more felony conviction offenses | | |
	One	Two	Three or more
All Violent Offenses	47%	31%	23%
Murder	9%	5%	3%
Rape	39%	23%	20%
Robbery	30%	21%	14%
Aggravated assault	61%	45%	38%
Other violent[a]	65%	51%	36%

Note: This chart reflects prison nonsentencing rates for felons based on their most serious offenses. For example, if a felon is convicted for murder, larceny, and drug possession, and not sentenced to prison, he would be represented in this chart under murder (the most serious offense) with three or more offenses.
[a]Includes offenses such as negligent manslaughter, sexual assault, and kidnapping.
Source: Bureau of Justice Statistics, *Felony Sentences in State Courts,* January 1995, 6.

Nationally, about one-third of all violent crimes are committed by persons who are under some form of community-based "supervision" at the moment they commit the crime. For example, over a 58-month period between January 1987 and October 1991, Florida parolees alone committed more than 15,000 violent and property crimes, including 346 murders.[31] Likewise, between 1990 and 1993, Virginia convicted 1,411 persons of murder; 474 (33.5 percent) of them were on probation, parole, or some other type of community release at the time they killed.[32]

Given the breadth and depth of the anticrime public consensus—not to mention the facts and figures that support it—why have public policies not drifted into conformity with public opinion on crime and punishment? Federal judges are a big part of the answer, we believe; so is the rise of federal-court intervention in the administration and management of state prisons and local jails. While legislative officials have attempted to respond to the reasonable fears of the public, federal judges have essen-

[31] Data from Statistical Analysis Center, Florida Department of Corrections, July 1993.
[32] Data from an ongoing Brookings Institution study of the legal status of convicted murderers, June 1995.

Table 11.3. *"Released violent offenders in 1992 served 48 percent of their sentence."*

Type of offense	Average sentence	Average time served[a]	Percent of sentence served
All violent	89 months	43 months	48%
Homicide	149	71	48
Rape	117	65	56
Kidnapping	104	52	50
Robbery	95	44	46
Sexual assault	72	35	49
Assault	61	29	48
Other	60	28	47

[a]Includes jail credit and prison time.
Source: Bureau of Justice Statistics, *Prison Sentences and Time Served for Violence,* April 1995, 1.

tially assumed control of making crime policy by taking a more active role in the adjudication of inmate litigation and in the resulting remedial measures. In our view, their policy choices have contributed to the outcomes that currently drive public opinion on criminal justice.

III: THE RISE OF JUDICIAL INTERVENTION IN PRISONS AND JAILS

Until the 1960s, in matters concerning prisons, courts traditionally practiced a "hands-off doctrine" of judicial nonintervention. This doctrine essentially held that inmates were "slaves of the state,"[33] and that courts lacked the jurisdiction to interfere in the practices of state and local correctional institutions. The conclusion of the U.S. Court of Appeals for the Tenth Circuit in 1954—that "courts are without power to supervise prison administration or to interfere with the ordinary rules or regulations"—was generally accepted by judges; it represents the majority of mid-twentieth-century decisions involving prison litigation.[34] The hands-off doctrine was based upon the idea that it was detrimental to the basic objectives of incarceration for courts to monitor or moderate the practices of prison officials. During this period, courts conceded that they

[33] *Ruffin v. Commonwealth*, 62 Va. (21 Gratt.) 790, 796 (1871).
[34] *Banning v. Looney*, 213 F.2d 771 (10th Cir.), *cert. denied*, 348 U.S. 859 (1954).

lacked both the authority and the capacity to make proper judgments about the operation of correctional institutions.

In the mid-1950s, the Warren Court initiated a profound shift in the role of the judicial branch. The Court's activism heightened the ability of judges to determine public policy and demonstrated an explicit willingness to become an "engine of social reform."[35] The most significant origin of this shift in judicial emphasis came via what Abram Chayes has referred to as "public law litigation"—cases in which the judge is the dominant figure in organizing and guiding the litigation and its resulting remedies. As Chayes points out, the judge in these cases develops and manages the relief that is determined to be necessary, thus "requiring the judge's continuing involvement in administration and implementation."[36] The centerpiece of the litigation is the judicial decree that "provides for a complex, ongoing regime of performance [and] it deepens, rather than terminates, the court's involvement with the dispute."[37]

The earliest instance of public-law litigation came in the form of the school-desegregation cases of the 1950s, beginning with *Brown v. Board of Education* in 1954.[38] These cases established the judicial power to intervene in the management and operation of state and local institutions. They also firmly entrenched the judiciary in the administration of social services through the imposition of judicial decrees.

As the boundaries of judicial activity expanded, many social groups turned to the courts as a means of winning their political struggles. The courts thus became the focal point of the social activism of the 1960s and 1970s as those groups sought to have their perceived rights constitutionally protected. In addition to increasing their involvement in social policy, the courts also expanded the concept of "civil rights" and began to delve into issues never before tested in litigation. The rise of judicial intervention in the administration of state prisons and local jails coincided with each of these developments as judges increasingly saw inmates as a social group with rights in need of constitutional protection. Judges began to issue and enforce orders that fundamentally changed the operation of prisons in America.

Beginning with the general activism of the Warren Court, the ability of prisoners to contest the conditions of their confinement was broadly ex-

---

[35] Jim Thomas, *Prisoner Litigation: The Paradox of the Jailhouse Lawyer* (Totowa, N.J.: Rowman & Littlefield, 1988), 85.
[36] Abram Chayes, "The Role of the Judge in Public Law Litigation," *Harvard Law Review* 89 (1976): 1281, 1284.
[37] Ibid., 1298.   [38] 347 U.S. 483 (1954).

panded and the hands-off doctrine was largely abandoned. Two decisions were especially influential in opening the floodgates of prisoner litigation. First, in *Jones v. Cunningham,* the Supreme Court held that state-prison inmates could employ a writ of habeas corpus to challenge not only the legality of their imprisonment but also the conditions of their confinement.[39] One year later, in *Cooper v. Pate,* the Court expanded prisoner access to courts and affirmed the principle of judicial review of inmate rights and prison policy.[40] The Court ruled that prisoners had a right to sue in federal court under Section 1983 of the Federal Civil Rights Act,[41] which provides for federal-court review in situations where the state is accused of infringing upon individual rights.[42]

In the years following the demise of the hands-off doctrine, most courts secured the rights of inmates through a piecemeal approach of guaranteeing specific rights. Numerous cases throughout the late 1960s guaranteed rights to inmates in areas of racial discrimination, corporal punishment, religion, and access to courts. Although this protection by the courts of specific rights was important in establishing the basic rights of prisoners, the piecemeal approach was widely seen as inadequate to solve the more basic problems of unsanitary and overcrowded institutions where inmates were denied adequate food, medical attention, and provisions for personal hygiene and were subject to attacks from other inmates and guards.[43] Many argued that active judicial intervention in the administration of prisons was the only means of securing adequate conditions there, because other branches of government were unwilling to devote the resources necessary to improve such conditions.

In response to perceived foot-dragging by state officials on prison reform, a number of federal courts in the early 1970s adopted the "totality of conditions" approach to prison litigation. In these cases, courts held that even if specific conditions in prisons may not, by themselves, be constitutional violations, the *overall* conditions of incarceration may be so poor that mere confinement in the institution constitutes cruel and unusual punishment.[44] In three separate cases decided in the early 1970s, federal courts utilized the totality-of-conditions approach to declare un-

---

[39] 371 U.S. 236 (1963).   [40] 378 U.S. 546 (1964).
[41] 42 U.S.C. § 1983.
[42] The jurisdiction to hear § 1983 cases is vested in the federal courts under 42 U.S.C. § 1343.
[43] Comment, "Confronting the Conditions of Confinement: An Expanded Role for Courts in Prison Reform," *Harvard Civil Rights–Civil Liberties Law Review* 12 (1977): 367, 369.
[44] "Confronting the Conditions of Confinement," 369.

constitutional the entire state correctional systems of Arkansas, Mississippi, and Oklahoma.[45]

Institutions in which the totality of conditions have been ruled unconstitutional have also been the subject of court-ordered decrees mandating reforms of the overall living conditions and the services provided. Although some courts specified which conditions needed to be remedied and gave prison officials time to draw up plans for alleviating these problems, others independently set forth detailed standards and ordered that they be met immediately.[46]

A frequently cited example of an early intrusive judicial decree is the one issued by Federal District Judge Frank Johnson in *Pugh v. Locke* in 1976, in which he set out an eleven-point program entitled "Minimum Constitutional Standards for Inmates of Alabama Penal System," offering detailed and comprehensive orders governing the operations of Alabama prisons. Judge Johnson's orders required extensive changes in virtually every aspect of prison operation, including maximum prison population, cell sizes, staff-to-inmate ratios, meal preparation, the amount and quality of medical care available to inmates, and the rules governing inmate correspondence and visitation. Judge Johnson's decree also required that educational, vocational, and recreational opportunities be provided for inmates.[47] Although Judge Johnson's order represented a significant departure from the traditional role of courts in prison reform, his decision merely reflected the trend that had been developing within the judicial branch since the mid-1950s. His comprehensive court order, modeled after previous decrees ordered in school-desegregation cases and in the reform of mental-health institutions,[48] became the standard for federal-court involvement in prisons for years to come.

In 1970, not a single prison system was operating under the sweeping court orders that are common today. By 1990, however, 323 state correctional facilities operated under conditions-of-confinement court orders or consent decrees (see Table 11.4). As of June 30, 1993, 39 state corrections systems had correctional departments or institutions under court order; in thirteen states, entire adult correctional departments were under court order.[49]

---

[45] *Holt v. Sarver,* 309 F.Supp. 362 (E.D. Ark. 1970); *Gates v. Collier,* 349 F.Supp. 881 (N.D. Miss. 1972); *Battle v. Anderson,* 376 F.Supp. 402 (E.D. Okla. 1974).
[46] "Confronting the Conditions of Confinement," 375.
[47] *Pugh v. Locke,* 406 F.Supp. 318 (M.D. Ala. 1976).
[48] See, for example, *Brown v. Board of Education,* 347 U.S. at 483; *Wyatt v. Stickney,* 325 F.Supp. 781 (M.D. Ala. 1971).
[49] *Sourcebook, 1993,* 115.

The prison-crowding "crisis"

The arguments driving court intervention in prison administration have been largely empirical rather than jurisprudential, and have focused on the perceived negative effects brought about by increasing prison populations. Although many aspects of correctional confinement have been the subject of lawsuits brought by inmates, the conventional judicial wisdom is that "overcrowding" is the primary cause of constitutional violations in prisons and jails. Proponents of judicial involvement have blamed high prison densities for producing increased stress and violence and for undermining administrative efforts to maintain order and provide essential services.[50] Indeed, as of June 29, 1990, of the 323 state correctional facilities under court order or consent decree for specific conditions of confinement, 186 were cited for conditions of overcrowding and 264 were ordered to limit their inmate populations (see Table 11.4). Moreover, many of these institutions have been ordered to conduct emergency releases of inmates to ease the perceived crowding.

It remains unclear, however, whether the empirical evidence actually supports the contention that crowding has caused Eighth Amendment violations. Recent studies have failed to find a significant correlation between increasing population densities in prisons and the violence, inmate health problems, or other tangible or psychological harms assumed to accompany them. In a recent review of the relevant empirical literature, Gerald Gaes, chief researcher for the Federal Bureau of Prisons, found that despite "the prevailing sentiments about the harmful effects of crowding, there is little consistent evidence supporting the contention that short- or long-term impairment of inmates is attributable to prison density"—and that is stating the case against the conventional judicial wisdom on "crowding" mildly.[51] Indeed, the court orders themselves may be partially responsible for the crowding "crisis," as judges have often crafted definitions of crowding that seemingly have little to do with the realities of how prisons operate.[52]

Since the first filing of prison-overcrowding litigation in 1965, overcrowding litigation has been waged in forty-seven states. The American Civil Liberties Union (ACLU), which spearheaded this litigation drive, boasts that the inmate plaintiffs have won total or near-total victories in

---

[50] Jeff Bleich, "The Politics of Prison Crowding," *California Law Review* 77 (1989): 1133.
[51] Gerald G. Gaes, "Prison Crowding Research Reexamined," *Prison Journal* 74 (September 1994): 329–63.
[52] Bleich, "Prison Crowding," 1127.

more than 90 percent of all cases.[53] As a recent article in the leading magazine for corrections professionals proclaimed, the courts' power to intervene in prison and jail cases "extends to doing whatever is necessary," including "ordering inmates released or facilities closed."[54] The article was aptly entitled "A History of Recent Corrections Is a History of Court Involvement."

In reaction to this trend, the Supreme Court has frequently implored lower federal courts to restrain themselves with respect to conditions-of-confinement cases. To cite just a few key decisions, in *Bell v. Wolfish*,[55] the court declared that double celling did not violate due process. In *Rhodes v. Chapman*,[56] the Court held that double celling was not cruel and unusual punishment. In *Wilson v. Seiter*,[57] the Court ruled that constitutional violations had to be based on specific conditions rather than "totality." And in *Rufo v. Inmates of Suffolk County Jail*,[58] the Court endorsed flexible standards for modifying consent decrees in light of changed circumstances. Indeed, in *Chapman*, the Court acknowledged the problems inherent in judicial intervention in prisons and jails. The Court held that the problems faced by prisons are "within the province of the legislative and executive branches of government," and that "courts are ill equipped to deal with the increasingly urgent problems of prison administration and reform."[59]

Although some scholars argue that these Supreme Court decisions signified the beginning of a "new hands-off doctrine,"[60] the actual trend in judicial intervention in correctional institutions in the 1980s refutes this contention. In the years following *Wolfish* and *Chapman*, the rate at which lower federal courts sided with inmates filing complaints did not decrease, as many courts essentially disregarded the admonitions of the Supreme Court. Research by Jack Call in 1988 indicated that in prison- and jail-overcrowding cases, during the eight years since *Wolfish*, lower federal courts issued rulings in favor of inmates in 73.8 percent of the

---

[53] Edward Koren, "Status Report: State Prisons and the Courts," *National Prison Project Journal* (1993): 3–11.

[54] William C. Collins, "A History of Recent Corrections Is a History of Court Involvement," *Corrections Today* (August 1995): 150.

[55] 441 U.S. 520 (1979).   [56] 452 U.S. 337 (1981).

[57] 111 U.S. 2321 (1991).   [58] 112 U.S. 748 (1992).

[59] *Rhodes v. Chapman*, 452 U.S. at 351 (quoting *Procunier v. Martinez*, 416 U.S. 396 [1974]).

[60] Ira P. Robbins, "The Cry of Wolfish in the Federal Courts: The Future of Judicial Intervention in Prison Administration," *The Journal of Criminal Law and Criminology* 71, no. 3 (1980): 219.

cases.[61] Call discovered that in more than half of these cases, courts blindly accepted the plaintiffs' arguments that overcrowding created harmful effects, rather than actually examining the consequences. In 35 of 65 cases, Call noted, the courts required little or no evidence that crowding had harmful effects on the inmates.[62]

It is universally accepted that court orders and consent decrees have been significant and far-reaching. Few studies, however, have examined their actual impact on correctional systems, on inmates, and on our criminal-justice system generally. The city of Philadelphia's enduring struggle with two consent decrees, imposed and enforced by a federal district judge, illustrates some of the negative institutional, financial, and public-safety effects of federal district-court intervention in state prisons and local jails.

IV: THE PHILADELPHIA STORY

Even if we regained control of our system tomorrow [from the court], we would feel the effects of this for a long time because we've had almost a generation of criminals who have been told that there are certain freebie crimes and that the system is powerless to do anything about it.[63]

—Sarah Vandenbraak
Chief, Civil Litigation, Philadelphia District Attorney's office

Philadelphia's jail system is governed by consent decrees. But as city Assistant District Attorney Sarah Vandenbraak argues, these consent decrees do not "enjoy the consent of the governed."[64] The decrees, implemented and overseen by Federal District Judge Norma Shapiro and agreed upon by city officials from the administration of former mayor W. Wilson Goode and inmate attorneys in 1986 and 1991, limit the classes of crimes for which defendants can be held in jail, provide for the early release of pretrial detainees, and place significant prison construction and management decisions within the jurisdiction of the federal district court. These agreements have resulted in the virtual decriminalization of drug crimes and the micromanagement of the jail system by the court, causing

---

[61] Jack E. Call, "Lower Court Treatment of Jail and Prison Overcrowding Cases: A Second Look," *Federal Probation* 52, no. 2 (June 1988): 34.

[62] Ibid., 36.

[63] Interview with Assistant District Attorney Sarah Vandenbraak, Chief, Civil Litigation, Philadelphia District Attorney's Office, October 26, 1994.

[64] Sarah Vandenbraak, "Bail, Humbug!" *Policy Review* (The Heritage Foundation, Summer 1995).

Table 11.4. *State correctional facilities under court order or consent decree, June 29, 1990 (by reason and whether ordered to limit the population)*

| | Number of facilities | | |
Reason	Total	Ordered to limit population	Not ordered to limit population
Total	1,207	264	943
Not under court order or consent decree for specific conditions of confinement	965	81	884
Under court order or consent decree for specific conditions of confinement[a]	242	183	59
Crowding	186	172	14
Medical facilities	172	34	38
Administrative segregation	121	99	22
Staffing	155	135	20
Food services/nutrition	136	116	20
Education	139	117	22
Disciplinary policies	114	93	21
Recreation	127	109	18
Visiting/mail policies	130	109	21
Fire hazards	114	105	9
Counseling programs	106	88	18
Inmate classification	121	103	18
Library services	122	93	29
Grievance policies	113	94	19
Other	41	19	22

Note: No federal correctional facility was under court order or consent decree at the time of the census. A total of 323 state facilities were under court order or consent decree either to limit population or for specific conditions of confinement, or both.
[a]Detail adds to more than the total number of facilities under court order or consent decree for specific conditions of confinement because some facilities were under court order or consent decree for more than one reason.
Source: U.S. Department of Justice, Bureau of Justice Statistics, *Census of State and Federal Correctional Facilities, 1990*, NCJ-137003 (Washington, D.C.: USGPO, 1992), 7, Table 10.

a dramatic decrease in the city's ability to effectively manage the criminal-justice system and control crime. In the words of veteran Philadelphia police detective Patrick Boyle, whose son, Daniel, a rookie cop, was murdered by a felon released because of the federal court order:

Yes, the prison cap works. It works for the criminals who know the system better than those of us who work in the justice system. It works for the drug dealers who know the limit they can carry without posting bond or going to court. It works to the benefit of every criminal who can commit any crime they wish without fear of bail or jail. But what of the honest, law-abiding citizens of Philadelphia? They have been victimized and held hostage by the prison cap long enough.[65]

The 1986 and 1991 consent decrees arose out of a civil-rights suit brought in Judge Shapiro's federal district court by ten inmates in Philadelphia's Holmesburg Prison in April of 1982, who alleged that conditions in the prison deprived them of their Eighth and Fourteenth Amendment rights. Although the inmates complained of many aspects of their confinement, the alleged violations were held to be primarily the result of jail overcrowding. Accordingly, the remedies initiated in the resulting consent decrees focused on reducing the current number of inmates in Philadelphia's jail system and stemming the flow of criminals into the city's correctional facilities.

Judge Shapiro, who was appointed to the United States District Court for the Eastern District of Pennsylvania in 1978 by President Jimmy Carter, has been the subject of intense controversy in Philadelphia because of her role in helping to formulate the 1986 and 1991 consent decrees and because of her orders blocking efforts to modify the decrees. First, in Judge Shapiro's order approving the 1986 consent decree, she accepted the inmates' request for certification of a plaintiff class to include all individuals who have been inmates of the Philadelphia prison system since April 30, 1980, and all future inmates.[66] Judge Shapiro also appointed a special master specifically to guide the parties through the negotiation of the 1991 consent decree; this gave the judge unrestricted control of millions of dollars and numerous construction projects and criminal-justice policies.

Although Judge Shapiro held that there was a need for improvement in many areas of the prison system, especially regarding those conditions allegedly impaired by overcrowding, she never found conditions of confinement in Philadelphia prisons to be unconstitutional. Moreover, Judge Shapiro concluded that even a trial might not uncover unconstitutional conditions in the prisons. There was a risk, she held, "that plaintiffs could not succeed at trial in demonstrating that the conditions of confinement . . . are unconstitutional such that any relief is warranted."[67] Thus, since

[65] Testimony of Detective Patrick Boyle of the Philadelphia Police Department before the Committee on the Judiciary, Subcommittee on Crime, U.S. House of Representatives, Concerning H.R. 3 and H.R. 554 (the "Stop Turning Out Prisoners Act"), January 19, 1995.

[66] *Harris v. Pernsley,* No. 82-1847 (E.D. Penn. Dec. 31, 1986) (order approving settlement agreement).

[67] Ibid., 3.

a trial would undoubtedly delay, and perhaps even deny, relief to which plaintiffs "may be entitled," it was deemed necessary to provide immediate relief by means of the consent decree arising from the settlement agreement.

In her defense, Shapiro's supporters point to the fact that the decrees were not imposed, but rather were consented to by Mayor Goode's administration. However, although the Goode administration was indeed a party to the consent decrees, the Philadelphia district attorney's office and current city officials have relentlessly pursued modification of the consent decrees, only to be repeatedly thwarted by Judge Shapiro. Arguing that the consent decrees threaten their right to prosecute criminals and are therefore not in the public interest, the district attorney's office attempted to intervene in the litigation and contest the consent decrees. Judge Shapiro, however, blocked every intervention attempt or challenge to the consent decrees. She even denied the DA's motion to intervene after the Pennsylvania legislature had enacted a statute explicitly conferring automatic standing on the district attorney in prison litigation under which inmates might be released or defendants prevented admission.[68]

Although Judge Shapiro should not bear the entire blame for the negative impacts resulting from the 1986 and 1991 consent decrees, her attempts to block the district attorney's intervention and her repeated refusals to allow modification of the consent decrees—even though there has never been a finding of a constitutional violation—have contributed significantly to the perpetuation of mandates that current city officials deem to be harmful to the public interest. Indeed, the evidence suggests that the court's intervention has resulted in quantifiable public-safety, institutional, and financial harm to the city.

Public-safety impact

The public-safety impact of the early-release and nonadmission provisions of the 1986 consent decree was apparent almost immediately after the provisions went into effect in June 1988. For crimes considered inadmissible under the cap, bench warrants increased dramatically; overall, the bench-warrant rate doubled in a matter of months. As Sarah Vandenbraak points out, by August there were instances in which an individual with ten or more open bench warrants would be arrested, only to say, "You can't hold me, the cap's on tonight."[69] By the end of 1988, it was evident that

---

[68] 18 Pa. Cons. Stat. § 1108.   [69] Vandenbraak interview, October 26, 1994.

the decree's permissive provisions regarding defendants charged with drug possession had essentially decriminalized drug dealing in the city.

By 1991, when the city began negotiations for a new consent decree, the problems caused by the cap had not subsided. As Democratic mayoral nominee Edward Rendell and District Attorney Lynne Abraham wrote in a June 27, 1991, plea to Mayor Goode to disavow the new, 1991 consent decree, "The releases and the cap paralyze the criminal justice system and present a real danger to the safety of all Philadelphians."[70]

In November 1992, a study by the Crime and Justice Research Institute (CJRI) reported that 67 percent of these released defendants did not show up for trial. The failure-to-appear rates were especially high among defendants charged with drug dealing, who had a 76 percent failure-to-appear rate, burglary (74 percent), and theft (69 percent). The overall failure-to-appear rate, reported the CJRI, was "roughly four times the rate found in earlier studies of Philadelphia defendants."[71]

The widespread release of pretrial detainees under the nonadmission provision and the high failure-to-appear rate have also resulted in an explosion in the number of outstanding bench warrants for misdemeanor and felony cases. The unconditional release mandated by the decrees in the *Harris v. Pernsley* case, concluded the CJRI, "has hampered the efforts of the courts to adjudicate cases expeditiously by increasing the number of missed appearances." This has translated "into bench warrants which need to be reviewed and disposed when defendants are again arrested."[72] Indeed, as the *Harris* defendants assert in their 1994 Motion to Vacate the 1986 and 1991 Consent Decrees, the number of outstanding bench warrants increased from 16,595 on December 31, 1987 (before the prison cap went into effect) to 46,637 in March 1994. In the first six months of 1994 alone, 11,682 new bench warrants were issued, 74 percent of which were issued for criminal defendants released under the prison cap.[73] The admissions moratorium and release mechanisms instituted by the consent decrees, declare the defendants, have effectively stripped the state-court judges of the "ability to compel persons accused of serious crimes to appear for criminal proceedings."[74]

---

[70] *Business Wire*, "Rendell and Abraham call on Goode to disavow city's consent to prisoner release in light of recent Supreme Court ruling," June 27, 1991.
[71] Crime and Justice Research Institute, *An Alternatives-to-Incarceration Plan for Philadelphia: Findings and Proposed Strategies*, November 1992, 20–21.
[72] Ibid., 37.
[73] *Harris v. City of Philadelphia*, "Defendants' Motion to Vacate the 1986 and 1991 Consent Decrees," U.S. District Court for the Eastern District of Pennsylvania, Civil Action No. 82-1847, September 14, 1994, 6.
[74] Ibid., 5.

The most important impact of the prison cap on public safety, however, is not the increase in the number of fugitives in Philadelphia, but the additional crimes committed by these individuals—who represent a riskier pool of defendants than those normally released on bail—while they are on the streets. As the defendants note in their Motion to Vacate, citing another CJRI study, 18 percent of the defendants released under the decrees are rearrested for new crimes within ninety days, compared with rearrest rates of only 5 percent for defendants released under state-court bail programs and 8 percent for cash-bail defendants during the same time period.[75] As District Attorney Abraham commented in her January 1995 testimony before Congress, the crimes committed by defendants released because of the cap have not been solely "petty" in nature. Throughout 1993 and the first six months of 1994, these individuals committed 9,732 new crimes, including 79 murders, 959 robberies, 2,215 drug deals, 701 burglaries, 2,748 thefts, 90 rapes, and 1,113 assaults.[76] To date, the total number of murders by defendants released under the cap has risen to more than 100.[77]

However shocking these statistics may be, they do not reflect the personal losses that have occurred as a result of the prison cap. In chilling testimony before Congress in January 1995, Detective Boyle recounted the story of how his 21-year-old son, Danny, was brutally shot and killed by the driver of a stolen vehicle that he had pulled over. Danny's murderer had earlier been released without posting bond and had ignored two outstanding bench warrants. "Danny's death was a direct result of the prison cap," argued Detective Boyle; the cap forces "police to put themselves in danger time and time again, by the very fact that they must arrest and rearrest the same criminals." In his plea to Congress to "restore some sanity to the criminal justice system in Philadelphia," Boyle asked, "Can anyone explain to the families of the over 100 murder victims [resulting from the cap] why their loved ones had to die? Can anyone explain to me why Danny had to die?"[78]

Despite the numerous tragedies resulting from the prison cap, the admissions moratorium means the police can do little to prevent released arrestees from committing new crimes. Nowhere is this more evident than

[75] Ibid., 7.
[76] Testimony of the Honorable Lynne Abraham before the Committee on the Judiciary, Subcommittee on Crime, U.S. House of Representatives, Concerning H.R. 3 and H.R. 554 (the "Stop Turning Out Prisoners Act"), January 19, 1995.
[77] Vandenbraak interview, October 26, 1994.
[78] Detective Patrick Boyle testimony, January 19, 1995.

in the area of drug dealing. Most dealers are well aware of how much drugs they must be caught with in order to be held in jail. They therefore "exploit the gaping loopholes of the prison cap to conduct a relatively cost-free drug enterprise,"[79] resulting in the city of Philadelphia becoming a highly desirable location for dealing drugs. For example, the *Philadelphia Daily News* reported an instance where a phone tap installed by the district attorney's office recorded the following conversation between dealers in New York and Philadelphia:

They're turning up the heat here in New York.
No sweat, man. Come on down to Philly. The town's wide open.[80]

In another instance, a now-convicted drug dealer, negotiating with undercover detectives, attempted to move a drug deal from the Montgomery County side of City Line Avenue to the Philadelphia side of the street because he knew he would not go to jail if he got caught in the city. Indeed, had this dealer been successful in moving the sale, he likely would have been released immediately rather than being held in the county jail and eventually convicted. As the district attorney's office confirms, of the 6,555 people who were charged with dealing drugs in Philadelphia in 1993, 5,490 were immediately released to the streets because of the admissions moratorium. Only 220 of these individuals bothered to post bail.[81]

Administration of the "planning process"

In addition to raising public-safety concerns, the 1991 consent decree has created what city officials have called a "bureaucratic nightmare"; it has resulted in the district court's direct governance of the funding used by the city to construct both the new detention facility and the Criminal Justice Center. These aspects of the agreement between city officials and plaintiffs have turned over to the federal district court many governmental functions, allowing Judge Shapiro, as District Attorney Abraham argues, to "micro-manage the Philadelphia criminal justice agencies."[82]

Under the 1991 decree, the court was allowed direct supervision of the prison-planning process, meaning that every decision now required extensive consideration by numerous parties. In a recent interview, Sarah Vandenbraak explained the bureaucratic process, mandated by the con-

[79] *Harris v. City of Philadelphia,* "Defendants' Motion to Vacate," 7. [80] Ibid., 8.
[81] Ibid. [82] Abraham testimony, January 19, 1995.

sent decree, that goes into every decision regarding prison planning. First, city officials—in conjunction with their consultants—devise a plan, prepare a report, and review a draft of the report with individuals in prison-management positions. The plan is then reviewed by the plaintiffs' lawyers and their consultants, who have the right to make objections to the draft. Finally, these objections are reviewed by city officials, as well as by their consultants and lawyers. By the end of the process, as Vandenbraak commented, "you have taken the decision out of the hands of the professional administrator" whose job it is to make such decisions. Aside from the obvious costs related to the process, these procedures, she contended, are "not really conducive to sound decision-making."[83]

Although some may argue that such a process is necessary to ensure that city officials and prison administrators comply with the relief mandated by the 1991 consent decree, Judge Shapiro's micro-management has extended beyond those decisions that would reasonably be considered vital to the interests of the inmate plaintiffs. For instance, debates have occurred between Shapiro and lawyers for both sides of the litigation over issues such as the placement of flagpoles in prisons, the location of inmate barbers, seating in courtrooms, the power of light fixtures, and the selection of artwork in the Criminal Justice Center and new prison.[84] During one hearing, Judge Shapiro expressed concern about the smoking policy in a new facility. Despite the fact that lawyers from both sides had agreed that smoking should be allowed throughout the facility, Shapiro ordered that one of its four sections be nonsmoking, thus directly governing the administration of the facility even in the absence of a dispute between the parties to the litigation.

In addition to granting control of the prison-planning process to Shapiro, the 1991 settlement between city officials and the court also allowed the district court to directly control the proceeds of the 1991 Philadelphia Municipal Authority bond issue of $224 million.[85] It is clear that Shapiro has used this control to oversee every aspect of prison construction and renovation, as well as the appropriation of funds to com-

---

[83] Vandenbraak interview, October 26, 1994.

[84] Abraham testimony, January 19, 1995.

[85] The court's control of the bond fund was established in Section 4.01 of the Trust Indenture, which states: "Pursuant to *Harris, et al. v. Reeves, et al.*, C.A. No. 82-1847, notwithstanding any other provision of this Indenture or the Lease, all contracts for the construction of the Detention Facility and the Criminal Justice Center, and any change orders which increase the total project budget for the Detention Facility and the Criminal Justice Center, must be approved by the U.S. District Court for the District of Pennsylvania prior to their award."

plete the projects. Throughout the hearings, Shapiro repeatedly emphasized that no monies could be expended from the bond funds without her approval. At one point, refusing to approve a project the mayor had proposed, Shapiro declared, "Well, the point is it's not his [the mayor's] money, it's bond money, in a sense it's the court's money."[86] At numerous other occasions, Shapiro made similar statements regarding her intention to maintain control over both the bond funds and the Philadelphia prison system.

In response to the managerial actions by the district court, the Philadelphia district attorney's Office and current city officials have contended that Judge Shapiro has overstepped her judicial authority and should be removed from the case. In a draft of the "Memorandum of Law in Support of Defendant's Motion to Disqualify," the defendants alleged, among other things, that Shapiro has used her fiduciary control as an instrument of substantive control over construction issues, as well as to assume governance over matters not covered by the 1991 consent decree. As Vandenbraak noted, "The judge is supposed to be a neutral arbitrator of a dispute between parties. . . . They are not supposed to set themselves up as the administrators."[87]

Financial costs related to the consent decrees

The expanded bureaucracy created by the 1991 consent decree has had implications beyond questions of judicial authority. The previously described decision-making process imposed by the agreement also creates tremendous—arguably unnecessary—financial costs to Philadelphia taxpayers, because the city is compelled to pay for the services of each party involved. By the time a decision is finally implemented, the city ends up having to pay for its own consultant, the plaintiffs' consultant, lawyers for both sides, and the fees of the special master. The need for court approval of construction changes has also resulted in avoidable costs to the city. In one instance, the Philadelphia court system wanted to spend $5,000 to expand one room in the courthouse for court reporters. Judge Shapiro, however, rejected the proposal, requiring the change to be completed post-construction—at an estimated cost of $30,000.

Philadelphia's businesses and citizens have also suffered financial losses

---

[86] *Harris v. City of Philadelphia*, draft of "Memorandum of Law in Support of Defendant's Motion to Disqualify," Civil Action No. 82–1847, October 25, 1994, 7, citing Notes of Testimony from December 4, 1992.

[87] Vandenbraak interview, October 26, 1994.

that can be directly related to crimes that have occurred as a result of inmates' being released because of the prison cap. First, the inability of the city to hold individuals charged with burglary and theft allows criminals to "plunder Philadelphia businesses with impunity, causing direct theft losses, increased security costs, and increased insurance premiums."[88] The resulting increase in the cost of doing business undoubtedly leads many businesses to leave the city, taking their tax dollars with them. Second, the virtual decriminalization of drug dealing and property crimes by the admissions moratorium leads many private citizens to flee their crime-ridden neighborhoods and move outside the city, further eroding the tax base.[89] Finally, any financial analysis of the impact of the consent decrees must consider the millions of taxpayer dollars that have been spent arresting offenders who are immediately returned to the streets. Although it is difficult to quantify the financial costs related to these impacts of the 1986 and 1991 consent decrees, the evidence suggests that Philadelphia taxpayers have suffered substantial economic and human losses.

V: FEDERALISM, CORRECTIONS, AND COURTS

In *Federalist* No. 78, citizens are instructed not to worry about the power of federal judges, who have neither "the purse" nor "the sword" but only "will." But as the Anti-Federalists warned, these judges can wield great power contrary to the public interest. In corrections, federal judges may lack both purse and sword, but they have managed over the last generation to take possession of the keys to the prison gates.

It is clear that federal judges have a proper and legitimate role not only in the adjudication of prison-conditions cases but also in providing for the implementation of remedies that remove existing constitutional violations. During the nineteenth and early twentieth centuries (when prisoners were considered "slaves of the state") and into the hands-off era of the mid-twentieth century, it is indisputable that prison conditions were sometimes harsh and inhumane, and that the rights of inmates were often breached. In these cases, court intervention through remedial orders was not only a legitimate use of judicial authority but a legally and morally necessary one.

Many federal court remedies, however, have gone beyond the protection of fundamental liberties. Furthermore, these remedial orders have of-

---

[88] *Harris v. City of Philadelphia*, "Defendants' Motion to Vacate," September 14, 1994, 10.
[89] Ibid., 11.

ten been justified not by proof of actual rights violations but by dubious empirical arguments regarding prison crowding. Despite the fact that research has failed to establish a solid link between prison-population densities and conditions that constitute cruel and unusual punishment, courts have frequently determined their own arbitrary definitions of "crowding"; they have crafted remedies accordingly, ignoring factors such as the psychological and environmental elements within the prison under consideration. Therefore, the resulting population limits or minimum-floor-space-per-inmate requirements set by the courts have often established a standard far above one acceptable under the Eighth Amendment's cruel-and-unusual-punishment clause.

In addition to crowding remedies, court decrees mandating expanded services for inmates—including increased access to law libraries, increased medical services, and expanded programs for the receipt of mail packages, just to name a few—have gone far beyond merely addressing rights protected by the Constitution. Most Americans want prisoners to have basic amenities (decent food, adequate medical care) and services (educational opportunities, drug treatment). But they do not want prisons to be virtual resorts, and they certainly do not want another generation of violent and repeat criminals returned to the streets because of seemingly arbitrary judicial remedies arising from expansive applications of judicial authority.

Indeed, when the negative impacts (institutional, financial, and public-safety problems) of intrusive court orders and consent decrees are not balanced or outweighed by positive impacts such as the protection of constitutional rights, judicial intervention cannot be justified. Any financial or human costs incurred because of remedies that go beyond setting a constitutionally minimum standard are both unnecessary and undesirable.

As the Philadelphia case demonstrates, the negative effects of judicial intervention in correctional institutions have been significant. These impacts, however, are by no means peculiar to Philadelphia. In 1993, the nation's inmates filed 53,713 lawsuits in federal court, up from just 218 in 1966.[90] Litigating these cases has cost states millions of dollars. But the most significant financial costs to states have been the costs of compliance with court orders emerging from successful lawsuits. For instance, studies have estimated that compliance with the prison order in *Pugh v. Locke* cost the state of Alabama more than $35 million, representing a two-

---

[90] Wesley Smith, "Jailhouse Blues," *National Review* (June 13, 1994): 40.

thirds increase in the state correctional budget.[91] Judge Frank Johnson's order in *Pugh* required extensive changes in virtually every aspect of prison operations, including the maximum population of Alabama prisons, cell sizes, staff-inmate ratios, meal preparation, the amount and quality of medical care to be available to inmates, and the rules governing inmate correspondence and visitation. Additionally, the state of Louisiana appropriated more than $106 million for capital improvements, and another $18 million in operating funds following a court decree concerning the Angola state penitentiary.[92]

Scholars have also suggested that court orders often undermine existing institutional authority and result in increases in violence behind bars. One such study, by Kathleen Engel and Stanley Rothman, concluded that a rise in prison violence coincided with the abandonment of the hands-off doctrine. "When guards now need to employ stern measures to maintain security or to protect inmates from one another," they noted, "they lack both power and respect."[93]

In Texas, for instance, a 1980 federal-court ruling in the case of *Ruiz v. Estelle*[94] affected nearly every aspect of the state's correctional operations and required significant changes in prison operations. Soon after the court's ruling, institutional order broke down and prison-operating budgets skyrocketed. Between 1973 and 1980, Texas had 19 prison homicides.[95] In the years following the court order, however, inmate violence increased dramatically. Incidents of violence per 1,000 inmates jumped from 4.65 in 1980 to 18.61 in 1984.[96] In 1984 and 1985, 52 inmates were killed and more than 700 were stabbed.[97]

Texas has also been forced to spend hundreds of millions of dollars to implement *Ruiz's* reforms; the state's annual prison-operating budget rose from about $91 million in 1980 to more than $1.8 billion in 1994.[98] Moreover, Texas's average yearly cost per inmate in 1979 was approxi-

---

[91] Malcolm Feely, "The Significance of Prison Conditions Cases: Budgets and Regions," *Law & Society Review* 23 (1989): 274.

[92] Gerald E. Frug, "The Judicial Power of the Purse," *University of Pennsylvania Law Review* 126 (1978): 727.

[93] Kathleen Engel and Stanley Rothman, "Prison Violence and the Paradox of Reform," *The Public Interest* 73 (Fall 1983): 103.

[94] 503 F. Supp. 1265, 1276 (1980).

[95] John J. DiIulio, Jr., *Governing Prisons* 53 (New York: Free Press, 1987).

[96] Sheldon-Eckland-Olson, "Crowding, Social Control, and Prison Violence," *Law and Society Review* 20 (1986): 391.

[97] DiIulio, *Courts, Corrections, and the Constitution*, 54.

[98] John Sharp, *Behind the Walls: The Price and Performance of the Texas Department of Criminal Justice* (Texas Comptroller of Public Accounts, April 1994).

mately $2,700, and it had been stable for at least three years. By 1984, however, that cost had risen to nearly $6,500; by 1990, it exceeded $13,500.

Finally, *Ruiz* has driven an increase in the number of inmate early releases.[99] In the years following the 1980 court order, the state parole board increased early releases by 400 percent. Today, in large part because of the *Ruiz* prison cap, inmates spend an average of only two months in prison for every year of their sentences.[100]

Even more important than these apparent financial and institutional costs is the impact that court-ordered prison reform can have on public safety. In response to the "crowding" of correctional institutions, judges have often ordered prison-population caps that have resulted in the early release of thousands of inmates. Any crime committed by an individual who would have otherwise been behind bars decreases the freedom and safety of law-abiding citizens, who suffer the personal losses associated with crime. For the families of rookie cop Danny Boyle and the approximately 100 other Philadelphians killed by court-released detainees between January 1993 and October 1994,[101] it is too late.

Clearly, not all federal courts—or even a majority of them—are responsible for enacting and overseeing orders that seize managerial responsibilities from prison officials to the public's harm. But as the case of Judge Shapiro in Philadelphia indicates, activist judges have the luxury of disregarding basic constitutional and legal doctrines when it suits them. In April 1992, then–Attorney General William P. Barr offered the support of the U.S. Justice Department in lifting the limits on Philadelphia's inmate populations mandated by the 1986 and 1991 consent decrees. Citing the Supreme Court's 1992 decision in *Rufo v. Inmates of Suffolk County Jail*,[102] as well as the absence of a finding of unconstitutional conditions in Philadelphia, Barr declared, "The cap has no basis in the Constitution; it is wrong as a matter of law, of policy and of public safety. It is wreaking havoc with public safety and victimizing innocent Philadelphi-

---

[99] There is no existing survey of the crimes committed by inmates released early because of the *Ruiz* prison cap. The results of early releases in other jurisdictions, however, indicate that these individuals often resume their lives of crime soon after their release. For example, the Virginia Governor's Commission on Parole Abolition and Sentencing Policy reported in 1994 that in Virginia "68% of all murders, 76% of all aggravated assaults, and 81% of all robberies" are "the work of repeat offenders." Governor's Commission on Parole Abolition and Sentencing Reform, *Final Report, State of Virginia* (August 1994), 72.

[100] Smith, "Jailhouse Blues," 40.

[101] Vandenbraak interview, October 26, 1994.

[102] 112 U.S. 748 (1992).

ans. It should be removed immediately."[103] Judge Shapiro, however, threw out the city's 1992 motion to vacate the 1986 and 1991 consent decrees, leaving Philadelphia to continue to suffer the consequences of the decrees agreed upon by the previous mayoral administration.

The central lesson here is that it is not enough to raise public awareness or pass new laws. For representative democracy to work on crime policy, more fundamental changes are needed. The first and most crucial step is to prohibit judges from becoming de facto legislators and corrections czars. The 1994 federal crime bill took a small step in the right direction. In December 1994, the National District Attorneys' Association (NDAA), a nonpartisan body representing concerned prosecutors throughout America, approved a resolution calling on federal lawmakers to adopt more detailed legislation to deal with the reality that "federal court orders in prison litigation often have severe adverse effects on public safety, law enforcement, and local criminal justice systems."

Inspired by the NDAA's proposal, the House in February 1995 passed Title III of the Violent Criminal Incarceration Act of 1995—the "Stop Turning Out Prisoners" (STOP) provision. After being held up in the Senate for more than a year, the bill finally emerged as the Prison Litigation Reform Act (PLRA) of 1996,[104] included in the budget package signed by President Clinton in April 1996.

The PLRA significantly limits the remedial powers of federal judges in conditions-of-confinement cases. After asserting that relief may extend only far enough to remove the deprivation of the rights of a specific plaintiff, the bill provides that courts "shall not grant or approve any prospective relief [including consent decrees]" unless that relief is "narrowly drawn . . . and is the least intrusive means necessary to correct the violation of the Federal right."[105] Also, the court must give "substantial weight to any adverse impact on public safety or the operation of a criminal justice system caused by the relief."[106] Finally, the act provides that in any civil action regarding prison conditions, no prisoner-release order shall be entered unless a three-judge court finds "by clear and convincing evidence" that crowding is the "primary cause of the violation and that no other relief will remedy the violation."[107]

The PLRA also offers states and localities an unambiguous right to seek and obtain relief from existing or future court orders and consent de-

[103] Jerry Seper, "Justice Will Fight Population Limits at Jails, Barr Says," *The Washington Times* (April 24, 1992): A3.
[104] 18 U.S.C. § 3626.   [105] 18 U.S.C. § 3626(a)(1).
[106] Ibid.   [107] 18 U.S.C. § 3626(a)(3)(E).

crees. First, any prospective relief is to be terminated no later than two years after its enactment, and remedies may be continued only if actual constitutional violations are proven. Second, any relief granted in the absence of a finding that the relief was narrowly drawn and the least intrusive means to correct the violation is to be terminated immediately.[108] Finally, the PLRA limits the powers of special masters in prison litigation and grants state- and local-government officials the right to intervene in prison-conditions cases in order to challenge court-ordered prison caps.

Whatever the ultimate impact of the Prison Litigation Reform Act, certain facts about the constitutional propriety of such laws should be noted.

Article III, Section 2 of the Constitution states that "the Supreme Court shall have appellate Jurisdiction, both as to Law and Fact, with such Exceptions, and under such Regulations as the Congress shall make." But Article III also makes the jurisdiction—indeed, the very existence—of federal "inferior courts" purely the province of Congress. Any reasonable doubts about the meaning of Article III vis-à-vis the power of Congress over lower federal courts is answered plainly by Edward S. Corwin's classic, *The Constitution and What It Means Today:* "The lower Federal courts derive *all* their jurisdiction immediately from acts of Congress. . . . Also, all writs by which jurisdiction is asserted or exercised are authorized by Congress. . . . The chief external restraint upon judicial review arises from Congress's unlimited control over the Court's appellate jurisdiction, as well as of the total jurisdiction of the lower Federal courts."[109]

Judge Shapiro and her like-minded brethren on the bench are right that "Congress can't do whatever it wants."[110] But they and the prisoners' rights and anti-incarceration lobby need to be reminded of the clear language of the nation's seminal political document with regard to the power of Congress to set the jurisdiction of the lower federal courts.

If followed, the Prison Litigation Reform Act should limit the remedial powers of federal judges and return the responsibility of managing correctional institutions to state and local officials. Perhaps even more important, its passage represents the enacting of the will of a persistent popular majority without trampling the rights of incarcerated citizens.

---

[108] 18 U.S.C. § 3626(b)(1)(2).

[109] Edward S. Corwin, *The Constitution and What It Means Today* (Princeton, N.J.: Princeton University Press, 1978), 213, 225.

[110] Judge Norma Shapiro, as quoted in Henry Goldman, "Judge open to prison-cap hearing, but says crime bill is crowding her," *The Philadelphia Inquirer,* November 1, 1994, B3.

Afterword

Federalism and community

PHILIP SELZNICK

The essays in this volume have given us a close look at local democracy in the United States. They have explored transformations of localism, and of the federal system, during several centuries of change and upheaval. At many points, concern is expressed for the vitality of relatively small-scale communities; the authors display a robust faith in what such communities can contribute to effective citizenship in a differentiated but unified nation.

In this brief afterword, I turn to some closely related but more general issues. I draw on a few strands of moral and social theory to cast light on federalist thought, especially by grounding it in a theory of community. Such a theory points to ideals as well as realities, to tensions and dilemmas as well as integrative principles.

A UNITY OF UNITIES

When we think of community, what comes easiest to mind is the *sense* of community, that is, shared feelings and beliefs about who we are and where we belong. But community is about structure as well as belief, about ways of relating as well as feelings. To understand community, we must look to that structure and to the special work it does.

Communities are best understood as frameworks within which diverse interests are served and ordinary life goes forward. Thus we readily distinguish communities from disciplined special-purpose organizations. The "Catholic community" is much wider than the church hierarchy; the "law-school community" includes alumni, staff, students, and associated enterprises as well as faculty. The European Community is an evolving confederation of independent states. Moreover, the tight discipline that might make sense in a monastic community would distort and suffocate a more ordinary community whose well-being depends on initiative, variety, and plurality.

As frameworks for the conduct of ordinary life, communities have this remarkable feature: They build on, and are nourished by, other unities—persons, groups, practices, institutions—that characteristically claim respect and protection. They demand and are granted a variable but irreducible autonomy; they are invested with intrinsic worth; they are treated as moral agents and as objects of moral concern. Hence what we prize in community is not unity of any sort at any price, but unity that preserves the integrity of the parts. This is very different from the unity we associate with administrative or military hierarchies. There, an ethos of efficiency and instrumentalism prevails. Subordinate units are fully deployable, manipulable, and expendable. They can be modified or rearranged at will, in the light of externally determined purposes and policies.

A persistent preoccupation with the integrity of the parts lends a special significance to the experience of community. To be sure, community is about integration; effective communities are indeed well integrated. But what kind of integration? That is the nub. A "unity of unities" requires integration of a special kind, one that allows and fosters the self-preservation—the survival and flourishing—of its fundamental constituents.

Thus understood, community presumes separateness as well as integration. Although all persons are alike in important ways, and connected to others, they are also unique and separate. This idea does not require us to think of people as disaggregated or "abstract." Individual persons are not detached from their social contexts; they are not necessarily arm's-length participants in contracts of limited obligation; they do not necessarily believe that all their choices should be autonomous; they do not necessarily claim inviolable rights of property or a right not to be taxed for the benefit of others. Rather, people can be dependent in some respects and distinct in others; moreover, kinds and degrees of separateness must be considered. People can be treated as distinct persons even if they are also socially embedded, socially implicated, even socially encumbered. As persons, they do make choices; they often struggle against authority; they sometimes cast off received identities. There is nothing objectionably "individualistic" about recognizing these facts, or in treating the well-being of persons as the criterion by which we judge policies and practices.

A healthy tension between autonomy and integration, so important to community, is also central to our understanding of moral experience. To be moral is to accept the claims of fellowship—including other-regarding virtues of respect and concern. However, as I have noted elsewhere, "fellowship does not entail the extinction of self-regard or the dissolution of self into collective life. There is a dual concern for the interests of others and for one's own integrity."[1] In moral development, self-regard is transformed, not lost. If people are to be morally competent, they must have psychic competence as well. They must be capable of making appropriate moral choices—including effective commitments. They must be able to transcend narrow or unmitigated self-regard. Thus understood, selfhood is a mainstay of morality, not an enemy.

This fundamental feature of moral experience is confirmed and reinforced by the conclusions of modern psychology and sociology. Studies of socialization and social participation tell us much about the need for a stabilizing center in human life. For such a center to exist, there must be psychic autonomy within a framework of bonding to specific persons, such as family members, and to person-centered activities, such as a satisfying occupation. Formed in part by these commitments, the centered self is coherent and autonomous, not fluid or free-floating. It affirms connections as well as independence.

We need not embrace, as genuine autonomy, the bleak freedom we associate with lack of restraint, gratification of impulse, or psychic manipulation of self or other. Genuine psychic autonomy is manifested in responsible emotion, belief, and conduct. Responsibility is underpinned by an array of competences—especially the capacity to defer gratification and form steady attachments. In this way, psychic autonomy shades into moral autonomy.

In sociology, theories of "mediated" and "core" participation echo these moral and psychological truths. They speak to the interplay of autonomy and integration. The argument is that social life works best, for individuals as well as groups, when people participate *in self-preserving ways*. This requires a kind of participation—I call it "core" participation—that satisfies the need for intimacy and, more fundamentally, for connections that are central to a person's life experience and identity. (This we may distinguish from "segmental" participation, in which only a part or the periphery of a person's life is touched or implicated.) Core participation takes place mostly within relatively intimate person-centered groups, which are capable of offering nurture, support, and protection. Ideally, participation in more distant, more impersonal groups, such as large organizations and communities, is *mediated* by participa-

[1] Philip Selznick, *The Moral Commonwealth: Social Theory and the Promise of Community* (Berkeley: University of California Press, 1992), 32–3.

tion in so-called "primary" groups, which may be families, friendship networks, or formally recognized but person-centered units of employees or soldiers.

The lesson is that social life—life in community—must be person-centered in important ways. This follows from the basic imperatives of socialization, which every community must meet. Socialization has everywhere a dual mission: transmission of a social heritage (including skills, understandings, and norms) *and* the transformation of unformed human animals into effectively functioning, competent, responsible persons. Communities (and most special-purpose associations) do not work well if they do not produce or recruit motivated and disciplined members. To meet that need, the members must be shown respect for their personhood and concern for their well-being. People want freedom *from* unbearable intrusion, and freedom *for* the opportunity to experience uniqueness and self-worth. This is the root, in human nature and social reality, of irrepressible demands for limited authority and the perennial quest for an appropriate balance of autonomy and integration.

A corollary is that people-in-community are not a "mass" of detached, unrelated individuals. Nor is "mass society" a congenial setting for the flourishing of persons. "Mass" connotes a loosely bound aggregate rather than a densely textured social life. In mass society people are disconnected from one another, and they have diminished opportunities for core participation. Bonds to other people, to sustaining ideas, and to clear self-conceptions are weak and fluctuating. As a result, people are less secure—and, at the same time, less committed. The theory of mass society tells us that moral competence declines as personal attachments become less compelling, and as the texture of society is thinned. The specters of mass society and mass culture remind us of the need for a closely woven social fabric within which the integrity of persons, and of vital institutions, is nurtured and protected.

THE FEDERAL PRINCIPLE

In *Federalist* No. 51, James Madison rejoiced that it would be practical to advance the republican cause "by a judicious modification and mixture of the *federal principle.*" What is this principle? Is its meaning exhausted by an arrangement of national and state jurisdictions? Is the vitality of local governments a relevant concern? Should we find, in the federal principle, a more basic guide to freedom and order?

The federal principle has been traced to Hebraic and Christian theology. The root meaning of "federal" derives from the Latin *foedus* (or "treaty"). In Biblical history, the transactions of God and humanity take the form of covenants or treaties with Adam, Noah, Abraham, Moses, David, and, in the Christian version, ultimately through Christ to all believers. God promises His favor on condition of faith and obedience. This giving and receiving of promises—the heart of so-called federal theology—creates expectations that God will be bound by His word, and that he will act justly, not arbitrarily or despotically. For their part, the covenanted people accept subordination as free persons entering a sacred compact. Faith based on covenant carries a message of limited power, a message of authority based on consent. Hence it may properly be called a constitutional faith.

Furthermore, the religious commitment to God and His commandments is personal as well as communal. "The league with God is directly with the smallest units, and Israel is not a pyramid joined to the deity only at the top."[2] This tradition is an assertion of human dignity. It is a way of saying that people-in-community are responsible actors, capable of holding their own—even against God. They have an irreducible claim to respect and concern. It is this inviolability of constituent units that justifies calling the relationship to God a "federal" union.

Federal theology was developed mainly by Protestant thinkers. As a result, the sharpest focus is on the faith, commitment, and ultimate autonomy of individual persons. But the federal idea is also presented as a principle of social order. Thus in the thought of Althusius (1557?–1638), covenant pervades social life. Society is the product of many interwoven social unions, all based on tacit or explicit agreements. Bonds of mutuality and reciprocity create a federated unity. The outcome is a political structure with increasingly comprehensive levels. But the more inclusive entity does not negate the significance, participation, and consent of the covenanted groups that compose it. Each level retains its importance and its integrity as an operative community with appropriate governmental functions.[3]

These are not the covenants of feudalism, where freedom is forgone in exchange for protection. Nor do they quite match the social contract of

[2] Delbert R. Hillers, *Covenant: The History of a Biblical Idea* (Baltimore: Johns Hopkins University Press, 1969), 78.
[3] Charles S. McCoy and J. Wayne Baker, *Fountainhead of Federalism: Heinrich Bullinger and the Covenantal Tradition* (Louisville: Westminster/John Knox, 1991), 57–8.

later generations. Althusius's conception of a federated unity is more pluralist than individualist in spirit and structure. He could not accept the view expressed by his younger contemporary, Thomas Hobbes, that autonomous groups are "lesser Commonwealths in the bowels of the greater, like wormes in the entrayles of a naturall man."[4]

A closely related idea is the doctrine of *subsidiarity.* This is an important theme in Catholic social doctrine. In what has come to be a canonical formulation, Pope Pius XI wrote:

It is a fundamental principle of social philosophy, fixed and unchangeable, that one should not withdraw from individuals and commit to the community what they can accomplish by their own enterprise and industry. So, too, it is an injustice and at the same time a grave evil and a disturbance of right order, to transfer to the larger and higher collectivity functions which can be performed and provided for by lesser and subordinate bodies. Inasmuch as every social activity should, by its very nature, prove a help to members of the body social, it should never destroy or absorb them.[5]

In subsidiarity, consent and agreement are not so important. They do not ground the federal principle. Rather, local groups and institutions have intrinsic worth because they make indispensable contributions to human flourishing, especially the flourishing of individual persons. What matters is well-being, not contract or even covenant.

Subsidiarity derives from the Latin *subsidium,* meaning "support, help, protection." The constituent units of society are to be nurtured and protected. They are helped to grow in inner strength, or to recover failing strength—that is, the capacity to perform their distinctive functions. They are protected as objects of moral concern and as social units whose well-being demands self-determination. Thus the underlying model is parental. The good parent helps the child grow, and provides direction, but is always aware of the child's intrinsic worth and of the vital need for independence.

Thus subsidiarity cannot be equated with delegation or decentralization. Those modes of ordering are compatible with the premise that local or functional units are in principle *expendable* as well as subordinate. They can be extinguished, or radically reconstructed, if that serves the needs of a more comprehensive and higher authority. In such a regime the local units are derivative, not constitutive.

The two doctrines—covenantal federalism and subsidiarity—come to much the same conclusions. Each sees major social groups as invested

---

[4] Thomas Hobbes, *Leviathan* (1651; reprint, London: Pelican Books, 1968), 375.
[5] Pius XI, *Qaudragesimo Anno,* 1931.

with moral agency and as necessary components of society. Social groups are responsible actors; as such, they can be held accountable for how they perform, or fail to perform, their special tasks. These conclusions are wholly compatible with our understanding of community as a unity of unities. This is not a unity without tension, nor is it a social order based wholly on shared outlooks or traditions. Pluralism is the keynote—a pluralism tempered by allegiance to wider unities of region, nation, and beyond.

Properly understood, pluralism is not a recipe for disunity, still less for fragmentation. Rather, pluralism calls for a certain kind of order within a complex polity. It does not deny the legitimacy of a central authority, but it says such authority is to be exercised with due respect for multiple sources of initiative, energy, and power. Pluralism informs and regulates, it does not negate, the claims of constitutional unity.

It is therefore unhelpful to counterpose decentralist and nationalist conceptions of the American political community. We can readily accept that "We the people" (not "We the States") created the United States of America. But the unity thus established was to have its own name and nature. It would be, among other things, protective of (and responsive to) local self-government. For this new nation, federalism was to be a covenantal principle.[6]

It should be noted that neither covenantal federalism nor subsidiarity is mainly concerned with democracy. The compelling theme is liberty, especially freedom from domination and for self-determination. The latter may take undemocratic forms. The federated unity is anticollectivist, opposed to any central authority that would have the will and the power to extinguish claims of locality and function. Intimations of democracy may be drawn from principles of consent and countervailing power. But there is no guarantee—indeed, no prominent expectation—that democracy will be nourished in a federated community governed by norms of subsidiarity and stewardship.

HISTORICAL CONTEXTS

The foregoing discussion suggests that the "federal principle" invoked by Madison has a deeper significance and a wider reach than is usually understood. At the American Founding, the principle was given a special ap-

---

[6] Note that a covenantal principle is not static. "As constitutional challenges are met, underlying commitments are clarified and elaborated." Selznick, *The Moral Commonwealth*, 482.

plication—the design of a federal republic. The Constitution reserved to the states broad powers of self-government. These powers were comprehensive and unspecified; indigenous, not derivative. Moreover, the state governments retained "sovereign" authority over counties, cities, private institutions, and individual conduct. This supremacy was qualified in important ways—above all, in that citizens of the states were to be citizens of the United States as well, and as such were to be guaranteed certain rights and immunities. However, the states were to have a primary role in the lives of citizens—indeed, *the* primary role. They were to be semi-independent republics, or "core polities," as Martha Derthick says in Chapter 5 of this volume. But the Constitution contained no guarantee that the federal principle would prevail *within* the states. Much was taken for granted, and the task of creating a national government on federal principles seemed sufficient to the day.

The American experience reminds us that the federal principle, like all such principles, is necessarily applied in response to the genuine problems of a particular community. The historical context gives center stage to some issues while brushing others aside. At the time of the Founding the former colonies were compelling political realities, and it was of paramount concern that they should survive and flourish within the new republic. This commitment to the *original* states had profound implications for the *future* states that would in time be fashioned from newly populated (and conquered) territories. These would be more casually cobbled, yet they would have the same dignity and power as the original thirteen.

In their grand design, the Founders left much for the future to decide. They could not know just how national-state relations would evolve, nor what would be the fate of the federal principle within a world made new by vastly expanded commerce and industry, technological revolutions, and international obligations. For American democracy, the great problem is how to give effect to the federal principle while recognizing the constraints and seizing the opportunities of history and circumstance.

Thus a fundamental indeterminacy afflicts the federal principle, as it does all political, legal, and moral principles. Such principles offer guides and touchstones, but by themselves they cannot provide unambiguous rules and definite conclusions. Nevertheless, despite the imprecision, there is much to be gained from keeping the broader conception of federalism in mind. Doing so establishes a standpoint from which to assess current institutions and practices. To be sure, Americans are committed to the states as major units of self-government. That is a political reality as well as a constitutional command. However, commitment to the states has its own ambiguities, as American history has shown. We have not been indifferent to the need for national solutions to national problems; we have had to assess the competence of the states to perform vital tasks, and to understand the variable and changing nature of that competence; we have had to learn the limits as well as the benefits of self-determination. Nor does the problem of national-state relations exhaust the meaning of federalism. We still need to ask, as has been asked in this book: What are the true constitutive units of social, political, and economic life? How should they be recognized, and how protected, by legislatures, courts, and executive agencies?

This approach shifts attention from national-state relations to a larger question: how to give effect to the federal idea as a principle of *community* and not only of *government?* In posing such a question, we refuse to take for granted, or as settled, the worth of government at any level, however organized. We cannot simply assume that local governments are seedbeds of democracy, that state governments are especially "close to the people," or that the federal bureaucracy is inherently unresponsive to the needs of communities and local institutions.

We should be wary of abstractions like "the people," or "close to the people." In a living community, the "people" are highly differentiated along many dimensions. Some have easy access to power and influence; others are relatively powerless. Whether and to what extent a unit of government is close or responsive depends on how the people are organized and what resources they have. The "people's institutions" may in fact represent an entrenched establishment. They may be out of touch with new interests and incapable of listening to voices routinely unheard. Responsive government—even at its best—is likely to be more selective than evenhanded. For many reasons, some groups may be favored and others ignored.

Local governments with limited resources are especially vulnerable to the pressures of powerful interests. We cannot presume that such agencies, just because they are local, will expertly define and diligently attend to the public interest. James Madison warned that this might be so when he argued that the evils of "faction" are likely to be greater in a small polity than in the extended republic envisioned by the Constitution, where a variety of factions would counter one another.[7] Of course, Madison took

---

[7] *The Federalist*, No. 10.

the importance of local governments for granted. He knew they would deal with most of the issues that touch people's lives. Nevertheless, his generalization had a prescience perhaps greater than he knew. The danger of faction in local affairs increases as national or multinational interests bring their influence to bear on relatively hapless local officials.

This is not to say that local governments are irredeemably captive or supine. Many are vigorous, independent, and dedicated to the public interest. The point is, rather, that the federal principle is not self-evident in meaning; not self-enforcing in practice; not likely to be permanently realized by a particular institutional design. Its application must be sensitive to change and context. A special lesson is that we must consider, at the same time, the limits of localism and the dangers of centralization: Each carries a virus of oppression; each can sap the vitality of community; each must be checked by a countervailing principle. Neither is self-limiting.

THE UNIVERSAL AND THE PARTICULAR

Localism and centralization, taken together, belong to a distinguished family of moral and social polarities. These include justice and compassion, rule and discretion, public and private obligation, broad and narrow self-interest. All display an irrepressible tension between general and special obligations. These polarities account for many of our most important perplexities. They reflect a wide-ranging, many-faceted competition between universalism and particularism. The success of federalism depends, to a large extent, on how that competition is managed.

Federalism creates comprehensive unities—notably national or international communities—and in doing so invokes abstract ideas and impersonal norms. However, if the federal principle is honored, the integrity of the parts must be nurtured and protected. As we have seen, this is the distinctive ethos of federalism compared with other, more integral forms of social and political organization.

The virtues of particularism are often disparaged, but they are not difficult to defend. There is a sense in which, as James Q. Wilson notes in Chapter 2 of this volume, "people are by nature locals." Indeed, most people mature and thrive in concrete settings, especially particular families and localities. From these they derive rootedness, authenticity, and loyalty. Abstract ideals and distant allegiances are pale reflections of a morality that stems from special and local affinities. Moral development begins with caring and concern for others who are "significant" because they share bonds of interdependence and responsibility. This person-centered experience is a necessary component of what I earlier called "core" participation.

Particularism is deeply rooted in biological bonding, and this accounts in part for its great power and persistence. Of course, we know there is a dark side to this power: isolation, exclusion, chauvinism, bigotry, and worse. These failings of intelligence, sensibility, and fellowship interfere with the enlargement of human communities. In response, an alternative ethic of *inclusion* has evolved. This ethic is "universalist" because it looks outward rather than inward, ultimately to all humanity (and beyond), and because it invokes general principles and abstract categories.

The virtues of universalism include tolerance, impartiality, and fidelity to principle. These virtues, which are more distinctively human than those of particularism, ease the transition from small to larger communities. A crucial step treats strangers as kindred, belonging to one's own kind. This step has been taken innumerable times in human history for quite practical purposes, such as forming alliances, consolidating conquests, and gaining material and spiritual prosperity.

Although universalism appeals to abstract thought and rational principles, it does not encompass all the findings of moral inquiry. Such findings point just as clearly to the benefits of particularism. The principles purport to be "universal" based on knowledge about all human communities, but not "universalist." They identify different virtues, different obligations, and different foundations of morality. Thus each morality can find support in a science of community. Each competes for preeminence, but neither leaves the stage.

For federalism, the great question is how to reconcile these competing claims and ideals. The universalist impulse transcends groups and embraces the rights of individuals. The ideal is a nation whose chief constituents are individuals, not states or local communities.[8] Local groups and governments may be respected for their special contributions, but not if they interfere with important rights. Insofar as a chief function of the national government is taken to be the defense of personal liberty, an original premise of the American Founding is preserved—that is, the national government may bypass the states in exercising its authority under the Constitution.

---

[8] On the views of Justice William Brennan, see Robert Post, "Justice Brennan and Federalism," in *Federalism: Studies in History, Law, and Policy,* ed. Harry N. Scheiber (Berkeley, Calif.: Institute of Governmental Studies, 1988), 37–44.

The price, however, is often a radical abridgment of local authority, especially on matters that affect schools, neighborhoods, and other aspects of everyday life. Most important is the effect on childrearing: An uncongenial moral environment can decisively limit the ability of parents to influence the character and conduct of their children. Indeed, it is difficult to uphold the values of family and communal life without significant deference to the authority of group leaders, including parents vis-à-vis their children and local officials vis-à-vis the community. Yet we cannot condone *abuse* of authority. We cannot abandon important rights, nor go along with whatever a local majority may decide. A jealous regard for principles of civility, including equal justice, remains relevant and necessary.

How can we resolve this dilemma? The following applications of the federal principle may point the way:

First, we are to uphold the autonomy and defend the vitality of particular groups, institutions, and communities. As in the larger realm of ethics and justice, *the moral primacy of the particular* is respected. Ultimately, particulars alone have intrinsic worth; their well-being is the touchstone by which we judge abstract concepts and principles. Thus if we ask what "moral equality" means, or what is a "human" right, we cannot answer by appealing to postulates and arguments alone. We must focus on the lived experience of degradation, lost opportunity, or arbitrary judgment. Only then can we know whether a universalist principle of fairness has been properly formulated, or makes sense in the context.

Second, we are to respect diversity without allowing its claims to override those of basic humanity and justice. There can be no set rule for striking such a balance, because too much depends on history and context. But we can do much to spell out what respect for diversity entails, and what it does not entail. We can draw on universalist ideals for principles of criticism and for guidance in reconstructing parochial experience. We can reject the extremes of radical multiculturalism, which would fragment society, and of cultural imperialism, which is indifferent or hostile to local sources of identity and authenticity.

Third, we can recognize that particular attachments are not only compatible with, but can preserve and strengthen, more comprehensive unities. If people feel that their cultural origins and distinctive identities are respected, they will more readily give their loyalty to a larger "community of communities." Indeed, loyalty to a larger whole can reinforce local life, as in traditional small-town America or among many religious communities, by providing compelling rituals, symbols, and beliefs.

And finally, each perspective must accept an ordinance of self-restraint. Advocates of "fundamental" rights need to limit their claims—especially their enforceable claims—to matters that are truly vital to the lives of citizens and the integrity of institutions. This is a caution against judicial overreaching, that is, formulating and applying abstract principles with insufficient attention to contexts and purposes. At the same time, defenders of particularism must accept the premise that parochial experience is not an unqualified good. Other goods—including the virtues of universalism—have an equally important part to play in the construction of human communities.

Contributors

ALAN A. ALTSHULER is the Ruth and Frank Stanton Professor of Urban Policy and Planning, with a joint appointment in the Kennedy School of Government and the Graduate School of Design, at Harvard University. He is also director of the Kennedy School's Taubman Center for State and Local Government. His most recent books are *Regulation for Revenue: The Political Economy of Land Use Exactions* (co-author, Brookings, 1993) and *Innovation in American Government* (co-editor, Brookings, 1997).

CHRIS COOKSON recently completed his doctorate in political science at the University of Houston. He is a research associate evaluating open-enrollment charter schools in Texas for the university's Center for Public Policy. His other publications are on education finance.

MARTHA DERTHICK is Julia Allen Cooper Professor of Government and Foreign Affairs at the University of Virginia and a former Guest Scholar at the Woodrow Wilson Center. She is the author of numerous books on American government, including *Policymaking for Social Security* (1979), *The Politics of Deregulation* (with Paul J. Quirk, 1985), and *Agency under Stress: The Social Security Administration in American Government* (1990). She has long had an interest in American federalism.

JOHN J. DIIULIO, JR., is professor of politics and public affairs at Princeton University and Douglas Dillon Senior Fellow at the Brookings Institution, where he founded the Brookings Center for Public Management in 1993. His dozen books include *Courts, Corrections, and the Constitution* (1990), *Deregulating the Public Service* (1994), *Medicaid and Devolution* (1998), and *American Government* (with James Q. Wilson, 7th edition, 1998).

KATHRYN M. DOHERTY is a doctoral candidate in the Department of Government and Politics at the University of Maryland. Her dissertation is entitled "Emerging Patterns of Housing, Community, and Local Governance: The Case of Private Homeowner Associations."

STEPHEN L. ELKIN is professor of government at the University of Maryland, chair of the Executive Board of the Committee on the Political Economy of the Good Society, and editor of the journal *The Good Society*. He is the author of *The City and Regime in the American Republic* and editor of *The Constitution of Good Societies* and *A New Constitutionalism*.

WILLIAM D. HAGEDORN graduated from Princeton University *magna cum laude* in 1995 with a degree in politics and from the University of Virginia Law School in 1998. He joined the law firm of McDermott, Will, and Emery in Washington, D.C., in the fall of 1998.

MARC K. LANDY is professor and chair of political science at Boston College. He is co-author of *The Environmental Protection Agency from Nixon to Clinton: Asking the Wrong Questions* (1994) and an editor of *The New Politics of Public Policy* (1995). He served on the panel of the National Academy of Public Administration that produced *Setting Priorities/Getting Results: New Directions for EPA*. He and Sidney Milkis are the authors of a forthcoming book, *First Citizen and the Politics of Presidential Greatness*.

PAULINE MAIER is William R. Kenan, Jr., Professor of American History at the Massachusetts Institute of Technology. Among her books are *From Resistance to Revolution: Colonial Radicals and the Development of American Opposition to Britain, 1765–1776* (1972) and *American Scripture: Making the Declaration of Independence* (1997). She is also contributing to a new history of the United States that will integrate the history of science and technology.

SIDNEY M. MILKIS is chair and professor of politics at Brandeis University. He is the author of *The President and the Parties: The Transformation of the American Party System since the New Deal* (1993) and *Political Parties and American Democracy: Remaking Constitutional Government* (1999), co-editor of *Remaking American Politics* (1989) and *Progressivism and the New Democracy* (1999), and co-author of *The Politics of Regulatory Change: A Tale of Two Agencies* (2nd edition, 1996) and *The*

American Presidency: Origins and Developments, 1776–1998 (3rd edition, 1999). He is currently working on two books: *The Progressive Party Campaign of 1912 and the Birth of Modern American Politics* and, with Marc Landy, *First Citizen and the Politics of Presidential Greatness.*

PHILIP SELZNICK is professor emeritus of law and sociology in the School of Law and the Department of Sociology at the University of California, Berkeley, and a former Fellow of the Woodrow Wilson Center. He was the founding chair for the Center of the Study of Law and Society and of the Jurisprudence and Social Policy Program in the School of Law, Berkeley. His books include *T. V.A. and the Grass Roots; Leadership and Administration; Law, Society, and Industrial Justice;* and with P. Nonet, *Law and Society in Transition.* He is the author most recently of *The Moral Commonwealth.*

CLARENCE N. STONE is professor of government and politics at the University of Maryland. He is the author of *Regime Politics: Governing Atlanta, 1946–1988,* which won the American Political Science Association's Ralphe Bunche Award. His most recent work is an edited collection of the politics of local school reform, *Changing Urban Education.*

RICHARD M. VALELLY is associate professor of political science at Swarthmore College. His publications include *Radicalism in the States: The Minnesota Farmer-Labor Party and the American Political Economy* (1989) and "Party Coercion and Inclusion: The Two Reconstructions of the South's Electoral Politics," *Politics and Society,* March 1993. He is at work on a book entitled *Making Black Ballots Count,* which traces black voting-rights politics since Reconstruction. He is a former Guest Scholar at the Woodrow Wilson Center.

GREGORY R. WEIHER is associate professor of political science at the University of Houston and a former director of the university's Center for Public Policy. He is co-principal investigator on the evaluation of open-enrollment charter schools in Texas, commissioned by the State Board of Education, and is editing a forthcoming issue of the *Policy Studies Journal* on charter schools.

JAMES Q. WILSON is the Collins Professor of Management Emeritus at the University of California, Los Angeles. He is the author of *The Moral Sense, Moral Judgment,* and *Bureaucracy,* among other books.

Index

371

Other books in the series (*continued from page iii*)

Blair A. Ruble, *Money Sings: The Changing Politics of Urban Space in Post-Soviet Yaroslavl*

Deborah S. Davis, Richard Kraus, Barry Naughton, and Elizabeth J. Perry, editors, *Urban Spaces in Contemporary China: The Potential for Autonomy and Community in Post-Mao China*

William M. Shea and Peter A. Huff, editors, *Knowledge and Belief in America: Enlightenment Traditions and Modern Religious Thought*

W. Elliot Brownlee, editor, *Funding the Modern American State, 1941–1995: The Rise and Fall of the Era of Easy Finance*

W. Elliot Brownlee, *Federal Taxation in America: A Short History*

R. H. Taylor, editor, *The Politics of Elections in Southeast Asia*

Šumit Ganguly, *The Crisis in Kashmir: Portents of War, Hopes of Peace*

James W. Muller, editor, *Churchill as Peacemaker*

Donald R. Kelley and David Harris Sacks, editors, *The Historical Imagination in Early Modern Britain: History, Rhetoric, and Fiction, 1500–1800*

Richard Wightman Fox and Robert B. Westbrook, editors, *In Face of the Facts: Moral Inquiry in American Scholarship*

Selig S. Harrison, Paul H. Kreisberg, and Dennis Kux, editors, *India and Pakistan: The First Fifty Years*